Contested Ground

The Southwest Center Series

Ignaz Pfefferkorn, *Sonora: A Description of the Province*

Carl Lumholtz, *New Trails in Mexico*

Buford Pickens, *The Missions of Northern Sonora: A 1935 Field Documentation*

Gary Paul Nabhan, editor, *Counting Sheep: Twenty Ways of Seeing Desert Bighorn*

Eileen Oktavek, *Answered Prayers: Miracles and Milagros along the Border*

Curtis M. Hinsley and David R. Wilcox, editors, *Frank Hamilton Cushing and the Hemenway Southwestern Archaeological Expedition, 1886–1889*, volume 1: *The Southwest in the American Imagination: The Writings of Sylvester Baxter, 1881–1899*

Lawrence J. Taylor and Maeve Hickey, *The Road to Mexico*

Donna J. Guy and Thomas E. Sheridan, editors, *Contested Ground: Comparative Frontiers on the Northern and Southern Edges of the Spanish Empire*

Contested Ground

Comparative Frontiers on the Northern and Southern Edges of the Spanish Empire

EDITED BY DONNA J. GUY AND THOMAS E. SHERIDAN

The University of Arizona Press
TUCSON

The University of Arizona Press

⊗ This book is printed on acid-free, archival-quality paper. Manufactured in the United States of America

03 02 01 6 5 4 3 2

Library of Congress Cataloging-in-Publication Data

Contested ground : comparative frontiers on the northern and southern edges of the Spanish Empire / edited by Donna J. Guy and Thomas E. Sheridan.

p. cm. — (The Southwest Center series)

Includes bibliographical references (p.) and index.

ISBN 0-8165-1859-9 (alk. paper). — ISBN 0-8165-1860-2 (pbk. : alk paper)

1. Latin America—History. 2. Frontier and pioneer life—Latin America. 3. Frontier thesis. I. Guy, Donna J. II. Sheridan, Thomas E. III. Series.

F1410.C747 1998

980—dc21 97-33730

CIP

British Library Cataloguing-in-Publication Data

A catalogue record for this book is available from the British Library.

Contents

Acknowledgments

SHORTLY AFTER Donna Guy became director of the Latin American Area Center at the University of Arizona in 1989, Joseph Wilder, director of the Southwest Center, made an extremely generous offer to fund a conference on a topic of interest to both centers, one that would eventually lead to an edited volume. It took very little time to agree on the basic idea of comparing the northern and southern edges of the Spanish Empire from original exploration and settlement in the early sixteenth century to the advent of railroads in the 1880s. Tom Sheridan was immediately invited to coordinate the Southwest and northern Mexico component of the project.

Guy and Sheridan initially invited five specialists from each region to attend a preliminary three-day conference at the Westward Look Resort in Tucson in the spring of 1992. The invitees consisted of historians, anthropologists, and a sociologist. Although we were aware that specialists in the Southwest and northern Mexico rarely participate in the same sessions at academic meetings as their counterparts in the Río de la Plata, we believed that it would provide both groups with a rare opportunity to compare and contrast these two regions in new ways. A second conference was held in April 1993 to coincide with the Inventing the Borderlands conference sponsored by the Ford Foundation and the Arizona Humanities Council, among others. At that time an additional anthropologist joined the Contested Ground group.

This book is the outcome of these meetings and conversations. The editors would like to thank a number of people for their contributions. First and foremost, we would like to thank Joseph Wilder of the Southwest Center for his unflagging economic and intellectual support for this project. Additional support came from the Latin American Area Center and the Southwestern Mission Research Center. The former staff at the Latin American Area Center, Gloria Durán and Lynn Shade, helped us coordinate the first conference and provided important secretarial support. Eva Johnson typed and organized the bibliographies into one final work. Finally, we thank Joanne O'Hare, Senior Editor at the University of Arizona Press, for believing in our ideas.

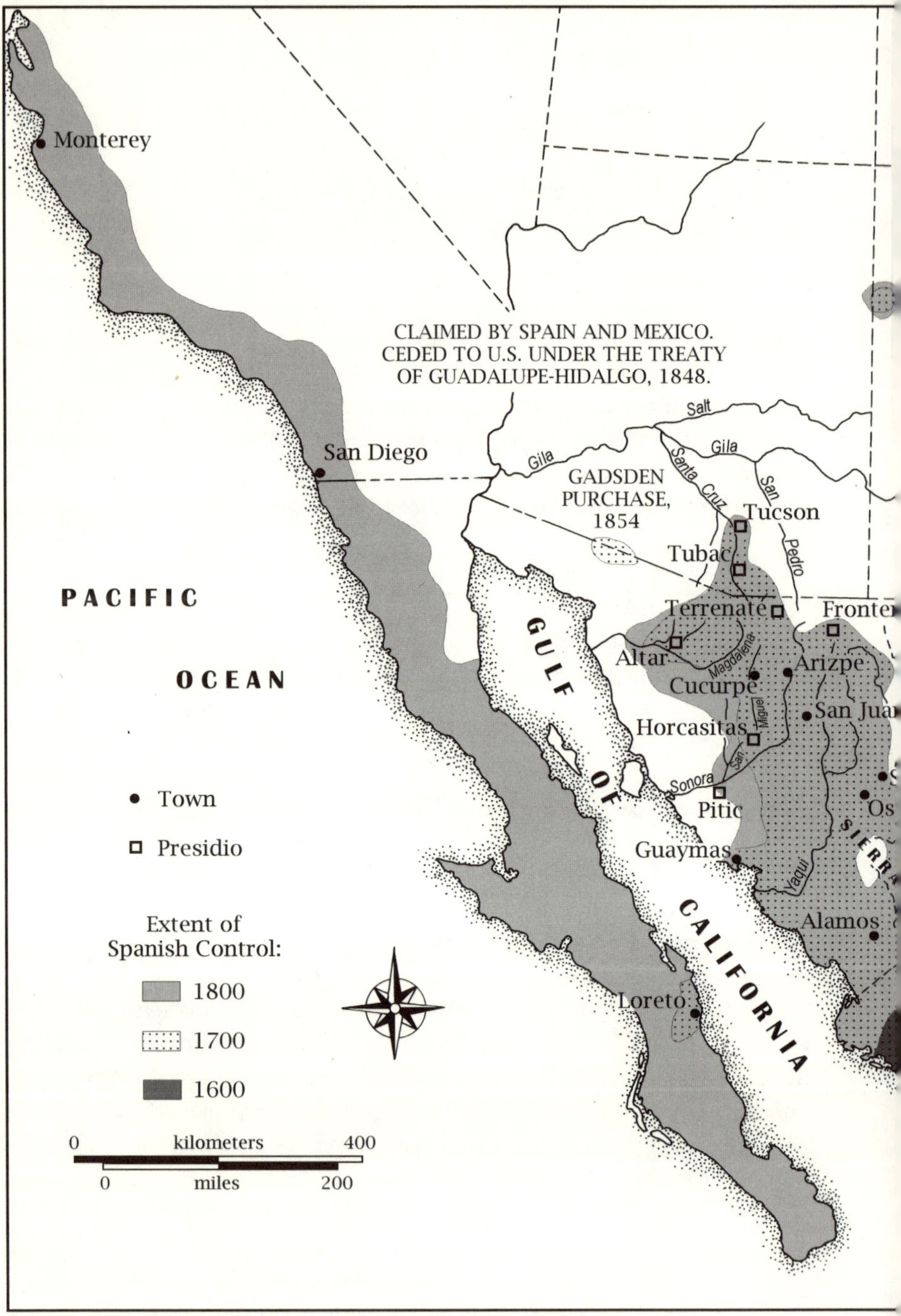

MAP 1. The Greater Southwest in 1800.

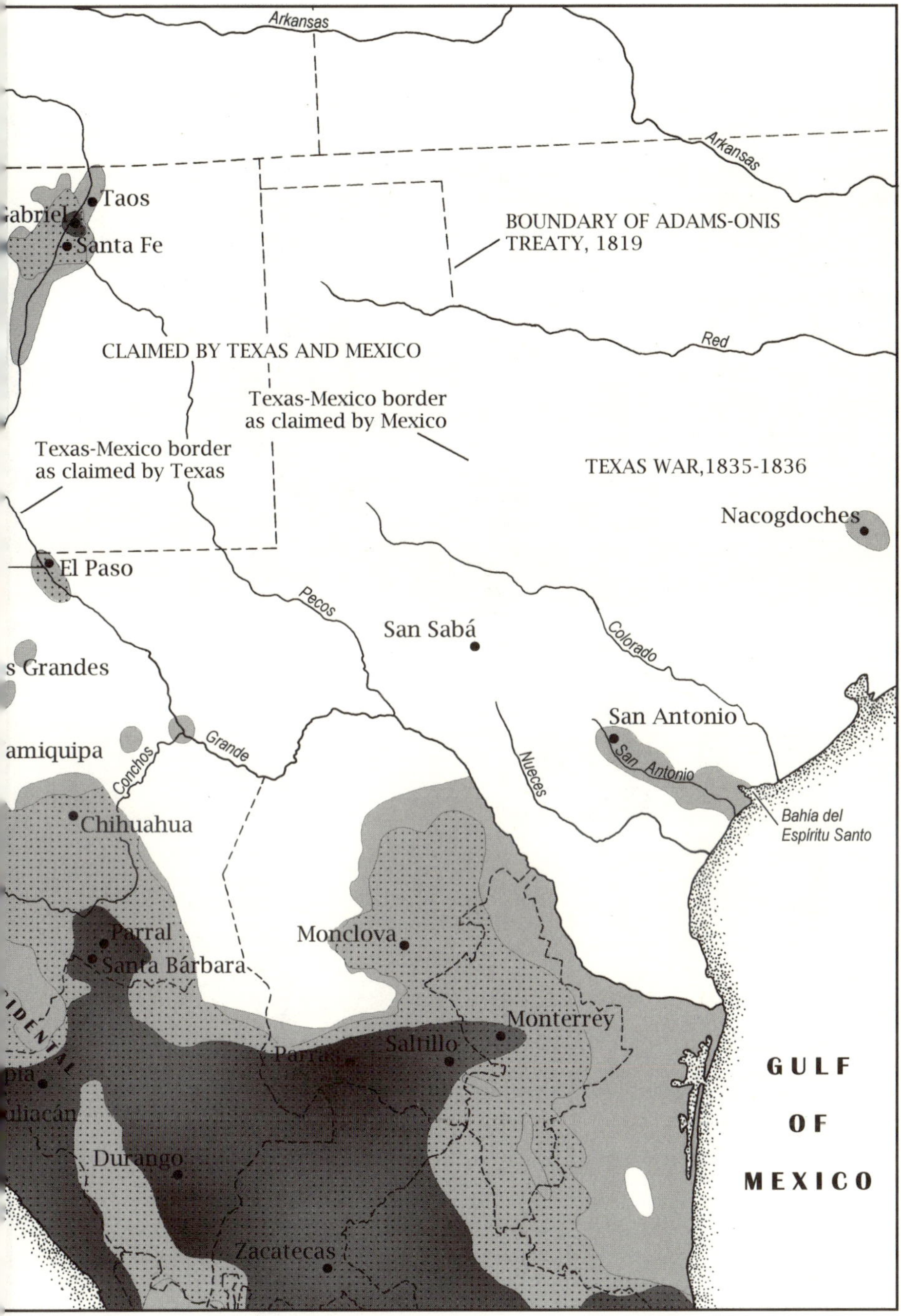
Arkansas
Arkansas
Taos
abriel
Santa Fe
BOUNDARY OF ADAMS-ONIS TREATY, 1819
Red
CLAIMED BY TEXAS AND MEXICO
Texas-Mexico border as claimed by Mexico
Texas-Mexico border as claimed by Texas
TEXAS WAR, 1835-1836
Nacogdoches
El Paso
Pecos
San Sabá
Colorado
s Grandes
San Antonio
San Antonio
amiquipa
Grande
Conchos
Nueces
Bahía del Espíritu Santo
Chihuahua
Monclova
Parral
Santa Bárbara
Monterrey
Parras
Saltillo
GULF
OF
MEXICO
Durango
Zacatecas

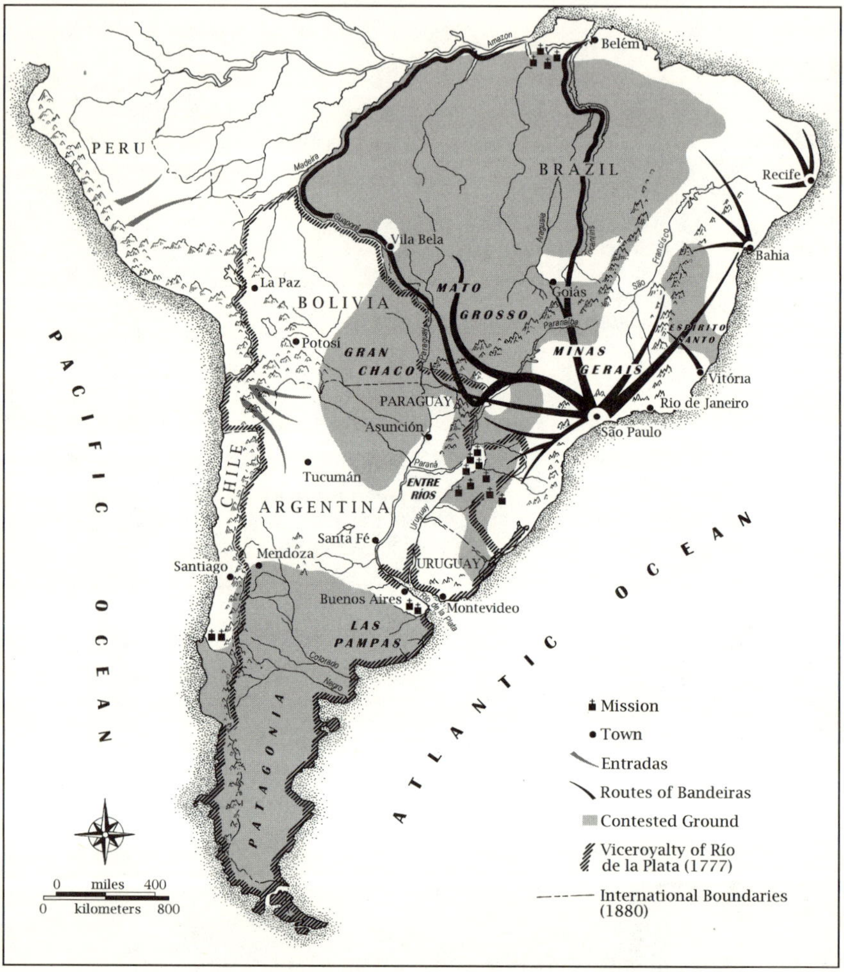

MAP 2. South America south of the Amazon.

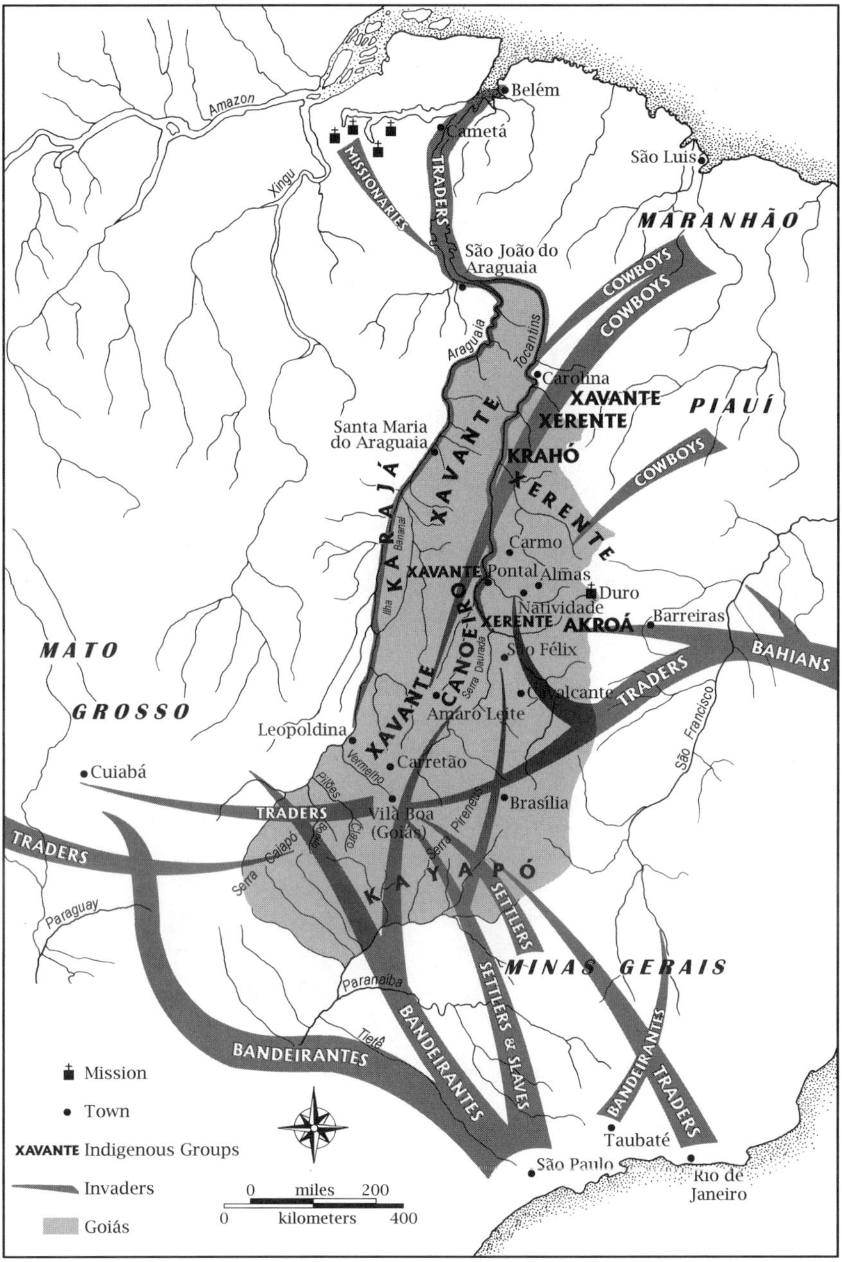

MAP 3. The Rio Araguaia, the Rio Tocantins, and the Goiás Region.

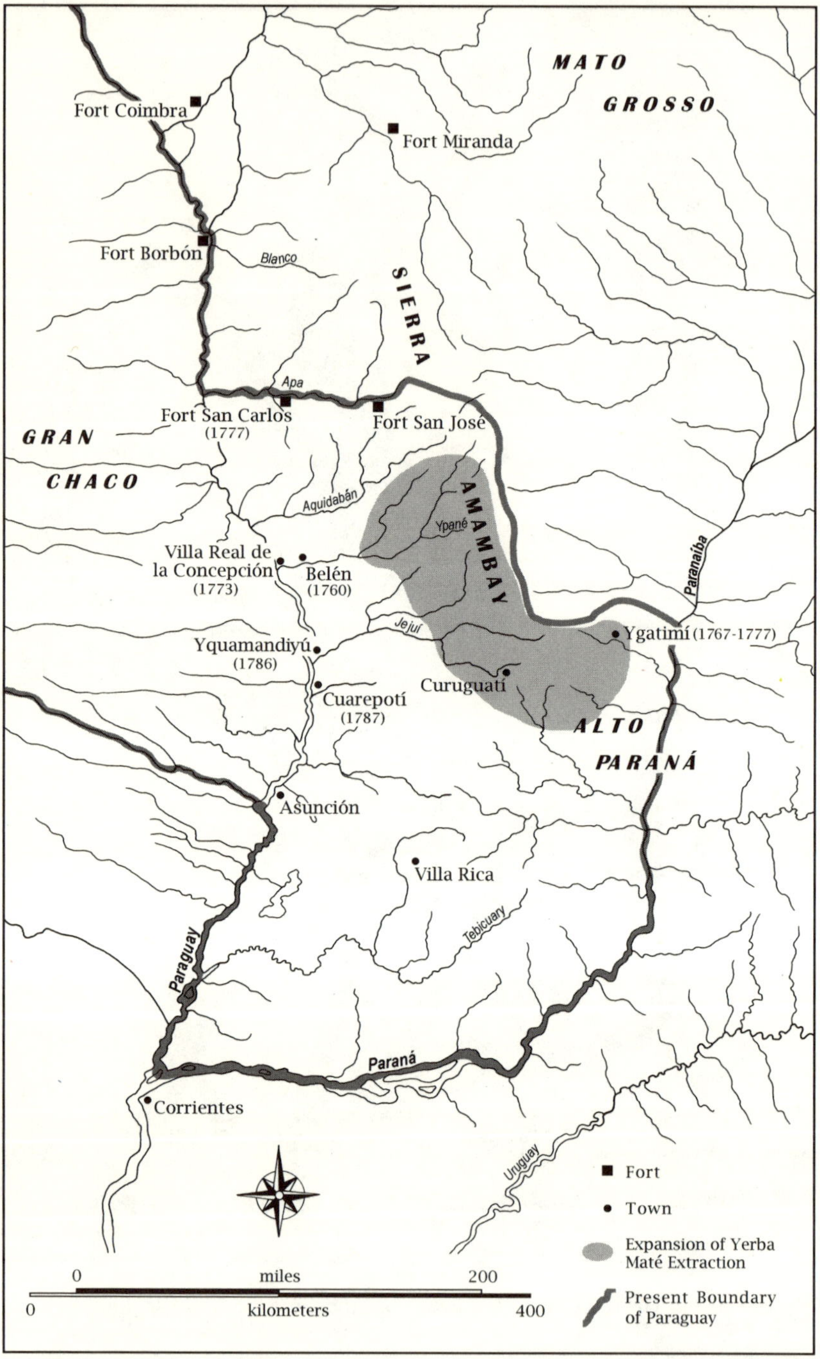

MAP 4. Paraguay and its major river systems.

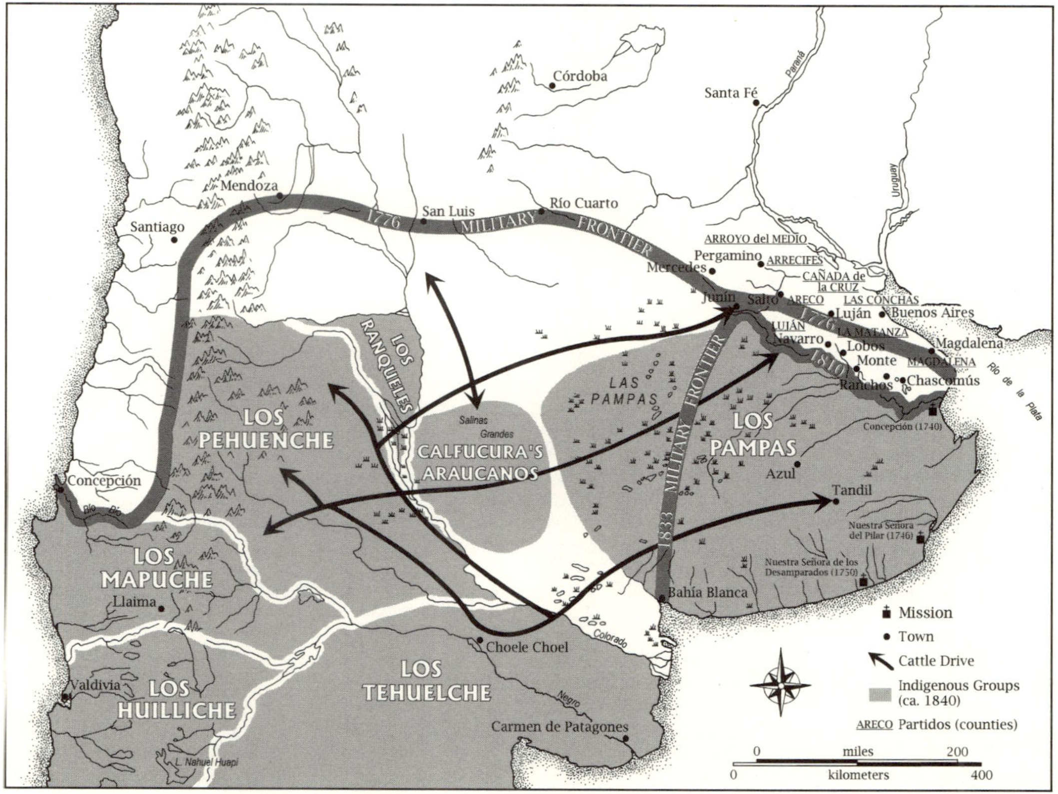

MAP 5. The Buenos Aires region.

Contested Ground

1

On Frontiers

The Northern and Southern Edges of the Spanish Empire in the Americas

DONNA J. GUY AND THOMAS E. SHERIDAN

WHEN THE SCHOLARS participating in the first Contested Ground working group came together in the spring of 1992, everyone was struck by the apparent similarities between northern Mexico and the Río de la Plata region. Both areas were peripheral to the centers of power in the Spanish Empire. Because secular Spanish settlement was slow and sparse, the Spanish Crown turned to members of various religious orders, particularly the young and dynamic Society of Jesus (founded in 1540), to incorporate thousands of Indians into its empire. The historical parallels between the famous Jesuit missions among the Guaraní in Paraguay and the Jesuit missions of northern New Spain intrigued all members of the group and begged closer examination.

Both regions also possessed extensive grasslands where Old World livestock proliferated and stockraising became a major industry. The presence of these animals, in turn, attracted many Native American groups—the Apaches and Comanches in the north, the Pampas Indians in the south—who came to rely upon stock raiding as a vital economic endeavor. On the pampas and along the northern frontier, these Indian raiders posed the most serious and immediate threat to the security and expansion of Hispanic society.

Both regions faced threats from other European and Euro-American powers as well. France, Britain, and Russia all nibbled at the edges of northern New Spain. Portuguese Brazil contested the eastern borders of the Río de la Plata. Later, in the nineteenth century, the United States moved relentlessly westward and eventually seized more than half the territory claimed by the Republic of Mexico. To defend itself against Indian and European enemies in the Río de la Plata and northern New Spain, the Spanish Empire developed a piecemeal defensive strategy that included the establishment of professional military garrisons, known as *presidios,* as well as the formation of civilian militia units and an enduring reliance upon Indian allies.

The writing of this book was prefaced by two conferences. As the first conference session commenced, we feared that others would not see the similarities we had perceived. Fortunately, our fears were unfounded because the conference took on a life of its own and prepared topics disappeared as individuals brought up issues they believed were central to the volume. From the outset, there was general agreement that participants were interested in analyzing zones of constant conflict and negotiation over power—economic, political, and cultural. We also realized that when we spoke of frontiers, we were discussing areas whose geographic delineation was constantly in flux over time. There were many frontiers in the Americas: ecological, political, social, cultural, and economic.

The topic of cowboys and their South American equivalents, the *gauchos,* also became a point of commonality and divergence. The image of the cowboy and the gaucho evolved in profoundly different ways. Whereas in the United States the cowboy was a hero on a romanticized frontier, Latin Americans viewed frontier life in a much more ambivalent light. In Latin America, particularly in Argentina, the gaucho was originally seen as a political threat to national development. Often of mixed racial heritage and disdainful of the law and contemporary methods of stockraising, gauchos often followed *caudillos,* local landowners or politicians who refused to relinquish authoritarian political privileges. The creation of the Argentine gaucho as a mythic figure occurred in the late nineteenth century only after gauchos no longer posed a danger to nation building.

The U.S. cowboy, in contrast, was rarely seen as a menace to the body politic. On the contrary, traveling Wild West shows and penny novels portrayed cowboys as the very essence of the frontier—rugged individualists who fought the Indians and tamed the wilderness, making it safe for American democracy and the march of progress. The United States has always romanticized its frontier past, endowing it with the virtues of self-sufficiency and individual freedom. Only recently has the image of the cowboy—and ranching in general—come under serious attack in the United States as some environmentalists have tried to eliminate grazing on public lands and have portrayed stockraising in the West as an ecologically destructive endeavor.

Nonetheless, both cowboys and gauchos assumed mythic proportions in historical scholarship as well as the popular imagination. According to these deeply embedded representations, cowboys and gauchos seemed to embody the best and worst of individualism and masculinity. They lived in masculine worlds where females only occasionally appeared. They were almost always portrayed as young, single men, free from the constraints of marriage, family, and the life cycle itself. Participants realized that such representations begged many important questions about the nature of cattle-ranching frontiers and the ways in which ranching societies were reproduced in both the biological and the cultural senses. Several participants argued that women and families played much more important roles on those frontiers than previously acknowledged.

Ecological and Historical Differences

During the course of the discussions, significant ecological and historical differences between the Río de la Plata and northern New Spain began to overshadow the similarities that had attracted us in the first place. Northern Mexico and the Southwest are much more arid than the Río de la Plata region; except for the mountain highlands, most of the Greater Southwest receives fewer than fifteen inches of rain a year. In contrast, twenty to forty inches of rain fall annually on the pampas north of the Río Colorado, while forty to eighty inches drench the grasslands and forests east of the Río Paraná.

Moreover, the topography of the Greater Southwest is considerably more rugged, particularly west of the Great Plains. The Andes formed the western boundary of the Río de la Plata region, and even though there was considerable contact between the mining districts of Alto Perú and the area that eventually became the Viceroyalty of the Río de la Plata, the two regions followed very different historical trajectories. Northern New Spain, on the other hand, sprawled across both the Sierra Madre Oriental and the Sierra Madre Occidental. Desert valleys alternate with mountain ranges to give the Greater Southwest a landscape of topographical extremes. Those extremes isolated Sinaloa-Sonora from Nueva Vizcaya and Nuevo México, making commerce and communication among the northern provinces difficult and expensive. They also provided regions of refuge and resistance for Indians fleeing Spanish dominion, and impregnable bases of operations for Native Americans raiding Spanish settlements.

Perhaps the most important geographical difference of all, however, was the presence of a major river system on the southern frontier. The Paraná, Paraguay, and Uruguay Rivers provided major avenues of transportation and communication that did not exist in northern New Spain. Those rivers linked the communities of the Río de la Plata to one another and eventually to European trade via Buenos Aires. They allowed the region to diversify its economy beyond stockraising at an earlier date than in the north and to expand into commercial production of tobacco, cotton, yerba maté, and wheat. They also provided a ready avenue for the smuggling of silver from Potosí. Throughout the Spanish colonial period and most of the nineteenth century, in contrast, the most important industry in the Greater Southwest remained gold and silver mining, which stimulated the spread of stockraising and led to the development of what geographer Robert West (1949: 7) calls the "mine-ranch settlement complex." Only precious metals justified the enormous danger and expense involved in transporting material from the northern frontier to Mexico City and Spain.

The Río de la Plata river system led to another overwhelmingly important cultural difference—the rise of Buenos Aires as a major urban center. Initially an outpost, this port town remained closed to legal trade until 1778. Two years earlier, however, Buenos Aires had been named the seat of the new Viceroyalty of the Río de la Plata in order to contain the advance of the Portuguese Empire to the north, as well as to stimulate more trade between the region and Spain. Once the port was opened, the opportunity to exploit the feral horses and cattle on the pampas stimulated the nascent cattle industry as well as the raising of other regional crops such as tobacco and yerba maté, a popular local tea.

Buenos Aires soon became so powerful from its export trade—and the ongoing smuggling of silver from Potosí—that it could extend its authority over other Spanish cities of the Río de la Plata such as Montevideo, Córdoba, San Miguel de Tucumán, and Asunción. Furthermore, the city's *cabildo* (town hall) was the site of maneuvers to declare the entire region independent of Spanish domination in 1810. The province of Buenos Aires provided much of the wealth necessary to finance the wars of independence and the civil wars that followed. Furthermore, the material wealth of the province was used to negotiate treaties with indigenous groups. Nowhere on the northern frontier did a peripheral town become so important that it replaced the centers of power in colonial Mexico or in the British colonies. During the nineteenth century, Buenos Aires developed into one of the great cities of Latin America, while communities like Santa Fe, Chihuahua City, Saltillo, Monterrey, Hermosillo, and Alamos remained little more than provincial centers. In 1750, Buenos Aires had a population of 12,000; by 1800, its population had quadrupled to 50,000. No city in northern Mexico or the southwestern United States reached that size until the twentieth century.

One final difference between the northern and southern frontiers was the timing and nature of the threat from other European or Euro-American powers. Beginning in the 1580s, Portuguese settlers and their Indian allies in the São Paulo region of southern Brazil mounted regular expeditions, called *ban-*

deiras (after the banners they marched under), west or south to search for mineral wealth and Indian slaves. In their quest for gold, diamonds, and emeralds these *bandeirantes* helped promote the exploration of the Brazilian interior, but they also wreaked havoc on Indian communities, including the Jesuit missions in modern Argentina, Uruguay, and Paraguay. The bandeirantes began raiding Spanish Jesuit missions in 1609, marching off thousands of mission Indians as slaves. By 1639, the raids had grown so intense that the Spanish Crown gave unprecedented permission to the Jesuits to arm their Guaraní converts so they could defend themselves against the bandeirantes. Thereafter the frequency of raids declined, but not before slave raiding and epidemic Old World diseases decimated many Indian communities. Portuguese Brazil contested the Spanish occupation of the Banda Oriental, the eastern edge of the Río de la Plata estuary, and threatened the security of Spanish- and later Argentine-controlled Río de la Plata for three centuries.

The French, British, and Russians never threatened the security of northern New Spain to such an extent. On the contrary, Spanish expansion northward was thwarted by Native Americans, not Europeans. The Spaniards may have feared their European adversaries, but Tobosos and Seris, Apaches and Comanches halted northern New Spain in its tracks until the military force of the Provincias Internas took the offensive in the late 1700s. The recurring fears of European or Euro-American invasion did not materialize until the 1840s, when the United States launched a two-pronged assault on northern and central Mexico and wrested Alta California, Arizona, and New Mexico away from the bankrupt young Republic of Mexico.

On Frontiers

These ecological and historical differences between the northern and southern edges of the Spanish Empire have translated into intellectual differences as well. As David Weber and Jane Rausch (1994: xiii) point out, "with the exceptions of Brazilians and Argentines, Latin American intellectuals have seldom considered their own frontiers central to the formation of national identities or of national institutions." Yet no other word in North American historiography carries greater ideological freight than the term *frontier.* In 1893, a young historian from Wisconsin named Frederick Jackson Turner argued, "The existence of an area of free land, its continuous recession, and the advance of American settlement westward, explain American development" (F. Turner 1994: 2). More than a century later, the idea that the western frontier was the crucible of American identity and American democracy continues to dominate both academic debate and popular discourse. As historian Patricia Limerick points out in a recent article, "Frederick Jackson Turner's Frontier Thesis entered its second century in remarkably good shape" despite withering critiques in the 1930s, 1940s, and 1960s, and the assaults of the so-called "New Western" historians today (Limerick 1995: 697).

In both Latin American historiography and popular culture the frontier was a place to be feared, a spawning ground of barbarism and despotism rather than democracy (Weber and Rausch 1994). Turner, on the other hand, provided a triumphalist and exceptionalist paradigm for a restless and aggressive nation that wrested half a continent away from Britain, France, Spain, Mexico, and hundreds of American Indian societies during its first century of existence. The pampas, jungles, and mountains of Latin America had to be subdued and civilized by European urban civilization, by the center, the core, the metropole. The North American "wilderness," in contrast, was a place of regeneration where the European was stripped away and the American was created. That paradigm still shapes the psyche of the United States long after the "free land" of the frontier has filled up with farms, ranches, towns, cities, Indian reservations, bombing ranges, and national forests. John F. Kennedy's "New Frontier" and Ronald Reagan's "Shining City on the Hill" are just two examples of the ways in which our belief in the uniqueness of our national character has expressed itself in the political arena and drawn us into dangerous adventures abroad.

As numerous critics have pointed out, however, Turner's "wilderness" of "free land" was a cultural as well as geographical landscape that had been occupied by human societies for at least twelve thousand years. Even before the arrival of Europeans in the early sixteenth century, American Indians had contended for and laid claim to both North and South America; invested their landforms with mythic significance; and transformed their plant and animal populations through hunting practices, horticulture, and the use of fire (Butzer 1992; Martin and Klein 1984; Martin and Szuter n.d.; Pyne 1982; Szuter 1991). Contrary to romanticists and primitivists from James Fenimore Cooper to Kirkpatrick Sale and Stanwyn Shetler, the Americas were not "the First Eden" or a "pristine natural kingdom" where "the native people were transparent in the landscape, living as natural elements of the ecosphere" (Shetler 1991: 226). Instead, they were often densely populated networks of Indian societies organized into bands, tribes, chiefdoms, and even states. In the words of geographer William Denevan (1992a: 370), "by 1492 Indian activity throughout the Americas had modified forest extent and composition, created and expanded grasslands, and rearranged microrelief via countless artificial earthworks. Agricultural fields were common, as were houses and towns and roads and trails. All of these had local impacts on soil, microclimate, hydrology, and wildlife."

So why is the myth of the pre-Columbian Americas as primeval wilderness such a powerful one? Denevan (1992a: 370) goes on to say, "the evidence, pieced together from vague ethnohistorical accounts, field surveys, and archaeology, supports the hypothesis that the Indian landscape of 1492 had largely vanished by the mid-eighteenth century, not through a European superimposition, but because of the demise of the native population. The landscape of 1750 was more 'pristine' (less humanized) than that of 1492."

In other words, Turner's individualistic American pioneers of the nineteenth century were encountering a continent that had been scoured of people by three centuries of epidemics of Old World diseases such as smallpox, measles, influenza, and diphtheria. Social scientists continue to debate the magnitude of aboriginal American populations and the exact timing and extent of those epidemics, but most agree that American Indian populations in 1492 were much larger than previously thought. They also agree that those populations plummeted by 66 to 95 percent throughout most of the Americas between the sixteenth and nineteenth centuries (e.g., Cook and Borah 1971–79; Crosby 1972; Denevan [1976] 1992b; Dobyns 1966, 1976, 1983; Reff 1991 and this volume; Verano and Ubelaker 1992).

The depopulation of the Americas, coupled with European ethnocentrism and racism, fueled what Reff and others call the "civilization-savagery myth." Turner, like many of his anthropological contemporaries, was a unilineal evolutionist who believed that human societies could be ranked on an evolutionary scale culminating in the Caucasian capitalist industrial democracies of Western Europe and the United States. His frontier was "the outer edge of the wave—the meeting point between savagery and civilization" (F. Turner 1994: 3). He elaborates:

> The United States lies like a huge page in the history of society. Line by line as we read this continental page from west to east we find the record of social evolution. It begins with the Indian and the hunter; it goes on to tell of the disintegration of savagery by the entrance of the trader, the pathfinder of civilization; we read the annals of the pastoral stage in ranch life; the exploitation of the soil by the raising of unrotated crops of corn and wheat in sparsely settled farming communities; the intensive culture of the denser farm settlement; and finally the manufacturing organization with city and factory system. . . . Stand at the Cumberland Gap and watch the procession of civilization, marching single file—the buffalo following the trail to the salt springs, the Indian, the fur-trader and hunter, the cattle-raiser, the pioneer farmer—and the frontier has passed by. (F. Turner 1994: 5–6)

From the vantage of the late twentieth century, such notions of "civilization" and "savagery" seem murderously quaint. During the ten decades since Turner presented his seminal paper, the world wars, holocausts, gulags, and global ecological devastation inflicted by industrial societies have severely weakened our faith in progress and the inevitability of "social evolution." Many historians have even discarded the notion of the frontier itself. Limerick (1995) adroitly uses Turner's own words to challenge his frontier thesis of creative rebirth and illuminate the webs of dependency—upon external capital, upon imperial and national governments, upon European and Euro-American cultural models of land use, water use, and ethnic relationships—within which western pioneers were enmeshed.

In this volume, however, we choose to retain the term *frontier* because no other term suffices. Frontiers, as we define them, are certainly not boundaries between civilization and wilderness, or between civilization and barbarism, because those are nothing more than the value judgments of the conquerors. But neither are they "regions" or "peripheries" of empires or nation-states. Instead, we view frontiers as zones of historical interaction where, in the brutally direct phrase of Baretta and Markoff (1978: 590), "no one has an enduring monopoly on violence." Along frontiers in both North and South America, as around the world, different polities contended for natural resources and ideological control, including the right to define categories of people and to determine their access to those resources. Those polities often exhibited immense differences of organization, population, and technology, yet frontiers marked the social and geographical limits of power among the polities themselves. Frontiers were, in a most basic sense, contested ground.

The starting point of our analysis, then, is power and violence. Turner and his intellectual successors often talked about economic frontiers—fur-trading frontiers, cattle frontiers, mining frontiers, agricultural frontiers. Utilizing the insights of economic historian Frederic Lane, Baretta and Markoff note, "one cost of an economic activity is the cost of its protection from violent disruption. One of the major activities of a government is to supply this protection through control of violence, a service paid for by taxation" (Baretta and Markoff 1978: 589). They continue, "Frontiers are . . . boundaries beyond the sphere of routine action of centrally located violence-producing enterprises, although they may be within the range of isolated attacks" (590). No matter how much Spanish mercantilists may have wanted to move beyond Zacatecas or Chihuahua City or Buenos Aires or Asunción, their governments or their private means often were not strong enough to protect their enterprises.

Our conceptualization of frontiers extends the tripartite division of the modern world-system proposed by political scientist Immanuel Wallerstein.

Wallerstein argued that beginning in the sixteenth century, a modern world economy based upon a global division of labor emerged as Europe expanded into Asia, Africa, and the Americas. Each division of that world economy—core, semi-periphery, and periphery—was characterized by a distinctive form of labor. In Wallerstein's words, "The periphery (eastern Europe and Hispanic America) used forced labor (slavery and coerced cash-crop labor). The core, as we shall see, increasingly used free labor" (Wallerstein 1974: 103). Recent studies of New World labor systems acknowledge core-periphery dichotomies but argue that the differences between the core and the periphery were less clear (Stern 1988).

Frontiers, on the other hand, were areas where imperial or, later, national power was too weak to maintain stable patterns of coerced labor. Furthermore, frontier groups used slave raiding attacks and slave labor for different reasons. As Socolow, Jones, and Hall demonstrate in this volume, slave raiding along frontiers was often intense, but adult male captives were usually killed or marched off to areas where state power was more secure. The ones who remained behind were women and children incorporated into households as domestic servants or socialized into the enslaving societies themselves. Because power was tenuous along frontiers, either violent resistance or flight was a more viable strategy there than it was nearer the core. Hence, the economic and political costs of forced labor were often too high for the societies involved, especially when their economic and demographic resources were stretched thin by global imperial entanglements.

Even among groups who had been incorporated into empires or nation-states, the proximity of frontiers often forced the state to make concessions such as the legal recognition of a land base, exemption from taxation, or freedom from or reduction of forced labor demands. In this volume, both Cynthia Radding and Daniel Nugent describe *colonial pacts* forged between the Spanish Empire on the one hand and indigenous communities and military colonists on the other. Those pacts recognized a mutual interdependence among groups living on or near the frontier—a dependence continually reinforced by external threats. Missionized Indians and Hispanic settlers found an ambivalent common ground in the battle against their mutual adversaries—whether they were Portuguese bandeirantes or Apache raiders.

One final general point about frontiers needs to be made. The adversaries on the frontier were often, in a very real sense, creations of imperial expansion itself. In the oft-repeated phrase of historian Owen Lattimore, civilization was the "mother of barbarism" (Baretta and Markoff 1978: 592). Lattimore was talking primarily about China and the ways in which it engendered the nomadic raiders of the Asian steppes. But his phrase, in all its irony, can be applied to other frontiers as well. As Jones, Slatta, and Hall point out in this volume, the American Indian raiders of both the pampas and the Great Plains ran off Old World animals while mounted on Old World animals. Comanche, Apache, and Araucanian societies would have taken radically different trajectories without Spanish horses, cattle, and mules, or the European weapons that intensified raiding and warfare across both continents.

Indian Resistance and Incorporation

Indigenous groups who became allies or subjects of the Spanish Empire were transformed as well. The Sonoran *serranos* Radding discusses developed an agro-pastoralist economy based upon both small-scale stockraising and agriculture. Many of their winter crops such as wheat, lentils, and fava beans were Old World domesticates because the major New World crops—corn, beans, and squash—were not frost tolerant. By the mid-nineteenth century, the Akimel O'odham (Pima Indians) living along the Gila River had become the greatest agricultural entrepreneurs in the Arizona Territory, selling millions of pounds of wheat to forty-niners, the Butterfield Stage Line, and both Confederate and Union soldiers during the Civil War (Sheridan 1988b).

But the adoption of European material items—or European rituals and symbols—did not necessarily mean acculturation and assimilation. Indians pursued many different strategies to resist incorporation into the Spanish Empire, ranging from the violent rebellions Deeds talks about to less direct resistance. Those strategies included geographic retreat among groups like the Rarámuri (Tarahumaras), who isolated themselves in the precipitous *barranca* (canyon) country on the western slopes of the Sierra Madre. They also involved all the so-called "weapons of the weak" including sarcasm, subterfuge, and foot dragging (Scott 1985).

Above all, however, Indians imposed their own meanings on the religious, political, and economic structures that Spaniards imposed upon them. During Semana Santa (Holy Week), for example, Rarámuri ceremonial participants in former mission communities group themselves into two organizations—the Soldiers (*sontárisi*) and Pharisees (*pariséo*)—and perform rituals rooted in the Passion plays taught them by Jesuit and Franciscan missionaries. Yet the reasons the Soldiers and Pharisees beat drums and march around their churches have more to do with Uto-Aztecan than Christian ideas about theology and the order of the universe.

According to the Tarahumaras, the universe is arranged in a series of levels with God (represented by images of Jesus) and God's wife (represented by images of the Virgin Mary) occupying the highest level and the devil dominating the lowest. God and the devil do not represent absolute good and absolute evil, however: the Rarámuri emphasize balance rather than the ultimate triumph of good over evil, and for most of the year, God and the devil possess equal power. During Holy Week, however, the devil gets God drunk and seduces his wife with his brilliant guitar playing. Seriously weakened, God and his wife seek refuge in Tarahumara churches. The Soldiers and Pharisees march in order to protect God until he can regain his strength and restore balance to the universe. Otherwise the world will be destroyed. Promises of an afterlife and Christian redemption from sin play little or no role in Rarámuri religious philosophy. The ceremonies of Holy Week may spring from Europe, but their meanings are highly Tarahumaran (Merrill 1983).

Unfortunately, we understand the social and cultural dynamics of Indian societies on the northern frontier much better than those of the Río de la Plata. Nonetheless, similar processes of resistance and reinterpretation undoubtedly occurred among the Guaraní and other South American peoples. Spanish conquest was a biological and cultural disaster for many native peoples, but those who survived manipulated the symbols, material items, and even the legal system of the conquerors to protect their communities and pursue their own goals within the empire.

Race, Class, and Gender on the Frontiers of the Spanish Empire

It is impossible to end our analysis of frontier societies without discussing race, class, and gender. The construction of social relations within the Spanish Empire and the American Southwest was intimately linked to these issues, and frontier areas were no exception. Although European women did not initially accompany the Spanish conquistadores, populations of European women helped mark Spanish families as elites; transmitted European culture, particularly to Indian women who served as domestics in their houses; and introduced European grains, fruits, and vegetables (Clendinnen 1982; Lockhart 1968; Martín 1983). Spanish women also married Indian men. Some were taken prisoner by Indians on both frontiers and later chose to live with the Indians rather than return to Spanish society. Their children benefited from their knowledge of both Spanish and indigenous languages (Socolow 1992).

Indigenous and African women also played critical roles. They were prime targets for the religious conversion of their families, and their service in Spanish households introduced them to new foods, customs, and language. Their gender and lack of power made them vulnerable sexual targets for European males. At the same time, however, many women used this cultural and sexual contact to help their own families. Their knowledge of Spanish and their personal relationships, including their relationships with European men, equipped them to help their groups develop better political strategies (Clendinnen 1982; R. Gutiérrez 1991; Mörner 1967).

Although the frontier regions of the Greater Southwest and the Río de la Plata have often been characterized as being eminently "male," the system of wealth transmission in both regions was predicated on the availability of women, as well as a legal system based upon inheritance. Therefore male relationships with women became important indicators of both class power and racial formation because they affected the class status and racial identity of their children.

The existence of involuntary servitude, both indigenous and African, as well as the system of identifying the status of children based upon whether their mother was slave or free, Indian or non-Indian, led to communities where the legal definition of race superseded concepts of class until the advent of the wars of independence. Thereafter in both the north and the south the legal system relied principally on accumulation of wealth and family history to identify the class position of men, while family history and the economic and social background of husbands defined the status of females.

Within the Río de la Plata region, the importation of African slaves, along with the presence of indigenous groups and the frequency of interracial relationships, led to a range of mestizo and mulatto groups in addition to the white Spanish population. In the Paraguayan region, bilingualism in Spanish and Guaraní became a common feature among the population, while in the Buenos Aires area there was little use of Indian languages by the non-Indian population. Furthermore, in the port area of Buenos Aires, the influx of European immigrants attracted by increased international commerce after 1810 soon overwhelmed the once-significant non-white population.

No such influx characterized the Greater Southwest until the California gold rush in 1849, nearly three decades after Mexican Independence and a year after the Treaty of Guadalupe Hidalgo ceded most of the American Southwest to the United States. Yet largely Spanish elites, some of them of Basque origin, developed in the relatively few, relatively small urban centers of Sonora, Sinaloa, Nueva Vizcaya, and Nuevo León (Voss 1982). Northern mining districts also imported African slaves during the seventeenth and eighteenth centuries, but their numbers were never large (West 1949). Nonetheless, mining communities —both the boom-and-bust placer discoveries and the more-established vein-mining districts like Alamos and Parral—attracted multiethnic labor forces where considerable miscegenation took place (Sheridan 1992).

Recent studies of widows in the American Southwest from the nineteenth century until 1939 indicate that widows residing in states with community property laws, a Spanish tradition, benefited from their rights to at least one-half of the community property. This contrasted with the Anglo-Saxon custom of a widow's third. Yet women of non-white races and ethnicities faced economic realities distinct from those of white women. They worked longer and often at much more onerous tasks (Scadron 1988). Other studies have emphasized not only the independence of many of the women but also women's economic interdependence and the critical role women have played in race relations (Foote 1990; Moynihan et al. 1990; Myres 1982; G. Riley 1984). In matters of gender as well as race and class, frontiers were zones of intense negotiation as well as violence—zones where social identities were more fluid than they were in more established areas where states exercised greater political, economic, and social control.

As the following chapters demonstrate, the Contested Ground project began with tantalizing similarities and ended up exploring significant differences between the northern and southern edges of the Spanish Empire and the republics that followed. All of us came away with more questions than answers. None of us finished this intellectual exercise believing that the Greater Southwest and the Río de la Plata offered a truly controlled comparison at all levels of analysis—cultural, political, economic, or ecological. The two ends of empire were too vast and too variegated for facile generalizations. In the future, more limited comparisons between regions such as the pampas and the plains may yield tighter contrasts and similarities.

At the same time, however, we did recognize that the frontiers we investigated were analytically distinct from the cores and even the peripheries of the Spanish Empire in the Americas or its succeeding nation-states. These frontiers were not empty quarters waiting to be settled or zones of barbarism waiting to be civilized a la Turner. On the contrary, they were shifting membranes of contact between different peoples, where power was constantly being contested and negotiated and where relations of race, class, and gender were different than in areas where empires or nation-states did indeed exercise a monopoly on violence. That recognition of frontier vitality and frontier volatility is perhaps the greatest contribution of this volume. We hope it stimulates more comparisons and more questions about these zones of intense contestation and negotiation at the edges of established social control.

2

The Jesuit Mission Frontier in Comparative Perspective

The Reductions of the Río de la Plata and the Missions of Northwestern Mexico, 1588–1700

DANIEL T. REFF

Reff challenges the deeply embedded historiographic assumption that Indians in Paraguay and northern New Spain accepted Jesuit missionization because of the inherent superiority of European crops, tools, and organizational strategies. He argues instead that Indian groups who welcomed the Jesuits did so because their own native systems were collapsing as a result of Old World epidemic diseases. Reff demonstrates that the mission frontier was a disease environment; early encounters between Jesuits and Indians cannot be understood without understanding the devastating epidemiological consequences of the Columbian Exchange in the Americas.

Reff also contends that Jesuit missionaries assumed the rights and responsibilities of native elites, reconstituted native production and organizational strategies, and introduced Christian beliefs and rituals that helped Amerindians cope with the unprecedented consequences of disease. He believes that Jesuits were particularly successful because their own epistemology, theology, and philosophy were consonant, in some respects, with Indian beliefs. The Jesuits also placed a high priority on acquisition of native languages, which facilitated their program of directed culture change.

SINCE THE END of the Pleistocene there have been few areas of the planet that have constituted true frontiers; humans have been continuously exploiting all but the most inhospitable corners of the Earth for the last eight thousand years. When we speak of the frontier, then, we are almost always referring to *contested ground*—land that becomes subject to competing claims of usufruct or ownership. Throughout history, the victors in this competition have not only claimed the frontier itself but often the exclusive right to its historical representation. Invariably the victors have cast themselves in the role of God's chosen people, while the vanquished either have had their existence denied[1] or have been cast as barbarians, infidels, or "underdeveloped" people.

It has been five hundred years since the invasion of the New World, when Europeans relegated the Indian to the role of savage, reserving for themselves the role of civilizer.[2] Try as we may to reject these categories, the fact remains that our habits of thought (rationalism, humanism, capitalism) and many of our values and beliefs—particularly notions of progress and success, as measured in the accumulation of property, energy, and personal power—predispose us to conceptualize the frontier and its principal players in ways that hearken back to the Columbian encounter (Comaroff and Comaroff 1992: 4; Galloway 1991: 453; Stannard 1992: 233–34). It is not by accident that the frontier often is spoken of in terms of cattle, fur, mining, and other commodities. Our "predicament of culture" (Clifford 1986) is evident in scholarly interpretations of what are perhaps the two most successful Jesuit enterprises in the history of the Americas (Dunne 1951: 123–24). In 1588 the Society of Jesus initiated the "spiritual conquest" of the Río de la Plata region, and in 1591, that of northwestern Mexico. Over the course of a century and a half, the Jesuits persuaded more than a half-million Indians in Paraguay and a comparable number in northwestern Mexico to accept baptism and missionization.

Several factors contributed to native interest in and acceptance of the Jesuits, particularly during the late sixteenth and first half of the seventeenth century. To date, most explanations of Jesuit success have reflected an implicit (if not explicit) assumption that mission ways of life, and, more generally, European civilization, were "advanced" relative to their native counterparts. It has often been suggested that the Guaraní of Paraguay and the native population of northwestern Mexico accepted the Jesuits in order to gain access to new and presumably better crops, tools, cattle, and organizational strategies (e.g., agricultural, military). In contrast, I suggest that there was nothing inherently better about Jesuit or European ways of life, including European technology.[3] Rather, native interest in and acceptance of the Jesuits were consequences of profound dislocations caused by epidemics of smallpox and other maladies during the late sixteenth and seventeenth centuries. If native peoples took an interest in the Jesuits and elements of their material culture (e.g., cattle, wool cloth, guns), it was largely because their own native systems and the environmental and sociopolitical context in which they had evolved had been undermined by disease episodes. Indeed, I suggest that the Jesuits generally assumed the rights and responsibilities of native elites, *reconstituting* native production and organizational strategies. The priests at the same time introduced beliefs and rituals (e.g., scourging processions, confession, relics), which, while of dubious intrinsic value, nevertheless enabled native peoples to deal with the unprecedented suffering and trauma coincident with recurrent epidemics.

The disease argument pursued in this essay is based on more than a decade of research with Jesuit and other primary sources from northwestern Mexico (see Reff 1991). Comparable research on disease has yet to be conducted for the Río de la Plata region. Thus, the argument elaborated in this chapter concerning the Guaraní missions is presented as a plausible scenario emerging from a pursuit of the parallels between the better understood situation in northwestern Mexico and the less well researched Río de la Plata.

The evidence of disease and its consequences clarifies the context in which native peoples opted for missionization. We are still left to identify the factors that enabled the Jesuits to assume leadership of "alien" societies. I pursue this question in the second half of the chapter, maintaining that the Jesuits went further than many of their European contemporaries, including members of other religious orders, in recognizing the rational basis of Indian culture. This recognition was due to a complex set of interrelated factors, including the Jesuits' epistemology/theology/philosophy, which was in many ways consistent with native beliefs. In addition, comparative analysis has shown that a significant number of missionaries in both Mexico and the Río de la Plata were Creoles. In the latter part of this essay I suggest ways in which the Jesuits' particular backgrounds, coupled with their acquisition of native languages, may have contributed to their success as missionaries.

Comparison of the Missions of Northwestern Mexico and the Río de la Plata

The Jesuit mission enterprises in northwestern Mexico and the Río de la Plata region were well documented by Jesuit participants (e.g., Pérez de Ribas 1645, 1896; Ruiz de Montoya [1639] 1892) and have been the subject of innumerable analyses, particularly by Jesuit historians (e.g., Alegre 1956–60; Hernández 1913; McNaspy 1984; Melia 1988; Pastells 1912–49; Polzer 1976; Storni 1980). A comparison of both mission frontiers reveals significant parallels that have a bearing on the issue of the missionaries' success. The term *success* is used here with reference to the fact that the Jesuits, whose numbers were never great (there were never more than eighty to one hundred missionaries working at any one time in either Paraguay or northwestern Mexico), were able to establish a largely self-supporting mission system that encompassed several hundred square miles and dozens of missions. At their height, the Guaraní missions and those in northwestern Mexico each had between 100,000 and 150,000 Indians under Jesuit tutelage.

In both Paraguay and northwestern Mexico the Jesuits received considerable support at the outset of each mission enterprise from key civil-military officials. Indeed, the governors of Nueva Vizcaya (Rio y Losa) and the Río de la Plata region (Hernandarias de Saavedra) initiated the Jesuit mission enterprises in their respective areas (López 1976: 20, 35; Mörner 1953: 205). This support during the formative years was particularly important inasmuch as the missionaries often were opposed by civilians who coveted the Jesuits' large Indian following. The Jesuits in both regions succeeded in winning exemptions from *encomiendas* and tithes for their Indian converts (López 1976: 37). Encomienda exemptions in the Río de la Plata region irked Spanish landowners, who had become accustomed to exploiting Indian labor during the half century preceding the arrival of the Jesuits in Asunción. When the Jesuits arrived in 1588, there were close to three hundred small Spanish farms in the valleys and grasslands to the north, east, and south of Asunción (López 1976: 23). Many if not most of these Spaniards employed Indians to harvest *yerba maté*—the principal export and "life blood" of the colonial economy of the Río de la Plata region.

Yerba maté was for the Spaniards of the Río de la Plata region what silver was for hundreds of Spaniards who flocked to northwestern Mexico during the second half of the sixteenth century. After the discovery of silver at Zacatecas in 1546, hundreds of silver mines and small farms and ranches were established in the sierras and along the eastern slopes of the Sierra Madre Occidental, in Durango and southern Chihuahua. Although Spaniards could not legally enslave Indians to work the mines or in related tasks, many Spaniards apparently abused the *repartimiento* system, enticing or forcing Indians to work for nominal wages (Deeds 1989). Indians who accepted baptism and Jesuit tutelage in northwestern Mexico, much like their Guaraní counterparts in the Río de la Plata region, were largely freed from involuntary labor drafts and were protected by the Jesuits.

For the most part, the Indians who accepted reduction and missionization in both the Río de la Plata region and northwestern Mexico were sedentary agriculturalists. Aboriginally, the Guaraní lived in innumerable permanent and semipermanent villages between the Atlantic coast and the Río Paraguay. The Indians grew a variety of crops, the most important of which were maize and manioc; beans, tobacco, and cotton were other important cultigens that the Indians exploited, along with a wide variety of hunted and gathered resources

(Métraux 1949). The aboriginal population of northwestern Mexico, with a few exceptions, also was sedentary. Maize, beans, squash, and cotton were cultivated by many if not most groups, who, like the Guaraní, lived in permanent and semipermanent villages ranging in size from several dozen to several thousand people (Beals 1932; Reff 1991; Sauer 1935).

In contrast, the Jesuits were decidedly less successful with hunter-gatherers, both in Mexico and in Paraguay (Mörner 1953: 201; Spicer 1962).[4] During the decades preceding the arrival of the first Jesuits in Asunción in 1588, the nomadic Mbayás, Guaycurús, and Abipones (from north to south) of the Gran Chaco all adopted the horse and began raiding Spanish and Guaraní settlements to the east of the Río Paraguay. The missions founded by the Jesuits during the seventeenth century were not immune from attack, particularly from the Guaycurús and Abipones as well as the Charrúas, another nomadic group that harassed the missions of the east and the south (López 1976: 41). The Jesuits in northwestern Mexico also had to contend with hostile horse nomads, although not until the mission system had reached maturity. Beginning in the late 1600s and continuing long after the Jesuit expulsion in 1767, the Apaches constantly threatened the Jesuit missions of Sonora (Spicer 1962: 230–40).

Raids by horse nomads, and more important, by Paulistas or bandeirantes from São Paulo, contributed to what is perhaps the most striking difference between the missions of the Río de la Plata region and those of northwestern Mexico, and indeed, the rest of the Americas (Mörner 1953: 199–201). Tens of thousands of Indians in the Guayra and Tape regions of the Río de la Plata were enslaved or killed by bandeirante slave raiders between 1628 and 1631. The raids forced the wholesale abandonment of almost two dozen Jesuit missions along the upper Río Paraná and the Río Ibicuy. In response to these raids, the Jesuits initially consolidated and then expanded their mission enterprise southwest of the Río Tebicuary. This rebirth of the mission system in the 1640s followed an unprecedented request by the Jesuits, which was approved by the Crown, to train and arm a thousand converts with muskets. Beginning in the 1640s, and throughout the remainder of the Jesuits' tenure in Paraguay, the Jesuits maintained a well-armed and well-trained Guaraní militia, which checked not only nomadic and Paulista raids, but the designs of Paraguayan *encomenderos*. Researchers have suggested that this unique military organization and the protection it afforded enticed the Guaraní to settle in missions (e.g., López 1976: 38).[5]

Disease and Its Demographic Consequences

As noted at the outset, perhaps the most significant parallel between the mission frontiers in northwestern Mexico and Paraguay is that they were disease environments. Elsewhere I have discussed in detail the evidence regarding Spanish-introduced diseases and their consequences in northwestern Mexico (Reff 1991, 1992; see also Gerhard 1982), including the role disease played in Jesuit-Indian relations. During the third quarter of the sixteenth century, following the opening of mines in the mountains and along the eastern slope of the Sierra Madre Occidental, infectious diseases began to make their way northward from Mesoamerica into northwestern Mexico. This movement of disease agents was facilitated by the regular flow of goods and people to and from the Spanish mining frontier. As a result, native populations generally were reduced by 30 to 50 percent prior to Jesuit contact. Following the founding of Jesuit missions in the 1590s and the colonization of New Mexico in 1598, opportunities for the northward spread of disease multiplied. Accordingly, beginning in 1593, the annual reports compiled by the Jesuits frequently mention or discuss in detail epidemics of smallpox, measles, typhus, and other maladies that swept through the mission system and beyond at regular five- to eight-year intervals (e.g., 1593, 1601–2, 1607–8, 1611–12, 1617, and 1623–25). Within a few decades of reduction and missionization, native populations uniformly were reduced by 75 percent or more (Reff 1991, 1992).

The rate and extent of population decline is reflected in Jesuit figures on baptisms and mission populations. In 1638, for instance, the Jesuits reported that only one-third of the 300,000 Indians they had baptized were still alive. In 1678, when the number of Indians baptized exceeded 400,000, the mission population totaled only 63,000. At the time of the expulsion, in 1767, the mission population had declined even further to approximately 30,000 (Reff 1991: 210–13).

In the Río de la Plata region, scholars have only recently begun to acknowledge the dynamic role of disease in Jesuit-Indian relations (e.g., López 1976: 37; Palacios and Zoffoli 1991: 293ff.). Nonetheless, there, just as in northwestern Mexico, smallpox, typhus, dysentery, and other acute and chronic infectious diseases exacted a terrible toll on the native population, both before and after Jesuit contact (Cantón 1921; Hernández 1913: I:13–15; Mörner 1953: 204). As was the case in northwestern Mexico, the Río de la Plata region suffered from repeated epidemics that apparently originated in adjoining areas, specifically highland Peru, where population densities were much greater and where Spanish mining activity at Potosí encouraged frequent movement of goods, people, and disease agents to Paraguay. Note that by the early 1700s more than six hundred tons of yerba maté were being imported each year from Paraguay to Potosí (López 1976: 24). Significantly, within a year or two of an epidemic in highland Peru, the same disease(s) was often reported by the Jesuits of the Río de la Plata region. For instance, the epidemics that affected the Río de la Plata region in

1589, 1595–99, 1610, and 1614 all seem to be correlated with slightly earlier or contemporaneous epidemics in the Potosí region (Evans 1991: 150–51).

Between 1524 and 1620 the population of the central Andes was reduced from around 9,000,000 to 600,000 (Cook 1981; Cook and Lovell 1991). Most of this population decline occurred between 1524 and 1588, when there were numerous epidemics and at least three pandemics of typhus (1546), influenza (1557–58), and smallpox (1585–91) (Cook 1992: 210). The last of these disease episodes, the smallpox epidemic which lasted from 1585 to 1591, was one of the most devastating pandemics of the sixteenth century (Alchon 1991; Cook 1992). It is the first pandemic that we know for certain affected the Río de la Plata region. Shortly after the three Jesuits arrived in Asunción, in 1589, the three priests (Ortega, Saloni, Fields) were called to Villa Rica and surrounding settlements, where they worked for nine months, attending to the corporal and spiritual needs of thousands of Guaraní. Reportedly, some two thousand Indians died before the priests could even propose baptism. Another six thousand gentiles were baptized, many of whom perished; the three Jesuits reportedly interred more than four thousand Indians during their nine-month stay (Cantón 1921: 130–31).

After striking Villa Rica and its environs, the epidemic apparently spread to Asunción, where more than one hundred people died per day (Cantón 1921: 131; Hernández 1913: I:6). Many thousands of Guaraní in and around the city perished. The Jesuits reportedly heard the confessions of ten thousand natives and interred another ten thousand who died (Cantón 1921: 131). This figure may or may not include some four thousand gentiles who died after baptism. Ciudad Real and the densely populated Guayra region along the upper Río Paraná also were devastated by the epidemic. Although the Jesuits did not provide mortality figures, they reported attending to thousands of Guaraní, again, many or most of whom perished (Cantón 1921: 131).

The 1589 smallpox epidemic occurred twenty years before the Jesuits actually established permanent missions among the Guaraní. In 1595, when the Jesuits were still just visiting native settlements, the Indians were stricken by another epidemic of what appears to have been, in part, smallpox. Again, the Jesuits reported that many thousands died (Cantón 1921: 132). As was the case in northwestern Mexico, epidemics followed in 1605–6 (López 1976: 52), 1610 (Pastells 1912–49: I:181), 1614 (Cortesão 1952: 16), 1621 (Cantón 1921: 29), and throughout the remainder of the seventeenth century (Hernández 1913: I:11). Well into the eighteenth century, smallpox continued to exact a heavy toll among the Guaraní and their neighbors (Cantón 1921: 148). In 1764–65, for instance, the disease swept the Paraguayan missions, killing some twelve thousand Indians out of a total population of around ninety thousand (Hernández 1913: I:11).

In Paraguay as elsewhere, the native population suffered from both acute and chronic infectious diseases. Works such as Ruiz de Montoya's *Conquista espiritual* (1639: 46, 53, 68–69, 82, 177) abound in references to typhus, dysentery, fevers (possibly malaria), measles, and smallpox (see also McNaspy 1984: 72, 76, 115, 125; Palacios and Zoffoli 1991: 324ff). In 1631, some two thousand Guaraní who were fleeing Paulista slave raiders died of dysentery (Ruiz de Montoya [1639] 1892: 160–61). Dysentery, typhus, and what may have been malaria were common among the Jesuits themselves (Hernández 1913: I:10; McNaspy 1984: 100–101). In 1637, malaria apparently had become such a problem that Jesuit superiors instructed priests to be more careful in their choice of mission locations to avoid areas that were too hot and infested with mosquitoes (Palacios and Zoffoli 1991: 311).[6]

A number of scholars have suggested that the Guaraní population was reduced by upwards of 90 percent by 1732—from roughly 1,000,000 to 141,000 (Furlong 1962: 8). However, the size of the aboriginal Guaraní population is unknown. Relatively little archaeological research that might shed light on pre- and postcontact demographic trends has been conducted in Paraguay (Palacios and Zoffoli 1991: 32). The historical record, as is apparent, suffers from its own shortcomings. Comprehensive time-series data were compiled neither by Spanish explorers nor by the later Jesuits, although the latter did produce impressive reports with data on baptisms and mission populations. Moreover, it is difficult to determine the importance of disease as compared with raiding by nomads and the Paulistas and the evils of encomienda, particularly Indian mortality from harvesting yerba maté, which reportedly claimed thousands of lives (Ruiz de Montoya [1639] 1892: 35).

We may never know the precise demographic consequences of disease in the Río de la Plata region. Nevertheless, various figures compiled by the Jesuits are suggestive. By 1639, the Jesuits had baptized roughly the same number of Indians in the Río de la Plata region as in northwestern Mexico—approximately 300,000 (Pastells 1912–49: VIII:596). It is not known how many of the Río de la Plata Indians were still alive in 1639, although the number could not have been more than 100,000, of whom more than two-thirds (assuming they were still alive) were slaves of the Luso-Brazilians. Once the Jesuits effectively repulsed the incursions of slavers (in the 1640s) and missions were reconstituted between the Tebicuary and Uruguay Rivers, the mission population rebounded. By 1657 there were nineteen Jesuit Guaraní missions with a population of 30,000. This number increased to 56,000 by 1678; to 102,000 by 1710 (in thirty missions); and peaked at 141,000 in the 1730s (Hernández 1913: II:717; López 1976: 36, 53).

This last figure of 141,000, although it may seem large, pales in comparison with the half-million or more Guaraní who were baptized by the Jesuits (Astrain 1902: V:518; Palacios and Zoffoli 1991: 156–65) and the enormous populations (100,000–200,000) that were reported in the mid 1500s for individual districts or regions such as Guayra, Tape, and the region between the Río Uruguay and the Río Paraná (Hernández 1913: I:5, 7; Palacios and Zoffoli 1991: 154–55). In the Asunción region alone, the Guaraní population declined between 1556 and 1688 from more than 100,000 to fewer than 12,000 (López 1976: 51–52).

Jesuit Success and Native Acceptance of Missionization

It is apparent that introduced diseases had a profound impact on the Guaraní, much as they did on the native population of northwestern Mexico. Until very recently, the evidence of disease and its consequences has not figured prominently in scholarly assessments of the dynamics of Jesuit-Indian relations in either the Río de la Plata region or northwestern Mexico. Traditional approaches have been hampered by enduring images that were produced centuries ago by some of the first Jesuit missionaries to work among the Guaraní and in northwestern Mexico. In works by authors such as Ruiz de Montoya (1639) and Pérez de Ribas (1645), the Jesuits are cast in the role of "great civilizers," combating idolatry, drunkenness, warfare, laziness, and polygamy (see also Cardiel [1767] 1989: 51).

Subsequently, during the Enlightenment, the Jesuit mission enterprises of the New World, particularly the Guaraní missions (known as the "Jesuit state"), were championed by Voltaire and Rousseau as testaments to European intellect and its ability to fashion through reason and logic a society where there once was chaos or uncertain relations (Mörner 1953: 195). This view has persisted into the twentieth century. In one of his earliest and most influential works on the mission frontier, Bolton wrote that the missionaries "helped to not only extend, hold, and promote the frontier, but more significantly still, they helped to civilize it" (Bolton 1917: 52). Indeed, Bolton likened the mission to a "great industrial school," where besides learning good manners, agriculture, and self-government, "the women were taught to cook, sew, spin, and weave; the men to fell the forest, build, run the forge, tan leather, make ditches, tend cattle, and shear sheep" (Bolton 1917: 57). According to Bolton, once the missionaries taught the "erstwhile barbarians" the rudiments of civilization, they turned the wilderness of New Spain into a veritable bastion of progress, with imposing buildings, fertile farms, and great stock ranches (Bolton 1917: 58).

The conclusions reached by Bolton in this early work were amplified in many of his later publications and have generally been accepted by modern historians and anthropologists. Researchers interested in both Paraguay and northwestern Mexico have emphasized the importance of new crops, tools, cattle, and other Jesuit innovations in purportedly attracting Indian converts and then "revolutionizing" aboriginal culture. The Jesuits are said to have made possible native settlement in towns, permanent houses, intensive agriculture, crop surpluses, craft production, and other advances in native economic and sociopolitical organization, including, in the case of Paraguay, a sophisticated military organization (McNaspy 1984: 190; Métraux 1949: 646, 651; Palacios and Zoffoli 1991: 191; Spicer 1962: 285–98).

Elsewhere (Reff 1991) I have discussed the evidence regarding Spanish or Jesuit "innovations" and their purported contribution to Jesuit success. There is no question that native peoples were interested in obtaining such things as knives, axes, cattle, horses, and clothing and that the Jesuits distributed these items as gifts to win over native *caciques* or *principales.* It is misleading, however, to suggest that these goods played a truly dynamic role in Jesuit-Indian relations, fueling and sustaining native interest in missionization. If Western technology were in fact a key reason for native interest in missionization, one would be left to explain why the Jesuits did not import and distribute large numbers of knives, kettles, axes, plows, and other goods. In the case of northwestern Mexico, I have yet to encounter a Jesuit bill of lading or other documentary evidence that the Jesuits imported significant quantities of manufactured goods to the frontier. Indeed, each Jesuit received a modest stipend from the Crown (250 pesos), much of which the individual missionary spent on ornaments for the church, rosaries, candle wax, and similar items rather than on plows, iron tools, or fruit trees (Reff 1991: 256; Treutlein 1939). It is also significant that works like Pérez de Ribas' *Historia* and Ruiz de Montoya's *Conquista espiritual*—both of which were written in part as "textbooks" for novitiates and would-be missionaries—neither indicate nor suggest that the distribution of fruit trees, horses, or metal items was or should be an important part of any conversion strategy.

This is not to say that horses, metal axes, fruit trees, and Old World cultigens did not become important for native peoples, particularly during the *eighteenth and nineteenth centuries.* At issue is whether European animals, plants, and technology played a dynamic role during the first sixty years or so of the Jesuit mission enterprises in Paraguay and northwestern Mexico. It was during this period that the vast majority of Jesuit converts accepted mission tutelage. Seventeenth-century acculturative processes cannot be explained on the basis of eighteenth- and nineteenth-century realities.

In both Paraguay and northwestern Mexico the Jesuits and their Indian charges employed mostly native farming practices and cultigens; the vast mission system erected by the Jesuits during the seventeenth century was based on corn, beans, squash, manioc, cotton, tobacco, and yerba maté—not European cultigens (Ribeiro 1983: 223; Ruiz de Montoya [1639] 1892: 17; Schmidel 1986: 44). Although it is true that the Jesuits introduced large numbers and varieties of cattle that were welcomed by native peoples, domesticated animals are not inherently better than the abundant wild resources that native peoples exploited aboriginally (Palacios and Zoffoli 1991: 182; Reff 1991: 259; Ruiz de Montoya [1639] 1892: 18–23; Schmidel 1986: 44).[7] The main advantage domesticated animals offered over wild animals during the early mission period was that they were a more readily available source of nourishment during epidemics (Hackett, Bandelier, and Bandelier 1926–37: III: 100).

What contributed most to Jesuit success during the early mission period was the *reconstitution* of native productive and organizational strategies. Before the arrival of the Jesuits and the introduction of Old World diseases, the Guaraní and their native counterparts in northwestern Mexico were living in permanent and semipermanent villages with populations that numbered in the hundreds and occasionally thousands (Clastres 1981: 98; Palacios and Zoffoli 1991: 154–55; Reff 1991). In point of fact, the idea of living in villages or towns with permanent houses was not new to native peoples in either Paraguay or northwestern Mexico. This is true, for example, of the large, communal structures that came to characterize the Guaraní missions; the Jesuits modified aboriginal structures (*ogapiguasauva*) by including interior walls, reflecting the missionaries' privileging of the nuclear family (Palacios and Zoffoli 1991: 126). It was precisely because native peoples already had a cultural model of village life that so many natives were interested in missionization.[8] The production and husbanding of crop surpluses also was not new to the Guaraní or groups in northwestern Mexico (Hernández 1913: vol. I), nor was it necessary for the Jesuits to teach native peoples "artistry."

Both Spanish explorers (e.g., Hammond and Rey 1928) and the Jesuits (e.g., Pérez de Ribas 1645) spoke of caciques in northwestern Mexico who apparently were heads of localized patrilineal descent groups. Often these caciques recognized a "principal chief," who enjoyed differential access to land, goods, and services and who monopolized the means of war, being able to assemble thousands of warriors from numerous villages and *rancherías* (Reff 1991: 40–42). Similarly, the Guaraní were reported to live in villages that were governed by lineage heads (caciques) and chiefs (principal caciques) who exercised considerable power and influence (Clastres 1981; Métraux 1949; Reff 1991). In both Paraguay and northwestern Mexico, it was often these caciques who petitioned for priests and baptism, relinquishing in the process some if not all of their authority (e.g., Cortesão 1952: 23–26; Reff 1991: 40–41).

The Jesuits were able to assume many of the rights and responsibilities of native elites because they were better able to explain and deal with disease. In the relative absence of pre-Columbian epidemics, native cultures in northwestern Mexico and Paraguay had elaborated few behaviors and beliefs to deal with the unprecedented destruction wrought by maladies such as smallpox. By contrast, the Jesuits brought rituals and beliefs that had evolved in the Old World over the course of a millennium precisely to deal with disease. Indeed, the history of Christianity—here defined as the religious beliefs and practice of peasants and clergy rather than of princes and ecclesiastical councils—is very much a history of vows, relics, saints, shrines, prayers, and processions to prevent or ameliorate misfortune, especially epidemic disease (Amundsen 1986; Christian 1981; Flint 1991; McNeill 1976). Although one can question the intrinsic value of relics, rosaries, confession, or blood processions, they nevertheless can have profound benefits for individuals and communities gripped with fear. The fact that the Jesuits coupled prayer with clinical care of the sick also empowered them vis-à-vis native elites, who, again, had little experience in this regard. Lastly, as Pérez de Ribas noted, the Jesuits had one further advantage over native elites:

> It was noted that God took the lives of Indian principales who were obstacles to the teaching of the Gospel. He finished them off to the amazement of their people. On the other hand, these nations have seen and noticed that the priests among them live long lives. They generally enjoy good health, in spite of the fact that they are destitute of doctors and medicines. (Pérez de Ribas 1645: 339)

Jesuit Recognition of the Indian

To suggest that the Jesuits' success hinged on their ability to reconstitute native productive and organizational strategies presupposes that they understood and appreciated important dimensions of Indian behaviors and beliefs. The Jesuits' perception of the Indian was governed to a large extent by their unwavering belief that they possessed the truth (Christianity, civilization) and that they were called on by God to impart this truth to the Indians, who had been enslaved by the devil for millennia (Ruiz de Montoya [1639] 1892; Pérez de Ribas 1645). In point of fact, the Jesuits were hardly cultural relativists; they came to the New World to change (not to understand) Indian cultures. Ethnocentrism is never absolute, however, and ironically, the same priests who lamented the Indians' lack of civilization discovered significant parallels in thought and behavior with native peoples. This was true, for example, of the Jesuits' commitment to communal, nonpropertied living and ceremonial and ritualistic labor, as defined by the Jesuit Constitutions (Ganss 1970; O'Malley 1993). The Jesuit formula for living, as it were, was very much at odds with the individualism, materialism, and "buyer beware" attitude of emergent capitalism back in Europe. Jesuit celebration of obedience, poverty, and charity, on the other hand, was entirely consistent with the principles of seniority (particularly male), reciprocity, and redistribution that governed native economic and sociopolitical systems (Palacios and Zoffoli 1991: 185; Reff 1991: 265).

The Jesuits went further than many of their European contemporaries in grasping the rational basis of Indian culture, and it was precisely this understanding of the "other" that helped them to reconstitute Indian productive and organizational strategies. In this regard, there were several interrelated factors that may have empowered the Jesuits as observers and which may help explain their success in the Río de la Plata region and northwestern Mexico. First, in keeping with their Thomistic education and philosophy, the Jesuits were predisposed to view the Indian as a rational being;[9] it was centuries of isolation from the Old World and an ignorance of the word of God—not a lack of reason—that accounted for the Native Americans' "backwardness." It is significant in this regard that Jesuit missionaries in Mexico in the late 1500s remained strong advocates of a native clergy (see Zubillaga 1968–73: III:328–38) even when other regular and secular priests took no stand on or actively opposed an Indian priesthood (Morales 1973; Poole 1981).

The fact that the Jesuits and Native Americans had a similar worldview contributed further to the missionaries' recognition of Native American behaviors and beliefs. At a time when rationalism and nominalism were flowering in Europe, the Jesuits and other religious retained what was essentially a medieval epistemology and worldview, championing the idea of a mysterious God who constantly intervened on earth to change the course of events and to combat Satan (Moore 1982).[10] Jesuit "supernaturalism," particularly the idea of the inseparability of the natural and invisible worlds, was consistent with the aboriginal beliefs of their Native American converts (Moore 1982: 197; Rubert de Ventos 1991). Although the Jesuits and their converts may have disagreed about who was responsible for supernatural events, neither doubted reports of flying shamans, talking stones, or altar cloths that mysteriously began to bleed (Reff 1995). Presumably, the discovery of this shared metaphysics facilitated Jesuit understanding and manipulation of Indian culture. In this regard, it is apparent that the Jesuits retained, albeit modifying when necessary, many aspects of native life. In the Río de la Plata region, for instance, the Jesuits retained such

Guaraní customs as communal living, governance by caciques, and even the Guaraní word for God (Tupan) (Palacios and Zoffoli 1991: 107).[11]

The worldview, including the supernaturalism, that many Jesuits brought to the Americas was particularly characteristic of Mediterranean Europe, where the populace found satisfaction and solace in miraculous intervention and supernatural activity (Weinstein and Bell 1982: 193). Mediterranean Europe is precisely the origin of many Jesuits who worked in the Río de la Plata region and northwestern Mexico during the seventeenth century (Aspurz 1946). Many Jesuits who journeyed to the Americas during this period were Italians, Portuguese, and of course, Spaniards (Aspurz 1946; Fajardo 1974: 6; McNaspy 1984: 22–23).[12]

Another striking feature of the Jesuit enterprises in northwestern Mexico and the Río de la Plata region is the number of Jesuit Creoles—individuals born in the Americas of European parents—who served on the mission frontier. The Jesuits differed in this regard from the Franciscans, who resisted for many years the admission of novitiates who had been born in Mexico (Morales 1973: 54–75). Some of the founding fathers of the Río de la Plata missions, priests such as Antonio Ruiz de Montoya and Roque González de Santa Cruz, were Creoles (McNaspy 1984). Storni's (1980) analysis of the Jesuit *catálogos* indicates that roughly 25 percent of the Jesuits who worked in Paraguay were born in the Americas, particularly in what is today Argentina (14 percent), Chile (4 percent), and Paraguay itself (4 percent). Eighty-three Jesuits were born in Asunción; more Jesuits who served in Paraguay came from this city than from cities in Spain (McNaspy 1984: 22–23).

A cursory examination of Jesuit catálogos and other sources for northwestern Mexico (e.g., Pérez de Ribas 1896; Zambrano 1961–77; Zubillaga 1968–73: vols. III, IV) suggests that the Jesuits, in fact, may have encouraged Creole novitiates. Significantly, the first missions in northwestern New Spain were founded by pairs of priests, each of which included a Creole born on the northern frontier.[13] It is unclear whether this pattern held throughout the mission period, reflecting a strategy consciously devised by Jesuit rectors and provincials. In his discussion of missions in the Jesuit Constitutions, Ignatius Loyola drew attention to the importance of pairing priests to insure the most effective combinations (e.g., experienced versus inexperienced; very ardent and daring versus circumspect and cautious)(Ganss 1970: 277–78).

Because they were themselves discriminated against and considered less capable by "true Spaniards" (McNaspy 1984: 52; Mörner 1953: 210), Creoles understood the status of "other." As Mörner (1953: 202) has suggested, Creole Jesuits were more apt than non-Creoles to take a wider view of colonial affairs. Arguably, Creoles would have had more exposure to Indian peoples and culture, and would be more apt to acquire native languages,[14] which was of paramount significance in understanding Indian behaviors and beliefs (Dunigan 1958; Polzer 1976; Rubert de Ventos 1991: 46–47).

No skill was demanded of the Jesuit missionary more often than knowledge of Indian languages. Although scholars have disagreed about whether other orders such as the Franciscans routinely mastered native languages (e.g., Clendinnen 1987: 11; Gómez Canedo 1977: 154ff.; Kessell 1976: 9, 11), the evidence from northern Mexico reveals that the Jesuits did learn and use native languages, whereas their Franciscan counterparts did not (Griffen 1979: 55; Polzer 1976: 56–57; Zubillaga 1968–73 V: 21, 219).[15] Jesuit reports, rules, and correspondence repeatedly emphasized that priests should become proficient in the native language of their assigned mission (e.g., Zubillaga 1973: 631). Indeed, among the rules drawn up by Father Visitor Rodrigo de Cabredo in 1611 was one that stated, "All missionaries will procure with all carefulness the language of their assigned mission—no priest will content himself with a knowledge of the Mexican language. It is imperative if the Indians are to grasp the mysteries of the Catholic faith that preaching, confessing, etc., be done in the native language."[16] The seriousness with which the Jesuits took these rules is suggested by Pérez de Ribas' (1645: 436) observation that missionaries on the northern frontier often ran the risk of forgetting their mother tongues. Elsewhere he noted:

> For the evangelical minister there is no means so powerful for winning the Indians over, dominating them, and retaining the great authority that is required for effective instruction, than to speak the Indians' language, particularly if it is spoken well. . . . Through language the minister is more revered than are their lying preachers. Moreover, I can state on the basis of much experience that sometimes knowing the language will enable he who preaches in it to save himself from the mortal dangers, disturbances, restlessness, and uprisings that the devil causes among these peoples. Speaking to them in their own language calms and controls them, it wins them over and subjects them. (Pérez de Ribas 1645: 22)

In Paraguay, Jesuit superiors also insisted that their priests master Guaraní and other native languages; many if not most Jesuits heeded this rule (McNaspy 1984: 48; Palacios and Zoffoli 1991: 105).

Conclusion

The Jesuit mission frontiers in Paraguay and northwestern Mexico were similar in many ways. On the eve of Columbus' fateful voyage of "discovery," the aboriginal population of the Río de la Plata region and northwestern Mexico numbered somewhere between 500,000 and 1,000,000. Archaeological evidence as well as observations of the earliest Spaniards indicate that native peoples in both regions lived in permanent and semipermanent villages that enjoyed a relative abundance of food that was grown as well as hunted and gathered. Although we know relatively little about many other aspects of native life, there is no empirical basis for inferring that the aboriginal populations of northwestern Mexico and Paraguay were "backward" or somehow in need of advancement.

In this chapter I have argued that Jesuit success was not a function of native peoples seeking to rectify any inherent deficiencies in their culture by accepting Jesuit programs for reduction and missionization. It has been largely our belief in progress—our own cultural conceit—that has led many to conclude that the Guaraní and the native societies of northwestern Mexico were drawn to the missions by wheat, oxen, metal knives, or the Jesuit organizational strategies for work or military defense. This is not to suggest that wheat, cattle, guns, and other items were not important but rather that their importance was conditioned by the collapse of native economic, sociopolitical, and religious systems. The fact is that the mission frontier was a disease environment. It was in this context that the Jesuits proposed baptism—a ritual cleansing of the soul—along with native resettlement in villages and towns where nonpropertied living and work arrangements very much like those that existed aboriginally were pursued. Although the Jesuits did not explicitly acknowledge their indebtedness to native people, and, indeed, many were loathe to consider such a possibility (e.g., Cardiel 1767; Nentvig [1764] 1980), subconsciously at least, they recognized the logic and utility of many native behaviors and beliefs, particularly those that were consistent with Church teachings.

This recognition of the "other" was facilitated in part by the Jesuits' own particular backgrounds and worldview, which embraced the "immediate reality of an invisible world." Of perhaps greater importance was the Jesuit mandate to become fluent in native languages. This pursuit of native languages permitted, or perhaps implicitly forced, the Jesuits to contemplate alternative behaviors and beliefs. Thus, the geographically distinct yet conceptually similar cases of northwestern Mexico and Paraguay show that the Jesuits, paradoxically, were both destroyers and rebuilders of native cultures.

3

Indigenous Rebellions on the Northern Mexican Mission Frontier

From First-Generation to Later Colonial Responses

SUSAN M. DEEDS

Deeds compares and contrasts the Acaxee rebellion of 1601 with the Yaqui rebellion of 1740 in order to demonstrate how Indian resistance in northern New Spain changed in response to changing frontier conditions. The Acaxee Revolt, like other first-generation Indian rebellions in the region, was characterized by messianic leadership and promises of millennial redemption during a period of violent disruption and catastrophic demographic decline due to disease. Deeds argues that these rebellions were attempts to revitalize many precontact social and religious elements in worlds that had been turned upside down by recent Spanish conquest and colonization. In a sense, her argument is the flip side of the same coin Reff tosses into the air in this volume: Some factions among Indian groups welcomed missionization while others resisted, yet both responses can be understood only in the context of disease and death. The 1740 Yaqui rebellion, on the other hand, was a more limited endeavor to restore the colonial pact of village autonomy and territorial integrity Radding describes.

Deeds is far more critical of the early Jesuits than Reff, arguing that missionization facilitated and accelerated the exploitation of Indian labor by consolidating dispersed Indian communities into mission towns. She also criticizes later Jesuit intransigence as the missionaries sought to limit Yaqui autonomy. Yaquis responded by manipulating divisions between the Jesuits and Spanish civil officials to pursue their own agendas in the colonial world. Above all, Deeds challenges the notion that there were homogeneous mission or frontier revolts. Instead, Indian rebellion and resistance must be interpreted in the context of distinct frontier stages and conditions shaped by many different historical and geographic variables.

DURING THE seventeenth and eighteenth centuries, the northern frontier of New Spain experienced a number of revolts by indigenous peoples incorporated to varying degrees into Spanish institutional structures. Jesuit and Franciscan missions represented Spanish institutional presence at its most local level. In this chapter I will use the concept of mission frontiers to denote zones of intercultural contact where incorporation by the Spanish system was fragile and fragmentary. Missions were social spaces where disparate cultures met and contested one another, usually in very unequal relations of domination and subordination (Pratt 1992: 6–7).[1] Therefore the mission frontier has both cultural and geographic connotations for the modern reader. Although we cannot be certain about how precontact indigenous groups construed the concept of frontier, we might expect that they perceived it similarly to the Spaniards in one respect: as a region of warfare and danger. They may also have associated it with the appropriation of resources outside their traditional boundaries, but they probably did not fully understand the Spaniards' goal of conquest: the permanent appropriation of territory, resources, and people. Nor did they embrace the Spanish association of frontier with religious crusading—that persistent legacy of the reconquest of Spain from the Muslims. Furthermore, the idea that frontiers were relatively empty spaces that had to be demarcated and "civilized" by filling them with towns was especially alien to Indian consciousness, at least to that of the Indians along New Spain's northern frontier.

The northern revolts ranged from the Acaxee rebellion in 1601 through the Pima uprising of 1751. In between fell revolts by the Xiximes (1610), Tepehuanes (1616–20), Tarahumaras (1648, 1650, 1652), and Pueblos (1680–92); Tarahumaras and other Sierra Madre Occidental peoples (1690s); Baja California groups (1734), and Yaquis (1740).[2] The aim of this chapter is to compare and contrast characteristics of the earliest "first-generation" revolt of the Acaxees, which began in 1601, with the Yaqui rebellion of 1740, which occurred after more than a century of Spanish impositions, and to identify peculiarly frontier attributes of both.[3]

Historians have noted that central Mexico's more concentrated indigenous population did not rebel in mass during the colonial period; instead riots tended to be localized (Taylor 1979). Pan-village revolts occurred more frequently in comparatively politically decentralized areas on the fringes of New Spain (Gosner 1992; G. Jones 1989). Nonetheless, it is misleading to suggest that there is a category of *peripheral rebellions* or *mission revolts* that have homogeneous characteristics (Coatsworth 1988: 27–28).[4] Even on frontiers, the uprisings that occurred after at least a century of Spanish occupation arose out of a more complex, layered mix of political, economic, social, ideological, and ecological factors than did first-generation rebellions. This chapter will examine two main questions: To what extent did frontier status with its peculiar variables of time, space, population density, and culture contact affect the motivations and characteristics of the revolts? Furthermore, how do they fit within a wide range of local indigenous responses to Spanish intrusion?

Although there is disagreement as to the degree of complexity of northwestern Indian societies at the beginning of the sixteenth century (Deeds forthcoming 1998b; Reff 1991: 17–96),[5] by the time Acaxees and Yaquis began to be congregated in missions at the turn of the seventeenth century, they shared features of what Spicer (1962) called the *ranchería* pattern. Living in dispersed settlements of only a few to perhaps several hundred households (rancherías), they cultivated corn, beans, squash, chiles, and cotton. Ranchería locations shifted in accordance with seasonal cycles and soil fertility. Native peoples complemented agricultural production with hunting and gathering. Their political structure was decentralized, with no overall tribal leader; rancherías were governed by elders. During frequent intertribal warfare, war leaders sometimes united several rancherías under their control. A headman, or cacique, represented the consensus of elders in dealing with outsiders. Ceremonial rituals were designed to placate gods of water, fire, and other natural forces through ceremonies of gift giving and dancing, often accompanied by the use of intoxicants. Shamans (called *hechiceros,* or sorcerers, by Spaniards) had special supernatural powers.

Although Acaxees and Yaquis shared these features of the ranchería pattern in the early seventeenth century, they also had significant cultural and environmental differences. They spoke distinct dialects of the Cahitan subgroup of Uto-Aztecan languages. Some evidence suggests that Acaxees may have had larger population concentrations in fortified villages. Environmental differences are particularly striking. Acaxees lived in dispersed rancherías in the gorges and canyons of the Sierra Madre Occidental in northwestern Durango and east-central Sinaloa. These sites were separated by steep canyon walls and high summits that made communication difficult and travel hazardous. A journey of a few miles distance as the crow flies meant as much as ten times that distance ascending and descending precipitous ravines with scores of river crossings.

To the northwest, Yaqui rancherías were distributed along the river of the same name, which flows southwestward from the Sierra Madre into the Gulf of California near present-day Guaymas. The bulk of the Yaqui population lived in comparatively densely populated rancherías along the middle Río Yaqui, where they practiced floodwater recession farming. These warmer lowlands were capable of supporting two and sometimes three harvests per year (Hu-DeHart 1981). Population estimates for both groups at contact vary considerably, but it is likely that Acaxees numbered at least 20,000 and Yaquis perhaps

60,000. By the time the Jesuits arrived, the population of both groups was probably reduced by half (Gerhard 1993: 228–29, 240; Reff 1991: 108–11). The Acaxee and Yaqui regions both fell within the Spanish province of Nueva Vizcaya, established in 1563.

The Acaxee Rebellion of 1601

Until the 1590s, the main Spanish presence in Nueva Vizcaya was secular, consisting of several hundred civilians and a few soldiers associated with silver mining and its supporting activities (Cramaussel 1990). Labor for the mines came from imported black slaves, Indian slaves captured in warfare, and paid workers, including Indians from the south, mestizos, and mulattos. Encomiendas of local Indians, especially Acaxees and Conchos (from southeastern Chihuahua), also provided labor when sufficient Spanish force was present to coerce it. In northern Mexico, encomiendas afforded a Spanish conqueror the use of a specified group of Indians for labor only. Assigned by the governor and other Spanish officials, encomienda Indians were supposed to provide labor for a few weeks per year, but they often served much longer and some apparently became virtual chattels of Spanish estates. The more systematic congregation of Indians into villages by Jesuits after 1590 fostered the development of encomienda by making Indians more accessible to their encomenderos (Cramaussel 1991; Deeds 1989). A distinctive configuration of encomienda characteristics—the provision of labor alone as tribute, the tacit enslavement of Indians in the earliest encomienda grants, the resettlement of dispersed, seminomadic groups in pueblos, and the persistence of labor tribute into the late colonial period—seems to have obtained in peripheral areas at both ends of the Spanish Empire (Cuello 1988; Saeger 1981; Service 1951).[6]

The imposition of forced labor to produce surpluses for Spaniards was only one of the accoutrements of the conquest. Even more disorienting and disruptive to indigenous socioeconomic networks were epidemic diseases, which had begun to take their toll in the late sixteenth century. Episodes of smallpox, measles, and other diseases occurred at five- to eight-year intervals into the seventeenth century, producing mortality rates as high as 40 percent in the first twenty-five years. Jesuit reports during the 1590s mention a variety of indigenous responses to such catastrophic change, including abandonment and even burying alive of the sick. According to the Jesuits, child sacrifice was also practiced as a trade-off to restore health to dying adults (González Rodríguez 1984: 156; Reff 1991: 128–29).[7]

In the sierra of Topia, Acaxees felt a growing outsider presence after 1580, when several hundred Spaniards migrated from Chiametla in Sinaloa after the mines played out in the 1580s and local Indians were decimated by slaving expeditions from Zacatecas (Alvarez 1992). Spanish miners founded *reales* at Topia, San Andrés, San Hipólito, and Las Once Mil Vírgenes de Cosalá. When the black slaves and paid laborers who had accompanied the Spaniards proved insufficient to meet the demand for labor, Acaxee rancherías in the environs became the targets of slaving expeditions. A few Franciscan friars ministered to the inhabitants of the mining camps but made little attempt to convert Indians outside the towns.[8] Acaxees did not mount active resistance as long as the invasive threat was still piecemeal. Attacks by neighboring groups were not new to them; for some time they had been experiencing raids by Tepehuanes from the east and Xiximes from the south. Those unfriendly neighbors had been aggressive in seeking goods and taking female captives.[9]

The arrival of the Jesuit Hernando de Santarén from Culiacán in 1598 augured a shift to a more coercive Spanish presence. The Jesuits had sought and received permission to extend their newly established northern Mexican mission field up from the Sinaloan coastal plains. Santarén was welcomed by encomenderos who recognized that the Jesuits could help consolidate dispersed rancherías ravaged by the recent epidemics of smallpox and measles and resettle the survivors near the silver mines. In addition to providing mining labor, Indians could also produce grain to supply the mines. The Jesuits were apparently willing to cooperate if the labor and commodity exchanges took place under their supervision. They were able to stipulate that a fine would be imposed on any Spaniard who entered the missions without permission.

In a show of mutual support, Padre Santarén accompanied Captain Diego de Avila and other encomenderos, along with Indian allies, on a tour of the sierra in 1600. In what they called a pacification campaign, Spaniards presided over ceremonial formalities intended to awe the Indians with the power of the Spanish king.[10] In this "rehearsal of subordinate social reality" (Guevara-Gil and Salomon 1994: 6), Avila explained the proper forms of deference to the king's representatives and taught the Acaxees to kiss the padre's hand. Threatening to return in greater force to enslave Indians who did not comply, the encomenderos ordered them to build houses and plant *milpas* on lands granted to them in the name of the king. These sites were intended to merge Acaxees from several rancherías into larger, more compact villages.[11]

The Indians were also ordered to build a community house, to wear clothing, and to cut their very long hair. Following the stick with a carrot, the Spaniards furnished cloth, seeds, tools (knives and hatchets were especially popular), and livestock to each pueblo. Traditional headmen were named to offices and admonished to see that all these instructions were carried out. One of the main goals was to get the Indians to turn over idols and bones that served as war trophies and fetishes. When they did comply, the Spaniards burned these items in huge bonfires. Exemplary beatings were administered to some Indians who demonstrated their insubordination publicly. The visitation tour—the characteristic act of taking possession and dramatizing Acaxee subordination—was carried out over several months.

An added incentive to comply was the Spaniards' promise to protect the Acaxees from hostile incursions by Xiximes. To that end, Jesuits also attempted to convert Xiximes, and Spanish soldiers from the presidio of San Hipólito warned them to keep away from Acaxee settlements. Not easily cowed, Xixime shamans taunted the evangelizing fathers with embellished explanations of their preferences in ritual cannibalism. Indian flesh was ordinary, similar to beef. Blacks tasted more like salt pork, but Spaniards, savoring of lamb, were the most delicious of all (Pérez de Ribas 1992: book 9, chap. 5).

Jesuit efforts, backed by encomenderos, were more successful among the Acaxees, who not only began to plant corn and systematically provide labor for the mines but also to learn the catechism and to turn over stone idols to the padres. The priests performed thousands of baptisms and continued their efforts to enforce monogamous unions.[12] Gift giving seemed to mask the intrusions. Acaxees quickly caught on to the custom that allowed mine laborers a small portion of silver ore (*pepena*) (Nakayama 1974: 72–73; Pérez de Ribas 1992: book 8, chap. 3).[13] Some Acaxees bartered their corn with petty traders, who frequently attempted to cheat them and abuse their women (Gutiérrez Castillas 1961: 84).[14]

Grievances were mostly aired away from the villages. Vigilance did not extend to woods and caves, where native rituals continued to be nurtured by shamans. There, Acaxees still venerated former icons representing gods of air, fire, water, war, and fertility. Through ceremonies and offerings of food and drink, Acaxees attempted to appease the old gods as well as a more recent addition to the pantheon: the icon symbolizing bloody stools. In public speeches, elders warned that turning over more icons would bring starvation and death. They urged their peoples to make haste in restoring the time-honored ceremonies through which they played out the relations of reciprocity that assured their survival.[15] Unsure of the relative power of Christian and indigenous supernaturals, many Acaxees hedged their bets by continuing old practices while at the same time incorporating new ones.

The arrival of two more Jesuits in 1601 expedited the program of forced resettlement, narrowing the prospects for seeking refuge away from Spanish intruders. Unrest escalated in the area around Alaya, the home of the Acaxee subgroup of Sobaibos and a significant source of mining labor for Las Once Mil Vírgenes de Cosalá to the south and San Andrés to the west. Perico, a Sobaibo elder, was also anxious to restore ceremonial traditions, but some of his ideas were not completely autochthonous. After several months of conspiring with other Acaxee headmen and elders through messengers, Perico led a rebellion in December 1601 (Pérez de Ribas 1992: book 8, chaps. 8–10).[16] He called himself God, Holy Spirit, and Bishop. It is probably no coincidence that Bishop Alonso de la Mota y Escobar was at the time undertaking a pastoral visitation in Sinaloa. Perico claimed to have come from heaven to save the Indians from the false doctrine of the Jesuits. He performed the sacraments of baptism and marriage; he also dissolved marriages that had been performed by Jesuits. He said mass, taught the Indians new prayers, and named disciples, including Santiago and San Pedro, to carry news of the revolt to other pueblos and rancherías.

The object was to exterminate all Spaniards, including the Jesuits; Perico claimed that he could blind them and even change them into cows, sheep, and horses to make them easier to kill. During the next few weeks, Spaniards and other non-Indians were attacked in mining camps and on mountain roads, resulting in as many as fifty deaths, while the Jesuits managed to take refuge in San Andrés and San Hipólito. Rebels burned many of the rather primitive churches as well as other makeshift buildings that had been constructed in the mining camps. The insurgents carried banners fashioned from church vestments, and one warrior wore the cap and mantle of a priest. Certain icons such as bells and crosses were targets for desecration. Acaxees who refused to join the rebellion also became victims. Rebel contingents were scattered throughout Acaxee territory among both neophyte Christians and the unconverted, and although the initial uprising demonstrated coordinated planning, the attacks took on a more haphazard pattern after several months.

At first, Spanish authorities attempted to negotiate with the rebels. Bishop Mota y Escobar and Governor Rodrigo de Vivero bargained with various rebel factions but achieved no lasting peace. The insurrection was suppressed only in 1603 when incoming governor Francisco de Urdiñola led a militia composed of encomenderos and Tepehuan and Concho allies on a punishing campaign into the sierra. The campaign was particularly brutal, marked by summary trials and executions of hundreds of captured rebels. Perico was executed by burning; forty-eight other rebel leaders were hanged and their heads displayed on pikes along the roads. Other rebels were sold into slavery.

Official accounts emphasized the role of hechiceros, agents of the devil, in provoking the rebellion.[17] Not only for the religious but also for lay Spaniards steeped in medieval Christianity, the devil was a force to be reckoned with, just as real as agents provocateurs of modern insurrections (Cervantes 1994: 5–39). They did not doubt that the devil could change humans into animals or make his idols weep. It had to have been the devil who caused the revolt by inducing elders, "lying old men," to spread lies about the Spaniards. Even though some padres attributed the uprising to the exploitation of Indian labor by greedy Spaniards,[18] the tendency of the invaders was to minimize dissension in their own ranks. So it was that the Jesuits could argue that lay Spaniards wished the Indians no ill, that they had committed no offense by entering Acaxee territory and working the mines that the Indians did not have the good sense to exploit. The benefits of salvation and material accumulation indisputably outweighed the aggravations (Pérez de Ribas 1992: book 8, chap. 11).

The Acaxee Revolt initiated a series of first-generation rebellions that affected the Nueva Vizcayan heartland in the seventeenth century. Many of its features would reappear in the soon-to-follow uprisings of Xiximes and Tepehuanes. In the aftermath of these early revolts, Spaniards renewed efforts to impose their minimum requirements for "civilized" living and to create conditions for the resumption of mining. Some seventy Acaxee rancherías, diminished in size through casualties and starvation, were reorganized into twenty-four villages (Huerta Preciado 1966: 80).[19] Jesuits, whose numbers now doubled from four to eight, exercised more control in appointing Indian governors and officials whose loyalty was assured, partly through gifts and privileges. Some of these officials accompanied Jesuits on visits to Sinaloa, where they were supposed to observe in the more settled missions the benefits of compliance (Pérez de Ribas 1992: book 8, chap. 6). To overcome conditions of scarcity after the revolt, the new sites were located near rivers on lands that could be easily cleared and planted.

Conversion efforts focused on the young, who were boarded in the new villages and taught the *doctrina* in hastily constructed churches. Jesuits took great pride in telling stories such as one about a thirteen-year-old girl who on her deathbed disavowed her natural parents and celebrated her imminent reunion with her "true" father in heaven (Pérez de Ribas 1992: book 8, chap. 16). The paternal association was also explicit in the proper form of address for Jesuits: father (padre). The deliberate attempts to drive a wedge between parents and children surely rankled (Dunne 1944: 60; R. Gutiérrez 1991: 75–81).[20]

Shamans and elders did not desist in their attempts to discount Christian teachings. Their credibility was enhanced by the appearance of Halley's comet, that ancestral omen of pending disaster, in 1607. Shamans predicted great mortality from disease and continued to emphasize the association between Christian baptism and death, encouraging people to flee the missions. When smallpox struck the next month, thousands succumbed, especially the young and the very old—as one Jesuit noted, all those who had escaped it the last time.[21] Vindication of the prophecy did little to promote active resistance, however, as the survivors of the epidemic struggled to avoid starvation. Nonetheless, three years later Acaxee shamans persuaded some of their people to join the Xiximes in the next first-generation rebellion. In that case, messianic leadership and millennial redemption also provided important ideological underpinnings for the revolt, and they continued to be a feature of first-generation revolts in Nueva Vizcaya. Although some Acaxees participated in the Tepehuan rebellion of 1616, after 1620 a course of more passive resistance and continued epidemic disease spelled their eventual disappearance as a distinct cultural entity (Deeds 1995).

The Yaqui Rebellion of 1740

In the case of the Yaqui Indians of Sonora, strategies other than rebellion evolved first, and more aggressive resistance came only after a hundred years of Spanish control (Hu-DeHart 1981, 1988; Pérez de Ribas 1992: book 2; Spicer 1980). Although the Yaquis repulsed the first Spanish military attempts to extend control into their territory at the beginning of the seventeenth century, by the second decade they were making overtures to Jesuit missionaries working among the Mayos and other groups to the south. The reasons for this change of heart are not clear, but one explanation attributes it to the fact that the Yaquis had several years during which they were left alone to debate their own course of action and during which delegations of Yaquis had ample opportunity to observe Mayo-Jesuit interactions. This permitted a smooth transition in which mutual interests could be negotiated (Spicer 1980: 16–20). A more plausible explanation is that smallpox and measles epidemics in 1616–17 prompted the Yaquis to invite the Jesuits (Reff 1991: 158–60). Father Andrés Pérez de Ribas reported that some Yaqui shamans considered baptism to be a curing ceremony. Some, of course, became disillusioned with the many deaths (especially of young children) that followed baptism, but others decided they had little to lose by getting the Christian God on their side.[22] By 1623, and without a coercive military presence, the Jesuits had reorganized the Yaquis from about eighty rancherías into eight mission villages.

For more than a hundred years, Yaquis and Jesuits coexisted in a state of adaptive or accommodative resistance (*Historia General* 1985: chaps. 2–3; Hu-DeHart 1981: 29–57; Spicer 1980: 20–32). Jesuits introduced a new political-religious hierarchy, in which they were the final arbiters, and a new agricultural production system oriented toward the production of a surplus. Despite such far-reaching impositions, Yaquis still conserved spaces in which certain autochthonous social and religious practices endured alongside Christian concepts of baptism, allegorical plays, and icons. Native ceremonial sodalities seem to have persisted within new structures, and kinship networks were not severely disrupted. Yaquis appear to have adapted rather readily to the market economy, not only by participating in the collective endeavor of producing mission surpluses, which the Jesuits controlled, but also through the individual sale of either their own produce or labor to the small and slowly expanding Spanish secular society.

For many decades, Jesuits were successful in manipulating the election of Yaqui officials who were effective in brokering conflicting interests. Even more significantly, they were able to minimize the demands of Spanish secular society on Yaqui peoples for nearly a century.[23] Mining reales established in the late seventeenth and early eighteenth centuries in Ostimuri and other neighboring regions did produce repartimiento demands, but many Yaquis voluntarily sold their labor to mines on a temporary basis (Hu-DeHart 1981: 41–45).[24] The latter tendency has been interpreted by some scholars as a deliberate Yaqui strategy for maintaining autonomy through the accumulation of capital and uninhibited movement across regions. Yaquis also served as military auxiliaries in campaigns against Indians unsubdued by the Spanish (e.g., Seris, Baja California groups). As "ethnic soldiers" for the colonizers, some Yaquis earned privileges and extra goods.

If Yaquis had perceived the Jesuits' restructuring measures as generally advantageous to their welfare, by the third decade of the eighteenth century the situation had altered. The detachment of the province of Sinaloa y Sonora from Nueva Vizcaya in 1733 recognized the growth of a mining and ranching secular society in this northwestern region (Ortega Noriega 1993: 77–81). The burgeoning demand for scarce labor resources brought competing groups into steadily escalating confrontations after 1700. Colonial authorities attempted to regulate Yaqui movement between regions, often linking crimes of theft and pilfering to their makeshift camps near mining towns.[25] The rebellion and the motivations for it have already been perceptively examined by several scholars whose interpretations are summarized below (Hu-DeHart 1981: 58–87; Mirafuentes Galván 1993; Navarro García 1966; Spicer 1980: 32–57).[26]

In the 1730s, some Spanish miners and agriculturalists found an ally in Sonora's entrepreneurial governor, Manuel Bernal de Huidobro, against an entrenched Jesuit monopoly, supported by influential Basque landowners, over the region's most productive labor and land (Deeds 1979; Mirafuentes Galván 1993).[27] The governor also sought ways to loosen Jesuit control of local markets, thereby tapping into a grievance felt by Yaquis themselves. Their surplus production was channeled out of the missions with little tangible benefit to them, and to make matters worse, a large part of the surplus went to support the poorer Baja California missions (Radding 1982: 81). When droughts or floods provoked subsistence crises, Yaquis could not be certain of access to mission stores. Ignoring growing Yaqui resentment over lack of control of productive resources, an increasingly bureaucratic and inflexible Jesuit organization worked defensively to insure Yaqui deference. Jesuits obdurately disregarded Yaqui demands for autonomy in the selection of their own village officials and continued to impose non-Indian (or mixed-blood) leaders who did not have strong support in their communities. They also angered many Yaquis by removing costly ornaments from some of the missions to cover debts incurred by missionaries. As an independent Yaqui leadership asserted itself, Jesuit intransigence grew.

After a number of altercations with Padre Ignacio María Nápoli, the governors of Huírivis and Rahum, respectively Bernabé Basoritemea and Juan Ignacio Usacamea (known as Muni), began to discuss their grievances against the Jesuits with civil officials who were anxious to exploit the rift. In the face of this disobedience and lack of deference (Padre Nápoli was also outraged that they dressed in the same style as Spaniards), the priest removed Basoritemea and Muni from office. In addition, he charged that they were possessed by the devil. In a bid to assert his authority over the Jesuits, Governor Huidobro tacitly supported the two deposed Indian governors in 1739, sending them to Mexico City to present their grievances to the viceroy. There they demanded the removal and replacement of two Jesuits (including Nápoli); more autonomy in the administration of their lands, election of their officials, and disposition of their produce and their labor; and the right to carry arms. Archbishop Viceroy Juan Antonio de Vizarrón y Eguiarreta, not a partisan of the Jesuits, supported the Yaquis' petitions for more independence and appointed them to military posts in Yaqui territory. But before they reached their homeland, rebellion broke out in northern Sinaloa and southern Sonora in early 1740.

Rebellious activity over the next several months was sporadic and uncoordinated. Nearly all the fighting took place outside the Yaqui region, either to the south in Mayo territory or north in Lower Pima country. The several thousand rebels, mainly Yaquis and some Mayos, never acted in concert. The impetus for rebellion seems to have grown out of dispersed raiding by bands of eastern Yaquis who were also foraging for food after a poor harvest in late 1739. Severe flooding in 1740 exacerbated food shortages. As the Jesuits continued to export food and rumors that the absent Yaqui leaders were dead escalated, Yaqui discontent became more widespread. None of the secondary accounts mention epidemic disease in the years preceding the revolt, but it would be useful to ascertain whether the *matlazáhuatl* epidemic of 1738–39, which severely affected regions to the south and east, played any part in exacerbating the subsistence crisis (MacLeod 1986).[28]

Rebels did not aim to annihilate Spaniards, and there were relatively few Spanish deaths. Indian casualties were probably considerably higher. Spanish civilians and missionaries whose properties and churches were attacked fled to Alamos. Eventually the rebels were defeated by Captain Agustín de Vildósola (Huidobro's Basque antagonist) in August 1740. The end of military activity coincided with the return of Muni and Basoritemea, who then toured the Yaqui region with Governor Huidobro to encourage a return to normal activities. A number of rebel leaders were imprisoned. Muni and Basoritemea were elevated to leadership positions, but their fortunes soon declined along with those of their protector. The Jesuits succeeded in getting the new and more sympathetic Viceroy Duque de la Conquista to remove Governor Huidobro for alleged indecision and incompetence in suppressing the rebellion.[29] In 1741, his successor, Vildósola, accepting apparent Jesuit fabrications that Muni and Basoritemea were fomenting another revolt, ordered that they be executed and their heads displayed on pikes.

In analyzing the revolt, Spicer discerned no consistent set of objectives, but reasoned that most Yaquis supported the more moderate changes embodied in the petitions carried by the two Yaqui governors to the viceroy and did not conspire to obliterate the Spanish or mission presence. He elaborated on the widening gulf between Yaquis and Jesuits in the eighteenth century, arguing that Yaquis had become more sophisticated in manipulating the dominant culture and more frequently asserted their independence, even taking advantage of Spanish legal mechanisms to do so. At the same time, an increasingly fossilized Jesuit organizational structure not only failed to accommodate this change but even misinterpreted Yaqui intentions. Jesuits new to the area were no longer in touch with native traditions, and their suspicion and hostility toward local leaders pushed them to appoint outsiders to village offices. In their view, Yaqui officials had gotten far too "uppity," a tendency that Jesuits attributed to encouragement from civil officials.[30]

In an assessment consonant with more recent attempts to explain popular riots as protests against the deterioration of a reciprocal (although unequal) relationship tacitly understood by rulers and ruled (e.g., Scott 1985: 345), Spicer depicted a Yaqui people acting from within the colonial regime to restore the "custom" they had come to see as their due within the colonial order. He also referred to a seemingly unique event of the uprising in which a Yaqui rebel, calling himself "King, Pope, God, and Virgin," ordered a small detachment of Spanish and mulatto soldiers stripped naked and whipped in the Mayo town of Santa Cruz. Spicer speculated on how this relates to a possible tradition of vision-based leadership, but offered no analysis as to how religious beliefs and practices may have influenced the revolt (Spicer 1980: 44–45, 53).

Although Spicer's analysis alludes to the growing secular Spanish presence, the dissension between that society and the Jesuits, and the weakness of civil administration, he focuses most intensively on the breakdown in Jesuit-Yaqui relations. Hu-DeHart also emphasizes Yaqui grievances against Jesuits but is more inclined to characterize the revolt as a "classical, large-scale peasant rebellion" directed at missionary landlords (Hu-DeHart 1988: 153–54). Despite the fact that neither interpretation makes much of how the Yaquis perceived the confrontations of civil and religious sectors, or the competing interests among elites, it is tempting to speculate that some Yaquis saw rebellion as a feasible option given the rifts within the colonial order. Jesuit power was no longer undisputed, but neither was it flexible enough to insure Yaqui survival within the colonial order.

Comparison and Contrast

Examination of these two "mission" revolts separated by more than a century suggests a number of ideas regarding intercultural contact on mission frontiers. The most basic shared characteristic is that each group was responding at least in part to relocation in Jesuit missions. The most obvious difference relates to timing. First-generation rebellions were intermediate tactics that fell between the immediate reactions to conquest (both passive and hostile) and later responses to the impositions of well-entrenched colonial rule, manifested through resistant adaptation (Stern 1987: 8–13),[31] flight, or outright rebellion. Although Spanish demands on indigenous peoples were continuous throughout the colonial period, only in the early period of contact did they coincide with devastating population decline and the violent disruption of existing social networks and ritual activities for sustaining life. Later rebellions were not so much desperate attempts to maintain equilibrium in a world turned completely upside down as they were efforts to repair damages to a modus vivendi that had evolved over time in a colonial context.

The Acaxee rebellion was fought by leaders and participants who had experienced firsthand the transition from preconquest to colonial conditions. The Acaxees wished to revitalize many social and religious elements of their precontact world, particularly the reassuring ritual activity connected with subsistence and health. The revolt occurred in the period of greatest demographic decline due to disease. High mortality is, of course, a great dissolver of hierarchical structure and probably inhibited rebellious activity at first, explaining why the Acaxees accepted missionary overtures. Yet continuing high rates of decline had the effect of cementing the association between conversion, baptism, and death. Indians often explicitly connected missionaries and churches with death, and in the Acaxee Revolt, shamans effectively manipulated these associations in inciting followers to cast off the Spanish yoke (Gutiérrez Castillas 1961: 138).

Perico and other Acaxee leaders did not intend to completely reestablish a previous age and did not reject some aspects of Spanish material culture and technology, such as livestock and metal tools. Nonetheless, Acaxee rebels did attempt to remove the primary obstacles to the restoration of preconquest ritual and social practices. Since destruction and recreation of universes was a feature of native cosmology, millenarianism offered a path to redemption through revitalization of certain cultural practices (Beals 1933; Wallace 1956). The call to arms had special appeal for warriors whose powers no longer served as a source of prestige and for ritual specialists recently demoted. Their losses were countered by Perico's transformation into messiah. He combined aspects of native religion, invoking former gods and idols, with a few symbols of Christian religious authority. God, the Holy Spirit, bishop, rituals, prayers, and sacraments were expropriated and transformed to help legitimate the rebel cause. Although these symbols probably had mutating meanings in the evolving indigenous worldviews, they clearly had significance as instruments of hegemony.

Invoking Santiago is a case in point. The Acaxee who took on this appellation testified that he knew that Santiago was the patron and captain of the Spanish soldiers (Cervantes 1994: 52–53; Taylor 1994).[32] The reversals that occurred when Indians despoiled or appropriated Christian vestments, icons, and titles indicate that these introductions were perceived as powerful; they were forces that Indians needed to destroy or emulate. Selective borrowings by groups accustomed to a polytheistic, cyclical universe were not really in conflict with the goal of obliterating the Spanish presence when they could be used to enhance power (Guha 1983).

Although there is doubt about the degree of social stratification among Acaxees at the time of conquest, the evidence suggests a societal organization grounded in reciprocal relationships based on extended kinship. The Spanish-introduced hierarchy of officials—plus Jesuit insistence on monogamous relationships, the boarding of children away from home, and the prohibition of rituals associated with subsistence—disrupted traditional patterns for the entire community, not just former leaders. Gifts were used initially to attract Indians, but these declined as the Indians' labor obligations increased. Both religious and lay Spaniards were perceived as exploitive and were targeted for expulsion from Acaxee territory. Although Acaxees may initially have seen the Jesuits as buffers between themselves and a civilian population that had already begun to exploit them, in the final analysis they determined that the "civilizing" mission of the Spaniards was not in their interest, no matter who carried it out. Even though Jesuits often called on Spanish officials to carry out punishments (and often set themselves up as protectors by intervening to have punishments reduced), they also inflicted corporal punishment themselves.

The timing of the Acaxee Revolt was also based on the degree to which the Indians saw the enemy as vulnerable or weak. In first-generation revolts, the odds seemed more conducive to victory when the non-Indian population was still relatively small. When the revolt persisted and Spaniards adopted scorched earth tactics, however, the Acaxees were put at a greater disadvantage. In general, Indian subsistence patterns in agriculture and hunting and gathering did not lend themselves to the stockpiling of resources necessary for prolonged conflicts. Although barren, rocky precipices were ready-made fortresses against Spanish attack, they afforded very little consolation for the hungry. Participants in first-generation revolts, familiar with previous patterns of warfare, were not prepared to deal with an enemy who could outlast them. The ability of Spaniards to capitalize on previous Indian enmities and enlist Indian allies was another important factor affecting the outcome of first-wave revolts. In the Acaxee case, Conchos and other Nueva Vizcayan Indians served as ethnic soldiers, and Spaniards were able to erode rebel support through a combination of force and gifts. The Spanish policy of recruiting Indian allies was particularly significant in the early period of contact, when the Spanish presence was modest.[33]

Summary executions and display of bodies were also used to admonish the rebels, and Jesuits were unanimous in supporting this hardline policy. During the Acaxee rebellion, when Indian slavery was still widespread in the north, those leaders spared execution were enslaved. Harsh retaliation was not a unique feature of first-generation revolts, but Spaniards were more preoccupied by their smaller numbers in the earlier revolts and may have felt it necessary to make the exemplary punishments more indelible by their brutality. Therefore, considerable gift giving was combined with threats of future reprisals and increased attention to reducing Indians to a small number of villages in order to subordinate the remaining rebels. This policy was relatively successful in eliminating the threat of further rebellion. In addition, Indian governors and other officials increasingly served to mete out discipline directly and impose the obligations demanded by Spaniards.

What is the correspondence between these characteristics of the Acaxees' first-generation revolt and the later Yaqui uprising? One of the most perplexing questions is why Yaquis accepted, even invited, Jesuit missionization and acquiesced to its demands for more than a hundred years before militantly rebelling. Were they motivated by the destructuration of their society provoked by epidemic disease as Reff (1991) argues? Or was acceptance a hesitant, uneven process in which Yaquis disagreed among themselves while the Jesuits got a foothold? Pérez de Ribas certainly alludes to opposition from certain shamans, indicating that considerable internal dissension was present at the beginning. Spicer (1980) asserted that one reason for relative accord was that Jesuits, while preaching against drunkenness, tended to forego tirades against plural marriages, sexual practices, and the worship of idols. I find this to be wholly inconsistent with Jesuit efforts in other parts of the northwest. I would argue that the missionaries themselves and the slowly evolving civil administrative structure exerted more coercive force, and that the Jesuits were especially effective in using some Yaquis to intimidate others. During the hundred peaceful years, there were always competing interests within the Yaqui missions, but the Jesuits kept them in check while they worked hard to limit Spanish settlement in the area.

Whatever the reasons for accommodation, Yaquis did develop strategies of resistant adaptation that allowed them some autonomy. Spicer argued that the religious accommodations of Yaquis to Christianity were inextricably linked with the mission towns themselves; a household- and town-based syncretic worldview incorporated Christian rituals/teachings and new work patterns (Spicer 1980: 59–70). But a dream world with intangible sources of power existed outside the towns in the *huya aniya* (sacred uninhabited areas that the Spaniards perceived as *monte* or wilderness) where Yaquis could continue at least for a time to relate to older supernaturals, symbols, and meanings. This sacred space was also a metaphorical space that freed Yaquis from the intercultural transactions of the mission. In addition, Yaqui barrios adjacent to Spanish mining camps provided antihegemonic social spaces where Yaquis could not only remain relatively autonomous from religious control but also have a base from which to engage in acts of theft with little chance of detection. In other words, many Yaquis were able to create "hidden" or subversive spaces within an ecological environment that had few physical hiding places (Scott 1990: 23–28).[34]

As this colonial balancing act evolved, some Yaquis were able to acquire some degree of autonomy even as they ostensibly assisted Spanish incorporation efforts. Certain leaders like Muni and Basoritemea garnered military and administrative prestige within the Spanish system while strongly identifying with communal interests. Their ability to articulate those interests grew out of an evolutionary process that coincided with the growth of Spanish society in the region—and the concomitant incursions into Yaqui "wilderness"—and with an increasingly intransigent Jesuit administrative structure that more than ever sought outsiders to control its charges. The competing civil administrative structure allowed occasional acts of defiance and aggression to go unpunished, and even encouraged dissident Yaquis to adjudicate their complaints, thus undermining Jesuit control.

The priests recognized the growing insubordination as they decried the overstepping of bounds inherent in the Yaqui leaders' wearing of Spanish clothing. Adding to this conjuncture, a subsistence crisis involving floods, drought, food shortages, and perhaps epidemic disease created a climate in which increased militancy, in the form of raiding, led to more generalized aggression. A rebellion resulted, but an uncoordinated one, in which perceptions of the degree to which the colonial contract had been violated varied from place to place. Yaquis did not act as one, and several of the western missions apparently remained peaceful throughout the rebellion. The rebels never articulated an intention to kill all the Spaniards, or even the priests. Attacks on Spanish settlements did cause most Spaniards to flee to Alamos, but the rebels made no attempt to take that town. Jesuits and other Spaniards were able to travel throughout much of Yaqui territory during the six months when the rebellion was most active. On more than one occasion, Spaniards captured by Yaquis were stripped naked but not killed. Such incidents and another in which Yaquis reportedly vowed to "send priests naked to preach in their own lands" bear comparison with underclass or subordinate desires for social leveling or social reversals like those represented in carnivalesque pre-Lenten celebrations. As Guha (1983) has argued, the rebels' aim was not so much to reconstitute the world as to reverse it.

The degree to which Yaqui religion influenced the revolt has not been carefully analyzed. Spicer (1980) argued that after the rebellion and after the Jesuits were expelled, dual religious structures continued to evolve in the towns and the sacred spaces outside of them, but that eventually both had strong Christian components. Yaqui anger over the removal of religious ornaments from some of the missions indicates strong proprietary feelings attached to the places and symbols of Christian worship. Scholars have discounted messianism and millenarianism as factors in the revolt, but what are we to make of the seemingly isolated case of the Yaqui who proclaimed himself god and king? Did he anticipate the end of Spanish rule—a reversal of the social order—in which these symbols of temporal and supernatural power would devolve to Yaquis?

A century later, Yaquis (along with Mayos) were highly receptive to the millenarian prophecies of Teresa de Cabora (Vanderwood 1989). Recent scholarship has indicated that a number of Indian "kings" roamed the northern Mexican countryside in the late colonial period, attracting Indian and peasant followers as they tapped into latent resentments. In appropriating and redefining the monarchical figure, Indian kings both reversed hierarchies and legitimized their actions (Van Young 1986; Mirafuentes Galván 1992). Similar ambivalences characterized the Yaqui uprising, even though Spanish authorities attributed them to the resumption of nativist (demonically inspired) ceremonies and practices such as the scalp dances that took place before battle (Spicer 1980: 47). Ritual activity intended to appropriate the power of the enemy was common to most northern groups, and it would not be surprising to find that these practices continued among the Yaquis and their Mayo and Pima allies.

Spanish explanations for the revolt diverged markedly. Governor Huidobro continued to charge the Jesuits with mistreatment of natives. Meanwhile, the missionaries successfully undertook a major effort to get the governor removed. Branding Huidobro a coward, they courted Vildósola, the Basque leader of the Sonoran militia forces that had defeated the rebels, and were instrumental in his appointment to the governorship. The cross-blaming was particularly vicious in an area where economic resources had become more vigorously contested; it contrasts sharply with the attempt during the Acaxee Revolt to stress Spanish harmony against the onslaught of the devil.

The latter is only one of the factors that distinguish the Yaqui rebellion from the first-generation rebellion. A greater degree of accommodation afforded Yaquis more access to Spanish institutions to protect their interests and more potential to garner prestige; this helped produce a native leadership that was at odds with a more entrenched and dogmatic mission regime. Yaquis took advantage of the alienation of Jesuits from the civil society, but internal divisions within their own society worked against the articulation of a single, unifying strategy or set of goals. The attempt by Muni and Basoritemea to work within the system while other leaders took more aggressive actions represents such contradictions. Mixed signals and the divisions within Spanish society made the governor's response less decisive than it might have been. The later rebellion was not a reaction to the cataclysmic early pressures of population decline and profound restructuring, but rather a response to the intensification of a colonial regime that threatened the measure of autonomy worked out by Yaquis and provoked a public eruption of heretofore masked counterhegemonic aspirations (Scott 1990).

The contrasts between these two revolts, which occurred in Spain's northern fringe a century apart, belie the notion of homogeneous mission or frontier revolts. Although the Acaxee and Yaqui rebellions share certain features related to their location in semiarid frontier areas and their response to the mission regime, they also differ precisely because they derived from distinct frontier stages and conditions. Spain's northern frontiers were erratically constituted in time and space, and were not the result of state-imposed boundary lines. Instead they reflected the Spaniards' appropriation and exploitation of dispersed resource areas whose fortification and settlement varied with changing circumstances. As Thomas Hall (1989a) has pointed out, the northern frontier encompassed multiple peripheries, determined not only by their degree of incorporation into the world economy but also by local peculiarities. Frontier conditions are by nature idiosyncratic, and the points at which their acculturating pressures become unbearable inevitably differ.

This suggests a second consideration. The confluence of idiosyncratic northwestern Indian characteristics with the weakness of the Spanish state on that frontier fostered an atmosphere favorable to armed indigenous resistance. For one thing, a dispersed, numerically small Spanish population was susceptible to attack by groups accustomed to intertribal warfare. Acaxees had not lost their precontact warring strategies, and Yaquis had acquired new fighting skills as ethnic soldiers in continuing Spanish campaigns against nomadic groups. Although the Yaqui rebellion occurred at a time of intensified colonization, Indians perceived divisions within the ranks of the invaders just as the Acaxees had discerned vulnerability before the Spanish presence was completely entrenched.

Furthermore, even though neither Acaxees nor Yaquis were in total solidarity during these revolts (and the Yaquis much less so), the relative lack of assimilation or *mestizaje* of both groups (not yet overwhelmed demographically by Spaniards) meant that a distinct ethnic identity could serve as a powerful force in attracting sizable segments of their populations to the revolts. It is worth noting that whatever ethnic glue promoted solidarity in the two rebellions derived from different frontier stages. In the earlier period, Acaxees drew on their organizational strategies from preconquest networks. Much later, the Yaquis distinguished themselves as distinct from others based as much on tribalization (Ferguson and Whitehead 1992: 12–16) that had resulted from their profound reorganization by Jesuits as on indigenous factors. Yet, whether in the seventeenth or the eighteenth century, indigenous peoples on the sparsely populated, thinly defended northern frontier of the Spaniards could more readily contest the alien presence than could their counterparts elsewhere. A fragile ecology contributed to the volatility of the frontier area, and severe disruption of subsistence patterns not infrequently served as a catalyst for revolt. For Acaxees overwhelmed early by intrusive pressures, the revolt was the last gasp in the struggle for ethnic survival. For Yaquis, it was only one weapon in an arsenal of resistance strategies, but one that would serve them again in the nineteenth and twentieth centuries before incorporation of their frontier was total.

4

The Colonial Pact and Changing Ethnic Frontiers in Highland Sonora, 1740–1840

CYNTHIA RADDING

Radding explores the political and ecological reasons why Indian communities in central and eastern Sonora forged a colonial pact with the Spanish Crown. In return for labor and military service against unconquered Indian groups, Opatas, Eudeves, and Pimas demanded village autonomy and territorial integrity under the Jesuit and later the Franciscan mission systems. Beginning with the Bourbon Reforms and accelerating after independence in the nineteenth century, however, the colonial pact dissolved as the Mexican nation privileged private over ethnically based communal ownership of land. This was just one of the ways in which capitalist penetration of the northern frontier redefined ethnic identities, created new constellations of class and power, and engendered peasant resistance within highland Sonoran communities during the 1800s.

THIS CHAPTER focuses on social and cultural change in eastern and central Sonora during the late colonial and early national periods. Its discussion of frontier ecology, rooted in historical struggles over scarce productive resources in the semiarid environment of the Sonoran Desert, addresses the following questions: What was the colonial pact between the Spanish state and Indians in northwestern Mexico, and how did its rupture influence ethnic and class relations in the region? How significant were legal, economic, and cultural distinctions between *indio* and *vecino* in highland Sonora during this century? What was the impact of military service and the Apache wars on the indigenous and Hispanic peasant population? By substantiating the material basis for social conflict, the present study documents a secular process of class formation that cut across racial lines and created new constellations of power.

The *colonial pact* signifies the political ties between the Spanish Crown and Indian communities through which the communities asserted certain basic claims to their means of livelihood and to a degree of local autonomy for their internal governance. Indigenous community leaders understood this relationship as being regulated by a reciprocal arrangement through which Indians provided labor for Spanish enterprises and auxiliary warriors for military defense in return for protection from enslavement and the loss of village lands (Jacobsen 1991). Such a pact could not be assumed nor was it consistently observed; rather, it had to be negotiated and tenaciously defended over two centuries of colonial rule.

The dissolution of the colonial pact during the Bourbon colonial administration and the formative years of the Mexican Republic affected particularly the Opata and Eudeve peoples of Sonora. These highland villagers competed with seminomadic bands of hunter-gatherers and with Spanish and mestizo landowners and small farmers for both desert and riverine resources; they relied on irrigable cropland, forests and scrubland for hunting and gathering, and pasture for grazing (Sheridan 1988c). The unequal struggle for survival during the transitional period of the eighteenth and nineteenth centuries transformed the social structures through which ethnic communities recreated their cultures and the political implications of resource allocation in the region.

Shifting Ethnic Boundaries among the Indigenous Peoples

The Sonoran Desert and its surrounding uplands comprised an area of geographic, demographic, cultural, and political frontiers. The ecological bonds between the physical environment and the peoples who inhabited it changed the landscape over time through both destructive and regenerative processes, processes which underlay the alliances and conflicts that punctuated their history. Migrations, conquest, and the imperial economy created distinct zones of production which, in turn, established changing and often conflictual frontiers through the countervailing forces of population dispersal and concentration. The serrano (upland) village peoples of the western foothills of the Sierra Madre Occidental had settled the area several millennia before the arrival of European conquerors. Organized in rival chieftaincies, serrano peoples had fought among themselves for territory, scarce agricultural resources, and control of trade routes (Reff 1991; C. Riley 1987). The relative aridity of the environment meant that both foraging and horticulture were essential to survival and, for this reason, cyclical migratory patterns within the region marked the peoples' way of life. Nevertheless, highland Sonoran villagers on the northern frontier of Mesoamerica were settled peoples whose cultures distinguished them from the nomadic bands of the North American Great Plains and the central *cordilleras* of the northern Mexican plateau (Griffen 1969; T. Hall 1989a; John 1975).

The colonial province of Sonora extended from the Río Yaqui in the south to the river basins of the Gila and Colorado in the north. It was shared (and disputed) by village agriculturalists, who settled in the river valleys, and by gatherers, hunters, and fishermen, who camped along the California gulf coast and in the rugged terrain of the Sierra Madre. These indigenous peoples gleaned their sustenance from the abundant flora of the desert and from the coastal estuaries; likewise, the low scrub forest of the hills and canyons of the sierras provided shelter, medicine, food, fiber, game, and small, irregular plots for planting. Nomadic bands moved in seasonal patterns, creating defined territories in proximity to the established villages where they traded. All groups depended on a variety of resources in order to assure subsistence, especially since climatic variations from year to year affected planting cycles and crop yields. For this reason, as well as the ritual visitations associated with ancient migratory patterns, the movements of different peoples blurred and altered the ethnic boundaries that crossed and recrossed the Sonoran map.

The *Opatería,* identified as an ethnic territory, comprised various clusters of agrarian communities which, under colonial rule, converged into a "nation" with common linguistic roots and cultural traditions. At the time of European contact, the Opatas controlled the major river valleys of central Sonora, and maintained contested boundaries with the Sobaipuri Pima, Lower Pima, and Cahita peoples to the north, west, and south, and with nomadic groups of the eastern Sierra Madre (Barnes, Naylor, and Polzer 1981: 81, 87; C. Riley 1987: 50, 295–98; Spicer 1962: 23). They engaged in territorial wars among groups of villages for control over individual valleys or mountain ranges. Serrano political structures and alliances were fluid, largely because their ethnic organization was rooted in the community. The Opatas' relatively high population densities, their ties to long-distance trade networks, and their territorial expansion implied both a well-developed peasant base and a degree of social stratification which, in altered form, endured through colonial institutions (Doolittle 1988; Gerhard 1993; C. Riley 1987; Sauer 1935).

Eudeves, highland villagers similar to the Opatas in their culture and economy, but distinct in their language, formed discernible clusters of communities in two separate zones located to the southeast and northwest of the Opatería proper (Pennington 1981, 1982). *Nebomes,* highland Pima speakers who held territory between the Opata and Cahita nations, adapted their farming methods to the ecological conditions of the Sonoran piedmont in much the same way as the Opatas. Linguistically related to the O'odham (Papago) farmers and gatherers of the desert plains, their villages and rancherías covered the upland terrain of the middle portion of the Yaqui drainage. Together, the Opata, Eudeve, and Nebome peoples constituted the settled peasantry of central and southern Sonora.

The Apaches, diverse bands of hunter-gatherers related linguistically to the Athapaskan speakers of Alaska and western Canada, appeared in the Mexican northwest after European conquest. In the seventeenth and eighteenth centuries, they displaced or assimilated other groups of hunter-gatherers known as the Sumas, Mansos, Chinarras, Jumanos, Jocomes, and Janos, who did not speak Athapaskan languages (Beckett and Corbett 1992; Hadley and Sheridan 1995; Naylor 1981; Spicer 1962). The Apaches and their allies hunted and raided along the ill-defined mountainous frontier between Sonora, Chihuahua, and New Mexico. The pressure of constant warfare waged against these nomads coalesced in an imperial policy to maintain presidios, armed garrisons of paid soldiers, in Janos (Chihuahua) and in Fronteras, Terrenate, Pitic, Horcasitas, Altar, and Tubac (Sonora). The Apaches, in turn, responded to increased hostilities with important adaptations in their mode of subsistence, warfare, and social organization. As they became skilled horsemen, men and women formed highly mobile bands that eluded presidial troops (Griffen 1988a; Lange, Riley, and Lange 1970; Lejeune 1984; Lumholtz 1902; Spicer 1962; Zúñiga 1985).

The Struggle for Autonomy through the Colonial Period

Spaniards first invaded Sonora in the early sixteenth century, lured by the promise of mineral wealth. In contrast to central and southern Mesoamerica—where Spanish dominion rested on native tribute and a colonial aristocracy sought the privileges of encomienda—the colonial economy of the northern provinces relied on mining and ranching. On the mining frontier of Nueva Vizcaya, centered on Zacatecas, Durango, and Chihuahua, Spaniards imported Indian, mulatto, and mestizo laborers and created settlements in the course of waging war against the Chichimecas. Mining reached Sonora from Chihuahua during the second quarter of the seventeenth century and spread gradually throughout the western cordilleras of the Sierra Madre. Silver strikes in Bacanuchi, Nacozari, San Juan Bautista, San Miguel, Trinidad, and San Ildefonso de Ostimuri attracted Spanish prospectors and free workers from Nueva Vizcaya; however, the main source of labor for mining and ranching in Sonora was local serrano communities (Río 1979).

With the northward advance of the mining frontier, colonial governors turned to the mission enterprise of the Society of Jesus to bring the northwestern provinces under Spanish dominion (Manje 1985; Ortega Noriega 1985; Pérez de Ribas 1985). Jesuit missionaries pursued a program of religious evangelization and sociopolitical stabilization based on the serrano villages. They concentrated the population of numerous small hamlets in nuclear towns that controlled sufficient cropland to support a compact community, a policy known as *reducción.* In the interests of conquest the Crown supported the missions financially and provided the legal framework to protect the Indians' land-use rights and shield them from the worst abuses of forced labor.

For nearly 250 years, first the Jesuit (1591–1767) and then the Franciscan (1768–1842) missions served as effective political linkages between the Spanish monarch and his Native American subjects in the frontier provinces. Notwithstanding the cultural conflicts that surfaced repeatedly over differences between the missionaries' objectives and native practices, the institution of the mission came to symbolize a colonial pact of reciprocal obligations, as revealed by the Indians' protests against the nineteenth-century liberal reforms regarding land tenure and village governance.

Highland peasants contested the asymmetrical distribution of power under colonial rule and negotiated their ethnic territory on a number of fronts. Sonoran indigenous peoples demanded autonomy and respect for their territory in return for their labor and provision of militias to fight the unconquered tribes on the margins of Spanish dominion. Furthermore, Sonoran peoples defended their ethnic space and claimed new territory through their physical mobility.[1] They faced repeated threats from Spanish officials and miners, who tried to overrun the missions to gain access to land and cheap labor. When their lands were overrun or rendered unproductive by the expanding frontier of colonial mining and ranching, however, serrano peasants created new rancherías (hamlets) related to the parent villages through kinship and visitation, and thereby maintained the essential contours of their communities in new settings. Migratory patterns and shifting ethnic frontiers comprised both a way of life and a means of resistance for Sonoran peasants, who could survive through hunting and gathering in the monte away from their fields. Indeed, temporary flight from the pueblos afforded them relief from hunger, crop failure, and epidemic disease.

The ethnic boundaries of this northern peasantry were fluid, comprising a number of Indian groups as well as a mixed population of vecinos, *castas,* and *gente de razón.*[2] Culturally, the demarcation between "Indians" and "non-Indians" was ambiguous, but the terms were not meaningless. Their significance derived from a combination of race, kinship, and effective participation in the life of the community. Ethnic identity vied with market relations of production as defining principles for securing access to the land in the closing decades of colonial rule. The struggle over land in Sonora, as elsewhere in Mexico, had strong political and economic significance. Arable cropland represented a tangible village patrimony that supported the ethnic autonomy of serrano peoples. Village leaders' defense of communal lands before Spanish and Mexican authorities concerned not only the material wealth of this productive resource, but also their status as the recognized governors of their people. At stake were the opposing concepts of land-use rights predicated on recognized membership in the ethnic community versus property rights held by virtue of purchase or juridical title.

After Mexican independence, these highland Indian communities faced a new political alignment in their confrontations with the Sonoran notables who took control of the state government. The struggle for territory and power entered a new phase, one that was both decisive and paradoxical. During the first half of the nineteenth century, when the Mexican state was weak at both the national and provincial levels, Sonoran ethnic polities confronted powerful networks of criollo families (Romano 1987; Voss 1984). These regional oligarchs used both legislative and military means to dissolve the colonial pact and forge new political alignments that favored their rise to power and their accumulation of private wealth.

The Role of the Missions in the Native Economy and Political Structure

The missions provided an institutional framework for the survival of peasant agrarian economy and ethnic polity under Spanish dominion. Mission pueblos replicated Iberian town government in a colonial setting through the election of Indian officers, who received a cane of office and the titles of *gobernador, alcalde, fiscal, topil* and, for purposes of religious instruction, of *mador* and *temastián*. Native governors wielded authority within their villages: they meted out local justice and assigned the specific tasks required to complete the work of planting and harvesting in mission fields.

Colonial law also reserved for each mission town a nucleus of arable land for the support of the mission as well as the sustenance of Indian families (Rivera Marín de Iturbe 1983: 162–96).[3] While individual milpas were separate from the *labores* allotted to the missions, the irrigation canals built and maintained through Indian labor benefited both the common fields and the milpas. To be sure, the *hijos del pueblo* were required to labor in the mission fields on certain days of the week, and women were assigned tasks relating to the preparation of food and the maintenance of the church and religious ornaments. Nonetheless, mission Indians also farmed their own plots and frequently sought work outside the pueblos in mining camps and haciendas, which suggests a significant degree of freedom of movement, despite their complaints over the level of work demanded of them.

Religious conversion in the missions was hardly complete nor free of conflict, as attested by the missionaries' repeated denunciations of witchcraft among their neophytes. Nevertheless, Christian ritual, visibly enacted in ceremonies, processions, and the cult of the saints, created an additional arena for Indian officers and ceremonial leaders to display their prestige before their kinsmen and *paisanos* (Pérez de Ribas [1645] 1985; Pfefferkorn 1983–84; Polzer 1976; Radding 1997; Spicer 1962).

The Role of Military Service in the Native Economy and Political Structure

The Apache frontier was one of the defining principles of Spanish-Opata relations during the eighteenth century. Spaniards, Pimas, and Opatas formed an uneasy, but necessary, alliance against the Apaches and bands of Sibubapas and Piatos (Lower and Upper Pimas) who abandoned the missions. Spanish settlers and authorities depended on Indian warriors to secure their dominion over what was as yet unconquered territory, while serrano peasants sought to defend their villages, livestock, and fields threatened by ever-encroaching bands of hunter-raiders. Moreover, the serrano villagers used their status as presidial auxiliaries and their military prowess on the nomadic frontier to defend their status as corporate communities.

Military service in the frontier presidios opened a new avenue for ethnic persistence in the Sonoran highlands as well. From the mid-eighteenth century onwards, Pima and Opata auxiliaries were recruited to fight in punitive expeditions mounted against the Seris and the Apaches. In addition, the Spanish bestowed the title of "Capitán General de la Nación [Opata or Pima]" on certain leaders, who exerted authority over the warriors recruited from numerous villages.

Following the establishment of the Comandancia General de Provincias Internas (1776), a high military command for the northern provinces, the creation of presidial companies manned entirely by Indian militias marked a further innovation. Colonial authorities stationed Opata troops at San Miguel de Bavispe (1781) and at San Miguel de Bacoachi (1784), turning these mission *visitas* in the upper Bavispe and Sonora river drainages into presidios. The salaries and military ranks assigned to the Indians in presidial service created a hierarchy parallel to that of the missions. Serrano men took seriously the honor that public office and military rank conferred on them, and there is some evidence that certain families monopolized these offices over several generations.[4]

Military service on the Apache frontier undeniably put Opata warriors at risk and drained manpower from the pueblos. Presidial auxiliaries found a new source of income, however, and—at Bavispe and Bacoachi—access to land as soldier-vecinos. Opata and Pima militias that fought against the nomads used the Spaniards' dependence on them to negotiate certain privileges for their leaders and protection for their communities. These privileges included honorific titles, uniforms, and a monetary salary. Finally, Indian auxiliaries preserved warfare as a unifying ligament of their societies and a means of re-creating social rankings within their communities (Mirafuentes Galván 1987a, 1987b).

Despite a common enemy, however, Spanish-serrano alliances were unstable and fraught with tension. Military service itself became a point of conflict, as Indian warriors called away for extended periods of time on punitive expeditions deep in the Sierra Madre found it necessary to pay other kinsmen to tend their crops. In addition, Spanish governors, native captains, and missionaries disagreed on the amount of rations that the pueblos should supply to military expeditions, giving rise to disputes over the cost of frontier defense and over the limits of these different spheres of authority.[5] More generally, cumulative demographic and economic changes in Sonora, hastened by Bourbon policies, gave rise to deepening lines of conflict both within serrano communities and between Indians and Spaniards.

Population Pressures and Privatization of Landholdings

Eighteenth-century Sonora saw a significant increase in its population through both natural growth and immigration from Nueva Galicia and Nueva Vizcaya. Mining strikes at San Antonio de la Huerta, Baroyeca, and San Ildefonso de la Cieneguilla created sizable population centers; in addition, many *placeres de oro* (placer gold strikes) scattered throughout the Sonoran highlands attracted new settler-prospectors, who recruited *cuadrillas* (gangs) of Indian laborers to work in these mining camps. Furthermore, ranching operations that clustered around old and new mining centers such as Tepache, Motepore, Saracachi, Trinidad, Río Chico, and Alamos (in northern Sinaloa) increased the number of people and livestock that lived off the land. Military presidios brought new groups of soldier-settlers who either came with their families or married in the province and claimed farming plots in the environs of their garrisons. The presidios of San Carlos de Buenavista, San Pedro de la Conquista de Pitic, San Miguel de Horcasitas, Santa Gertrudis del Altar and, farther north, Fronteras, Tubac, and Tucson all gave rise to *villas* with a mixed Spanish, casta, and Indian population.

Just as significant was the differential growth between vecinos and Indians in Sonora during the late colonial period. Serrano population declined seriously in the sixteenth and early seventeenth centuries due to epidemics and, in later periods, recurring episodes of disease and crop failure (Jackson 1994; Reff 1991). Although serrano population was rising again by the last third of the eighteenth century, Spanish and casta populations were growing even faster.[6]

The growing number of vecinos resulted from the blurring of ethnic categories due to migration and to changes in the *calidad* or civic status of Indians who chose to leave the mission regime. *Naborías*, the pool of Indian laborers seeking wages in the mines or living as tenants on the Spaniards' haciendas, became confused with the vecinos or gente de razón, persons nominally of white or mixed racial origin who were not subject to the communal obligations imposed on Indians. Furthermore, an indeterminate number of Indians petitioned to change their status to that of vecino, motivated by the attraction of wages and commodities in Spanish settlements and by a desire to escape the burdens of communal labor obligations that seemed to outweigh the protection of traditional mission communities. In 1784, Bishop Antonio de los Reyes noted both that all the mission villages contained substantial numbers of vecinos and that many fields nominally belonging to the pueblos and assigned to the upkeep of the churches were unplanted. In Arivechi and Saguaripa, where the "vecinos and Indians who live in the class of vecinos" outnumbered the hijos del pueblo, Opatas and Eudeves had petitioned the alcalde mayor to be considered vecinos, while Indian *comuneros* of Movas, Cucurpe, and Mátape had sold or rented much of their land to private settlers (Radding 1992).[7]

Those Indians who left their pueblos or, without abandoning their villages, changed their status to that of vecino altered the ecological and social relationships that had sustained traditional systems of land use and distribution in the serrano communities. Market arrangements of purchase and rental of fixed plots of land vied with the allotment of usufruct rights to floodplain milpas among Indian families by village leaders. Changes in land tenure eroded the efficacy of farming techniques that had followed the seasonal rhythms of flooding and drought in the Sonoran piedmont. Indian commoners lacked sufficient land to support themselves and the missions, while vecinos expanded their holdings of both farmland and pastures. The gradual privatization of communal land and unbounded rangeland, considered *realenga* or public domain, through the legal instruments of *composición* (verification of land title) and *denuncia* (filing a claim on public land) seriously threatened the economic patrimony and political integrity of highland communities. At issue were two opposing concepts of property and two distinct polities: that of vecinos, or subjects of the realm, and that of the *común,* or membership in an Indian corporate community.

During the first quarter of the eighteenth century, when privatization of land in Sonora gathered momentum through registered composiciones, Indian communities took steps to protect their holdings.[8] The missions of Nuestra Señora de la Concepción de Movas and Santa Ana de Nuri, at the confluence of the Chico and Yaqui Rivers, and the mission of San Pedro de Aconchi, in the Sonora Valley, paid for land titles authorized by the governor of Nueva Vizcaya.[9] In 1716, Pima commoners of Obiachi, Xecatacari, and Buena Vista in the mission district of San Pedro de Cumuripa, petitioned the local magistrate to restore their lands and authorize the formation of a new pueblo in Buena Vista "in order to serve both Majesties."[10]

After the mid-eighteenth century, the population of Spaniards and vecinos (of diverse ethnic origins) reached a critical mass sufficient to expand private landholdings at the expense of native communities (Gerhard 1982: 285; Radding 1997: 171–207). Analysis of land titles recorded between 1790 and 1850 shows that during this period the pace of land enclosures accelerated.[11] Purchases through public auction increased after 1788, and peaked during the decades from 1810 to 1820 and 1830 to 1840. The size of realengos, measured in the number of *sitios* included in each property, tended to rise over time, and prices paid for rangeland increased noticeably throughout the period. This may be due, in part, to officially set minimum prices for land sold in public auction beginning in 1805. Nevertheless, the upward pressure on land values, especially after the turn of the nineteenth century, suggests that population growth (of people and cattle) spurred competition for land among the vecinos and created the conditions for a land market to develop on the Sonoran frontier.

Military presidios established under Bourbon rule in the central and northern portions of Sonora constituted the nuclei from which private landholding expanded. Presidial captains took advantage of their privileged position to develop family enterprises centered on ranching and local commerce. Numerous clans vigorously expanded their properties during the early decades of the nineteenth century, constituting a provincial landholding class (Voss 1982, 1984). Among the more outstanding examples are the Noriega (Pitic); Arvizu, Aguilar, and Iñigo (Horcasitas); and García, Escalante, and Elías-Gonzalez

(Fronteras, Bacoachi) families. These notable families prospered under official Bourbon policies that accelerated the privatization of landholding during the final decades of colonial rule.

The legal framework for an evolving land market in Sonora was established by Visitor-General José de Gálvez, the personal representative of the king in New Spain, who decreed the formal division of mission lands in 1769. Gálvez's orders were reiterated by Intendent-Governor Pedro Corbalán in 1772; by Pedro Galindo Navarro, advisor to the Commandant-General, in 1785; and by Commandant-General Pedro de Nava in 1794 (Escandón 1985; Kessell 1976; Río 1985).[12]

Bourbon directives for land redistribution reserved a nucleus of land for community support and, in theory, benefited each resident Indian family with a subsistence plot. In practice, however, these initiatives accelerated the transferal of land from communities to private estates and hastened population decline in the pueblos. The parallel and mutually reinforcing processes of a diminishing land base, intrusion of non-Indian squatters in the pueblos, and increased demand for wage labor in Spanish enterprises impoverished native horticulture and eroded the political foundations of Indian communities. Internal migratory patterns intensified as serrano villagers turned increasingly to paid labor as presidial auxiliaries, mineworkers, and transient day laborers or became tenants and *peones* on the haciendas that consolidated their holdings in the major river valleys during this period. Ethnic communities in Sonora experienced internal stratification and a deepening schism between vecinos and hijos del pueblo, which would lead to the breakdown of many of their corporate structures after Mexican independence.

Ethnic Rebellion as a Response to Converging Pressures

These different lines of conflict converged in three ethnic rebellions that shook the province in the mid-eighteenth century: the Yaqui uprising of 1739–1741; the Seri revolts beginning in 1748; and the Upper Pima rebellion of 1751 (Figueroa Valenzuela 1986; Hu-DeHart 1981; Kessell 1970; Mirafuentes Galván 1987b, 1989; Spicer 1962, 1980). The Yaqui and Upper Pima rebellions were suppressed, but bands of Pima rebels, known to the Spaniards as Piatos and Sibubapas, often joined with Seris to attack Spanish communities. Sibubapa resistance intensified after the expulsion of the Jesuits in 1767, when many Lower Pimas fled their pueblos and roamed through the highland ranges, robbing cattle and engaging in passing skirmishes with presidial troops. Their movements paralleled similar migrations across the porous ethnic boundaries of

Pima, Eudeve, and Opata territories during the confused period when ordered mission life was interrupted by the removal of Jesuit missionaries from the province (Pennington 1981).[13]

Each of these revolts was sparked by different sets of grievances and circumstances. Foremost among the causes were resentment against particular missionaries' disciplinary actions, territorial claims to lands usurped or occupied by miners and ranchers, and food shortages occasioned by drought and crop failure. Taken together, however, they make evident the combined pressures on Sonoran highland communities, which mounted in intensity during the last half-century of colonial rule. While Yaquis and Upper Pimas were not able to sustain a long-term rebellion, their revolts, combined with the prolonged resistance of the Seris and the ongoing wars on the Apache frontier, limited colonial dominion in Sonora. Spaniards never saw their ambitions for mining wealth fully developed nor brought to fruition their imperial project to hold a unified northern frontier.

Dissolution of Community Autonomy Following Mexican Independence

The wars of independence affected the province of Sonora only indirectly, drawing presidial troops away from frontier defense to support the royalist cause against the *insurgentes* of the central plateau (Officer 1987: 84–86; Vidargas del Moral 1985: 321–27; Villa 1984: 153–60). Nevertheless, once Mexican independence was consummated in the Republic of 1824, Sonoran landed notables exerted their influence to take control of the governorship and legislature of the state of Occidente and, later, of Sonora and Sinaloa.[14] Like other peripheral elites in early republican Mexico, the Sonoran oligarchs changed the terms of negotiation with the ethnic communities in their province and, in so doing, altered irretrievably the operative legal definition of property and the relations between the state and these serrano *naciones*. The new regime pushed aggressively to privatize the land and to change both the civic status of Indians and the internal governance of their pueblos (Tutino 1986: 216–28; Voss 1982).

The deputies of Occidente and Sonora passed legislation during the decade from 1825 to 1835 that, in theory, established equality between Indians and vecinos, and defined citizenship in terms of landed property. This new legal framework sought to impose the sovereignty of the state over the pueblos through the institutions of municipal government and the division of communal lands. During the same period, the expulsion of the Spaniards from Mexico, ordered by federal law on December 20, 1827, and applied in Occidente on February 15,

1828, deprived those Sonoran pueblos that had remained under mission tutelage—primarily in the Pimería Alta—of their missionaries and left their communal property in the hands of civilian commissioners.

The most important of these laws was Decree 89 of 1828, which focused on the corporate holdings—*fundo legal*—and all arable lands in the communities. Despite the appearance of equitable treatment—as suggested by the first two articles of the decree, which called for the restitution of "those lands which have been unfairly taken" from Indian communities, and by the citation of the appropriate sections of the colonial *Recopilación* of 1681 and a similar decree issued by the Cortes de Cádiz of 1813—the root purpose of Decree 89 concerned the demarcation and division of communal lands. It stated, "The lands known as the fundo legal, as well as mission property restored to the pueblos and vacant lands in their environs, shall be reduced to private property to the exclusive benefit of the Indians."[15] The legislators recognized as legitimate property only those holdings authorized by legal title, thus favoring large landowners and undermining the ancient tradition of the común. Concerning ethnic polity, the authors of this law took note of the racially mixed population that characterized many communities and opened their councils and militias to both vecinos and Indians, altering the system of internal governance that the pueblos had received from the missions. In point of fact, contemporary observers criticized the deleterious effects of Spaniards and castas who had gained control of political offices in the communities (Radding 1979: 28–29, 88–90; Romero 1995: 70–80).[16]

The state of Sonora passed a series of laws between 1831 and 1835, based on the tenets of Decree 89, which made it easier for private citizens to register "vacant lands" as their own and subordinated Indian pueblos to municipal governments.[17] That Sonoran governors enforced the new laws to the benefit of local elites is evident in the reports and correspondence that reached the president of Mexico from different sources during these years. State officials had measured and divided village lands in the Opata villages of the Sonora River valley and in the Eudeve area of eastern Sonora. These legal innovations placed valuable communal resources in private hands and set in motion two parallel processes: the consolidation of a regional landed oligarchy and the social stratification of peasant communities. The division of alluvial cropland in the pueblos separated peasant cultivators into classes of vecinos and Indians, smallholders and "proletarians." By the 1830s, villages like Mátape, Batuc, Nacameri, Cumpas, Aconchi, and Baviácora comprised dual communities of Indians and vecinos, distinguished by their opposing claims to the land. Conflicts over land arose in the former missions of Mátape, Batuc, and Tepupa over measurements begun during the colonial period and extended through purchase and inheritance over half a century. Nacameri was the scene of litigation between vecinos and a nucleus of Pima and Eudeve families who remained from the mission and, later, between non-Indian smallholders and *hacendados* from the powerful Robles, Aguilar, and Gómez del Campillo families (Radding 1997: 234–38; Romero 1995: 125–78).[18]

Taken together the legal distinction between Indian citizens and hijos del pueblo, the division of communal lands, and the dissolution of the pueblos' internal governance constituted an unprecedented invasion of Sonoran ethnic communities. Responding to events, Opata governors protested the loss of village land, the disintegration of the común, and the corrosion of their authority as concomitant parts of the same process. Indigenous leaders resisted the new political order through negotiation, political appeal, and armed revolt. Between 1825 and 1833, Opata and Yaqui warriors confronted presidial troops in numerous skirmishes in the mountain ranges between the Bavispe and Yaqui Valleys. Opata leaders Dolores Gutiérrez, Juan Güiriso, Antonio Baiza, and Miguel and Bautista Sol joined with the famed Yaqui leader Juan Banderas. They launched an ambitious rebellion to create an autonomous state in eastern Sonora. They opposed the division of communal lands and taxes imposed by the state government; furthermore, the Opatas called for restoration of the colonial mission regime and, with it, the restitution of the común. These uprisings, occurring simultaneously with new Apache incursions through the sierra, seriously shook the fledgling regime, but state troops suppressed the Indians' movement with the capture and execution of their leaders (Spicer 1962: 61–64, 100–3).[19]

Even while engaged in armed revolt, Opata leaders turned again to negotiation, appealing their case to the highest authorities of the Mexican nation. In 1831, Opata representatives obtained an executive order from President Anastacio Bustamante directing the governor of Sonora to recognize their communities' fundo legal and to restore alienated land to their villages. Bustamante's ruling had little effect, however, because state authorities ignored the federal directive. After their military defeat and several violent confrontations with landowners in different localities, the Opatas again sent representatives to Mexico City in 1836. José Anrríquez, the governor of Cumpas, and Juan Ysidro Bohórquez, "a native of Oposura representing himself and thirty-six pueblos who comprise the Opata nation," gave a formal petition to the Secretary of State and of the Interior. In the petition they reasoned that the core problem of land was linked with their status as leaders and legitimate representatives of their people. What they defended was the land itself, valued as an ethnic territory, and a political order that was receding from their grasp in a time of transition marked by changing agrarian structures and a new configuration of power.[20]

The Secretary of State reiterated Bustamante's directive of 1831, but in ambiguous terms referring merely to compliance with the law. By midcentury, the Opatas had lost their communal lands, and within several decades their ethnic territory was considerably eroded. The Opata nation suffered disintegration not because its leaders lacked political acumen or a sense of their own history, but rather because the power structure they confronted had economically and militarily surpassed the resources they could marshal in defense of their ethnic community.

Diverse ecological, cultural, and political frontiers collided in Sonora during the century between 1740 and 1840. After Mexican independence Sonoran provincial elites overturned the colonial pact between Indian communities and the state. Leading frontier families buttressed their rise to power with the ideological tenets of liberalism and federalism, which supported their regional autonomy vis-à-vis the central government and defined citizenship as a status conferred on individuals independent of corporate entities such as ethnic communities, guilds, or the Church. Equally significant, the juridical bases of land tenure were irrevocably changed, elevating private property over communal holdings.

But early republican liberalism did not go uncontested. Peasant cultivators of the Sonoran highlands articulated a different discourse rooted in the común. Their ethnic polity evolved from pre-Hispanic origins, and was remolded and preserved through colonial institutions. Serrano villagers persisted in their defense of ethnic autonomy, linked to communal agrarian structures and the physical mobility that permitted them to live in the semiarid environment of the Sonoran piedmont. Ethnic traditionalists confronted emerging social classes which, in turn, developed from an expanding market economy and the privatization of the land.

Agrarian conflict would continue in the Sonoran highlands throughout the nineteenth century, contributing to the explosive events of the Revolution of 1910. The social landscape and ethnic frontiers of this frontier province were never fixed or immutable; indeed, the piedmont and desert lowlands of Sonora have remained contested ground. It was during the transition from colony to republic, however, that serrano peoples ceased to be a peasantry based on ethnic ties to the común and became rural workers and producers—*rancheros*, tenants, and sharecroppers—whose claim to the land depended on contractual relations of purchase, rental, and service.

5

Women of the Buenos Aires Frontier, 1740–1810

(or the Gaucho Turned Upside Down)

SUSAN MIGDEN SOCOLOW

Socolow explores the myth of a ranching frontier occupied by males—Indians, Europeans, and mestizos. By examining 1744 census returns from various districts of rural Buenos Aires, she discovered that the sexual imbalance in this part of the Río de la Plata frontier was far less extreme than imagined, and that women and children were found in all rural areas studied. Furthermore, these family units were central to the raising of crops and small farm animals important for food. This presence of women and children offers a more useful explanation of how gaucho cowboys were socialized.

TWO YEARS AGO I received a lovely Christmas card from friends in Argentina. Indeed, it was the archetypical Argentine Christmas card—a beautiful, somewhat stylized line drawing of two men around a campfire sharing the sublime camaraderie that comes with a close friend and some yerba maté. My friends had sent me a modern version of their nation's most heroic figure: the gaucho.

That gaucho needs no introduction to any student of Latin American or even world history. The so-called "Argentine cowboy" is an integral part of the history and historiography of his country. A product of the pastoral economy and the *vaquerías* (roundups of wild cattle), the gaucho is the quintessential frontier figure. Indeed he has become a mythical figure—macho, independent, and inhabiting an exclusively masculine world. From time to time the gaucho encounters a *chinita* (a nubile young woman), the temporary object of his affections, but the general vision of rural society is so male-centered that one is at a loss to explain how the population of the region was able to reproduce itself. While there is some disagreement among historians as to exactly when, why, and where the first gaucho appeared, the literature on the gaucho, and on the rural world of the pampas in general, paints the rural frontier as an exclusively male domain.[1] Although recent historical debates have questioned whether the rural population during the late colonial period consisted of nomadic gauchos or salaried peons, the discussion is still centered exclusively on men and male workers (Amaral 1987; Gelman 1989; Mayo 1984; Mayo et al. 1987; Salvatore and Brown 1987).

During the eighteenth century, most of the Río de la Plata frontier was synonymous with the rural areas of the city of Buenos Aires. Although the frontier lay close to the capital city, relatively little is known of life in either the hinterland of Buenos Aires or any other rural zones during the colonial period. Because one of the enduring myths of Argentine history is that the frontier was overwhelmingly male, even less is known about the role of women in the rural society that developed on the ranches, farms, and forts established to hold back Indian attacks. The literature makes no mention of women as participants in the labor force and only occasionally recognizes them as inhabitants of the rural regions.[2] This chapter attempts to redress this silence by drawing on census and other data. It questions the extent to which the pampas was a masculine world and analyzes gender roles along the frontier from the mid-eighteenth century until the end of the colonial period.

Demography

If we use the simplest definition of an American frontier—that is, a region where indigenous populations and non-indigenous settlers came into continuous and hostile contact with each other—much of the province of Buenos Aires lay within the frontier in the eighteenth century. (For other Spanish American colonial frontiers see R. Gutiérrez 1991; Rausch 1984; and Weber 1992.) Rural districts of Buenos Aires covered a roughly oval-shaped region approximately 270 miles long by 80 miles wide, running parallel to the Río de la Plata. Traveling from northwest to southeast the specific *pagos* (districts) were Arroyo del Medio, Arrecifes, Areco, Cañada de la Cruz, Luján, Las Conchas, La Matanza, and Magdalena. Although the Indians theoretically were found only in the vast plains to the west and south of the Río Salado, the region was extremely permeable. It was not until the 1750s that a series of forts was founded in an attempt to draw a firm border between "civilization" and the lands of the "infidels" (Comadrán Ruiz 1969: 58–59).[3] No district in the rural zone, including the immediate outskirts of the city of Buenos Aires, lay more than one hundred miles from the Indian frontier.

From the beginning of Spanish settlement, the ranches, farms, and settlements of the Río de la Plata were periodically threatened by raids organized by Pampas, Pehuenche, Tehuelche, and Araucanian hunting parties (Angelis [1836–37] 1969; Falkner [1744] 1935; K. Jones 1984; Socolow 1987, 1992; Tapson 1952, 1962: 11). The usual Spanish response, when possible, was to organize a counter-raid, or *entrada* in hopes of punishing the offending Indians. At times an endemic state of war existed, as Indian raids and Spanish entradas broke out along the frontier.[4] The line of forts established in the 1750s was reinforced during the 1770s and 1780s, in an attempt to control the fluidity of the frontier (Azara 1969a; Marfany 1940b). The Crown also encouraged settling a civilian population close to each fort.

The Spanish combined this line of forts and missions with a program of pacification and cooptation of hostile Indians. Sporadic incidents continued along the frontier,[5] but in general Spanish policies after 1780, combined with adverse natural phenomena (such as drought), contagious disease, and widespread food shortages, weakened Indian assaults and imposed an uneasy peace. Nonetheless in 1744, the year the first census of rural Buenos Aires was taken, Indian raids were still an ongoing problem. In fact, during the same cabildo meeting where a census was first discussed, the need to investigate how many captives were held by Indian 'infidels' in the region was also mentioned.[6] Although the census was not taken for specific military reasons, defense of the region no doubt was a major consideration.

At midcentury virtually the region's entire rural population lived in a frontier zone, although those districts to the northwest of Buenos Aires (Las Conchas, Cañada de la Cruz, Areco, Arrecifes) constituted what we may call a more "settled" frontier. These areas were sparsely populated, but the route linking Buenos Aires to Córdoba and to the silver mines of Alto Perú crossed this district. Regions to the south (Luján, La Matanza, and Magdalena) represented a more isolated, "newer" frontier.[7] Nonetheless, the entire rural district, both to the north and the south of Buenos Aires, was vulnerable to Indian attack.

According to the census of 1744, the total rural population of the province of Buenos Aires was 4,664 (Moreno 1989). Age and sex data are available for 86.1 percent (4,014) of the individuals. These data show that while males were in the majority, the sexual imbalance assumed in much of the literature was nowhere as large as implied. Overall, 55.5 percent of the rural inhabitants were male while 44.5 percent were female. Indeed, among those who identified themselves as Spaniards (the overwhelming majority, 84.6 percent of the entire group), males outnumbered females by only 53.4 percent to 46.6 percent. Among the non-Spanish population (mestizos, mulattos, indios, and free

TABLE 5.1
Masculinity Index by Age Group, 1744

Age	*White*	*Non-white*
1–19	101.8	133.7
20–59	125.4	256.0
60+	235.0	767.0

and enslaved blacks), the sex ratio was very different; here men outnumbered women by two to one.

Information from the 1744 census allows us to reconstruct the age profile of the rural *porteño* population. This population was a young one, with approximately 54.2 percent of inhabitants under age twenty. The masculinity index in table 5.1 shows that in the "white" population there was a slight surplus of males among those under twenty, a surplus much increased in the adult population, and even greater among the elderly.

Why this population imbalance? Age pyramids by race show that among whites the discrepancy between the numbers of males and females begins to be dramatic only above age thirty, an indication of the effect of mortality among women of childbearing age (see figs. 5.1–5.3). Indeed these data suggest that rural women survived the births of their first few children, only to die after bearing a fourth or fifth child. Although Concolorcorvo, a traveler who made his way from Buenos Aires to Lima in 1773, praised the healthfulness of the pampas, reporting that "two-thirds of those who die are the result of falling from a horse or being gored by a bull" he clearly did not take female mortality into account (Concolorcorvo 1942: 56–57).

A second possible reason for the predominance of males among the adult population was internal migration. Third, the 1744 census was taken during a period of ongoing Indian raids, and the population patterns in the age pyramids probably show the effect of these raids. Indian raids, for example, might have been a factor in the relatively small number of male children aged birth to nine years, for young male children were frequently taken captive in Indian forays (Socolow 1987: 120). These raids, and the resulting death of adult males in battle might also explain in part why the cohort of males in their thirties is slightly smaller than might be expected. As females of all ages were also taken captive by Indian invaders, the effect of the raids is not clearly visible in the female age pyramids.

While these numbers go far in adjusting the "male-only" picture that has become part of the mythology of the frontier, in themselves they do not provide a vision of the life of the women who lived along the frontier. Here we must rely on a closer analysis of the census supplemented with other historical evidence. In order to construct the role of women (and men) along the colonial frontier, I have looked at two pagos, both on the edge of the region, that represent slightly different economic and settlement patterns.

Areco, a region located along the traditional route that linked Buenos Aires with Potosí, represented the more settled frontier. This pago lay eighty-four miles (twenty-four leagues) to the north of Buenos Aires, and was, according to Concolorcorvo, a region of "many hacendados . . . with spacious lands, where all types of livestock are raised, but where the raising of mules, which are sold young to the invernadores of Córdoba, is most important" (Concolorcorvo 1942: 57). To the south, Magdalena, a more isolated region of relatively recent settlement, was involved in ranching (cattle, sheep, and horses) mixed with largely subsistence farming. Only four years before the 1744 census enumeration, Magdalena had been the scene of a large-scale Indian raid in which more than one hundred settlers had been killed and many had been taken captive. Both regions were well within the humid pampas, an area of relatively abundant, fertile land (Gelman 1992: 106).

Examining the male-to-female ratios in both frontier zones reveals a general pattern not all that dissimilar from the global data. In Areco, of a total population of 491 inhabitants, 56.6 percent (278) was male, 41.1 percent (202) was

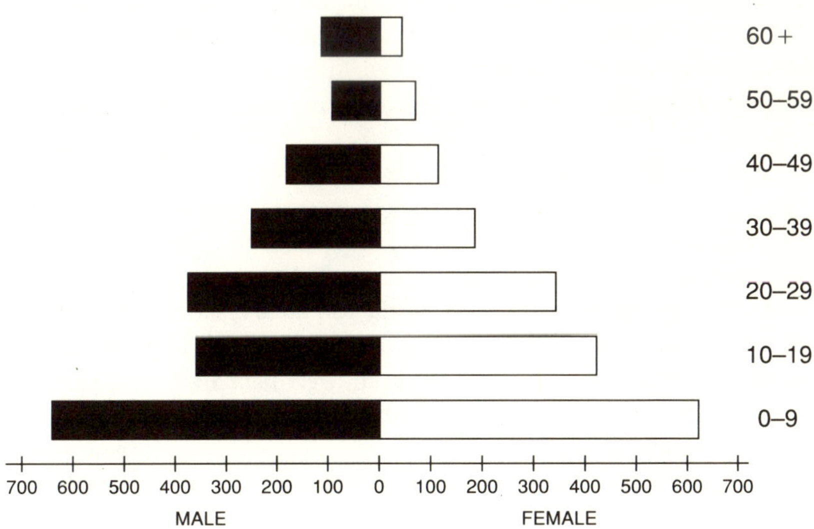

FIGURE 5.1. The white population of the Buenos Aires region in 1744.

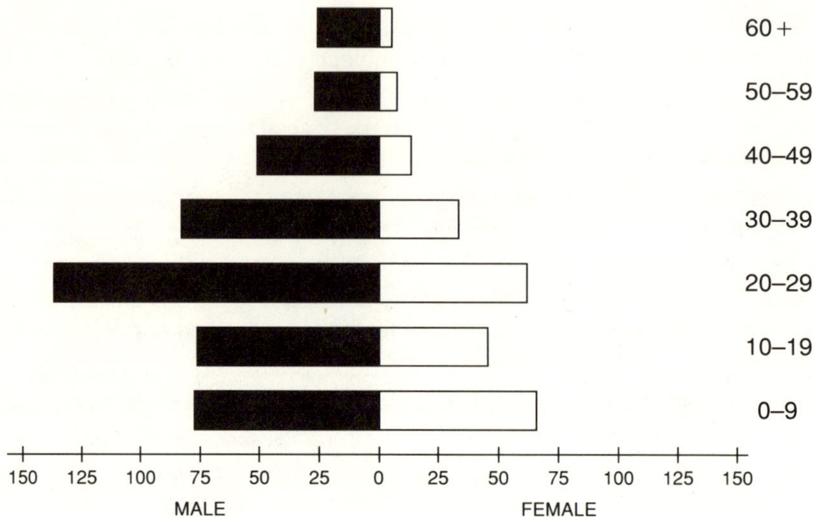

FIGURE 5.2. The non-white population of the Buenos Aires region in 1744.

female, and 2.2 percent (11) was indeterminable from the information in the census. In Magdalena (population 677), 52.4 percent (355) of the population was male, 39.4 percent (267) was female, and 8.1 percent (55) was indeterminable. By identifying those in the indeterminable category who were children (listed vaguely as *hijos menores*) and assuming that the sex distribution of these children was the same as those for whom gender was clearly given, we can correct the sex ratio figures as follows: for Magdalena 57.1 percent male and 42.9 percent female; for Areco 57.9 percent male and 42.1 percent female (see table 5.2).

Census data for Areco and Magdalena also allow measurement of the effect of migration on the sex ratio. In Areco, in-migrants accounted for 13.4 percent of the population. In Magdalena, a less prosperous and less accessible region, in-migrants were 5 percent of the inhabitants. In both regions, immigrants were predominantly from the north of the Río de la Plata region, principally Córdoba, Paraguay (including Misiones), Corrientes, and Santiago del Estero. Regardless of birthplace, migration was an overwhelmingly male phenomenon, in part because of traditional cultural patterns and in part because there were more economic opportunities in the region for men than for women. Men made up 89.4 percent of the newcomers to Areco, and 97.1 percent of the same group in Magdalena. The few women whose birthplace was outside the region

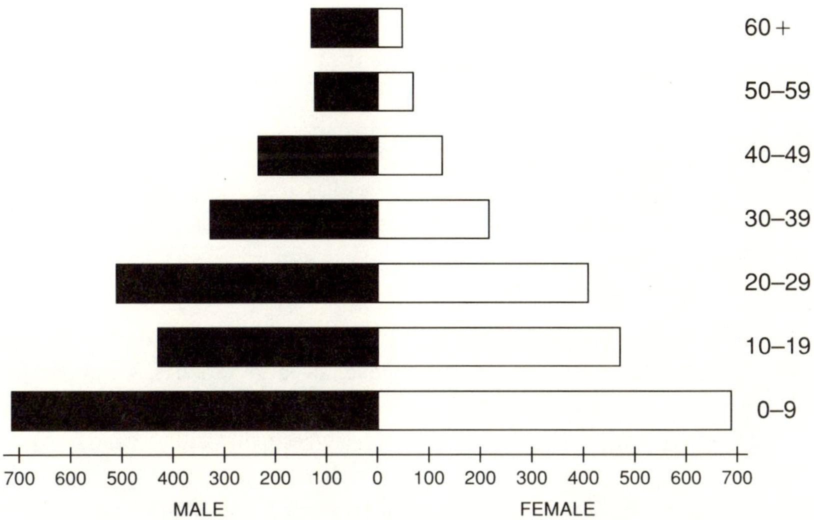

FIGURE 5.3. The total population of the Buenos Aires region in 1744.

tended to be Indians from Misiones. Table 5.2 shows the effect immigration had on the sex ratios of the two frontier zones.

In both regions, heads of household were overwhelmingly male. Indeed it was rare to find women filling that role along either the southern or northern frontier. In Magdalena only 4.5 percent (6 of 134) of the households was headed by a woman; in Areco the percentage rose to 11.5 (6 of 52), still a rather insubstantial number, but one that suggests that women were better able to survive as heads of household in wealthier, more settled regions. In those few cases where women were heads of household, they were always widows.

It is interesting to note that the incidence of property ownership was much higher among these few female heads of household than among the population at large, suggesting that most poor widows, those whose husbands had not owned land, were forced to migrate to towns or cities or to take refuge with kinfolk. There was also a shortage of employment openings for poor widows; very few rural families, for example, were wealthy enough to employ female servants. Rural life allowed few options for non-propertied women to survive as heads of household, for they lacked the gender, the economic opportunity, and the socioeconomic position that would have given them the wherewithal to continue living on the frontier.

Nonetheless, a few propertied widows, able to combine their wealth with the

TABLE 5.2
Sex Ratios, 1744

	Areco		Magdalena	
	M	F	M	F
Overall	57.9	42.1	57.1	42.9
Corrected for immigration	52.5	47.5	54.8	45.2

social position and authority which came from being the *viuda* of an important man, continued as at least the nominal heads of large ranches. Whether these few women actually managed rural property is difficult to determine; the fact that all lived with at least one adult kinsman suggests that the actual day-to-day administration of their property was left to others. Four of the six female heads of household in the Magdalena region owned solid homes and large numbers of livestock—including Clara Márquez, widow of Juan Jimenez, who owned one thousand cattle and four hundred sheep, and Doña Martina Luola, widow of Masiel de Aguirre, with fifty head of cattle and one thousand mares.

In addition to their property, these two women also headed relatively large household establishments. Clara Márquez lived with four adult children (ranging in age from eighteen to thirty), a free mulatto male servant and an *agregado* (farmhand) in a house described as being made of *teja y adobe* (tile and adobe). Doña Martina headed an eight-person establishment including her daughter, a nephew related to her late husband, an elderly male slave, a younger female slave, and the slave's three children. The home was described as being of *adobe y teja*, featuring five *tirantes* (ceiling beams); it was the largest private residence in the Magdalena region.

Not every widow was wealthy. Two were found on *tierras arrendadas* (rented property); each lived with only one son, one in a *casa* and the other in a *rancho de paja* (straw-roofed hut). Gregoria de los Ríos and her sixteen-year-old son owned one hundred head of cattle. Teresa Nieva, widow of Francisco Díaz, owned no livestock. She and her twenty-six-year-old son listed their occupation as farming (*labranzas*).

Neither of the frontier regions under discussion was an egalitarian society. Race, wealth, and social position, although perhaps less important than in urban areas, were still potent social markers. The Magdalena census contains specific information on landholding that allows reconstruction of social distinctions. Only 10 of the 139 households in the region were described as *estancias* (ranches). Furthermore of the 125 households where ownership can be determined, only 37 (29.6 percent) owned the land they lived on; the other 88 households (70.4 percent) farmed rented land (tierras arrendadas). The vast majority of the inhabitants of the region therefore did not live on ranches, but rather on small subsistence plots or farms, which they usually rented.[8]

The type and size of landholding were closely correlated with the family organization of those inhabiting the property. Patriarchal families (a nuclear family plus other individuals living under the tutelage of a paterfamilias) were found only among the *grandes propietarios* (owners of large properties) (Moreno 1989: 272). Subsistence farms were overwhelmingly inhabited by nuclear families.

Indeed the nuclear family was the survival unit of the frontier. Few households in either Magdalena or Areco were described as containing only one individual or two or more unrelated individuals of the same sex. To the north and the south, inhabitants of the frontier were overwhelmingly found living in what were essentially nuclear family units composed of a married couple and their children. Adult women in both frontier zones were primarily listed as "wives"; younger females were children within nuclear families.

For most men taking a "wife" meant setting up an independent household. Indeed taking a wife was the motivating force behind creation of new households. Unmarried adult children, regardless of age, continued to live with their parents, and new households were formed only at time of "marriage." It is clear that small farmers were overwhelmingly dependent on members of their own families for labor in order to survive. Individuals could not survive without their families, for men, women, and children all contributed to the household economy.

"Marriage" was the almost universal norm, although at least one late-eighteenth-century traveler believed the living arrangements of the inhabitants to be far more casual. Félix de Azara (1969b: 285–86), traveling through the pampas and the Paraguayan countryside, remarked on the casual living arrangements of the inhabitants. He doubted that there were any females over the age of eight in the entire region who were still virgins. Formal church marriage was probably less frequent in the countryside than in the city, in part because the rural population was only tenuously served by the Church. Nonetheless, the degree to which households were formed around couples and the repeated use of the term *casado* in the census records themselves suggests that Azara misconstrued stable concubinage or common-law marriages as licentiousness.

The traditional social role of wife and mother was found in all social groups from *estancieros,* or owners of large properties, to dependent farm laborers. In Areco, 81 percent of all households were made up of at least a man and wife;

in Magdalena, this figure reached 85 percent. In addition, another 19 percent of households in Areco and 9.6 percent in Magdalena were headed by widows or widowers, people who had once comprised part of a stable couple. Indeed, these households represented a transformation of the nuclear family produced as a result of the life cycle. Only in Magdalena were any households headed by single people found; these households, all headed by men, accounted for only 5.2 percent of the total.

Women and the Rural Economy

To better understand the economic contribution of rural women we must distinguish between estancias and farms and between the production of each type of unit. The primary function of estancias was raising so-called *ganado mayor* —cattle, horses, and mules—for distant markets. Other products were hides, *sebo* (tallow), *grasa* (suet), and cattle tongues, as well as various meat products, including *charque* (jerked beef), *cecina* (dried beef), and *tasajo* (hung beef) (Millau [1772] 1947: 48). While no doubt occupying large expanses of property, estancias were relatively rare along the mid-eighteenth-century frontier. Although some women lived on estancias (primarily the wives and daughters of the foremen [*capataces*]), women were excluded from the central equestrian labors of the livestock economy (Slatta 1983: 57). The estancia owner himself might be present on his ranch, but his family often resided in Buenos Aires.

Cattle were rarely raised on small farms, although the owners may have had limited access to animals culled from wild herds. Rather, farms held *ganado menor,* or smaller animals. Much of the production of rural farms was for domestic consumption, and here women played an essential role. Women were active in caring for domestic animals, primarily sheep and goats, which allowed for a small production of wool for domestic use. Women participated in the shearing of sheep and then carded, spun, and wove the coarse wool into ponchos and other garments. Women were active in growing food crops, and aided with planting and harvesting of wheat and corn. They also were in charge of processing and storing food, and grinding wheat into flour, and corn into cornmeal. Sebo, grasa, and smoked dried meat products were also produced in small amounts by rural women working alongside their menfolk. In addition, food preparation, cleaning, candlemaking, and medical services were part of the female domestic economy. Indeed, because of female labor, relatively few goods consumed by the frontier inhabitants of Buenos Aires would have been purchased in a rural *pulpería.*

How much work did women perform? Beginning in the 1780s, travelers to the pampas occasionally made note of the region's inhabitants. These reports were usually rather negative as to the work ethos of both men and women, but at least one observer of rural life in the early nineteenth century found women to be far more hardworking than men, noting that "the poor females perform all the drudgery, waiting upon [the men] with the greatest humility" (Alexander Caldcleugh in Slatta 1983: 57). The same travelers also remarked that rural women were often ill-clad, dirty, unkempt, and prematurely aged by the harsh conditions of frontier life (Slatta 1983: 57).

To a certain degree, rural women had few economic options in those regions. Domestic textile production seems to have been extremely limited, with each household producing only enough for its own consumption and none supplying any local or regional market. Women were also clearly not included in the part-time salaried labor market that employed men in seasonal tasks on nearby estancias. The lack of any opportunities to supplement their personal or family incomes probably reinforced the subordinate social position of females in this society. On the other hand, the centrality of some form of marriage to the creation and survival of the independent household might have given women, especially those in their late teens and early twenties, some degree of power and flexibility. But at best this power was transitory and limited to an age-specific cohort of women: those on the marriage market.

Frontier women were nonetheless not tied to their hearth and home. Like the men who lived along the frontier, they learned to ride horses and, at least according to one witness, were at least as skilled in horsemanship as rural men. Horseback riding was not an elite activity in eighteenth-century Río de la Plata but rather a universal skill essential to any and all human movement. "Horseback riding is a continual activity of those who live in the countryside, where women participate, with great skill, as frequently as men" (Millau [1772] 1947: 45).

The socialization of children along the frontier was accomplished by men and women operating together within the nuclear family, not by solitary men. Indeed, there were few solitary men, or solitary women, on the frontier. Although the overall density of population was only 0.4 inhabitant per square kilometer, men and women not only lived in households, they often had family nearby. Marcos Pavón and his wife María Villegas Isarra, for example, lived with their five children in a casa de paja in the Magdalena area. Pavón, who rented land, owned fifty head of cattle and two hundred sheep. In another household on the same plot of land, his son, the son's wife, three children, and six other young female children could be found. Two of Pavón's older daughters, both married, one with a young child and the other rearing an orphaned child, also lived with their husbands in the same compound.[9] These women living in proximity to other female kin not only helped one another in their chores, they also participated in the creation of feminine culture on the frontier.

The degree to which frontier women were engaged in procreation can be gauged to some extent by constructing a child: woman ratio, that is a ratio of children between birth and fifteen to women aged sixteen and older. In Areco, there were 1.48 children for every woman, while in Magdalena there were 2.36 children per woman. The lower child: woman ratio in the north is tied more to the relatively greater prosperity of that region than to differing levels of fertility; there was a larger group of slave women with no children in the Areco region.

Although the census cannot be used to reconstruct the average number of children born per woman or to calculate rates of infant mortality, there is reason to believe that both were high. The average number of sons and daughters living with at least one parent was 3.2 in Areco, but only 2.2 in Magdalena. This difference suggests that infant mortality might have been higher in the more isolated Magdalena region. The case of María Villegas Isarra demonstrates that a woman might have five children, ranging in age from eight to fifteen (8, 11, 13, 14, 15) at home, and three older children who were already married and had formed their own households. High birthrates probably resulted from early "marriage" for women, as well as a lack of birth control. These birthrates did insure a large and constant source of child labor, but at the same time they increased the mortality risk for rural women, who were bearing children in rustic conditions. Rural women probably bore their first child relatively early and continued to have children throughout their fertile years. Like women, children of both sexes were critical for the survival of the rural household, for they too provided needed labor; those households with few sons and daughters tended to compensate by including kin (brothers and sisters or in-laws of the head of household), and/or orphaned children within their numbers.

Treatment of Women

What general type of treatment did these frontier women experience? This is a most difficult question to answer, but at least some aspects of women's lives are reflected in the criminal records of the courts of Buenos Aires. While we have no way to know how much crime against women went unreported, the records allow us to reconstruct the most extreme treatment of women and view interpersonal relations between women and men.

From the criminal records, it is clear that rural women, especially those who were poor, were frequently victims of men's violent behavior. The most common crimes against women were physical abuse and wife beating, followed in frequency by rape and kidnapping. These crimes were usually committed by family, friends, acquaintances, or neighbors. The localized nature of crime reflected the familiar parameters of the feminine world. In addition, most crime against women was committed in the home, again suggesting a limited social milieu for women.

In order to better understand the treatment of women, we can divide the crimes into the larger categories of domestic disturbances and sexual offenses. The first category of crimes—which included beating, stabbing, and attempted homicide—usually occurred within the family. Most typically a wife was the victim of her husband's anger, although women were also abused by kinsmen.[10] Male anger could be set off by unseemly conduct on the part of the woman, especially by her failure to conform to the norms of expected female behavior with regard to sexual conduct. The right of a husband to discipline a wife suspected of unseemly conduct (*mala conducta*) applied to all men regardless of race or legal condition. Several cases also reflect a man's right to use violence to control the female members of his family. Within the culture of eighteenth-century Argentina, male violence, within certain limits, was also a mechanism for asserting dominance and masculinity, and was considered within the norm of expected male behavior.

Nonetheless, the most grievous examples of domestic abuse also reflected the high level of personal violence and frustration that was a normal part of lower-class male life. Men of the rural sectors—subsistence farmers, peones, and ranch laborers—lived in a world over which they had little control. Armed with knives, they turned their frustrations at their economic and social roles on the nearest available victim, their wives—who were in a socially sanctioned subordinate position. Testimony in these cases suggests that a high degree of physical abuse was tolerated by some women, often over long periods of time.[11] The ubiquity of nuclear households may well have tended to remove any constraints that kin might have exercised in controlling male violence against women.

The second major group of offenses against women—sexual offenses including rape, kidnapping, and haircutting—also tended to be committed by men from within the same social world as the victim. Sexual offenses were almost uniformly committed by men known to their victims: by neighbors, acquaintances, or kin, fictive and real. Although lust was frequently the motivating force, these crimes were not random crimes of passion, but crimes in which the victim was well chosen by the assailant. When the victim of violent sexual crime was a married woman, the violence directed against her was at times just one act in a personal dispute between the assailant and the woman's husband.

Arguments between men that had started over land, personal insults (*palabras injuriosas*), or affronts to a man's honor sometimes escalated to involve the married woman. A married woman was the perfect victim in these disputes, for she was the means by which an enemy could assail her husband's manliness (Aufderheide 1976: 168, 171).

Any attack against a man's wife was inevitably an attack against him. It was the man whose honor had been jeopardized, and it was the man who sought legal redress. Even in the very act of reporting the crime to a local magistrate, however, the man was publicly admitting his vulnerability and the fact that he was too weak to seek his own retribution. This is perhaps the reason why so many of the sexual offenses reported to local magistrates were charges of "attempted rape," rather than rape.[12] Successful rape and kidnapping were seldom reported to the authorities as such because of the attendant shame involved, but cases of attempted rape often included testimony on previously committed rapes and kidnappings that had gone unreported.

In cases of sexual assault against unmarried women, again the assailant was almost always an acquaintance of the woman involved, someone she had known, even fleetingly, before the crime was committed. Some single women with male protectors were victimized to destroy a male kinsman's honor. Underlying this pattern of violence was the reality of a strongly male-dominated society that viewed unprotected females as fair game for sexual advances. A woman who was even temporarily without a husband, father, or brothers was viewed as unprotected property, waiting to be claimed through male sexual prowess. In the countryside, both married and single women left alone could become the victims of rape and other violence, attacked by men described as *guapos* or *gauderíos*—roving precursors of the nineteenth-century gauchos. Once a woman had been sexually attacked, her violator often felt free to return and reclaim her whenever he pleased.[13]

Testimony from many of the cases suggests that in rural areas kidnapping and rape of unmarried girls were part of the local courtship pattern. After meeting an eligible young woman, a man would steal her from her home, usually at night or when the girl's male relatives were temporarily absent. After riding some distance from the "bride's" family, the girl was deflowered and the marriage thereby consummated without benefit of clergy. The couple then set up household, publicly living as man and wife. Only when the girl's family disapproved of her suitor, or when her new husband continued to "court" other women in the same way as he had wooed her, was any formal complaint lodged.[14]

Haircutting, although of lesser violence than rape or kidnapping, also had sexual significance. Cutting a woman's hair was tantamount to publicly branding her as morally loose. Jealousy or rejection was often the motive behind this crime, but again women were also slandered in this way in order to attack the honor of their male kinsmen.

Conclusion

In conclusion, there is no doubt that women were found along the rioplatense frontier. Although their numbers were never as great as men, they were by no means a small component of the population. Furthermore both men and women lived principally in nuclear families; that is, a man, his wife, and their children. On the farms that provided the livelihood of most nuclear families, women (and children) were basic to the rural household, undertaking some tasks considered to be specifically female roles and sharing other chores with men. For the vast majority of frontier inhabitants, men and women, adults and children, life was physically hard and material conditions notoriously sparse. But for female inhabitants along the frontier, gender combined with Indian raids placed them at special risk for capture, while gender combined with a culture of male dominance made them susceptible to male violence within a household setting. While this chapter has, I hope, opened some possible avenues of future research on frontier women in colonial Latin America, there are still many issues that need to be addressed.[15] We still need to know more about the myths and realities, the daily life of hearth and home, and the moments when ranches and *chacaras* (small farms) were under attack. The home was a female workplace, but we still have very little information about the material culture of the frontier: housing, clothing, possessions, and food.

Although I have spoken about domestic labor, we need to know more about women's work and the gender division of labor. What were the work relationships between men and women and among women, especially among frontier women, domestic slaves, and agregadas? I have tried to sketch out women's work in food processing and manufacturing, cleaning, growing crops, gathering seeds, soapmaking, candlemaking, weaving, and sewing, but we know nothing about other roles such as doctoring. Indeed we need information about sickness in general, and women's sickness in particular, as well as childbirth and childbirthing and mutual aid in times of sickness. Most of all, we need to consider issues related to the value given to women's work, as well as qualities prized and scorned in a frontier woman.

In addition to labor, we should seek to better understand the power of kinship in the lives of frontier women. I have spoken briefly of household formation, but we know little of kinship formation and its relationship to creating stable communities on the frontier. For example, was "intermarriage" among neighbors a common pattern? For those few who owned land, we need more research on inheritance patterns of the land; we also need to know what happened to the majority of families living on tierras arrendadas. I have spoken briefly of family size, but there is still much to be learned about rural women's family lives, including courtship, "marriage," childbearing, the relationships of men and women in marriage, and relationships of women to their children. I have also alluded to the condition of women without husbands—that is, single women and widows—but we know nothing about remarriage of widowed women. Although we can begin to speak of female patterns of sociability, much remains to be done; we do not know, for example, whether any informal communal organizations existed in which men or women participated.

Although this chapter speaks briefly of migration into the frontier zone, we know little of migration out of the area, although the scarcity of widows suggests it occurred. How transient or rooted was the frontier population, and was migration linked to gender? Some work has been done on women's relationships with Indians, but we know nothing of the images and stereotypes that frontier women held of the Indians, nor of how they viewed the hardships and dangers of their lives.

There is a need for a total reassessment of the frontier in Latin America, to take into account the lives and experiences of women in these settlements. Indeed our very concept of frontier in Latin America is heavily gender-laden; masculine values such as rugged individualism, independence, taciturnity, strength, and restlessness are central to the myth of the frontier. One North American historian has stated that "women did play highly significant and multifaceted roles in the development of the American West . . . their lives as settlers displayed fairly consistent patterns . . . these shared experiences and responses of frontierswomen constituted a 'female frontier' " (G. Riley 1988: 2). Can the same be said of colonial Latin America or of eighteenth-century Argentina? In the case of the Río de la Plata, did a female frontier become more masculine in the nineteenth century as a result of first the Rosas and then the Avellaneda campaigns? Only after such research will we be able to come full circle, back to the gaucho which whom I began this chapter, and answer whether the gaucho is a valid figure of premodern Argentina or a romanticized creation of a phallocentric culture.[16]

6

Spanish Colonial Military Strategy and Ideology

RICHARD W. SLATTA

Spanish military strategy against hostile indigenous groups, according to Slatta, was ineffective and deleteriously affected by Eurocentric attitudes. His comparison of the frontier areas of New Spain and the Río de la Plata reveals similarities in the limited numbers of troops, recruitment of ill-paid and often unsuitable soldiers, efforts to save money on defense, and an inability to defend the area against indigenous groups who were far more knowledgeable of the terrain. He concludes his essay by pondering on what might have happened if Spanish policy had been more enlightened on both frontiers.

SPAIN DEVELOPED similar, mostly ineffective, frontier military priorities and strategies at the northern and southern extremes of its New World empire. Officials generally used a defensive strategy but intermittently took the offensive against hostile Indians. The realities of conflicting royal priorities, frontier social forces, and determined Indian resistance repeatedly forced the Spanish to modify official strategies. Despite these modifications, however, Eurocentric ideologies, not frontier social realities, generally set the parameters of military strategy (Archer Jones 1987: 177–94).

In order to explore those strategies, Spanish policies in northern New Spain, primarily Nueva Vizcaya and New Mexico, are compared with those in the pampas to the south and west of Buenos Aires, Argentina (Hu-DeHart 1981: 8). Many differences existed between the northern and southern frontiers. With the exception of Paraguay, missions had a much greater impact in the north. The two regions differed in indigenous populations, terrain, aridity, and availability of livestock. Despite these important differences, however, clear similarities emerged in Spanish military policy at the far northern and southern extremes of its empire (Slatta 1992b: 25–48).

The Spanish enjoyed initial quick successes, even against formidable enemies such as the Aztecs. From the 1520s on, however, Spanish frontier strategy became more defensive. Indians in the northern and southern extremes of the Spanish colonial empire proved difficult to subdue. Many had no wish to subject themselves to Spanish rule or religion and effectively resisted domination. The vastness of the frontier created major logistical headaches for Spanish forces. In addition, chronic shortages of manpower and money generally denied frontier commanders the option of launching major offenses. Occupation and control of already claimed territory, not continuous expansion of the frontier, became the primary goal (Elliott 1984: 152, 156–57, 163, 165; Moorhead 1975a: 5–11).

Spanish defensiveness increased in the mid-sixteenth century in the face of sharp Indian resistance. The Mixtón and Chichimeca Wars of the 1540s and 1550s forced a defensive posture on the overwhelmed Spanish. The various "nations" labeled Chichimeca attacked supply trains en route to mines, estancias, and towns. Viceroy Luis de Velasco responded feebly and tentatively, launching generally unsuccessful entradas and building presidios (Naylor and Polzer 1986; Powell 1952: 29–31, 57, 60, 204).

"Both fortress and farce" was Odie B. Faulk's evaluation of the presidio. "It could withstand siege, but it could not halt Indian incursions into the interior of New Spain" (Faulk 1979: 74). Early presidios housed only six to fourteen soldiers. By 1585, the general failure of military conquest in the north forced the Spanish to adopt a more conciliatory frontier policy. Missions, diplomacy, and peace gifts became more important than military units (Moorhead 1975a: 5, 7, 10–11).

Spain's initial forays into the Río de la Plata met with stout Indian resistance. In 1516, Querandís or Charrúas summarily killed the first European to enter the Río de la Plata, Juan Díaz de Solís, a Portuguese-born navigator sailing under the flag of Castile (Rock 1987: 8; Vidal [1820] 1944: vi). Pedro de Mendoza established a humble outpost at Buenos Aires in February 1536. Within months Indians laid siege to the Spanish camp. Their attacks and siege killed some two hundred Spaniards and reduced the force to one-third its original size. The Spanish resorted to eating cattle, horses, rats, snakes, and even shoe leather to survive. According to Francisco de Villalta, "Some kept their dead companions around for three and four days, that they themselves might take his food ration and so survive; it happened that others, seeing themselves so hungry, ate human flesh" (Nichols 1939: 121). By 1541, Buenos Aires stood deserted and burned (Rock 1987; Serrano 1947: 208–10; Vidal [1820] 1944).

After rebuilding Buenos Aires in 1580, Spaniards began competing with

Pampas Indians for wild livestock. As on the northern frontier, military funding remained scarce. Beginning in 1745, the Cabildo de Buenos Aires levied a series of taxes on carts, mules, salt, and hides. After slowly gathering funds for seven years, in 1752 the cabildo paid to build new forts at Luján, Salto, and Zanjón (Nichols 1968: 43; Tapson 1962: 12).

Radiating out in concentric circles to the south and west of Buenos Aires, these crude, makeshift sod huts (*fortines*) were an attempt to push back the frontier line. Poorly armed frontier troops warned ranches and villages of Indian attack, often by cannon shot. Soldiers manned rickety watchtowers to afford a longer view across the flat, treeless plains. Similar watchtowers were proposed for the northern frontier of New Spain. The better manned forts mounted occasional expeditions against hostiles. By 1781, the line of forts had pushed out only to Chascomús, northwest to Ranchos, Monte, Lobos, and Navarro. Beyond the Río Salado, however, the plains remained the domain of the Indian (L. Gutiérrez 1968: 35–37; Marfany 1940a: 102; Rodríguez Molas 1968: 120–21; Walther 1964: 108–9, anexo 1).

On the far northern fringe of the empire in New Mexico, Spanish military force existed hardly at all. Officials left seventeenth-century frontier defense in New Mexico up to a handful of resident encomenderos. The Pueblo Revolt of 1680 forced the Spanish to retreat from New Mexico and to devote more attention and money to frontier defense. Settlers and missions remained highly vulnerable throughout the next century. Officials repeatedly but unsuccessfully requested more presidios and soldiers (Simmons 1968: 112–14).

Spanish defensiveness stemmed as much from competing royal priorities as from strategic planning. Royal officials responded to more proximate problems and to noisier, better situated lobbies. European affairs, of course, claimed highest priority. The British sack of Havana in 1555 and more than one hundred other corsair attacks focused Spain's attention on the Caribbean. The vast distances from Spain to its frontiers and the slowness of communication hampered policy implementation. In addition, tiny white frontier populations did not constitute a very formidable political lobby (Burkholder and Johnson 1994: 70, 142–46).

Lack of finances left frontier commanders with few tactical choices. Major offensives cost more than the Crown would commit. Defensiveness permitted frontier policy on the cheap. For example, Francisco de Urdiñola, governor of Nueva Vizcaya from 1603 to 1613, coped with budget cuts by reducing frontier forces. After quelling a rebellion by the Acaxees in 1603, he mustered out troops to save money. Six years later, another rebellion by the Xiximes killed many Spaniards in the thinly defended province. A self-defeating cycle developed.

The Spanish repressed uprisings, cut forces to save money, and then suffered renewed Indian rebellions in the poorly defended north (T. Hall 1989a: 75–101; Naylor and Polzer 1986: 172).

Spain's infrequent attempts to mount offensives against the "*indios bárbaros*" generally failed. Viceroy Alvaro Manrique de Zúñiga (1585–90) had to pursue what he termed a "peace offensive." He concluded that mass force further inflamed frontier conflicts, so he reduced troop levels and closed some presidios (which also saved money). He left a single roving unit of thirty-one men to provide material assistance to the Indians—food, clothing, land, tools, religious instruction, and protection. His successor, Luis de Velasco the Younger (1590–95), built more missions than presidios, pursuing a policy of "peace and persuasion" (Meinig 1971: 141–45; Moorhead 1975a: 13; Naylor and Polzer 1986: 37–39).

Borderlands defensiveness continued into the seventeenth century. The Spanish built fewer but somewhat stronger presidios with a garrison of twenty-five to thirty soldiers each. In 1667 the governor of Nueva Vizcaya proposed constructing ten watchtowers and adding a few troops to the frontier. The Spanish also built two-story adobe and stone towers (*torreones*) in villages and towns in New Mexico, in order to provide needed intelligence and help coordinate responses from different presidios. Like many policy reforms, this one was stillborn. Divided military authority and petty politics also hampered policy coordination (Moorhead 1975a: 18–19; Simmons 1991: 62–63).

Particularly devastating attacks, such as the "Great Northern Revolt" (1680–98)—which actually was a series of revolts sweeping across Nueva Vizcaya, New Mexico, and Sonora—forced the Spanish to reevaluate their defensive policy. They increased the number of presidios and the number of soldiers guarding roads. Some of the new presidios had fifty men apiece, double the size of earlier contingents. *Flying companies* escorted travelers and merchandise and rapidly moved to assist areas under attack. Nonetheless, when *Maestre de Campo* (Colonel) José Francisco Márin inspected the northern presidios in 1693, he found only 381 soldiers and officers thinly spread over the frontier (Moorhead 1975a: 20–24).

A century later, strategy remained defensive. The marqués de Rubí warned in 1768 against overextending into "imaginary dominions" controlled by hostile Indians. Crown military spending for the interior had nearly doubled since 1700, but defenses remained precarious. Rubí resurrected the idea of a ring of presidios to protect settlements south of the thirtieth parallel. Isolated garrisons farther north at Santa Fé and San Antonio would need reinforcing. Economy again held sway over security in the proposals. The entire frontier force would number only 910 men (Moorhead 1975a: 58–61; Weber 1992: 205).

In his 1768 report, Rubí reasoned that the Comanches attacked Apaches rather than Spaniards in pacified areas. He urged the Spanish to ally with the Comanches against the Apaches. In his "Instrucciones" of 1786, Viceroy Bernardo de Gálvez minced no words. "The vanquishment of the heathen consists in obliging them to destroy one another" (Weber 1992: 229). From the days of the first conquistadors, Spanish policy had skillfully turned intra-Indian conflict to European advantage (Moorhead 1975a: 58–61).

The desire to "privatize" frontier defense was a recurrent theme in Spanish strategic thinking. By attracting settlers to the frontier, officials could reduce expenditures and transfer defense to civilians. Settlers would, in theory, fight hard to defend their homes and property. But the far northern frontier, especially Arizona, attracted few Spanish settlers. Civilian militias supplemented professional soldiers even after the formation of presidios. In Sonora and the Pimería Alta, militias effectively quelled the Yaqui Revolt of 1740 and the Upper Pima rebellion led by Luis Oacpicagigua in 1751. During a frontier inspection in 1766, Nicolás Lafora observed "eighty militiamen, well mounted and armed" in Albuquerque. Most reports, however, indicate that militia units, like presidios, generally lacked both arms and expertise. According to Edward Spicer (Spicer and Thompson 1972: 298), civilian settlements proved much less effective than missions in promoting pacific Spanish-Indian relations (see also Polzer and Sheridan 1997; Simmons 1968: 147–48).

Some clerics opposed locating Spaniards near Indians because of the former's corrupting influence. Pedro de Arriquibar, writing from Bacoachi in 1795, complained that, owing to bad Christian influence, "there is no lack of concubinage, improper speech, oaths, maledictions, insults, envy and so forth" (Matson and Fontana 1977: 122).

Attempts to populate the frontier in Argentina also met with frustration. Powerful estancieros opposed ceding land to smallholders on the frontier. Besides competing for grazing land with the estancieros, freeholders would reduce the available supply of landless laborers (gauchos) needed for ranch work. Labor and social control, not a Jeffersonian agrarianism, motivated the landed interests of Buenos Aires (Azcuy Ameghino 1991: 199–208; Rock 1987: 48, 65–66).

From the earliest days of the conquest, the Spanish used bribery and gifts to buy off indigenous groups they could not defeat outright (T. Hall 1989a). Officials used special funds to purchase gifts and food for Indians in hopes of making Indians dependent. New Spain's Viceroy Bernardo de Gálvez's "Instrucciones" of 1786 cynically described the goal. Indians "should be made accustomed to the use of our foods, drinks, arms, and clothing, and they should become greedy for the possession of land" (Simmons 1968: 143–46). Apaches seeking peace should be given "defective firearms, strong liquor, and such other commodities as would render them militarily and economically dependent on the Spaniards" (Officer 1987: 62).

Friendly chiefs could expect about fifteen to twenty pesos worth of goods, including tobacco and food. Other gifts included jerked meat, salt, clothing, sugar, gunpowder, livestock, and minor trade goods. By the spring of 1787, Gálvez's policy brought the Utes, Comanches, and Navajos into alliance against the Apaches. Following the campaigns coordinated by Jacobo de Ugarte y Loyola, who served as *comandante general* of the Provincias Internas (the "interior provinces" encompassing all of northern New Spain) from 1786 until 1790, many Apaches sued for peace as well, settling in *establecimientos de paz* (peace establishments) near northern presidios (Griffen 1988a; Weber 1992). The buy-off or rationing system broke down during independence when Spain had to divert troops and supplies elsewhere. Indians reverted to raiding, and by the 1820s, the tenuous peace of the late colonial period had largely collapsed (Moorhead 1975a: 100–13; Simmons 1968: 146–47; Weber 1982, 1992).

Spaniards occasionally altered their defensive posture of building forts. On the northern frontier, greater offensive action coincided with two or three waves of heightened exploration and expansion. The activities of Francisco Vásquez de Coronado, Juan de Oñate, and Sebastián Vizcaíno highlighted the period from 1540 to 1610. Strategy remained defensive during the seventeenth century. During the next wave of expansion, the 1680s and 1690s, Spain took the offensive in response to threats from major Indian uprisings and to heightened French activity in the Mississippi Valley. A century later, Bourbon reformers sought to counter frontier threats from Russia and England. Spain usually took offensive action when it feared threats from other colonial powers to its vulnerable northern frontier (Kessell 1991: 69–70, 73; Weber 1992).

Offensive expeditions in colonial Argentina usually met with failure. Indians enjoyed superior knowledge of the terrain and usually outnumbered their pursuers (see Jones in this volume). In 1663, the Cabildo de Buenos Aires sent fifty soldiers in pursuit of Indians raiding frontier estancias. In a three-hour battle, soldiers killed fifty to sixty Indians. More Indians drowned as they tried to escape across a river. But such punitive offensives yielded only temporary respite. Spaniards tried to take the offensive by fielding itinerant patrols. In 1712, the city of Santa Fé sent out roaming patrols. The poorly trained and ill-equipped troops had little deterrent value against Indian raiders. The vastness of the pampas and the Indians' superior geographical knowledge gave them a decided tactical advantage. In 1724, when rural militia forces took the offensive to pursue raiders, Indians attacked Buenos Aires itself (Argentine Republic 1973, I:12; Marfany 1940a: 20–24, 48–49).

Fierce attacks close to Buenos Aires during the 1740s forced the cabildo to alter its purely defensive strategy. Spanish pursuit had proved fruitless, and ragtag militia units proved poor deterrents. The cabildo instructed Governor José de Andonaegui to build new forts and to create companies of *blandengues* (gaucho cavalry units) to patrol the countryside. The first three blandengue units, formed in 1752, served at Mercedes (Luján), Salto, and Magdalena. Each unit consisted of fifty men plus officers (K. Jones 1984: 27; Moncaut 1978: 12–15; Rodríguez Molas 1968: 102, 119–21; Vedoya et al. 1979: 17–18).

In the Borderlands, Spain fielded well-armed light troops (*compañías volantes*) during the Chichimeca Wars of the sixteenth century. More mobile than presidial units, the "flying companies" guarded roads and traveled quickly wherever they might be needed. In 1772, Commandant Inspector Lieutenant Colonel Hugo O'Conor (born in Dublin) moved aggressively to chastise the Apaches. In September 1775, his 340 troops killed 130 Indians and recovered much booty. Apache raids, however, did not diminish. In 1778, the commandant general of the Provincias Internas, French-born Teodoro de Croix, created companies of *tropas ligeras* (light troops). Of special appeal to the royal treasury, these troops were more cost-effective than the heavily equipped *soldados de cuera*. As was often the case, however, European threats and other imperial distractions pulled resources away from the frontier (Simmons 1968: 27, 155; Moorhead 1975a: 68–72, 82–84, 93, 97; Weber 1992: 225–26).

Bourbon strategists also gave the Río de la Plata more attention. Increased trade, legal and contraband, brought the region greater economic significance. Conflict with the French and British over the Malvinas (Falkland Islands) a few years earlier and expansionist threats from the Portuguese in Brazil increased security concerns. Foreign threats preoccupied the first viceroy, Pedro de Cevallos. Nevertheless, he proposed to José de Gálvez that a massive force of ten to twelve thousand men take the offensive against hostile Indians in the south (Tapson 1962: 16).

In 1778, the more cautious Juan José de Vértiz y Salcedo succeeded Cevallos and authorized a study of the planned offensive. Vértiz did not wish to spend the large amount of money necessary for the offensive. His frugal motto, according to historian Jorge Cabodi, was "to govern is to save" (Moncaut 1978: 29). His fiscal conservatism, coupled with rancher opposition, doomed the offensive (Tapson 1962: 16–18).

Mistreatment by officers alienated many frontier troops. Royal officials sent criminals to serve as low-ranking frontier soldiers. In 1606, the marqués de Montesclaros complained to King Felipe III that "the infantry being recruited in this kingdom is regularly committing many excesses, and those delinquents who are not soldiers are being protected by the infantry. . . ; [they are] apt to become worse because the companies are made up of reprobates, *gente de mal vivir,* who are fleeing Spain because they are not safe there" (Naylor and Polzer 1986: 143–44).

Poor recruitment could derail the best military planning. A report of 1738 complained that Argentina's regular frontier army was comprised of "vagabonds, including Indians and mestizos and the rest Portuguese" (Marfany 1940a: 68–69). Florián Paucke, a Jesuit, visited a small fort at Pergamino in 1750. He expressed grave dismay at the activities of the officer and his men who "play cards, eat, drink much, sleep, and curse" (Rodríguez Molas 1968: 121).

The soldiers' meager pay came late or not at all. Paymasters sometimes gambled away the payroll. Some Sonoran commanders received kickbacks from local merchants (often relatives) on goods and horses purchased for presidios. Gregorio Alvarez Túñon y Quirós, captain of Fronteras presidio from 1708 until his removal from office in 1726, used soldiers as his own personal labor force and collected salaries on vacant positions (Polzer and Sheridan 1997). Frontier soldiers, however, found alternative civilian jobs scarce. For some men, the poor pay of soldiering was better than starving (Moorhead 1975a: 27, 201, 213–14; Officer 1987: 41–42; Simmons 1968: 122).

Of course, not every frontier commander was a corrupt profiteer. An exhaustive audit in 1603 turned up no malfeasance by Captain Gabriel Ortiz de Fuenmayor. Alonso de Nieva of San Luis Potosí testified that "the captain has always met the obligations of his charge to visit the frontier as he was ordered without failing to do service to his majesty" (Naylor and Polzer 1986: 115). He kept order and delivered goods to Indians punctually and fairly.

Reform-minded Bourbons sought to reduce corruption and improve the lot of frontier soldiers. They alternated paying soldiers in cash with providing provisions, but abuses marred both systems. Rubí found little discipline, no instructions from officers to enlisted men, and no drill or training. Weaponry lacked uniformity. Many troops suffered shortages of food and equipment. Many were in debt. The more adaptable frontier soldiers managed to survive and in some cases prosper. David Weber (1992: 328–29) documents some cases of upward mobility for frontier troops (also see Moorhead 1975a: 56–57; Simmons 1968: 134–35).

New regulations in 1772 placed force above compromise and diplomacy. They reinforced a 1729 policy of exiling intransigent Apaches to Mexico City and environs. Beginning in the late 1780s, Spanish conflict with the Apaches hardened. Enterprising Spaniards could earn rewards for a pair of Apache ears. Soldiers marched captive Apaches to Vera Cruz for shipment to Havana, where they worked as forced laborers. The draconian policy failed. Apaches escaped or resisted so fiercely that the Cuban governor protested the practice. Escapees able to return to the north fully and violently vented their hatred on the Spanish (Moorhead 1975b: 206, 209; T. Hall 1989a: 126; Weber 1992: 215–16, 232).

Meanwhile in the Río de la Plata, Félix de Azara, a Spanish scientist, noted with disgust that the frontier boundaries of 1796, "because of a few annoying barbarians, are approximately the same as those which [Juan de] Garay took with sixty men 216 years ago" (Tapson 1962: 25). He urged increasing the frontier population by granting land in exchange for military service. He also revived the idea of itinerant "early-warning" patrols based at small frontier installations.

In May 1804, Captain Sebastián Undiano y Gastelú seconded Azara's goal of populating the frontier. He emphasized the importance of utilizing natural barriers against the Indians. He urged Viceroy Sobremonte to push settlements and forts to the Río Negro to gain "the peaceful conquest of 17,000 square leagues of land, with the best soil in the Universe" (Vedoya et al. 1979: 31–32; Walther 1964: 160–61).

Relative calm prevailed on the frontier toward the end of the colonial era until independence disrupted frontier policy. Indians came to "corrals" in many cities to trade hides and skins. Feliciano Antonio Chiclana suggested in 1804 that Indians be given a monopoly on the salt trade to end conflict over that critical resource. The Spanish paid tribute or protection money to friendly Indians in exchange for peace and intelligence on the movements of hostiles (Tapson 1962: 26).

Despite several centuries of strenuous Spanish efforts, however, the far frontiers of New Spain and the Argentine pampas remained perilous places for Spaniards and Creoles. Not until Julio A. Roca's "conquest of the desert" in 1879 did Argentina achieve a "final solution" to its frontier Indian threat. The northern frontier was not pacified until the 1870s and 1880s, when the Western Apaches and Yavapais were confined to the San Carlos Reservation in 1874, the Comanches were finally defeated at Palo Duro Canyon in west Texas in 1875, Victorio and his group of Chiricahua and Mescalero Apaches were run down in Chihuahua in 1880, and Geronimo surrendered for the final time in 1886 (T. Hall 1989a; Sheridan 1995).

Many Indian groups successfully resisted Spanish domination. Spanish strategy and actions also contributed to their failure at complete military conquest. The conquistadors held an initial edge in firearms, horses, and other technology vital to their success in much of Latin America. Indian acquisition of the horse and mastery of cavalry warfare, however, tipped the tactical balance in their favor (see Jones this volume). Indians possessed a dangerous arsenal, including bows and arrows, lances, and light armor. Skillful lance warfare by Indians generally carried the day over primitive Spanish firearms. Spanish artillery served more to intimidate than to seriously injure Indians. On the vast flat pampas, cavalrymen proved the most potent force to counter the superb horsemanship of the Indians. But Spanish cavalrymen there—in contrast to the presidial soldiers of the northern frontier, who relied upon the lance—considered using lances degrading. They preferred pistols and carbines. Not until the late nineteenth century did the balance of technology tip in favor of whites against equestrian plains Indians (Forbes 1960: 192).

Some early frontiersmen, with fresh memories of the Reconquest, regarded Indians as they had "Moors," infidels to be defeated and enslaved. Soldiers (frequently unpaid or underpaid) and freelancing explorers held slave sales to be a legitimate source of profits. By the 1530s, Indians as far north as Sonora and New Mexico already exhibited hostility toward Spaniards because of slave raids (Forbes 1960: 7, 12–13, 41; Weber 1992: 20, 51).

Frontier events often blunted Las Casian reform efforts. On the northern frontier, the outbreak of the Mixtón Wars nullified the abolition of Indian slavery decreed in the New Laws of 1542. "Treasonous" Indians could be enslaved. The ferocity of the Chichimeca War (and the need to reward soldiers) provided further rationales for enslavement. Under New Spain's fourth viceroy, Martín Enríquez de Almanza (1568–80), the de facto policy of total war, *guerra a fuego y a sangre,* became official. Slave raids continued to be a factor in regional Spanish-Indian and later Mexican-Indian relations along the northern frontier until the mid-nineteenth century (Cuello 1988: 685–88; T. Hall 1989a: 68; John 1975: 33–34; Meinig 1971: 14–15; Naylor and Polzer 1986: 37–39; Powell 1952: 64, 73, 105–12).

Residents of Buenos Aires (porteños) engaged in *malocas* or slave-hunting expeditions to counter their chronic labor shortages. These slaving expeditions did not have the same grand scale as those of bandeirantes from São Paulo, Brazil. But slaving did nothing to enhance Spanish-Indian relations. Enslaved Indians worked at many tasks, particularly in the necessary agricultural labors despised by many Spaniards. Despite official denunciations, Indian slavery continued in New Spain and in Argentina until at least the 1680s. In neighboring Paraguay, Indian slavery persisted until at least the 1750s (Burkholder and Johnson 1994: 114–15; James Saeger, personal communication).

Despite tactical shifts, Spanish grand strategy on the frontier ossified during the colonial period. Unable to learn from or adapt to failures of the past, Spanish officials waged an unsuccessful centuries-long war against "barbarism." Local interests, such as miners and ranchers, lobbied successfully for the right to exploit Indians. Native resistance to incorporation was a logical response to long-term Spanish encroachment and enslavement.

Both regions suffered relative neglect and insufficient support throughout the colonial era. European exigencies and pressures elsewhere in the empire frequently pushed distant frontier issues to last place. Religious wars and imperialist competition drained the Hapsburg treasury. The dynasty sank into ineffectual decay during the seventeenth century. To the Crown, the meager potential benefits of expanding remote frontiers did not justify increased expenditures (John 1975: 37, 38, 44, 91).

Whenever possible, the Crown pushed the costs of settlement onto private individuals, who saw greater potential gains. Freebooters, such as Francisco Leyva de Bonilla in New Mexico, operated outside the law. Exploitation by Spanish settlers outraged Indians and poisoned relations. One Indian blamed a Pima uprising in 1690 on "Spaniards who took away their land and populated it with horses and cattle" that damaged and ate the crops (Hu-DeHart 1981: 57). Father Diego Miguel Bringas de Manzaneda y Encinas complained in his report of 1796 that at Tucson, "the Indians' crops are also badly damaged by the cattle and other animals belonging to the inhabitants of our presidio" (Matson and Fontana 1977: 66). Quechan Indians likewise protested crop destruction by Spanish livestock and other abuses by killing the Spaniards while they were attending mass in the summer of 1781. That brought to a bloody end the short-lived Spanish colony on the Colorado River and severed the route between Arizona and Alta California pioneered by Juan Bautista de Anza less than a decade earlier (Forbes 1960: 41, 74; Kessell 1991: 75; Officer 1987: 57; Sheridan 1995: 33).

Frontier policy on the cheap largely failed to eliminate or even deter skillful equestrian raiders of the pampas or the Borderlands. Philip Wayne Powell (1952: 89) deemed the Spanish policy during the Chichimeca War "penny wise, pound foolish." In 1764, Juan Nentvig (1980: 134), a Jesuit, petitioned the king to increase frontier defenses. "If the Crown does not provide greater numbers of soldiers, I am of the opinion that the few we have will do more harm than good." Nentvig pointed out that "Apaches take triple revenge" in retaliation for expeditions by small Spanish forces.

The Spanish had more success at incorporating Indians on the northern than the southern frontier. Colonial policy on the pampas lacked the missions and adaptability found in northern New Spain. Spaniards temporarily transformed some groups, such as Pueblos, Opatas, O'odham (Pimas and Papagos), and after 1786, even Comanches, into "friendly" Indians. Thousands of Apaches even settled in peace establishments near presidios, some of which, such as the one in Tucson, lasted for decades (Officer 1987). Many bands, however, successfully resisted inclusion. Even incorporated Indians rebelled against forced deculturation, as the Pueblos did in 1680.

On the southern frontier, the Spanish sought to exterminate and subjugate, not to incorporate, pampas nomads (Moncaut 1978: 10–11). Thomas Falkner ([1744] 1935: 104–6) placed primary blame for a series of major uprisings from 1738 through the 1740s on Spanish actions. According to the Jesuit, in 1738 "the Spanish, very injudiciously, and indeed ungratefully, drove Mayu Pilqui-Ya [Mayulpilqui], the only Taluhet Cacique who was their friend, to his destruction, by forcing him to retire to a distance, exposed to the enemies which he had gained by defending their territories."

Following Mayulpilqui's death, other caciques attacked ranches on the southern plains. Maestre de Campo Juan de San Martín indiscriminately slaughtered peaceful Indians led by Calelián the elder in revenge for the raids. The slain cacique's son with a force of three hundred revenged the massacre with a bloody raid on Luján. They drove off thousands of cattle. The maestre de campo raised a militia troop of five hundred and slaughtered and enslaved other innocent Indians. These Spanish outrages touched off uprisings all along the long frontier line (Falkner [1744] 1976: 104–6; Moncaut 1978: 10–11).

History is full of "what-ifs." What if, instead of striving to crush indigenous cultures, Spaniards had worked to integrate themselves into successful, existing Indian trade relations? What if Spaniards had practiced cultural acceptance instead of forced subjugation? Spaniards and Indians might have established peaceful multicultural trade networks instead of suffering from prolonged, bloody conflicts. History is full of implausible but functional pragmatic cooperation between very different societies.

On the northern frontier, many Indian nations had long-established trade relations. Pueblos traded corn, textiles, and pottery with Plains nomads in exchange for salt, and buffalo and deer products (John 1975: 6, 30; Spielmann 1991). The rapacious Vicente de Zaldívar observed in 1598 that Apaches in New Mexico "sell meat, hides, tallow, suet, and salt in exchange for cotton, blankets, pottery, maize, and some small green stones [turquoise?]" (Forbes 1960: 83). In 1599 Alonso Sánchez described the Pueblos as "excellent and intelligent farmers; they are much given to commerce, taking from one province to another the fruits of their lands" (Forbes 1960: 94).

In his report of 1803, Governor Chacón described the extensive trade between Spaniards and nomads (*naciones gentiles*) in New Mexico:

> The products traded by the Spaniards to said nomad Indians are horses, saddlebags, *anqueras* (leather skirt covering the horse's rump), bits, hatchets, war axes, lances, knives, scissors, scarlet cloth, serapes, cloaks, woolens, indigo, vermilion, mirrors, [illegible interlinear word], loaf sugar, native tobacco, corn in flour and on the ear, bread, and green or dried fruit. In exchange, the nomads give Indian captives of both sexes, mules, moccasins, colts, mustangs, all kinds of hides and

> buffalo meat. The result is that the balance of the trade between the two parties always comes out in favor of the Spaniards. (Simmons 1991: 171)

Indians of the pampas and Andes developed an extensive cattle trade between Argentina and Chile (see Jones this volume). By the early seventeenth century, Indians traded ponchos for weapons, liquor, and other goods in Buenos Aires and other towns on the pampas (Rodríguez Molas 1968). In the mid-eighteenth century, Falkner ([1744] 1976: 86) suggested that "a commerce might also be established with the Indians; who for sky-coloured glass beads, cascabells of cast brass, broad swords, heads of lances, and hatchets, would exchange cattle for the use of the colony, and fine furs to send to Europe." Many Indian groups showed considerable pragmatism and willingness to compromise in their relations with the Spanish. The Yaquis, for example, worked out a modus vivendi after the expulsion of the Jesuits in 1767. They successfully maintained their traditional agrarian economy and villages established during the Jesuit mission period but also worked as miners for Spaniards. Both Yaquis and Spaniards derived some benefits and coexisted (Hu-DeHart 1981: 28, 102–3).

The porous membrane of the frontier permitted cultural transmission in both directions (Slatta 1990b: 19–20). Spaniards living in frontier regions did not reject and attack all elements of Indian culture. For example, some Spaniards came to appreciate the utility of buffalo hides. By the 1580s Athapaskan deerskin clothing had passed to Pueblo tribes. According to Joan de Ortega, in 1601 Spanish women in New Mexico wore deerskin clothing as well (Forbes 1960: 120). With less cultural rigidity, Spaniards could have found many other indigenous elements worthy of trade and emulation.

Spaniards sometimes showed sparks of accommodation. Some profit-minded officials, such as New Mexico Governor Bernardo López de Mendizábal (1659–61), established extensive trade relations with the Apaches using Pueblo intermediaries. Regrettably, the avaricious governor poisoned Spanish-Apache relations by launching massive slave raids and selling the captives in Sonora (John 1975: 89). As the rapid expansion of worldwide trade today amply demonstrates, groups of widely differing even antithetical political cultures can set aside their differences in the name of mutually beneficial economic exchanges.

Even the highly resistant Apaches on one occasion reached an accommodation with the Spanish. Following a series of military defeats in the late 1780s, a number of Mescalero and Warm Springs (Chiricahua) Apaches made peace with New Mexico Governor Fernando de la Concha. In the 1790s, the Indians settled with permission in the Río Grande Valley at Sabinal, between Belen and

Socorro. Spaniards furnished tools and seed, taught the Apaches to irrigate, and provided rations while the crops were growing. Unfortunately, Concha became ill and left New Mexico. His successor, Governor Chacón, abandoned the Sabinal Apaches. They in turn abandoned the settlement and returned to mountain homelands (Simmons 1991: 56–60).

Obviously, the Spanish had little control over the impact of the diseases that they brought to the New World. But slavery, forced relocations, and reductions exacerbated Indian-Spanish relations and worsened epidemics and famines. Forced reduction touched off the great Tepehuan rebellion of 1616. Despite the use of force, the Spanish failed to force most Indian villages into their cultural model. Within a century of Spanish contact, the Pueblo had been reduced from between 110 and 150 villages to only 43. Nor did efforts to populate the frontier with Spaniards fare much better. According to Fray Francisco de Ayeta, in 1679 on the eve of the Pueblo Revolt, New Mexico contained about seventeen thousand mission Indians, including Hopis and Indians living in the El Paso area, while the non-Indian population was less than three thousand (Forbes 1960: 139, 175, 285; Gerhard 1982: 321; Spicer 1962: 26, 463; Weber 1992: 90).

Jesuit Juan Nentvig's opinion of the Seris and Pimas in 1764 is revealing of the Spaniards' unfortunate, static, intransigent view of Indian society. The Seris, he wrote, "are so blood-thirsty that so long as the seed remains, the evil cannot be rooted out" (Nentvig 1980: 133–34). He recommended deportation. Nentvig expressed equally negative views of Pimas and Apaches. Little wonder that many missionization efforts failed.

Fiscal constraints, corruption, the ignorance of newly arrived officials, and a desire for easy wealth hindered effective military policy. Eurocentric ideologies, however, straightjacketed Spanish policy throughout the colonial era. This ideology demanded total victory of Spanish "civilization" over Indian "barbarism." Over the centuries, Spanish officials seemingly forgot little and learned little. Jack Forbes (1960: 285) summarized the outcomes of Spanish colonial frontier military policy succinctly: "an epoch of warfare, population decline, and cultural decay."

Without question, Spaniards living in frontier regions came to understand that social relations required significant negotiation and accommodation with Indians. Unfortunately European ideology, not New World frontier realities, most often shaped overall Spanish strategy. Ideological rigidity stymied any hope for the level of intercultural arbitration that might have resulted in more inclusive, pacific frontier relations (Slatta 1989: 177, 190–91; Spicer 1962: 281).

7

Comparative Raiding Economies

North and South

KRISTINE L. JONES

Indigenous groups throughout the Americas quickly learned to incorporate horses and cattle into their cultural universe. Jones examines the significance of raiding and trading of horses and cattle on the northern and southern frontiers of the Spanish Empire, particularly in those areas with grasslands. She argues that ethnohistory enables us to understand more clearly how Indian trading affected nation building and offered an important strategy that was intimately linked to the militarization of these areas.

AS THE SPANIARDS expanded their colonizing activities to the north from central Mexico and to the south and east from the Andean strongholds, they often encountered particularly fierce guerilla resistance from loosely organized groups of indigenous "nomadic" peoples. This was particularly true in the regions of desert grasslands. While in many cases transhumant groups were incorporated into the colonial system and settled life through missionization and labor drafts—for example, the Yaquis, Pimas, and many of the Tarahumaras/Rarámuri in New Spain, the Guaranís of Paraguay, and the Promoaucaes of Chile—in other instances native peoples retained positions of cultural and political autonomy well into the nineteenth century. One particularly potent strategy for resistance—guerilla raids for livestock and captives—contributed to the emergence of strikingly similar raiding economies in both North and South America. The fearsome raids of horse-bound Apache and Comanche warriors in North America were matched in many ways by the dreaded *malones* of Araucanian war parties in the sparsely defended frontier in South America. In this chapter I will examine some of the reasons for the success of this strategy, and consider some of the relative costs and benefits in a comparative context.

Until recently, faded or forgotten recollections of frontier conflicts, particularly those of the nineteenth century, relegated the vanquished to marginal and silenced status as ethnographic subjects. However, for both North and South America (K. Jones 1994b: 107–8), scholarly investigation of archival sources, including tax records and census data, reveals the important political and economic role of individual Indian entrepreneurs and tribal confederations in opening up the "deserts" to modern commercial ranching.[1] Although the extralegal nature of economic and social relations associated with raiding and trading makes it difficult to document the quantitative extent of raiding or trading, it is clear that the process was not simple, nor were the terms primitive. Furthermore, Indian participation was not marginal in an economic sense.

Comparison of raiding economies on the northern and southern frontiers of the Spanish colonial empire before and after independence also raises interesting questions about state formation, because the very definition of national borders ultimately depended upon the resolution of hostilities in the frontiers. In this context, a transnational perspective casts a different light on the historical record.

Because the act of either raiding or trading, separately or in combination, involves social exchange and economic redistribution, it is necessary to locate the analysis in social as well as geographic terms. Furthermore that exchange takes place within a territorial zone of interaction between two or more societies. This territorial zone, which in this book we are calling *contested ground,* is distinct from the more precise and linear boundary that is used in a strictly political context. In this chapter I will follow the convention of political geographers when using the word *frontier* to convey this zonal dimension with its broader social context (Sahlins 1989: 4).

The Colonial Margins

By 1600 the northern and southern limits of the Spanish colonial frontier in the Americas were defined mostly by military outposts and missions. Scattered frontier settlements emerged to support and defend mining activities such as those in Saltillo in New Spain and Potosí in Peru. Their demographic and economic influence within the Spanish colonial world was minimal. For well more than two centuries after sixteenth-century expeditions, the arid grasslands and deserts of North and South America remained relatively unexplored by the Spanish.

In South America, the lush grasslands and more arid regions (*pampas húmedas* and *pampas secas*) south and west of the Spanish colonial frontier remained open to the various hunting and gathering Pampas groups.[2] Patagonia, that region south of the Río Negro, remained the domain of the closely related

Tehuelches.[3] Those Araucanians who had not fallen under the encomienda system in Chile centered their mostly horticultural activities in the western and eastern foothills and southern Andean highlands along the Pacific coast south of the Bío Bío River, but they also hunted in the grasslands east of the Andes.

Social relations in the southern plains and deserts of North America were similarly diverse and dynamic. Regional differences had developed over centuries of interethnic relations that included trade as well as warfare and led to cultural developments differentiating the Navajos from the Apaches. The arrival of the Spanish in the sixteenth century upset the balance of power. By the 1690s, after the 1680 Pueblo uprising had been quelled by Spanish forces, the regional balance of power began to shift in favor of the Spanish.

The introduction of European livestock into grasslands in both North and South America in the 1500s had profound consequences, leading to intensified use of grasslands and extending ranges for seasonal hunting and gathering activities. Settled groups (including some groups settled in the Río Grande Valley in North America, and the Pehuenche and Huilliche, who settled in different southern Andean valleys) began to expand into grasslands to supplement horticultural activities. Native people in some desert regions, such as the Tehuelches in southern Patagonia and the Utes in the high northern deserts, never fully adopted the horse, probably because of inadequate water supplies and the damage horses wrought on the fragile but fruitful desert ecology.

The horse seems to have been favored as a source of meat as well as transportation among native people in both North and South America, although cattle were also prized. Networks of barter exchanges, which helped to regularize inter-band distribution of goods and resources, expanded with the horse to include increasingly wider social spheres. The Spanish also used the native fondness for horsemeat to rid themselves of mares, which were scorned as mounts.

The introduction of European-manufactured products, particularly iron implements such as axes and hoes, into pre-existing trading networks also began to alter the intertribal balance of trade (Holder 1970). In the North American case, for instance, Apache trading parties annually entered the pueblos of Taos, Pecos, and Picuris to trade meat, hides, and salt for Pueblo blankets, pottery, and corn (R. Gutiérrez 1991; Kessell 1979). In the Southern Cone, Pampas (Puelche) trading parties traveled up the Río Neuquén and over the Andean cordillera to trade *avestruz* (South American ostrich) feathers, guanaco and horse hides, and salt for woven blankets, Pacific shells, and Araucanian beads.[4]

Increased intercultural relations sometimes led to intensified raiding activities, which in turn regularized and distributed material resources, marriage partners, and status. The acquisition of the horse improved success in raiding activities. Among the Araucanians, inter-band raids known as *malones* (or *malocas* in Chile) originally followed allegations that malevolence and witchcraft were affecting the health of individuals in a community. The Apaches, on the other hand, initially distinguished raiding from war parties, and resorted to raiding to meet short-term needs for supplies (Opler 1978: 368–92). In both cases, these culturally specific institutions were eventually transformed by military encounters with Spanish forces.

By the end of the seventeenth century colonial authorities in both frontiers finally settled on defensive fortifications to protect colonial boundaries. Each foray of Spanish militia brought retaliation, disrupted pre-existing patterns of exchange, and brought about extensive loss of lives and property among all parties.[5] Both the northern and southern frontiers of the Spanish colonial empire were defined and confined by fully developed raiding economies within a few years. Small raiding parties plagued Spanish settlements located at the margins of what was called Apachería and Comanchería in North America and Araucanía or *los desiertos* (the deserts) in the Southern Cone. As colonial military forces quickly discovered, hostile indigenous groups possessed a dangerous arsenal. The bow and arrow had a surprisingly long range. On both frontiers, ambush, sneak attack, and extraordinary horsemanship enabled the indigenous peoples to wage war effectively.

In North America, the eighteenth-century southern migration of Utes and Comanches—pushed by pressures from European expansion in the north and French activities in the east, and pulled by increased opportunities for hunting and trading—had several consequences. These included the exchange of firearms and intensified interethnic relations in what the Spaniards called Apachería. Apaches often ambushed Spanish forces, and over time learned to adapt the colors, weapons, and tactics of their enemies.[6] During the early eighteenth century, French firearms reached the Plains nomads of the Borderlands. According to Tom Hall (1989a: 93–95), the gun and horse made the Comanche "Lords of the South Plains."

A similarly profound transformation occurred on the southern frontier. The eighteenth century witnessed "the Araucanization of the desert." Militarized Araucanian inter-band malones spread east of the cordillera, incorporating related groups such as the Pehuenches, as well as some Tehuelches and even Pampas bands through trade, wife-exchange, and warfare. The Araucanian language (Mapundungun) became the lingua franca within the Indian world. Frequent Araucanian-sponsored hunting and raiding parties exploited the enormous herds of wild cattle and horses that had proliferated to the east.

Opportunities for raiding and acquiring captives increased in proportion to Creole settlement, and Araucanian raiders moved deeper and deeper into the pampas.[7] At the same time, Pampas Indians, also dependent on the horse, variously competed and cooperated with the Araucanians according to the needs of individual bands (K. Jones 1984; Mishkin [1940] 1992; Secoy [1953] 1992).[8]

As in North America, the Araucanian and Pampas people quickly learned that Spanish firearms could be devastating against bow-and-arrow attacks. They supplemented bows and arrows with other weapons, including lances up to twelve feet long (Molina [1808] 1973: 2:65). Pampas Indians used *bolas* or *bolas perdidas,* multiple balls or a single ball on a rawhide thong, to strike potentially fatal head and body blows.[9] Small pointed cudgels, knives, and leather armor completed the stock of weapons (Estrada 1981: 143–44; Falkner [1774] 1935): 128–29; Tapson 1962: 6–7). The English Jesuit missionary Thomas Falkner described the leather armor used by Pampas Indians in the 1740s as bulletproof (Falkner [1744] 1976: 129).[10]

Not all intercultural relations in the northern and southern frontiers were hostile, nor was the militarization of the frontier the only result. Indeed, opportunities emerged that contributed to social conditions unique to the frontier because they were related to the expansion of colonial empire. In his book, *Maloqueros y conchavadores en Araucanía y las Pampas, 1700–1800* (Raiders and traders in Araucanía and the Pampas), Leonardo Leon Solís (1990: portada) described a unique frontier society that mirrored mid-seventeenth-century conditions on the northern frontier. In his words, "The human universe that flourished . . . was picturesque and violent; there were mingled mestizos, gauchos, friendly *capitanes,* settlers, peons, frontiersmen, bandits and petty criminals [*maloqueros* y *mal entretenidos*], in an independent world of its own that recognized neither the rules of the ancestral *admapu* [Araucanian/Mapuche world] nor the dictates of imperial legislation."[11] According to Leon Solís, the *malón,* in which spoils were simply consumed, was the defining characteristic of this frontier society. These activities ultimately led to the consolidation and militarization that defined the frontier until the late nineteenth century.

Was this militarization an inevitable process? One traditional model holds that raiding activities were the only alternative in an uneven contest between the mercantilist colonial state and the primitive economies of the hunting and gathering peoples. What this model does not explain, however, is why raiding activities continued and actually flourished over the centuries.

We know that raiding was not a postconquest innovation in Araucanía or among the Pampas or Querandís; evidence of raiding tactics dates from the very first encounters with Europeans. In his study of the Chiricahua Apaches,

D. C. Cole (1988: 48) points out that Apache raiding *preceded* the arrival of the Spanish. We also know that military defeat of the hostile tribes by colonial forces in both the northern and the southern frontiers was by no means inevitable at the end of the eighteenth century, as is clear from Spanish attempts to pacify the raiders through treaties and rationing systems.

We know much less about the scale of the raiding—be it Apache or Comanche or Tehuelche or Mapuche—and how it may have changed over time. However, while raiding economies clearly impeded the development of colonial settlements, raiding was not intrinsically detrimental. This process simultaneously opened up tremendous new opportunities for trade for all parties involved. Therefore colonial judgments of the raiders as enemies must be explained in the context of the larger social phenomenon. The concept of raiders as a force outside of, or in contradiction to, the process of consolidating the colonial state belies the obvious—that increased raiding in one region often facilitated increased trade in others. This exchange both directly and indirectly benefited and promoted the expansion of the Spanish Empire.

Unfortunately, archival research does not immediately reveal the extent of this trade because raiders in both regions—described in contemporary documents as the enemy "other"—seemingly bear no relation to reports of *indios amigos* or *indios fieles* who provided horses, hides, woven blankets, or other goods in frontier markets.[12] Hence, the full dimensions of intercultural economic exchanges in the frontier are obscured. The costs of the raids to frontier settlements in terms of lost livestock, captives, and casualties can be documented. The benefits of trade—which in the frontier was uncontrolled, undocumented, and considered by colonial authorities as contraband at best—is much more difficult to measure.

Controlling the Frontier: Pacification and Frontier Societies

The reforms initiated by the Bourbon monarchy to better control and administer its American colonies, beginning with the expulsion of the Jesuits from the Americas in 1767, had dramatic consequences in the northern and southern frontiers. Where Jesuit missions had once stood with presidios as the bastions of centralized western authority on the frontier, Creole commercial and ranching activities now proliferated.[13] The Crown attempted both to defend borders and to control and regulate the expansion of Creole activities in these frontier regions. This led to the creation of the Provincias Internas, including frontier provinces (Texas, Coahuila, the Californias) and Intendencias (Chihuahua 1785,

Durango 1787, Sonora 1787, Arispe 1791); the Viceroyalty of the Río de la Plata in 1776; and the Captaincy-General of Chile in 1778 (TePaske and Klein 1986: 15). All were intended to bolster the greater interests of that empire (Lombardi and Lombardi 1983: 31–32). Professional military officials were dispatched from Spain to reorganize and secure the northern and southern boundaries through both offensive and defensive measures. Their goals were to thwart competing French, Russian, English, and Portuguese colonial pretensions as well as to protect the area from Indian raids.

In the northern frontier of New Spain, the reinforcement of the presidio system in 1790 followed a decade of increasingly hostile and damaging Apache raids. These threats were compounded by the institution of scalp bounties paid by colonial officials. Spanish authorities instituted pacification policies involving the payment of rations, which they believed was a less costly alternative to prior policies of slavery and extermination. Between 1790 and the 1820s relatively peaceful frontier relations facilitated continued Creole development and settlement in the north, and at the same time linked some Apaches (and later Comanches) into patterns of dependency on the rations provided through peace treaties.

The direct costs of maintaining the northern frontier against Indian raids between 1791 and 1815 are documented in the records of the Caja Real for the Intendencias of Arispe and Chihuahua (TePaske and Klein 1986). Between 1791 and 1800 military expenditures represented the largest portion of governmental expenses for Arispe, and they continued to consume more than half of the budget after the turn of the century. In Chihuahua, more than a third of the budget went to maintain the presidios between 1796 and 1814. In contrast, a relatively small amount was paid directly to the Apache indios amigos, in the form of rations (see table 7.1).

The extralegal informal trade involving friendly Indians can only be estimated. David Weber (1992) argues that decreases in hostilities in the last decade of the eighteenth century were a necessary precondition for frontier expansion, even though they did not exactly promote economic and population growth. "At heart," he claims, "economic interests and mutual security united Spaniards and Indians" (Weber 1992: 234–35, citing Griffen). Other factors, "including a growing demand for grain, livestock and textiles in the revived silver mining districts of Chihuahua and Sonora" (Weber 1992: 234–35) and markets for hides and tallow in Alta California, stimulated the growth of Creole ranching activities in the frontier.

By the turn of the century in the Intendencia of Arispe (northern Sonora), for instance, the population soared to 75,000 and the population of frontier

TABLE 7.1

Costs of Defending the Northern and Southern Frontiers, 1791–1815 (values in reales de ocho)

	1791–1795	%	*1796–1800*	%	*1801–1805*	%	*1806–1810*	%	*1811–1815*	%
Real Caja de Buenos Aires										
Total income	11,113,906	—	10,231,514	—	12,442,654	—	12,268,635	—	13,797,158	—
Total expenses	9,224,129	—	9,042,276	—	14,467,558	—	12,840,950	—	12,423,199	—
Amount to frontier zones	2,437,579	26	2,627,810	29	3,887,091	26	6,708,348	52	4,598,828	37
Amount to indios amigos	701	<1	—	—	4,478	<1	3,984	<1	7,043	<1
Real Hacienda de Arispe										
Total income	1,862,736	—	2,150,743	—	1,855,770	—	1,271,925[a]	—	521,595[b]	—
Total expenses	1,217,151	—	1,232,142	—	1,575,472	—	1,271,917	—	580,841	—
Amount to presidios and compañías volantes	991,349	81	968,320	78	1,037,984	65	631,235	49	27,295	5
Amount to gastos de Apache	48,651	5	41,490	4	35,935	3	27,295	4	6,614	24
Real Hacienda de Chihuahua										
Total income	—	—	3,974,879[c]	—	5,266,450	—	5,589,800	—	3,996,184[d]	—
Total expenses	—	—	3,974,877	—	4,981,868	—	5,589,799	—	3,996,184	—
Amount to presidios and compañías volantes	—	—	1,653,505	41	2,059,255	41	2,158,020	39	1,091,493	32
Amount to gastos de Apache	—	—	58,708	4	103,373	5	113,577	5	23,653	2

Sources: Data are from John J. TePaske and Herbert S. Klein, *Ingresos y egresos de la Real Hacienda de Nueva España* (México: Colección Fuentes del INAH, 1986), see especially pp. 16–23; and Tulio Halperín Donghi, *Guerra y finanzas en los orígenes del estado argentino (1791–1850)* (Buenos Aires: Editorial Belgrano, 1982), pp. 62–68 and 126–33

[a] Includes 1807–9

[b] Includes 1813 only

[c] Includes 1797–1800

[d] Includes 1811, 1813, and 1814

outposts like Arispe and Ures doubled (from 1,000 to 2,000) in a rush to acquire titles for stock ranches. According to Stuart Voss (1982: 23), the proliferation of cattle ranches was so great that the price of cattle dropped from ten pesos to three between 1797 and 1802. Barbara Tenenbaum's study of economic development in the Provincias Internas (1776–1846) documents the vitality of the frontier economy during the Bourbon period (Tenenbaum 1993: tables 1–8). Her analysis clearly demonstrates that revenues exceeded military expenses and that "far from being a drain on the imperial or national coffers, as was generally supposed at the time, the figures show that the [Creole] *norteños* actually provided more succor [to the viceregal and republican treasuries] than their counterparts in most other areas" (Tenenbaum 1993: 103). Looking at military expenses and rationing costs for Arispe and Chihuahua, 1791–1815 (see table 7.1, "gastos de Apache"), we see that the cost of the treaty system relative to total costs of frontier military expenses (4 percent) was a small price to pay for the benefits gained by the Bourbons through increased bureaucratic control of the frontier.

The Spanish pursued similar policies to protect the southern frontier as part of the overall Bourbon Reforms. After Buenos Aires became a viceroyalty in 1776, military officers from Spain moved south and west of Buenos Aires to organize the rough forces of blandengues, described as "vagabonds, including Indians and mestizos" (Slatta 1989: 180) manning the *postas* and fortines. They negotiated peace treaties with Pampas people, who agreed to refrain from any activities north of the Río Salado in exchange for rations. Frontier expenses in the province of Buenos Aires represented a much smaller proportion of total administrative expenses, and payments to indios amigos represented only a tiny fraction of those costs (see table 7.1).

In contrast to the situation on the northern Mexican frontier, government revenues in Buenos Aires did not even meet administrative costs in some years. However, potential profits to be gained from the hide market prompted a demographic shift to the south. The population in the southernmost cattle ranching region of Chascomús grew more than two and a half times between 1781 and 1798 (Comadrán Ruiz 1969). This frontier commerce, in which Creole, mestizo, and Indian alike participated, was a direct result of *both* liberalized trade policies that stimulated population and economic growth in the port city of Buenos Aires *and* a locally negotiated peace treaty with the Pampas Indians.[14] The frontier region west of Buenos Aires between Río Cuarto and San Luis, on the other hand, was not protected by peace treaties, and continued to be plagued by raids.

In Chile, the Bourbons moved to institutionalize *parlamentos de paz* (ceremonial peace treaties involving the exchange of great quantities of commodities) with Araucanians along the southern border. In a fascinating description of the organization of these late-eighteenth-century gatherings Chilean historian Luz María Méndez Beltrán (1982: 109–73) details the materials and ornate staging of these ritualized intercultural events. While the costs of the parlamentos probably did not amount to much relative to total frontier expenses, in all frontier regions the value of peace was inestimable. To the Araucanian participants, the acquisition of axes, metal spurs and bits for harnesses, felt hats, and the usual tobacco was also great. Frontier peace—and conflict—in Chile was negotiated through more than seventeen parlamentos throughout the eighteenth century (Leon Solís 1990: 145).

As in the northern frontier, treaties and pacification in the southern frontier permitted the expansion of Creole activities. The frontier population grew much faster in Buenos Aires, especially in the "new south" opened up by treaty with Pampas groups, than it did in the rest of the province (Comadrán Ruiz 1969). The rush for land titles soon converted open grasslands into private property.

In contrast to the northern frontier, the cost of maintaining the frontier forts and rations in the Intendencia of Buenos Aires amounted to less than a third of the expenses to the Real Caja of Buenos Aires between 1791 and 1805, although most of the expenses were incurred by the military (Halperín Donghi 1982). Between 1806 and 1810 the costs of frontier maintenance shot up to more than half of the total expenses, in part because of the British invasion of 1806.

The benefits of the pacification program for Buenos Aires are quite clear, particularly when examining the virtual explosion of commerce in the southern frontier. In 1811 the total (taxed) production of the interior of Buenos Aires was valued at 31,147 pesos, and hides and tallow represented 82 percent (25,516 pesos) of that production. Forty percent of those hides and tallow came not from the old "livestock corridor" oriented to the northwest, but from the newly opened southern frontier regions. It is particularly suggestive that more than 80 percent of the goods consumed in this new south were stimulants such as *aguardiente*, yerba maté, sugar, tobacco and cigarette papers, all highly popular items in the uncontrolled but flourishing trade with the "Indians."[15] Comparing the costs of maintaining the treaty system to the growth in revenues from the Provincias Internas (see table 7.1) reveals similar benefits of the rationing program in North America as well.

How did Indian participants fare in the treaty system? While Spanish frontier settlement and ranching activities had expanded into the grasslands under the protection of Bourbon defensive strategies, Indian hunting and trading in the same area had also expanded. The vastness of the South American pampas and the North American deserts and plains, and the unlimited possibilities for relatively unimpeded travel by horse permitted and encouraged increased opportunities for intercultural and interethnic encounters. As economic activities shifted to the margins for the Creoles and Indians alike, intercultural trade networks grew more complex and interconnected.

Up until the late eighteenth century raiding activities had primarily been another means of meeting subsistence needs, but the wide opportunities for trade opened up by the pacification measures of the treaty system changed this balance. The institutionalized rationing of *vicios*—"vices" such as aguardiente, tobacco, and yerba maté in South America (K. Jones 1994b: 103–23), and sugar and tobacco in North America (Moorhead 1968: 18)—into the trading network fueled a demand for these items that continued long after rationing programs broke down. This potential market among non-allied native peoples, much greater than the rationing system could supply, soon gave impetus to increased raiding and trading.

Frontier Economies and Regional Adjustments after Independence

A breakdown of colonial control over the northern and southern frontiers of the Spanish Empire accompanied the transition from colonial rule to independence, and regional struggles were resolved according to local interests during the first few decades of the nineteenth century. Frontier policies of defense and rationing initiated during the Bourbon Reforms began to erode during the wars of independence. When frontier troops and resources were called upon to quell rebellion, the forts were left unmanned and rations went undistributed.

When their rations were cut after independence, Pampas groups renewed their raids against southern agricultural settlements. In Chile Araucanian troops tended to ally themselves with royalist troops against independence fighters, who also tended to be the southern *latifundistas* who had most opposed treaties and rationing systems (Leon Solís 1990). When the system of parlamentos ultimately collapsed with independence, intensified malones followed in both Chile and in Argentina. In northern Mexico, the presidio system went into rapid decline after 1821, and by 1830 the Apaches returned to raiding (Griffen 1988b: 121).

Following independence, the responsibility for the "defense" of the frontier fell to Creole settlers. By this time, however, the nature of frontier relations had been profoundly transformed by the disappearance of the rationing system. The scope and scale of raiding activities and the quantity of captured booty in the early nineteenth century in both North and South America far exceeded the capabilities of locally organized small bands of raiders. Indeed, the situation Sweeney (1991: 17) describes in Apachería holds equally true for Araucanía: "The Indians had prospered and become more dangerous during years at peace; many Indians could read and write Spanish, many leaders understood Spanish [Mexican] tactics, many of them had become adept in the use of European [Mexican] weapons."

The removal of restrictive trade barriers following independence stimulated economic growth throughout the Americas, and this was particularly true in both the northern and southern frontiers. In fact, the new opportunities in the frontier regions prompted dramatic demographic reorientations that began to reshape postcolonial frontier societies and economies. Creole settlements in the frontier provinces exploded, especially around ports and other centers of the new export trade, and Indian encampments mushroomed in the northern and southern desert grasslands.

Frontier Economies and the World Market

Distinct frontier societies with unique forms of social relations emerged in each region, independent of both the old colonial order and more traditional native systems. Local responses to raiding and trading were negotiated differently. At this point comparisons begin to fall apart, and the unique strategies forged in different frontier regions can tell us a great deal about the specific historical processes that contributed to the formation of very different states.

In both the North American plains and the South American pampas the transition from hunting to husbandry of the vast herds of wild horses and cattle for trade can be traced to this post-independence moment (Brown 1979). The disappearance of colonial trade restrictions with foreign powers, improved maritime transportation, and the ability of steam-powered vessels to penetrate interior river systems, plus increasing demand for hides and tallow, made intensified ranching more profitable.

Traditional Mexican and Argentine frontier ranchos were reorganized on a more commercial basis. Holders of land titles asserted their rights to control the hoofed resources of the grasslands, and traditional usufruct or communally based tribal systems eroded as ranchers began a paper-based claim to grazing lands. In the next few decades access to commercial markets was increasingly closed to all but those who managed to wrest control over land rights.

Traders appeared to take advantage of commercial opportunities in the

1820s, and while trading posts spread into the North American grasslands, *pulperías* (rural general stores and taverns) sprouted in the pampas. This trade soon pulled the Indian world directly into the market economy. The shift from hunting to husbandry favored hunting ceremonies and war parties because livestock was increasingly acquired by raiding rather than by hunting *cimarrones* (wild animals). Militarization and social hierarchization resulted. The increased numbers of livestock and captives taken in raids required greater attention to care of the herds, and women were diverted from traditional activities of some horticulture and gathering wild seeds and fruits (Leon Solís 1990: 136–42). The balance in the sexual division of labor shifted as increasing numbers of hides and tons of charque (jerked beef) had to be cured by women for trade. The importance of captives in carrying out this and other tasks stimulated a greater demand for captives.[16]

Caudillismo and Tribalism: Defining the Frontiers of the States

The power vacuum and striking regional economic developments in frontier regions that resulted from the withdrawal of royal authorities led to intense political struggles. Local and regional elites assumed greater prominence and played important roles in building the new American states. Historians have characterized this period as the era of *caudillismo,* and the frontier experience shaped more than one of these caudillos.

Caudillos in the frontiers (such as Juan Manuel de Rosas and Justo José de Urquiza in Argentina in the 1830s and 1840s) and so-called "Big Men" in Sonora and Chihuahua began to build upon their military and diplomatic experience in negotiating frontier relations with raiding parties. Indian leaders also emerged. Caciques (chiefs) who negotiated terms favorable to the continued sovereignty of native peoples began to attract increasing numbers of followers.

There are clear similarities in the development of tribal structures and the emergence of pivotal intertribal chiefs in the North American and South American grassland frontiers. Parallel success in equestrian raiding and trading is clearly related to the Spanish introduction of the horse. International trade, too, had its impact. Despite distinct cultural and symbolic systems, in the larger picture, the technology and equipment necessary for the equestrian raiding and trading lifestyle (including ultimately the Remington rifle), ranked military societies, and shared war ceremonials were all linked to the pressures of the world market for scarce resources.

Intercultural social relations involving Indians and Creoles in these frontier zones during the first half of the nineteenth century caused temporary alliance networks to be forged in one region as they broke down in another. In the absence of a strong central state, or even, for that matter, clear authority for local governments, competition for political power devolved into the hands of local leaders. In both the northern and the southern frontiers, Creole and mestizo caudillos often led local militias to conduct trade with individual caciques from some tribes while defending local interests against raiding activities of other tribes.

Under the auspices of the new provincial government in Argentina, in 1825 local ranchers instituted a rationing system they called *negocio pacífico con el indio* (peaceful exchange with the Indian) to distribute rations in exchange for truce via the *guardias* (military outposts).[17] Building on this rationing system plus a series of military expeditions and peace treaties between 1825 and 1833, the ranchers and various Pampas and Araucanian tribes soon worked out the terms of coexistence in the grazing lands south of the pampas. Treaties guaranteed the purchase of Indian goods, named specific ranchers as protective *patrones* of new allies, pledged support against enemy Indians, and specified providers of the annuities. As in the colonial era, these locally negotiated agreements included the exchange (redemption) of Creole captives and *regalos* (presents) marking the terms of the agreement (Academia Nacional 1979; K. Jones 1984; Socolow 1992).

By no means were all of the Indians pacified, however. In contrast to Buenos Aires province, residents in other regions did less to defend their southern boundaries, and although provincial authorities took some measures to establish peace treaties to protect agricultural interests, malones around Mendoza, San Luis, and Río Cuarto continued (Archivo Histórico 1985: 9–40). The Bío Bío frontier remained stable in Chile as some Araucanian groups began to move permanently onto the pampas.

In 1835 an Araucanian cacique named Calfucurá moved his followers from Llaima in Chile to settle near the *salinas grandes* (salt flats) in present-day La Pampa, where, after a brief struggle with Mariano Rondeau, a "pacified" ally of Juan Manuel de Rosas, he emerged as leader of the Araucanian forces that dominated frontier relations in Argentina for the rest of the century (K. Jones 1989: 179).

Just as Calfucurá was building political coalitions, so was Argentine rancher Juan Manuel de Rosas. After his successful 1833 military campaign, which advanced the southern border of Buenos Aires, he launched a successful political campaign that landed him the governorship of Buenos Aires province. Early on he transferred responsibility for annuity payments from the frontier landowners' association to his government. From 1835 until 1851 the Comisaría General authorized annual payments to allied Pampas and Araucanian entities that over time appeared more like tribes than bands.[18] Rosas and his supporters profited in those two decades both from lucrative government contracts and from a reprieve in raiding; however, his political opponents, Unitarian landowners in the interior provinces, complained that some malones against their property were carried out at Rosas' request.

For Buenos Aires province, the expanded alliance network successfully quelled post-independence malones from 1835 to 1851. In Chile frontier relations south of the Bío Bío River remained relatively stable because the attraction of the pampas pulled the Araucanians south and east of the cordillera. A major diaspora of thousands of Araucanians east into the Argentine pampas had begun in the early 1800s and continued into the mid-nineteenth century.

During this period, non-allied Pampas Indians, witnesses to the plight of their "pacified" relatives caught in bonds of dependency, began to act to maintain political autonomy and sovereignty over their remaining territorial stronghold. Effectively closed out of opportunities for commerce and denied rations, the non-allied Pampas Indians saw that joining the Araucanians and organizing larger and deadlier malones was their only remaining option. Powerful and charismatic individuals took on prominent political and military roles, and war chiefs like Calfucurá and Llanquetruz, leader of the Ranqueles, gained notoriety for their increasingly hostile raids of unprotected ranches. They captured tens of thousands of head of livestock and hundreds of captives, all of which were traded along a series of well-worn trails leading over the cordillera into Chile, where Chilean *conchavadores* (itinerant traders) continued to profit handsomely. This trade led to the commercialization of frontier settlements such as Laja in Chile.[19] Other leaders such as Sayhueque, head of the Huilliche Manzaneros in the cordilleran highlands, opted for neutrality. However, maintaining neutrality grew more difficult, especially when Chilean pressure for farming lands south of the Bío Bío River began to threaten traditional Araucanian sovereignty after 1849. The gold boom in California had stimulated the market for Chilean wheat, and the Chilean government began to turn its attention to the southern frontier in a series of measures that eroded Mapuche territorial rights.

Although similar economic forces applied in the old Spanish northwest as trade restrictions disappeared after independence, local conditions were very different. Unlike the Argentine case, the breakdown of the presidio system in Mexico in the late 1820s was followed by decades of bloody warfare and raids, and the hostilities were particularly intense from the 1830s to the 1860s. Also in contrast to the southern frontier, several local markets competed for the northern frontier trade instead of the European export market.

Apache raids into Sonora and Chihuahua were directly linked to increased opportunities for commercial trade in Texas, California, and New Mexico, particularly with Anglo-American traders. In Sonora, though the acquisition of private land grants continued to grow and though population grew by 25 percent along the coast (Weber 1982: 183), the northern frontier lost population because of Apache raiding that began when military forces and rationing disappeared during the independence struggles. An initial attempt to raise a volunteer army failed, and local Mexicans reverted to exterminations (Basso 1983: 466). The Apaches, however, held the upper hand in this situation, striking deeper into Sonora to raid a valuable "supply" depot (Getty 1963: 7). In fact, anthropologist Keith Basso (1983: 466) argues that the Apaches viewed Sonoran ranchos as "valuable economic resources that could be counted on throughout the year to produce substantial amounts of cereal grain and livestock." James Officer (1987) argues that in Hispanic Arizona isolated local Mexicans were forced into fragmented truce making with the Apaches because they desperately depended on the trade. The Apaches traded the livestock and booty from raids with other tribes and with North American traders moving into the desert plains.

The New Mexicans were much more interested in defending their local interests than in maintaining a common front with Sonora or Chihuahua against Apache and Comanche raids. Accordingly the New Mexicans constructed their own buffer treaty alliance with the Mescalero Apaches prior to 1810. In this treaty the Mescaleros received rations and rights to "a sizable area in Chihuahua and lands in New Mexico stretching from the vicinity of El Paso northward to the Sacramento Mountains" (Griffen 1988b: 129). As a result of the alliance, New Mexico, which had become an "exploited internal colony" (Opler 1978: 421) during the last years of colonial rule, enjoyed a "burst of commercial activity along the trail between Santa Fe and St. Louis."

In Texas, Weber (1982: 86–96) states, "dealing with the Indians was sufficiently lucrative . . . that some Americans set up trading posts along the Red River." The Texas ranching industry, stimulated in the 1780s, rapidly expanded after independence. Texas attracted settlers, and its population grew at a rate of 100 percent per year from 2,500 in 1821 to 40,000 in 1836, including Anglo-Americans. Between 15,000 and 20,000 head of cattle were said to be driven from Texas to Louisiana annually after 1780, and observers lamented the "disorderly slaughter" that had reduced their number (Chipman 1992; Teja 1990; Weber 1982: 86–96).

In California, new trading relations with the same British merchant fleet that traded in the port of Buenos Aires began shortly after independence. Maritime merchants from New England also began stopping along the California coast in the 1820s in a search for sea otter pelts, and also entered the trade in cowhides and tallow. As was the case in Buenos Aires province, cowhides and tallow became California's largest export commodities at the turn of the nineteenth century (Weber 1982: 135, 206). The population of California more than doubled (3,320 to 7,300) between 1821 and 1845, growing at a rate of 5 percent (compared to 1 percent for the rest of Mexico). That the production of cowhides and tallow in California far exceeded that of either Texas or New Mexico, even though it had less than a quarter of the population, suggests considerable contraband trade, probably with Indian traders from the Southwest.

The Apaches and Comanches now clearly recognized the monetary value of booty obtained through raids and traded with other tribes, competing with colonists and North American traders, converting goods into gold when possible to purchase guns and powder from traders in Louisiana. The western Apaches, bounded by hostilities to the west and the north and thus unable to participate in the booming intertribal trade in bison hides in the high Plains, fared less well (D. C. Cole 1988: 48). Others (Navajos, Chiricahuas, Mescaleros, Jicarillas) flourished as trade intermediaries.

The tactical advantage enjoyed by the eastern Apache and Comanche tribes against the northern Mexicans was very much a result of the struggles between centralists and federalists, which caused diversion of resources from frontier defense. In contrast to the southern frontier, where uncontrolled commerce was co-opted and consolidated by landowners to create the formidable livestock economy that drove the Argentine economy well into the twentieth century, the northern frontier was increasingly divided by competing regional interests.

By the mid-nineteenth century we can no longer speak of a "northern frontier" and a "southern frontier." Instead, we are looking at the creation of four distinctly different states: Argentina and Chile, Mexico and the United States. Boundaries and national projects of the modern nation-states were by no means worked out, and it was paradoxically in these frontiers that many of the problems of nationalism were to be resolved. The consolidation of the modern nation-states, in fact, very much depended on the resolution of border issues—

and resolution of border issues depended on military conquest of the raiding tribes.

Why military conquest? Because centuries of frontier relations that were built on intercultural trade had also contributed to the formation of formidable armies of raiders, and, in that particular historical context, little option remained for the new states.

However, by challenging the paradigm in which nineteenth-century frontier development is seen as having evolved *despite* the obstacles to progress posed by Indian raids, I suggest that frontier development expanded *because* of Indian trade. Clearly frontier relations were hostile and the colonial legacy of scalp bounties and slave raids colored the transactions. It is also clear that frontier raiding economies initially contributed directly to the formation of nineteenth-century capitalist development and ultimately pulled all the players into that market through trade. Much as the contemporary discourse of the time may have argued, military conquest of the Indians was not the a priori or inevitable solution, but rather the result of failure of prior frontier strategies that had excluded and subordinated Indian traders.

By challenging the conceptual marginalization of the "raiders" as an outside force obstructing the consolidation of the modern nation-states, we discover that frontier raiding and trading economies involving Indians and Creoles alike not only facilitated the formation of the modern ranching industry but also played a central role in the process of state building.

8

Interethnic Conflict and Resistance on the Brazilian Frontier of Goiás, 1750–1890

MARY KARASCH

Are all frontiers successfully controlled by their conquerors? Karasch explains the Portuguese failure to dominate a series of indigenous groups in the Brazilian region of Goiás. An area surrounded by rivers, forests, and savannah grasslands, this frontier region attracted Portuguese miners, indigenous groups, and runaway African slaves for its gold deposits and potential for agriculture and ranching. The indigenous groups living in the area responded with a varied mixture of resistance, partial accommodation, and extinction.

SOME STUDIES of frontiers have approached the subject as representing little more than a boundary between "civilized and barbaric," a moving line of settlement into new "unsettled territory," or a conquest process involving European subjugation of "less civilized" non-Europeans. Recent frontier studies have focused on stages of development and suggested a natural progression to full integration (Chappell 1990).[1] In reality, numerous frontiers did not meet such an ideal. Indigenous populations held sway, diseases disrupted European penetration, and geography limited outsider intrusion. European settlers were not uniformly successful everywhere, most notably in Africa, but also in some parts of the Americas. This chapter will examine one frontier shaped by many complex variables, in which a colonial power tried and failed to impose its European way of life, values, and objectives of civilization and Christianization on the indigenous populations.

The colonial power was Portugal, the region of its concern the Captaincy of Goiás, and the people it failed to assimilate to its values were the Kayapó, Xavante, Xerente, Canoeiro, Krahô, and Karajá, among others. Why did Portugal fail? Or, conversely, why and how were these peoples able to endure and preserve their languages and culture in spite of more than a century of forcible conquests and missionary efforts? Several variables made resistance possible and survival probable. First was the physical environment, including infertile soils and such endemic diseases as malaria and Chagas' disease;[2] second, the Portuguese imperial policy that focused on gold to the exclusion of all else; third, the failure of the missionary enterprise; and fourth, Indian resistance strategies of varying types.

The most successful indigenous populations followed multiple strategies, sometimes accommodating to the Luso-Brazilian invaders, at other times escaping to the forests, and on still other occasions engaging in warfare or making treaties with the Portuguese. In all cases, they operated as sovereign "nations" and were so recognized by bureaucrats in Lisbon.[3] Indian choices also shaped the frontier and ensured the survival of their people. This chapter will examine the ways in which the invaded and enslaved were "actors" in the history of the Goiano frontier.

Environments

The terrain of the Captaincy of Goiás was extraordinarily diverse. Immense in size, the area was dominated by three enormous rivers (Gomes and Teixeira Neto 1993).[4] To the south, the waters of the Rio Paranaíba flow into the Paraná and ultimately into the estuary of the Río de la Plata. To the west is the Rio Araguaia, which rises in central Brazil and flows north to meet the other great river in the east of Goiás, the Tocantins. Their waters join near São João do Araguaia, and one great current flows north to empty its waters into the Amazon Delta near Belém.

Between the rivers was a lush, forested land occupied by numerous populations in the early eighteenth century; a century later, however, many would be extinct due to the impact of warfare, disease, and the slave trade in Indians to Belém. To the north and east of the Tocantins were grasslands suitable for cattle raising. It is unclear when or where the forests ended and the *cerrado* (semiarid savannah) began. A pattern of alternating rainfall (approximately six months of rain followed by six months of dry season) dictated the cerrado's vegetation. Rainfall and the rainy season were apparently more intense and longer lasting in the eighteenth century than today. Eighteenth-century governors reported periods of extraordinarily heavy rain and intense heat, and they favored the dry season because it made travel possible and brought relief from flooded terrain and intermittent fevers. The dry season was the time of war, when the Portuguese left their towns and mounted expeditions of conquest.

Agriculturally rich lands were in the south between the City of Goiás (formerly Vila Boa de Goiás) and the Rio Paranaíba and between Vila Boa and the Rio Araguaia. Other fertile soils existed in and near the sources of the Rio Araguaia, along its banks, and on Bananal Island, where the Karajá claimed the lands for their crops and cattle. Beyond the Araguaia to the west were the unknown "wild lands" of Mato Grosso. During the eighteenth and nineteenth centuries, the Rio Araguaia was the border between the "civilized" and "uncivilized" worlds. But even this border was crossed by Luso-Brazilians, who traveled frequently between Mato Grosso and Vila Boa. The gold trade, both contraband and legal, furthered commerce and communication among Luso-Brazilians and provided new sources of plunder to the Kayapó.

The last major environmental factor influencing settlement on the frontier of Goiás was the low mountains of the Pireneus and Serra Dourada, among the many sources of gold. Although the Indians of Goiás apparently did not mine for gold, they collected nuggets from the Rio Vermelho. There is little evidence that they commonly occupied the mountainous regions of Goiás, although by the eighteenth century the mountains formed refuges for *quilombolas* (fugitive slaves).

Because of the gold, Vila Boa was settled by outsiders and linked by overland *comboios* (convoys) to Bahia and Rio de Janeiro. Months of dangerous travel separated Goiás from Belém, São Luís, Salvador, or Rio de Janeiro, with still more months between one of these port cities and Lisbon. Expeditions sent to guard gold convoys or to explore for still more gold lost men to accidents, malaria, bandits, fugitive slaves, and Indians. Narratives of trips to Goiás treated such deaths as routine, unless they involved men of quality from noble families. Along the rivers, fevers claimed many lives, but in general Goiás was not as deadly to Europeans as Africa.

The disease environment of Goiás was also less pernicious than that of coastal Brazil. Because of its isolation and low population density, Goiás often escaped major epidemics of smallpox and other diseases that depend on urban densities. Heart disease, probably due to Chagas' disease (Allison 1993), and leprosy were common in the eighteenth centuries, while malaria increased notably along the rivers in the nineteenth century. Medical practitioners in the late eighteenth century treated fevers with quinine, and the only disease known to have seriously impeded Portuguese settlement was malaria.

Indigenous populations, however, experienced significant fatalities due to measles and respiratory infections upon contact with Europeans, and those who had been resettled along the rivers in mission villages (*aldeias*) were decimated by malaria. Bureaucrats rarely recorded high rates of population decline in the late eighteenth and nineteenth centuries. Those who bore the brunt of the first impact of disease appear to have done so in the seventeenth century—

or earlier. Although aldeia records report high death rates, they are not comparable to sixteenth-century rates (Karasch 1992: 408–9).

The Invaders of Goiás

What brought the Portuguese to hazard their lives in Goiás was gold, discovered by expeditions (bandeiras) from São Paulo in the 1720s. The gold mines stretched from the Rio Vermelho, the site of the City of Vila Boa de Goiás, capital of the Captaincy, to Carmo in the north near the Rio Tocantins. Each successful strike attracted adventurers from Portugal and its empire, who founded aldeias (hamlets or villages), and *vilas* (towns), where the "good men" of property ruled through the city council (*senado da câmara*). Once enough gold had been accumulated, they built a chapel or church and constructed houses for their large households (including slaves), as well as stores, shops, and market stalls. Outside the vilas, the thatched-roof houses of local Indians, who were agregados (semi-assimilated and "attached" to local whites), proclaimed their apartness from Luso-Brazilian lifestyles.

Not only the Portuguese entered this frontier, but also non-Europeans. The first of these were from other parts of Goiás or other regions of Brazil; they were strangers to the land between the rivers, although they shared the same phenotype and distant history. Because of its centrality and access via river transport, Goiás had received Tupí-speaking migrants since Portuguese disruptions began on the coast in the sixteenth century. By the mid-1700s, many "Indians" in Goiás had already had years of contact with the Portuguese; some had ancestors who had fought with them against the Dutch in Maranhão, while others had been Christianized in Jesuit missions; still others, such as the Canoeiro, had fled slavery to take refuge in central Brazil. Hence the Gê-speaking populations of central Brazil confronted semi-assimilated Indians with different languages, values, and lifestyles, who wanted access to good lands. Thus, war was also endemic between the original inhabitants of the land and the new "Indian" invaders (Toral 1984–85: 292–93).

Assimilated Indians, known as *caboclos* in the modern Amazon and as Carijós in São Paulo, also moved onto the frontier as cattle drovers, agricultural laborers, *roceiros* (small farmers and dependents on large ranches), and riverboatmen or soldiers. Speaking Portuguese, practicing folk Catholicism, and living in the forests by subsistence agriculture, hunting, and fishing, they often joined the Luso-Brazilian forces that waged war on other nations or labored in service positions for their white patrons. Cabocla women served in

TABLE 8.1

Slaves in the State of Goiás, 1804–85

Census Year	Total Population	Slave Population: Male	Female	Total	Percentages: Female Slaves	All[a] Slaves[a]
1804	50,365	12,094	7,933	20,027	39.6	39.8
1825	62,478	7,329	6,046	13,375	45.2	21.4
1832	68,497	7,220	6,041	13,261	45.6	19.4
1848	79,339	5,681	5,275	10,956	48.2	13.8
1856	121,992	6,416	5,918	12,334	48.0	10.1
1861	133,565	5,787	5,661	11,448	49.5	8.6
1872	158,920[b]	5,337	5,211	10,548	49.4	6.6
1885[c]	—	2,857	2,961	5,818	50.9	—

Source: Mary Karasch, "Slave Women on the Brazilian Frontier in the Nineteenth Century," in *More than Chattel: Black Women and Slavery in the Americas*, ed. David Barry Gaspar and Darlene Clark Hine (Bloomington and Indianapolis: Indiana University Press, 1996), p. 81.

[a] Percentage of total population.

[b] The census records 158,920, but my calculations yield 158,929.

[c] Only the slave population was counted in 1885.

white households as domestic servants, concubines, and wives or headed their own households of children and slaves as single women.[5]

Men and women of African ancestry also invaded Goiás as enslaved miners and domestic servants, fugitive quilombolas, and free men and women of color. Because so many blacks (*prêtos*), mulattos (*pardos*), and *cabras* (other racial mixtures, but including some African ancestry) were enslaved in Goiás, by 1804 the subjugated population numbered about 40 percent (see table 8.1). These Afro-Brazilians followed their own survival strategies, which sometimes involved accommodation to Luso-Brazilian culture, and at other times resistance and flight to fortified *quilombos* from which they warred with Indians as well as their former owners.

As early as 1750, the invaders of Goiás were a truly multicultural group. The Portuguese, mostly males, were few in number and largely limited to the major administrative centers, especially Vila Boa and São Félix, where the mints were located. As gold output declined and contraband trade made it more difficult for the Portuguese to control its export, the number of Portuguese adventurers and priests who remained in Goiás also fell. They took their gold and returned to Lisbon or moved on to other parts of the empire. After the expulsion of the

Jesuits (1759), the missionary effort also declined. By the 1780s, the remaining Portuguese were largely those who had married into the local white population or formed consensual unions with women of color. Their ties with non-white women and their pardo children held them to an increasingly violent frontier, as Luso-Brazilian town life collapsed and many mining towns reverted to forests. As Portuguese strength eroded, white Goianos challenged a Portuguese governor in 1805, and a rebellious Desembargador led an act of secession in the north (now the state of Tocantins). Taking advantage of elite divisions, the Indians of Goiás staged their own insurrections and initiated a century of war against those who had invaded the land between the rivers.

The Original Inhabitants of the Land

The Goiano indigenous populations in the eighteenth and nineteenth centuries were also diverse and constantly changing, migrating to new lands in response to slaving expeditions and settler invasions. Early historical records track the habitations of the once densely populated region at the juncture of the Araguaia and Tocantins Rivers, a region closely linked with the river trade to Belém. Although few Portuguese, other than Jesuit missionaries, dared to travel south of Cametá because of the fierce resistance of the riverine peoples, once gold was discovered, daring prospectors and their slaves traveled down the Tocantins to reach the mines. Two of many nations living along the river that tried to impede Portuguese transit in the 1730s were the Tembéassu and Tembemeri (Martins de Lima [1738] 1986: 131).

Further south was another partially assimilated group, the Krahô, who had also reached the eastern banks of the Tocantins from Maranhão. Once cattle predators, they had abandoned raiding in preference for cattle husbandry and were so adept that they were challenging ranchers for the best grazing lands. The ranchers influenced the government to relocate the cattle-keeping Krahô to the aldeia at Carolina, where they were henceforth subjected to forced labor under military directors in the nineteenth century (Karasch 1992: 408; Melatti 1967).

Immediately to the south of the Krahô and sometimes allied with them were other Gê speakers, the Xerente and Xavante, once one people, living east of the Tocantins, who split over resistance tactics to the Luso-Brazilians. The Xerente pursued accommodation in order to survive along the Tocantins.[6] The Xavante chose armed resistance and later withdrawal west of the Araguaia, where they now live and use international alliances and the modern media to defend their current land claims.

Competing with the Xavante and Xerente for lands before 1880 were the Canoeiro, who roamed through the same region, especially after some Xavante abandoned the Tocantins for settled aldeia life at Carretão. A mysterious people, the Canoeiro (canoers) must have been river dwellers at some point in their history. Tupí speakers, they had been in contact with Luso-Brazilian settlers for some time in the eighteenth century. They clearly knew Luso-Brazilian customs and spoke some Portuguese. Feared by their enemies as the most violent and "barbaric" nation on the frontier, they were indomitable in their opposition to pacification and settlement in Christian villages (Pedroso 1992; Toral 1984–85).

In the south of Goiás lived the Southern Kayapó, a Gê-speaking people who are among the best-known nations in the historical record (Chaim 1974: 56–61; Karasch 1981; T. Turner 1992: 311–38). The Kayapó (Caiapó in the eighteenth century) first took the brunt of Paulista expeditions in the late seventeenth century along with the now-extinct Goiases. In 1741, some eight thousand Kayapó were enslaved by the Paulistas, and survivors took refuge in the south of Goiás near Vila Boa. In the eighteenth and nineteenth centuries, the Kayapó were found over a vast region centering on the Claro and Pilões Rivers, the Serra do Caiapó, and Caiapônia of Goiás. Some Southern Kayapó survive in Xingu National Park, while the Northern Kayapó confront 1990s-style miners, cattlemen, and land-hungry peasants.

North of the Kayapó lived the Gê-speaking Karajá, who occupied Bananal Island and the banks of the beautiful Rio Araguaia. Pacified as early as 1775, the Portuguese intrusion came later because of the distance of most of the Karajá from the gold mines (Hemming 1987: 68–69).[7] In both the 1700s and 1800s, the Araguaia was principally important to the Luso-Brazilians as a waterway for trade and communications between Belém and the gold-rich captaincies of Mato Grosso and Goiás. But in the nineteenth century, the provincial government established a string of military garrisons and mission villages to "civilize" and Christianize the once-independent Karajá.

Population Trends

Another important determinant of culture change or successful resistance and survival is linked to frontier demographics, such as the size of the indigenous population in contrast to that of the invaders. Unfortunately, we have few precise population data for Goiás until 1804. Because of the difficulties of census taking on a violent frontier, official figures largely concern the Luso-Brazilian population and their African slaves; and estimates of the size of Indian nations are suspect because the Portuguese authorities exaggerated the numbers to glorify their conquests. However, we can trace the following population trends after 1804: a general increase in the free Luso-Brazilian population; a decline in the Afro-Brazilian population, including the number of those living in quilombos; and a decline in Indians in state-sponsored mission villages (see table 8.1).

Although some regions were more seriously affected by settlement than others, we cannot identify an overwhelming influx of land-hungry settlers in the eighteenth or nineteenth centuries. There were always areas open to Indians seeking to escape Luso-Brazilian intrusion. Because most European immigrants and Luso-Brazilian settlers searched out the dynamic poles of growth linked to coffee plantations in the southeast, the Goiano frontier did not "close" in the nineteenth century. Furthermore, economic development in Minas Gerais, São Paulo, and Rio de Janeiro drained off African slave labor, leaving few black slaves to provide the necessary labor or guns with which settlers could hold their lands against Indian offensives. Without massive influxes of new Africans, the number of quilombos also declined. Population growth did occur in this region in the nineteenth century, but it was minimal compared to that of southeastern Brazil (see table 8.1).

In terms of gender and ethnicity, the Luso- and Afro-Brazilian populations were predominantly male; free women, especially white females, were few in number as late as 1783.[8] As is true of most frontiers, one characteristic of the Goiano outpost was intense male competition for female labor and companionship. The most powerful and wealthy men dominated the female minority in extended households of wives and slave concubines, many of whom were Indian. One of the principal causes of conflict between Luso-Brazilian, Afro-Brazilian, and Indian men was raids for women. Luso-Brazilian slaving expeditions "exterminated" adult male Indians and captured women and children, who were brought back to settlements as slaves or agregados. Some women and children were branded as slaves and traded north to the markets of Belém.[9] Most fugitives from the mining camps (quilombolas) were African males, and they too sought wives from among the Indians.

Enslaved African women were also used for their labor and as sexual partners and wives. Their two principal occupations were cooking or other household responsibilities and agricultural labor. They raised foodstuffs (manioc, corn, and beans) and plantation crops, such as cotton, coffee, and sugar. As slaves, they and their children were also subject to capture by Indians, but more often they were coerced into sharing their lives with free men of color or white men (Karasch 1996).

Population data—at least from 1783 and thereafter—also provide some insight into ethnicity. Groups included in the census data were usually categorized as *brancos,* pardos, or prêtos (whites, mulattos, or blacks) or free, freed, and enslaved. In late-eighteenth-century Vila Boa, those classified as free whites comprised 17.4 percent of the population; the Portuguese would have comprised only a small portion of this population, since the branco category of the 1780s also included Brazilian-born whites, many of whom had an Indian or African female ancestor. Pardos comprised another 15.3 percent, and black and pardo slaves 57.5 percent.[10] As mineral output in the region declined, Portuguese out-migration increased, although census data fail to document this trend.

Settler Society

The colonial government, society, and economy that the Indian nations confronted in the eighteenth and nineteenth centuries were complex institutions. In the 1700s, the Captaincy of Goiás was ruled by Portuguese men of quality appointed by the Crown on the basis of their high-born status, imperial service, education, and/or connections at court. Lower bureaucratic offices were acquired through "donations" of Goiano gold. Less exalted men grew wealthy through trade as merchant-capitalists, controlling access to credit and capital and the long-distance trade between the coast and the mining towns. Portuguese priests met the religious needs of the colonists, while their slaves earned the priests wealth from mining and agriculture. Ambitious military men of Portuguese ancestry monopolized the ranks of officers of the regiments that guarded the gold control points (*registros*) and the gold caravans to Salvador and Rio. According to surviving official documents, all aspects of eighteenth-century colonial policy were centered on capturing the king's fifth of the gold and preventing its loss. A related preoccupation was removal of Indians from lands reputed to be rich in gold. As the ability of the Portuguese to extract and export gold from Goiás declined, due to widespread smuggling as well as the placer mines playing out, policy shifted to the search for new mines or new sources of wealth from ranching and agriculture and the river trade to Belém.

After gold, the missionary effort supported by the Crown was the next priority because royal authorities valued the religious conversion of their vassals and viewed it as their Christian duty. They funded mission villages and appointed priests, many of whom lacked the dedication of the Jesuits. Some priests came to Goiás in search of gold and in order to increase their chances of acquiring an ecclesiastical position in Portugal after their "perilous" service to the Crown. Those who remained in mining towns entered politics and occupied bureaucratic positions. As men of property, they were often the largest slave owners in mining towns, and they devoted themselves to administering their estates instead of proselytizing Indians (Jayme 1973).[11]

By the nineteenth century, the priests were few in number and generally attached to parish churches located in towns or hamlets. The imperial government turned to Italian Capuchins and French Salesians to combat the shortage of priests. Few missionaries, however, risked their lives on this frontier. Whereas eighteenth-century Jesuits had worked alone in their aldeias, the Capuchins depended on the assistance of armed garrisons (Primerio 1942: 292–300). The vast majority of eighteenth- and nineteenth-century Indians never came in contact with a Catholic priest, and indigenous religions survived intact, with minimal Christian or African influence. In contrast, a small minority of Christian Indians who did not live at the state-supported mission villages searched fruitlessly for Catholic priests to visit their villages and perform essential rites, such as the baptism of children.

The third major group in Goiás influencing Indian policy was the Portuguese military, supplemented by white, pardo, and black militias. In the colonial period, the Portuguese officers stationed in Goiás formed part of a worldwide empire. Ambitious officers obtained patents to serve in Goiás because the captaincy offered career opportunities and access to gold. Most senior officers sought only one or two tours of duty before moving on to service in Portugal or its empire. Junior officers who married local white or non-white women were more likely to remain in Goiás.

The principal responsibility of the Portuguese officers was to defend the Crown's share of gold, the *quinto*. Only these officers received the responsibility—and the opportunity—of guarding the mints and the captaincy's checkpoints for imports and exports. Portuguese officers usually did not fight in the Indian wars, unless an exceptional officer organized and led an official expedition to conquer nations obstructing trade and attacking gold miners. Those who fought were organized in bandeiras and militias. In the eighteenth century, Portuguese governors appointed Portuguese officers to lead official bandeiras of exploration to locate gold and subdue hostile nations. Included in the bandeiras were local whites anxious to avenge family deaths and obtain Indian "servants," racially mixed persons who were experienced frontiersmen and Indian fighters, and an auxiliary of black or Indian slaves who provided food and supplies.

After 1822, the presidents of Goiás continued to organize bandeiras, but many in this period were hastily assembled and semi-organized posses designed to exterminate hostile Indian nations or avenge settler deaths. "Offensive wars" of extermination had been forbidden by the Portuguese Crown in the eighteenth century. With the connivance of Goiano presidents, however, settlers in the nineteenth century attacked the Indian nations whom they viewed as competing predators and whose elimination was necessary to secure their own control over land, cattle and horses, and slaves (Karasch 1992: 409–11). Also participating in the bandeiras and sometimes in the Indian wars were the white, pardo, and black militia regiments, as well as a fourth, a barefooted force known as the *pedestres* that included semi-assimilated Indians. Local men organized by color formed local militias that provided protection to frontier towns. Basically, they were skilled frontiersmen rather than members of a foreign army.

After independence, the presidents of the province faced even more serious Indian warfare provoked by settler slaving expeditions and massacres, and exacerbated by a desperate shortage of white men to defend Goiano settlements. Eventually, the presidents created provincial forces and accepted National Guard regiments. Once again, the number of men in any regiment remained low, due to disease and desertion by free men of color who had been forcibly recruited. Although garrisons were constructed, especially along the Rio Araguaia, provincial authorities were unable to staff them adequately, and some fell quickly under attack (Hemming 1987: 395–96).

The fourth group that traditionally has an impact on indigenous populations is that of invading settlers, such as the Boers in South Africa, the Anglos and their slaves in Texas, or Spanish and mestizo settlers in New Mexico. In Goiás, however, settler populations are not easily characterized, because of their diverse regional origins, ethnicity, and class backgrounds. The first settlers to arrive in the 1720s were Paulistas with their Indian slaves. The Portuguese and Spanish followed, usually with African slaves drawn either from Angola or the Costa da Mina in West Africa. The early settlers, including those from Minas Gerais, focused on mining, although as the century progressed, they diversified the sources of their wealth and applied for land grants to raise cattle and horses or plant sugarcane. They also joined with merchants and invested in business and trade. These ambitious men and their Goiano descendants were attracted to whatever was profitable.

Their slaves, including Africans who translated skills in gold mining from the Gold Coast of West Africa, sought freedom for themselves and their families through self-purchase in gold. A minority of black slave women, who ran the shops specializing in foodstuffs and cheap liquors, bought their own freedom or that of their children with gold dust acquired from their miner patrons. The descendants of these freed persons became the free black and pardo populations of the region. Although many continued to live in the towns because of the black brotherhoods there, others escaped discrimination by moving out on the frontier and forming free black communities (Baiocchi 1983). Thus, settlers in Goiás were likely to be black or racially mixed, and we cannot describe the frontier in terms of an Indian-white dichotomy.

More often, however, freed and free blacks and pardos lacked autonomy and lived in dependent patron-client relationships with former slave owners or their descendants. As peasants, they raised subsistence crops or worked as cowboys. Their wives wove clothing and cared for gardens. They were among the principal targets of Indian attacks, as the Xavante and Kayapó raided for women, foodstuffs, and cattle and took revenge for settler attacks on their communities.

Like the free blacks, once-enslaved fugitives who had established quilombos were also targets of Indian raids. They too were invading lands Indians claimed. The most successful quilombolas remained hidden from both Indians and settlers, surviving to the present. These include the inhabitants of Kalunga and other black villages recently discovered near Cavalcante, Goiás. Since almost all quilombos were small and dispersed, they did not pose as significant a threat to the Indian nations as did other settlers (Dos Quilombos Fez-se Kalunga 1992: 12–13; M. Silva 1974).

Nineteenth-century land invasions by settled agriculturalists in the south; cattlemen in the north, east, and west; and riverboatmen were far more significant. Agricultural production served the miners, and most farming and ranch labor was done by Indian and African slaves living close to the mining towns. Settler-cultivated land was an oasis in the midst of forest held by Indian nations. Cattle ranches were also close to Vila Boa or other mining towns. Some semi-assimilated Indians lived in state-sponsored aldeias, where they also cultivated the land. Population density was still light, however, and settler-agriculturalists were not a severe threat in the 1700s.

Land-hungry settlers entered Goiás throughout the nineteenth century. Population increases in part reflect this in-migration of free men and women from São Paulo and Minas Gerais. Although links among Goiano, Paulista, and Mineiro families reached back to the 1720s, the size of this migration to Goiás was much greater, as was the scale of cash crop production; crops were raised not only for sale to neighboring mining towns but also to the coffee economies of Minas Gerais and São Paulo. Slaves on large Goiano plantations cultivated coffee, cotton, and sugar, while dependent peasants on the same estates raised quince for marmalade and tobacco for export throughout the interior, as well as foodstuffs. During the second half of the nineteenth century, these settlers began the agricultural development of one of modern Brazil's richest agricultural states.

To the southwest of the region in which Vila Boa was located were the lands of Caiapônia, a region straddling the road between Vila Boa and Vila Bela in Mato Grosso. In the eighteenth century, agriculturalists and ranchers had emerged to sell their products to the mule teams plodding between Vila Boa and either São Paulo or Mato Grosso. The Kayapó targeted these settlers, and bandeiras were sent to "pacify" them. Once the Southern Kayapó were pacified in the 1780s, settlers could flourish. The region did not remain at peace, however, for Portuguese injustices led the Kayapó to flee the aldeias, and by the 1830s they had resumed warfare on settlers and travelers.

The settler frontier also expanded north along the Rio Araguaia, bringing the Karajá in contact with cattlemen and farmers in search of lands near the river. The first bandeira to contact the Karajá reached Bananal Island in 1755. Subsequently settlers worked cattle ranches and farms on the east banks of the Araguaia north of the road between Leopoldina (now Aruaña) and Vila Boa and south of Bananal Island. Generally, settler-Indian relations on this frontier were not marked by violence and war until the 1880s, when local settlers attempted to exterminate the Karajá living along the southern stretches of the Rio Araguaia (Couto de Magalhães [1863] 1975; Villa Real [1792–1793] 1848).

The situation in the north was a different story. Groups identified as *sertanejos* and cowboys from the *sertão* (backlands) of the northeast drove their cattle to Amaro Leite and São Pedro de Alcantara (now Carolina) on the east bank of the Tocantins. They displaced the Akroá, Krahô, and Porekamekra. And once settled between São Pedro and São Félix on the Tocantins, the sertanejos fought new nations (the Xavante, Xerente, and Canoeiro), who raided their cattle and tried to drive them from the east banks of the Tocantins. Some nations, such as the Krahô, took up cattle husbandry, but these backland settlers forced them out (Melatti 1967).

The north was a cattle frontier, where major conflicts centered on control of good, well-watered pastures and property rights to cattle and horses. Land tenure patterns were characterized by a dominant major family, usually white, while the labor force was composed of slaves (Indian or black) and dependent men of color who served as cowboys. On this frontier cattle replaced the Indians, as the cattlemen either subdued and assimilated the Indians in northern aldeias or drove them west of the Tocantins. The Xavante abandoned these lands in the eighteenth and nineteenth centuries, moving to aldeias or fleeing west of the Araguaia, but the Canoeiro kept up the attack through the 1880s.

The final group of settlers were the Bahians, who entered Goiás along the road that stretched via Barreiras to the Rio São Francisco and ultimately to Salvador, Bahia. They too were tough backlanders who settled in central Goiás or on the east bank of the Tocantins. Many were racially mixed or black. In the eighteenth and early nineteenth centuries, some enterprising pardos had taken over lucrative interior trade routes, and along with Portuguese peddlers they traded dry goods and exotic consumer goods from the coast to exchange for gold dust. Also accused of being *contrabandistas* in gold by Portuguese officials, the Bahians apparently thwarted Portuguese officials' control of gold exports in the late eighteenth century. To avoid the official checkpoints, they traveled throughout remote or difficult terrain and Indian-controlled territories.[12] One suspects they had trade relationships with some nations. In the north of Goiás, for example, the Krahô fought more effectively because of the assistance, including weaponry and gunpowder, they received in trade from local men.

Another eighteenth- and nineteenth-century illegal gold trade route was via the Tocantins and Araguaia Rivers to Belém do Pará. Non-whites who were experienced frontiersmen and canoers were especially important in the river trades, both legal and illegal. River expeditions along the Araguaia and Tocantins sometimes faced fierce Indian resistance, so traders had to travel in armed convoys of large canoes. By the time steamships were introduced in the 1860s, Indians supplied firewood. Until that time, however, many nations resisted white intrusion, and one of the key white policies of late-nineteenth-century Goiás was removal along the rivers of all non-assimilated Indians in order to facilitate the peaceful navigation of the great waterways and the entry of Luso-Brazilian settlers (Doles 1973).

Resistance Strategies

These then were the forces confronting the Indian nations on the frontier of Goiás: Portuguese bureaucrats seeking honors (*mercês*) and gold; priests who devoted more time to their business enterprises than to Christianization; ambitious men using military service to acquire gold and further their imperial careers; rapacious bandeiras avenging settler deaths and acquiring slaves by "right of conquest"; free and freed blacks who allied with the slave owners to save their own lives; quilombolas who hid from their enemies, both white and Indian; African slaves who served their owners by massacring Indians; land-hungry cattlemen and peasants of all races from nearby captaincies and provinces; and finally the river traders and backlanders who ran the interior trades that provided the lifeline of supplies to keep the whole system going.

Diversity among the invaders led to diversity in indigenous responses. It was not simply a choice between armed resistance and assimilation to the white man's culture. The problem in Goiás was that survival as a people demanded multiple forms of relationships with the invaders, most of whom were non-white. The groups who survived were adaptable, innovative, and often pragmatic and varied in their responses to the invaders. In modern times, they still demonstrate such qualities in dealing with state or national bureaucrats even as they pursue alliances with international organizations, anthropologists, and journalists.

While contemporary anthropologists can testify to the complex social organizations, political and economic structures, and religious values that make survival possible in the twentieth century, there is little direct evidence from eighteenth-century Goiás. Documentary evidence comes from the literate invading elites, who seldom took the time to examine indigenous social structures and customs. To most invaders, the Indian nations (also termed "gentiles") were "barbarous," fierce, hostile, wild animals, or "*bugres*" (a highly pejorative word). At most we are fortunate to locate ethnic indicators and generalized comments about Indian refusal to labor as slaves; failure to assimilate to "civilized customs" and wear clothing; refusal to live in tile-roofed houses; and inability to demonstrate an accurate understanding of Catholicism, even after baptism. Officials expressed dismay at the speed with which Indians fled aldeias and returned to warfare and raiding Christian settlements.

In spite of these limitations and biases, there are still other sources that enable us to define the diversity of responses by the Kayapó, Xavante, Xerente, and Canoeiro. Of these four only the Canoeiro, who pursued the single policy of armed resistance, almost entirely disappeared into obscurity and poverty. Many other nations died out because of frontier wars of extermination and enslavement or because of the spread of diseases. Only their names are known. What I hope to demonstrate here are the reasons some nations survived as a people and shaped the Goiano frontier over the course of a century.

Kayapó

After being enslaved by the Paulistas in 1741, the Kayapó began forty years of warfare on the frontier. They attacked invading miners and cattle ranchers and made the early gold strikes in the south extremely hazardous. Once expeditions waged "offensive war" against them, they retreated to raids on supply caravans, mines, and remote ranches, where they stole livestock and killed slaves. By the 1780s, they had succeeded in removing settlers from large regions of southern Goiás and delaying further invasions of their lands.

The arrival in 1778 of a new governor in Vila Boa, Luís da Cunha Meneses, led some Southern Kayapó to adopt new survival strategies (Karasch 1981; Monteiro 1951). To end the chronic state of intermittent warfare that slowed the flow of gold to the royal mint in Vila Boa, Governor de Cunha Meneses decided to make peace with the Kayapó. The first indication of a parallel shift in Kayapó tactics was the decision of Angraí-oxá, a Kayapó chief of the Rio Claro region, to send a small group of thirty-six (headed by an old man named Romexi) to verify the pacification promises of José Luís Pereira, a military officer who had contacted them. The governor welcomed the Kayapó to Vila Boa and sent them to inspect the state-run aldeia of São José de Mossâmedes, established in 1755 for other pacified nations. Subsequently six warriors returned to their people and brought more than two hundred Kayapó back to Vila Boa in 1781 to be received by the governor. Governor da Cunha Meneses treated the arrival of the Kayapó as a conquest and celebrated their submission as vassals to the Portuguese Crown by baptizing 113 children. The Kayapó were then settled at another state aldeia, Maria I, named for the Portuguese queen. Eventually Maria I attracted still other Kayapó, and as many as seven hundred soon lived in four villages. While Portuguese bureaucrats regarded this settlement as permanent, the Kayapó obviously did not. By the early nineteenth century, there were so few Kayapó living at the aldeia that it was closed and the surviving residents transferred to São José. At that time, both villages together had no more than three hundred Kayapó.

The Kayapós' choice of *aldeamento* in the 1780s was probably due to two factors: access to good lands and water in a time of severe drought combined with Portuguese gifts of food. Maria I offered fertile lands for agriculture, while São José had "good waters and many forests." Further gifts of textiles, iron tools, and corn (as well as the personal authority of Angraí-oxá and later his granddaughter, Damiana da Cunha) kept some Kayapó in the missions. Most, however, eventually fled because of forced agricultural labor and deadly diseases. By 1808, most Kayapó were living near the Rio Araguaia and even west of it. While a few remained in São José, the majority resumed warfare. In 1819, Goiás Governor Fernando Delgado Freire de Castilho turned to Damiana to lead an expedition to pacify her people once again, but she returned with only seventy. The wars continued with quilombolas joining in the violence. As the Kayapó attacked the invaders along the road to Mato Grosso, government troops slaughtered them in their villages.

The state-sponsored massacres led to further Kayapó resistance or flight. By 1824, only 124 Kayapó remained in São José, and they were increasingly surrounded by hostile settlers ambitious to seize their lands. More Kayapó fled, and by 1829 groups of Kayapó had spread to an area near Cuiabá and seriously disrupted trade between Mato Grosso and Goiás. Expeditions within Mato Grosso drove them back to the Araguaia and Claro Rivers, where the frightened settlers appealed to the governor of Goiás for help. He then sent Damiana on her last expedition. After nine months of travel, she returned with a virulent fever, possibly malaria. She died in 1831, and São José was virtually abandoned by the Kayapó. Eventually, the last of them were transferred against their will to Arinos, Mato Grosso, in 1833 and 1834. The Kayapó who were expelled from São José once again resumed warfare on the settlers and raided Rio Claro and Rio Bonito in the 1860s (Gallais 1942: 101–2; Hemming 1987: 397–98; Karasch 1992: 412, note 35).

For the Kayapó, the choice to live in aldeias had been one among many. But well into the 1880s, armed warfare was their principal form of resistance. They were more effective than the Canoeiro in surviving as a people, however, perhaps because of their temporary stay in the aldeias, where they acquired the food, weapons, and tools necessary for survival. They also learned more about their enemies. It is clear from the written record that the injustice of their forced removal from São José in the 1830s led some of them to return to warfare. They were still at war with settlers in the 1880s when a new set of missionaries reached the region and began yet another attempt to pacify and Christianize them—a century after their initial pacification by the Portuguese in the 1780s.

The Xavante and Xerente

Another nation that followed diverse resistance strategies was the Xavante. We can trace early Xavante populations living in Maranhão to the east of the Rio Tocantins. By the 1780s, they had crossed the Tocantins and engaged in offensive warfare in the north of the Captaincy of Goiás, where they attacked the mining towns and raided isolated ranches. Their attacks were so successful that Governor Tristão da Cunha received royal authorization to wage offensive war. In 1788, his forces pacified and resettled three to four thousand Xavante at the aldeia of Carretão about twenty leagues from Vila Boa. The Portuguese again provided gifts of food, textiles, and iron tools to a conquered nation. Eventually the Xavante, like the Kayapó, deserted the aldeia and resumed frontier warfare. By 1811, their challenge was so serious that the royal government in Rio authorized another offensive war against them, giving permission to enslave live captives. Especially targeted were the Xavante who had fled from Carretão, where they had learned Portuguese, the use of European weaponry, and knowledge of settler customs, which enabled them to attack at the most advantageous times. They were still at war in northern Goiás in 1836, when an expedition was organized to remove them from the Tocantins region (Karasch 1992: 397–411; A. Silva 1992: 357–78).

In their many wars, the Xavante often sought strength in greater numbers by forming coalitions with other nations. The Xavante allied with the Xerente, and together they raided and killed the settlers and slaves of Pontal, Carmo, and Almas. They also forged an alliance with the Karajá. When authorities built a presidio, Santa Maria do Araguaia, in the north in 1813, a coalition of Xavantes, Xerentes, and Karajás attacked and destroyed it (Karasch 1992: 403). While the Xavante showed flexibility in aligning with similarly threatened nations to fight the settlers, they also tried an innovation to shift the balance of power their way. Although it proved to be temporary, this strategic change documents their adaptability. Previously, the Xavante had routinely slaughtered male slaves working on the gold strikes and destroyed quilombos. In the 1700s, the Xavante tried to increase their own numbers by offering refuge to fugitive slaves (Chaim 1974: 127). A few black men turned to them for help, and reports soon reached the Portuguese of blacks who were fighting with the Xavante rather than against them. This new strategy soon broke down, however, and the Xavante resumed their wars on slaves and settlers.

In the following century, still other Xavante chose to reside in the state-run aldeias. The largest numbers apparently lived at Pedro III do Carretão. According to a French missionary visitor in the 1880s, Carretão had once sheltered ten thousand Indians of different nations, but between 1764 and 1888 the thousands of Indians had declined to “one man and two women of Indian race” (Gallais 1942: 74–75). Descendants of Indian women and black slave men, however, lived in Carretão’s environs. Among the nations at Carretão were the Xerente and Xavante, most of whom fled the aldeia because they had been tortured like slaves with stocks, chains, whips, and iron collars. As of 1849, only seventy or eighty Xerente and Xavante remained at Carretão.

Although the Xavante were among the first nations to be settled in eighteenth-century aldeias and were among those with the longest experience in aldeamento, Luso-Brazilian sources clearly detail their resistance and flight from the aldeias. The majority of them took up warfare after fleeing the aldeias or withdrew to west of the Araguaia to escape settlement. Historically, the Xavante were famous for their ability in war, being among the most feared nations in Goiás. Like the Kayapó they survived as a people by choosing a variety of strategies: temporary aldeamento, alliances with other nations, armed warfare, and flight to Mato Grosso, where they retreated from history to be recontacted and repacified in the 1940s (A. Silva 1992: 368–69).

Many Xerente, however, rejected armed resistance, choosing to settle down and assimilate. Some historians contend that they are actually Xavante, but Xavante "tamed" by contact with settlers and missionaries. Aldeia records usually link the two as living in the same villages, but they also distinguish between them. Both are placed along the Tocantins in the same localities in the nineteenth century; but eighteenth-century sources use only the term *Xavante.* In the nineteenth century, Xerente were living at the same aldeias as Xavante, working in agriculture and the river trade to Belém, adopting some Christian rituals such as baptism, and speaking Portuguese. The difference was that they chose to live along the Tocantins even though they grew increasingly impoverished. Nonetheless, the Xerente too have survived as a people, and they still maintain land rights in the north, in what is now Tocantins state.

The Canoeiro

In contrast, the Canoeiro (now Avá-Canoeiro) pursued the exact opposite strategy of the Xerente: implacable resistance (Toral 1984–85). Noted for their "ferocious and indomitable courage," they stood fast against their enemies, hurling insults at them in Portuguese. Their women and trained dogs accompanied them into battle and fought "as valiantly as the men." Their weapons included bows and arrows and long lances. Since they were comparatively few in number—Cunha Mattos estimated no more than three hundred warriors in the 1820s—small bands of Canoeiro used classic guerrilla warfare tactics of surprise attacks after careful intelligence. They avoided confronting armed men with guns but struck ranches when least expected. While some were clearly raiding for cattle and horses—their diet included horsemeat—others were engaged in revenge raids, killing rather than capturing the women, children, and slaves of ranchers.

Nineteenth-century governors' reports trace the Caneiros' unwillingness to accommodate or settle in missions. Their ferocity, however, was directly related to enslavement and the bitter depredations of the bandeira led by Joaquim Theotonio Segurado in 1819. As Miguel Lino de Morães reported to provincial authorities in Goiás in 1830, the Canoeiro were still "irreconcilable" because of what they had suffered in 1819. Through an interpreter they declared that "they were not [about] to be our slaves" (Pohl 1976: 213–15).[13] Apparently they never entered into negotiations with Portuguese officials or settlers or settled in state-run aldeias except along the Araguaia. According to Cunha Mattos in 1824 and Couto de Magalhães in 1862, they were originally Carijós Indians who accompanied bandeiras from São Paulo in the 1720s. Fleeing from the Paulistas, they established themselves in northern Goiás between 1724 and 1726, where they established an identity as canoe Indians and began a century of hostile interactions with the Xavante, Xerente, and Luso-Brazilians along the Tocantins (Pedroso 1992: chap. 2).[14] Perhaps they were among the hostile nations the Jesuits encountered as they descended the Rio Tocantins in the 1730s.

According to Toral (1984–85), the second phase of their history began about 1820, when settlers, beginning with Segurado in 1819, forced some of them to abandon the Tocantins region and migrate west to the banks of the Araguaia. Some Canoeiro remained behind, however, at Cavalcante and Formosa, and the Canoeiro splintered into two separate groups. Pacified in the twentieth century, small bands of five to ten still find refuge in caves in the hills between the Paraná and Maranhão Rivers. Although their survival in the upper Tocantins is now questionable, their resistance strategy in that region left them impoverished fugitives hiding in caves from their enemies.[15]

Isolated bands of Avá-Canoeiro, pacified and "docile" Xerente, rebellious Xavante, and resilient Kayapó all survived on the frontier of Goiás; they lived while others disappeared into extinction. How and why they endured as separate peoples remains to be studied, but what is certain is that they too shaped the character of Goiano society and culture. Although twentieth-century explorers often present the image of isolated Indians entering into contact with the civilized world for the first time, the Goiano nations studied here had experienced at least two centuries of cultural interaction with invaders. Their treatment as slaves, however, usually led the nations to return to warfare to obstruct "hegemonic resolution" in favor of Portugal or its successor state, imperial Brazil. Waves of immigrants did not inevitably flow into the region over two centuries; instead, settlers attempting to "disinfest" Goiás of its inhabitants often died in battles with competing peoples. The conflict over spheres of influence is unresolved. Some violence still persists, as ranchers and miners continue to contest the Indians for rights to land. In the last decade of the twentieth century, the Goiano frontier, especially in the north, has yet to close.

9

North to the Yerbales

The Exploitation of the Paraguayan Frontier, 1776–1810

JERRY W. COONEY

By the 1770s, the Río de la Plata region of Paraguay experienced an export-based boom based upon cattle and yerba maté, a local tea. Cooney explores the expansion of both these industries and their implications for the development of this riverine frontier in the late eighteenth century. The revenues gained through that economic expansion had important political ramifications.

IN THE 1760S, Paraguay was a stagnant, neglected, and isolated region with most of its population huddled closely around the provincial capital of Asunción. Its inhabitants were primarily engaged in subsistence agriculture and secondarily in the extraction of yerba maté—the latter at that time heavily dependent upon labor supplied by the archaic encomienda system (Cardozo 1959: 78–109). Within one generation, however, the territory effectively controlled by Asunción had increased at least 40 percent, and wage labor, particularly in the yerba industry of the province, had replaced encomienda labor. The barter-based agricultural and pastoral economy had given way to one based upon specie and the export of raw materials and agricultural products to the south in exchange for finished goods. New settlements extended the outer reaches of the province to the north, and from those settlements entrepreneurs exploited virgin stands of yerba while at the same time an expanding cattle frontier served the burgeoning export trade (Cooney 1990: 15–36; Velázquez 1965: 15–23).

Paraguay had always been a frontier region, continually assaulted by hostile, nomadic Indians from the north and west. By the 1750s, the impulse for provincial expansion sprang from the need to protect the province from such raids. That desire was reinforced by the greater imperial goal of blocking further expansion out of Brazil. On all sides the Portuguese appeared to be closing in. Paraguayans and imperial officials alike were concerned about the Lusitanian settlement of Ygatimí on Paraguayan-claimed territory (1767–77) and after that challenge had been met, they then worried about the Portuguese push south in the Paraguay River valley. Even to the southeast, officials in the former Jesuit missions of the upper Plata repeatedly called upon military aid from Paraguay in the face of Portuguese advances.

The first step to secure the northern frontier was the 1760 foundation of the reducción of Belén on the Río Ypané (Viola 1986: 30–37). That settlement, founded in an effort to "civilize" the often hostile Mbayá Indians, also served as a catalyst for the economic penetration of the region. Soon thereafter, Governor Agustín Fernando de Pinedo founded Villa Real de la Concepción near Belén to block Portuguese expansion in the north, as well as to aid the pacification of the Indian frontier (Ferrer 1985: 13–30; Quevedo 1959–60: 76–78). In 1777, an expedition under the command of the same governor seized and destroyed Ygatimí, and forcibly brought back many Brazilians to Paraguay.[1] At the same time Ygatimí was destroyed, Fuerte San Carlos was founded on the Río Apá in the far north to guard the frontier against both Indian attacks and Portuguese penetration. To fill in the regions between Villa Real de la Concepción and Asunción on the river, Yguamandiyú on the Río Jejuí and, farther south, Cuarepotí, were founded in 1786 and 1787 respectively.[2]

Governors had little difficulty in attracting settlers to the new frontier since pressure for land in old nuclear Paraguay had increased in the first half of the eighteenth century (Vives Azancot 1980: 196–201). The land in the north was fertile; well watered by the rivers of the region; and with hardwood forests, *palmares*, savannahs, and brushlands, not that different from traditional Paraguay. The government awarded settlers building lots in these new towns and *chacras* (agricultural plots) on the outskirts of the new villages. At the same time, *mercedes* (land grants) to be used for cattle raising were freely granted to offspring of the old traditional elite. And even the most humble Paraguayan eventually might find employment in the new yerbales or cattle estancias of the north. Many settlers in this region had earlier leased rather than owned lands in the areas around Asunción. Others had served as simple agricultural laborers and were described as *desarraidos o vagos* (vagrants). On the other hand, they were, by custom and earlier decrees, recognized as *españoles-americanos* and therefore not subject to the encomienda system. Free labor dominated the economics of the new frontier—whether on the chacras of the northern littoral, on the new cattle ranches of the same region, or in the yerbales.

Yerba maté (*Ilex paraguaiensis*), or Paraguayan tea, had long been Paraguay's main export, even after the Jesuits to the south had successfully seized the market with their cultivated crop in the seventeenth and eighteenth centuries (Garavaglia 1983). With the Jesuit expulsion in 1767, the extraction of yerba fell into the hands of Asunción entrepreneurs and reverted to the traditional harvest by gathering, rather than cultivation.

The shift of emphasis in the yerba industry from the Jesuit missions to northern Paraguay coincided with the great administrative and economic reforms of the 1770s and 1780s in the Río de la Plata. The creation of the viceroyalty in 1776, the Edict of Free Commerce in 1778, and the installation of Intendentes in 1782 all had a tremendous impact on this vast region, and no less upon Paraguay (Lynch 1958: 280–89). Internal trade restrictions were removed, and aggressive porteño and Montevidean merchants expanded both the internal and external trade of the viceroyalty. Paraguay and the yerba industry profited from an expanded market and easy credit supplied by Buenos Aires merchants. The *carrera del Paraguay* (the river trade of the Paraguay and Paraná Rivers) grew tremendously in the late colonial period, and yerba—a staple used throughout southern South America—played a central role in that commerce.

The first step in the yerba trade was locating virgin yerbales in hitherto unexploited regions. This was usually facilitated by friendly Indians who, in return for gifts, communicated to authorities the location of such yerbales.[3] By the 1780s, the greatest area of yerba exploitation in the north of the province was in the region of the Arroyo Estrella, the headwaters of the Aquidabán and Ypané Rivers, and from there to the rise of the Cordillera de Amambay. The second necessary factor was a merchant or estanciero financier (*beneficiador*) who possessed capital and/or credit granted him from porteño counterparts (Cooney 1990: 25–27). The beneficiador might be either an individual or a partnership.[4]

After the purchase of a license to exploit a *beneficio* of yerba, the beneficiador then hired a crew for an expedition to the yerbales. The most important employee was the foreman or capataz, in charge of the expedition itself. He received a salary of approximately thirty pesos per month, *vaqueros* (salaried cowboys) and escort soldiers received about sixteen pesos per month, and peones about one peso per day (Aguirre 1950: 272). One might assume that the latter earned nearly as much as the capataz, but stated wages are misleading as the system of *fomentos* (advances) and deducted expenses greatly diminished the real pay of a peon. Peones or *yerberos* were advanced hard cash, clothing, animals, and tools—all charged against their accounts—which had to be satisfied by gathered yerba.

The expedition transported as much gear as possible up the rivers that penetrated the yerbales. Then, after picking up their cattle, mules, and carts, which had trekked overland to a rendezvous point, they either followed old trails or blazed new ones to their destination (Aguirre 1950: 239–83; Robertson and Robertson 1839: 136–50; Whigham 1991b: 21–27). On arrival, they established several ranchos near water for their cattle and mules. The men's shelter was simple roofed sheds with no walls. For the processing of yerba, a *barbacuá* (trellis or grillwork placed upon four arching poles) was constructed.

From the base camp yerberos, often working in pairs, fanned out to extract yerba. Leaf-bearing branches of this bush were cut, and then a *haz*, a pile of eight to twelve *arrobas* (an arroba was about twenty-five English pounds), was formed. The peones then gathered firewood and carefully scorched the leaf-bearing branches which, along with loose leaves, were compressed within a leather-tied wooden framework. A peon, with the aid of his partner, balanced the load on his back with the use of a tumpline (leather cord slung across the forehead), which enabled him to carry a large load on his back. This burden of approximately 150 pounds of yerba was then ported back to the rancho. The peones repeated this trip several times.

At the base camp, the yerba was placed upon the barbacuá, there again to be toasted. Once ashes were removed and the ground cleaned, the peones placed the yerba on the ground below the barbacuá and beat it. Then it was placed temporarily in a sack made of hide (*guamí*). With these labors completed, the peones then rested. The next morning at two o'clock labor began again. Now it was time to grind the yerba into even finer pieces. The guamí was placed in a hole in the ground, then the yerba within was ground as in a mortar. With this task done, the yerba was then turned over to the capataz and the amount produced by the yerbero was credited to him. From initial gathering of the yerba in the woods to handing it over to the capataz, the process usually took three days.

The peon, however, was not yet finished with this yerba. He had now to place it in *percheles* (silos) where it would season until transported to market. The perchel was an enclosed wooden shed with a hide door entrance, inside which the yerba was stacked in layers. The peon entered and compressed the yerba until it was a semisolid mass. When a sufficient quantity had been collected and compressed, the yerba was ready for final packing. A cowhide, supported by two poles, was sewn into a sack with an opening at the top. This sack, with a normal capacity of about fourteen arrobas (one *carga* or two *tercios*) was then packed with yerba; *manijas* (handles) were attached for ease of handling. When a sufficient amount of yerba had been accumulated at the ranchos, the sacks were transported by oxcarts to a navigable stream for shipment to a river port.

In the yerbales, there was a well-established division of labor among the four occupations: capataces, peones, vaqueros, and soldiers. The first oversaw the labor of the peones; checked the quality of the yerba; controlled the distribution of food and tools, and the everyday life of the ranchos; supervised the vaqueros in their care of animals; and kept the accounts of peones' yerba handed to him. He also led the soldiers in the defense of this party against any hostile Indian attack.

Peones were classified into various groups. Some, known as *troperos,* were really labor bosses employed by beneficiadores to advance goods to yerberos or *conchavos,* contract the labor of such peones, and be responsible for ensuring each yerbero's payment of yerba to redeem his debt.[5] Other peones simply contracted directly with the beneficiador. A third group, termed *changadores,* were not conchavos as they accepted no advances and worked independently in the yerbal with their own tools, animals, etc., selling their collected yerba directly to the capataz of an expedition. Crews also had *boyeros* (ox drivers) and *picadores* (goaders) for the conduction of yerba to a navigable stream. Large beneficios that required security might have two or three soldiers who accompanied the party.

Working conditions in the yerbales were generally deplorable. Often the men were clothed in rags and, as Aguirre (1950: 268) observed, "hunger is the characteristic of the beneficios" as yerberos ate but once a day. As a consequence, their health often was precarious. Sores were common and, even though subject to strenuous physical labor, the peones often appeared pale and emaciated. Disease, insects, and venomous snakes plagued the workers as well. Yet their greatest burden, perhaps, was the system of fomentos. Contracted peones had to redeem with yerba advances of specie and goods for themselves or for the support of their families, as well as paying the costs of their daily rations. All too often, they never could erase their debts from the books, entering into a legal state of permanent debt peonage and condemning themselves eternally to the beneficios with a corresponding abandonment of their families. Too often the beneficiadores padded the debts of an illiterate yerbero and charged him double for his daily maintenance. Rather than clearing his account, the peon fell further and further behind.[6] At the same time, however, some beneficiadores, to ensure the continued work of a good yerbero, paid a subsidy to his family to keep him working in the yerbal.

Even those who avoided falling into a state of debt peonage often found themselves in the yerbales longer than anticipated. A normal fomento was two hundred pesos, generally in a combination of cash or goods for a peon's family, and supplies for his work in the yerbal.[7] Other charges against him were seven pounds of yerba a day or nine and one-half pesos a month for rations. On the fomento of two hundred pesos, he also paid a tithe of twenty pesos as well as ten pesos for severance taxes. Theoretically, to clear his books and pay the other charges, he would have to work eighty days, but generally it took twice that long or nearly half a year in the yerbales. Yerberos who were absent for long stretches of time from their villages and families reinforced the custom of women-led households in Paraguay (Potthast-Jutkeit 1994: 87–104). At the same time, however, yerberos who did clear their accounts but kept on working received their "overage" in silver. The yerbero who went on a spectacular binge with his money after emerging from the *campo* became a common sight in river towns by the 1790s. Yet for those provident few who were fortunate to contract with an ethical beneficiador and saved their money, work in the yerbales supported their families and might even promise a modest capital (Robertson and Robertson 1839: 148–50).

The transient nature—as well as the physical hardship—of the yerba industry was responsible for the absence of women in this industry. The yerbales were exclusively male—a state of affairs that at times led to bestiality, homosexuality, and even pederasty. Bestiality was a common offense in the yerbales, in both the colonial and national eras, and the criminal records of the Asunción Archive are replete with such cases.[8] There do not seem to be as many cases dealing with homosexual practices, but some occurred.[9] One practice that probably promoted perversion in the yerbales was the custom of contracting *guainos* (adolescent males) for camp work (Ferrer 1985: 68).

Conchavos had few means by which to rectify poor treatment by capataces or bad labor conditions in the yerbales. Local officials on the frontier enforced the terms of contracts and, if workers mutinied, they faced rapid repression. In 1788, some forty "peones españoles" from the village of Trinidad contracted to work in the yerbales of the upper Paraná. Some twenty-one mutinied against their capataz because, in the words of a local official, "they did not wish to work." The mutineers then returned to their village, where the ringleaders were arrested, placed in irons, and remanded to the governor for punishment.[10]

Mutinies occurred rarely, however, since workers realized they had little chance of prevailing against their capataces and the power of the state. Merchants and beneficiadores also dominated the Cabildo de Asunción, and that body made sure that in no way would the "masters of peones of the yerbales lose the advances made with the purpose of redemption through personal labor in the 'Minerales de la Yerba.' "[11] Cabildo members believed that workers were all too prone to take advances and then run away without fulfilling their contracts or, by feigning illness, avoid any work at all. And in all justice to the beneficiadores, at times the peones were the unscrupulous ones.

Discontented yerberos had another, more common method of protest. By the 1790s some changadores, or independent yerberos, converted themselves into illicit merchant-entrepreneurs. From stores in out-of-the-way spots, they supplied yerberos, settlers, militiamen, and cattle drovers with various goods. They also illegally exchanged locally made rum (*caña*) for yerba clandestinely extracted by yerberos (sometimes even extending credit to their customers) as well as providing places for illegal games of chance.[12] The governor ordered local officials to remove such establishments "ordering with an absolute prohibition the introduction by any person of said pulperías (stores) into *los minerales de Yerba.*"[13] Those orders had little effect since complaints about changadores (illegal merchants) not only continued, but in Curuguatí local merchants began to utilize the services of these shadowy entrepreneurs to avoid payment of sales tax on their yerba transactions.[14]

Beneficiadores were no more law abiding than were their peones. They evaded state fees for the licenses necessary to exploit yerbales.[15] Too often no attention was paid to the limitation of twelve peones to work each individual beneficio.[16] A blatant example by one charged with the enforcement of law in his jurisdiction was the beneficiador Lieutenant Colonel Benancio de la Rosa, militia commander of Cuarepotí. He had twenty-three peones in his beneficio.[17] Yerba smuggling was not as profitable as tobacco smuggling, but it did occur as beneficiadores evaded various taxes. Some yerba was diverted from yerbales in the Curuguatí region to the Alto Paraná and thus avoided inspection and tax charges at Asunción.[18] The Alto Paraná was poorly patrolled by the forces of the lieutenant governor of Misiones, making it relatively easy to evade the revenue police (*resguardo*) at Corrientes. From all indications, Asunción's authority over beneficiadores was weaker in the region of Curuguatí than elsewhere. The distance overland to that remote northern village and the traditional lawlessness of its inhabitants probably account for its beneficiadores' blatant disregard of the law.[19]

The exploitation of yerbales in the late colonial era proceeded with no thought of conservation. Everyone connected with the industry assumed that yerba maté was an unlimited natural resource.[20] That view coupled with a growing demand prompted a continual advance of the yerba frontier. By the 1790s, yerbales close to the Río Paraguay in the north had been exhausted, and yerberos started penetrating the region between the Aquidabán and Apá Rivers, working their way eastward toward the region then being exploited by peones from Curuguatí.

In the last generation of the colonial era, the yerba trade had expanded from a low of 26,429 arrobas exported from Asunción in 1776 to a high of some 327,150 arrobas in 1808 (Cardozo 1959: 106). Table 9.1 shows annual exports of yerba between 1781 and 1810.

TABLE 9.1
Exports of Paraguayan Yerba, 1781–1810 (in arrobas)

Year	Amount Exported	Year	Amount Exported	Year	Amount Exported
1781	125,271	1791	142,245	1801	281,790
1782	—	1792	234,787	1802	246,833
1783	247,290	1793	116,145	1803	231,928
1784	111,533	1794	130,163	1804	283,544
1785	—	1795	154,058	1805	263,344
1786	161,258	1796	201,172	1806	279,992
1787	166,207	1797	236,205	1807	297,800
1788	120,353	1798	330,480	1808	327,150
1789	169,875	1799	—	1809	204,547
1790	148,837	1800	217,110	1810	151,425

Source: Data are from Thomas Whigham, *La yerba mate del Paraguay (1780–1870)* (Asunción: CPES, 1991), p. 20.

The trade gave rise to a new merchant elite in the province, generally peninsular in origin and resident in Asunción. Merchant-associates in Buenos Aires granted credit to their upriver counterparts at an easy 5 percent, and the flourishing yerba commerce fueled imports of European finished goods. For the first time, the Paraguayan economy became integrated into that of the greater Río de la Plata (Cooney 1990: 22–24). River transport boomed from a low of 25 boats, canoes, or rafts leaving Asunción in 1776 to a high of 502 in 1808—and most carried cargoes of yerba, fully or in part (Aguirre 1949).[21] The expansion of river trade also resulted in a decrease in carrying charges. In the early 1780s, the cost of shipping an arroba of yerba to the estuary was two reales; by the turn of the century it was only one and one-half reales.[22]

The availability of cheap water transportation was critical to the development of the yerba trade. Without the tributaries of the Río Paraguay, it would have been difficult to tap the yerbales. Without the Paraguay-Paraná system, it would have been impractical to ship yerba. Of all the areas of Spanish America, the Río de la Plata has been the most blessed with navigable rivers, and the history of Paraguay itself, let alone the frontier exploitation of yerba maté, serves as a testimony to those waterways (Cooney 1990: 123–44).

During this era, Villa Real de la Concepción was the main center for the yerba trade in northern Paraguay. By 1804, more than sixty merchants of this villa engaged in that commerce. They employed more than two thousand peones in "labors in the montes, in which 200,000 arrobas a year are extracted." The viceroy of the Río de la Plata considered that commerce so important that he recommended to the Ministro de Hacienda in Madrid that a *diputado* of the Buenos Aires Consulado be appointed to that villa (in addition to the one resident in Asunción) to adjudicate commercial disputes.[23] That request was approved.

Not only did yerba fuel the private economy of Paraguay, the multitude of taxes and fees on this commodity financed the operation of the Intendencia. A beneficiador acquired a license to exploit a yerbal for a period of one year by paying forty pesos to the provincial treasury's Ramo de Guerra.[24] That particular treasury account was then used for provisioning militias in frontier presidios, purchasing arms and munitions, and supplying gifts to Indians. No legal justification for this *ramo* existed, but it had been in existence and used by governors since the 1500s to pay for defense of the province against Indian and Portuguese aggression. By the end of the colonial era, the Ramo de Guerra was under attack from Buenos Aires. Viceroy marqués de Avilés criticized it, claiming that its existence encouraged Paraguayan governors, most notably Lázaro de Ribera (1795–1806), to engage in unnecessary military adventures against Indians (Avilés y del Fierro 1945: 532–34). Such was not really the case. Ribera was an irritating, contentious subordinate, but he was no warmonger.

All exchanges of yerba maté bore a sales tax of 4 percent, and as a product of the earth it also was subject to the tithe—the 10 percent tax on incomes that went for the support of the Church. If yerba was transported to Asunción for shipment south—and most of Paraguay's yerba did pass through the capital—then the *derecho de estanco* was paid, which might best be termed a severance tax of eight pounds of yerba for every sixteen arrobas of that commodity extracted from the yerbales (Aguirre 1950: 278). Shipowners transporting yerba from the province paid a fee of eight arrobas for every one thousand shipped south, as well as a small fee for the trip permit. And finally, a small fee was paid for official paper (*papel sellado*) on which was issued the licenses to beneficiadores (Ferrer de Arrellaga 1985: 78–80).[25]

By 1780, the Intendencia de Paraguay lived off this beverage. Yerba alone was responsible for the fact that between the 1770s and the turn of the century, provincial revenues jumped at least fivefold.[26] Governors were well aware of the importance of this commodity and solicitous of its well-being. The magnitude of yerba's importance may be seen in the five-year period from 1788 to 1792, when Paraguay exported an average yearly worth of 292,653 pesos of that commodity. According to a well-placed observer, the Asunción Treasury received 11 percent of that amount, or 32,182 pesos annually (Azara 1847: 313–14).

The burgeoning yerba industry in the north prompted the rise of a new cattle frontier in the same region. A large quantity of beef was consumed by yerberos, either on the hoof or as charque. Oxen and mules, of course, provided transport into the yerbales and the extraction of yerba to navigable streams. However, the greatest demand was for hides for packing, and the ranches of central Paraguay could never hope to supply the quantity needed. In addition, that traditional ranching area was rather distant from the new yerba frontier. Governors achieved an easy solution to this problem by the grant of *mercedes de ganado mayor* (cattle ranch land grants) to any deserving español-americano, either in reward for his services to the Crown or even for the services of his family. A petition to Governor Pedro Melo de Portugal by the brothers José Marco Yegros and Martín José Yegros for a grant of land justified that request since:

> [The brothers] are well deserving on the account of the services of their father, grandfathers, and other ancestors, as well as the alacrity in which the supplicants have served the King and *patria.* It is well known that they [the brothers] have never been rewarded with encomiendas, tierras baldias, or other awards that are common recompense in the province for services.[27]

In the 1770s and 1780s, governors granted many mercedes on the northern frontier to members of the old landed elite. Governors were quite casual in granting land as it was plentiful. Pedro Melo de Portugal and his successor, Joaquín de Alós, paid little attention to the Laws of the Indies in this matter. Not all mercedes were large; better than half were five or six square leagues, which was considered medium-sized for Paraguay. At the same time one suspects that, in a time when the traditional Paraguayan encomienda was under attack from royal officials, these two governors took the administratively expedient (and doubtless wise) attitude that if grants were necessary to mollify the old elite who formerly had profited economically and socially from their encomiendas, fine and well.

Near new settlements in the north, cattle grants approached one or two square leagues in size, while further into the campo they ranged from five to eight square leagues (Ferrer de Arrellaga 1985: 33–40, 87). Peones in the cattle industry were generally under the command of the foreman who ran a particular ranch for an owner. These vaqueros found working conditions better than their yerbero counterparts, but their wages were rather lower. The owner supplied rations and the peones on such ranches led a more regular life, as women and children accompanied their menfolk to these stations in the north. Around the rough ranch huts women tended plots of mandioca and other vegetables, as women had done in Paraguay since before the conquest.

In the early 1780s, the cattle industry faced a crisis. Demand for hides for the packing of yerba and tobacco exceeded supplies, and the government placed restrictions upon their export. At the same time, the northern ranges had to be stocked and ranchers of that region resorted to outside purchase. Between 1780 and 1790, more than 100,000 head of cattle passed from Corrientes into Paraguay by the Paso del Rey (Maeder 1977: 343).[28] An unknown number from the former Jesuit missions also passed north, and that transfer sheds some light upon the disappearance of large numbers of cattle from inventories kept by the new government administrators. By 1791, the new cattle region of Paraguay was sufficiently stocked that it could sustain all demands made upon it. By 1800, perhaps as many as 1,500,000 cattle ranged throughout Paraguay and the former export restrictions on hides were relaxed (Aguirre 1951: 124–32; Azara 1943: 21).

The economic benefit to the province of the expansion of the cattle frontier was obvious. A hoped-for result was the increase of government revenues. An observer in 1801 stated:

> Fortunately the governors of Paraguay . . . have distributed lands in such a way . . . that estancias are common throughout the province. Two square leagues of unoccupied land produce nothing and when sold the Treasury receives at the most forty pesos. However, if given to a poor man free of charge who stocks it with cattle worth one thousand pesos — that is, more than two thousand head — it would contribute to the Treasury in only two years through transactions two hundred fifty pesos for the ramo de guerra, besides the alcabalas. . . . (Azara 1943: 14–15)

Governors also established on the frontier new, state-owned *estancias del rey* (king's ranches). Operated by a rural civil servant with control over state-employed peones, the ranches usually raised cattle to provision the garrisons of presidios that accompanied the cattle and yerba industries into the north. By the 1790s, estancias del rey were scattered throughout the new frontier, there even being one upriver in the Chaco serving Fuerte Borbón (Williams 1973).[29]

The old encomienda elite of Paraguay transformed themselves into a cattle elite and, in the late colonial period, benefited tremendously from this change. Why should they then resent new Iberian immigrants taking over the commerce of the province, or that the same immigrants became the most prominent beneficiadores of yerba? Paraguayan ranchers now found a very profitable niche in the infrastructure of the yerba industry. Out on the periphery of the province, ranchers concentrated on supplying cattle, oxen, mules, and other animals to the beneficiadores. And when needed they also supplied hides directly.

The cattle industry witnessed as much violation of the law as did the yerbales.

Rustling proved common and ranchers were well advised to brand yearlings as quickly as possible. The Laws of the Indies were consistently violated in the grant of mercedes (Bastos 1962: 449). Widows and minors were despoiled of the use of their land as rapacious neighbors simply moved their cattle in.[30] Maximizing profits and paying absolutely no attention to the revenue-producing desires of governors, ranchers consistently avoided payment of the sales tax on cattle—as well as the tithe. In some very good years for the yerba industry, the sales tax paid upon cattle sales in the Villa Real de la Concepción—the center for the northern yerba industry and site of a *subdelegación* of the Asunción Treasury—was for no more than eighty head.[31] Estancieros paid taxes only on cattle sold to the state—generally to provision the forts on the frontier when the estancias del rey could not meet their needs, or to the tobacco monopoly. They would not pay the sales tax on private sales.[32]

The drive north to the Río Apá in the 1780s had repercussions on more than the economy. Throughout Paraguayan history, settlers had been faced with the problems of an Indian frontier, and nomadic tribes of Guaycurús roamed on horseback from the Mato Grosso into the Gran Chaco, and also south to the Río Ypané. The attitude of the various Indian groups was always of concern to governors, who recognized the risk and expense of frontier war.[33] Militia action was not cheap. Just as in other areas of Spanish America, gifts to Indians and conciliation cost less and were more productive of tranquility as "it is the only method to achieve the benevolence of all these nations [of Indians] who could cause us notable damage if they combined with the Portuguese or refused to deal with us."[34] Governors repeatedly ordered officials to treat with the Indians and avoid harassing them. Governors encouraged secular and regular clergy to "civilize" the northern Indians by founding reducciones such as Belén on the Río Ypané (Blujacki 1972: 65–79; Saeger 1989: 61–68). Even so, the greatest obstacle to good relations with Indians was the general Hispano-Guaraní dislike and antagonism toward non-Guaraní Indian groups. This contempt has at times pervaded all segments of Paraguayan society and has been a blot upon the history of this region. Indians who were not "civilized" (i.e., not Christians and who led a nomadic life) were considered not quite human.

By the mid-eighteenth century, many Guaycurús had become dependent on certain aspects of European civilization. The use of iron tools and weapons had wreaked havoc upon the palmares (a source of food and fiber) and the animals they traditionally had hunted (Saeger 1989: 59). By the end of the colonial period, they greatly depended upon beef for food. Governors of Paraguay understood this. In addition to gifts of clothing and iron, as well as vesting chieftains with symbolic authority, they sporadically supplied cattle to tribes.

In return, the Indians were expected to keep the peace, refrain from close contacts with the Portuguese to the north, and limit their raids upon the herds of the new estancias.

Nonetheless, hostilities between Paraguayans and Indians in the north did occur. Yerberos were taken captive and regularly they were ransomed by the government. Indians at times raided the yerba camps, but their main target was not humans. Rather, they plundered the garden plots of humble Paraguayans and the cattle of the estancias—the latter for food and to sell to the neighboring Portuguese. Complaints about such cattle raids became common in the 1780s and 1790s. The northern ranchers, who were generally also militia officers, took matters into their own hands in 1796. In May, the militia of Villa Real de la Concepción assaulted a camp of "peaceful" Mbayás. One hundred fifteen Indians were killed with forty being "passed to the knife" after surrendering. An investigation ensued to ascertain the reason for that outrage but "it was managed in such a way that the aggressors escaped without punishment" (Lastarria 1914: 92). War then erupted in the north as other Mbayás took revenge for the massacre by raiding ranches between the Apá and Aquidabán Rivers. What Governor Lázaro de Ribera had feared came to pass—a full-scale and expensive Indian war and one that spilled over into the yerbales. Until an unsteady peace was secured in the late 1790s, little cattle raising or yerba gathering north of the Aquidabán was possible.

Militia service in the north was unpopular, both for the officers and the enlisted men. The general routine of the militia consisted of garrisoning forts and patrolling the avenues of Indian access into the cattle ranges. It was uncomfortable, boring, and poorly paid. Desertion was common as militiamen resented the time spent away from their chacras or from the more profitable yerba industry.[35] One might purchase from the Ramo de Guerra an exemption from militia service for a small fee, and many vaqueros had that release given to them by their masters. Still, the best proof of the unpopularity of militia service was seen in the flood of exemptions by cultivators under contract to the processing factory of the tobacco monopoly between 1800 and 1802—just as the province underwent a militia reorganization and in the midst of a war against the Portuguese (Frakes 1989: 494–95).[36]

The drive north not only brought the Paraguayans into closer contact with the Guaycurús but also with the Portuguese who at the same time were pushing south in the Mato Grosso down the Paraguay River valley (Bastos 1979: 25–87). A clandestine trade in cattle, horse, and mules out of the Concepción region rapidly ensued in return for gold from the Portuguese mines to the north. That was troublesome enough to governors of Paraguay, but they also worried about

Portuguese influence over Indians in the border area. Not only could Indians supply intelligence to the Portuguese at the fort of Coimbra, but they sold stolen livestock to the Lusitanians as well.[37]

Eventually, full-scale war against the Portuguese erupted and the Paraguayan participation in the War of Oranges (1800–1) was a fiasco. Governor Lázaro de Ribera rashly believed that he could fulfill the old dream of expelling the Portuguese from the entire Paraguay River valley and mounted an expedition against Coimbra in the Mato Grosso. Ribera's ambition was greater than his military skill and the assault failed. The province at the same time was weakened by the fruitless dispatch of other troops to help defend Misiones. On the heels of the Coimbra failure the Portuguese and their Indian allies stormed and destroyed Fuerte San Carlos on the Río Apá (Correa Filho 1925: 140–52). Only the conclusion of the war in Europe and a return to the status quo ante bellum in this region saved Ribera from further reverses (Frakes 1989: 506–8). The prompt response by Portuguese authorities in Mato Grosso to Paraguay's challenge essentially confirmed the Río Apá as the effective boundary of the province of Paraguay and signified an end to the northward territorial expansion of this era.

The expansion of Paraguay's yerba frontier was a result of a felicitous conjuncture of six critical factors: plentiful yerbales, an adequate labor supply, the internal administrative and economic reforms of the Bourbon era, a supply of easy credit from porteño merchants, a market for this commodity that transcended even viceregal borders, and the ease and low cost of river transport by which good returns were made on shipping high-bulk, low-profit merchandise.

While concern about Portuguese advances prompted royal authorities to expand Asunción's control to the north, it was the exploitation of the yerbales that really consolidated Paraguayan power in the region north of the Río Jejuí. The yerba industry pulled a significant population into the north and away from the Río Paraguay. At the same time, the littoral settlements prospered as shipping points for yerba from the interior as well as initial foci for agriculture and the cattle industry of this region. Asunción entered into a prosperous "golden age" in the late colonial era as immigrant merchants made it the center of yerba shipping for the entire upper Plata, while revenues on yerba exports fueled the greater tasks of government in the Intendencia era. Finally, even though frontier expansion was halted as a result of the War of Oranges, the present northern limits of eastern Paraguay were effectively solidified in this era—mainly as a result of expansion of the yerba frontier.

Certainly yerba maté was the most important product from the north in the Intendencia period, but it was the cattle frontier that had the greatest long-term impact upon Paraguayan society. Regardless of their disregard for the Laws of the Indies pertaining to cattle mercedes, governors did succeed in a significant distribution of land in medium-sized, legal portions. Félix de Azara (1943: 10–11) believed that this manner of distribution encouraged a frugal, diligent husbandry among recipients. At the same time, many landless Paraguayans became independent landholders. Was there an element of social mobility on the northern frontier? Any final answer awaits further research but it does appear that there was.

In addition, members of the old elite underwent a significant transformation. Many of them, or at least their second and third sons, ceased their petitions for encomiendas, abandoned the Asunción and Cordillera regions, and moved to the frontier to serve the yerba industry by their pastoral pursuits. The rapid peninsular-merchant domination of Asunción and the strange lack of a criollo response to that domination becomes more understandable in light of new frontier opportunities. Rather than losing social and economic influence during the Intendencia and Francia eras, as standard wisdom would have it, the old elite, now more firmly based in the campo than before, actually expanded its power. The new areas of settlement needed militia officers, *jueces comisarios*, and other minor royal officials. Recipients of cattle mercedes filled almost all of these posts, and the traditional directing elite of Paraguay flourished on the northern frontier just as it had in other times and other places in the province. It was this elite, with its origin in the mercedes of land in the late colonial era, that retained its pervasive power in the campo until the 1930s (Whigham 1991a: 27–29). The frontier expansion of the province in the late colonial era and the resultant exploitation of the yerbales produced a social and economic impact that extended far into the national era.

10

The Río de la Plata and the Greater Southwest

A View from World-System Theory

THOMAS D. HALL

Hall applies the insights of world-system analysis to processes of frontier formation and destruction on both the northern and southern edges of the Spanish Empire as the regions slowly and haltingly became incorporated into regional and global economies. Hall emphasizes that frontiers can only be understood as zones of interaction between both global and local forces.

IT IS A CLICHÉ that historians and sociologists study history in different ways. My approach is to examine historical evidence in order to discern general patterns and processes, and then devise systematic explanations—theories—for those patterns. These then suggest new ways to examine old and new evidence. Such investigations, in turn, typically suggest limitations, extensions, modifications, and rejections of the original theory. In this cycle, facts that do not fit current theory are of most interest precisely because they point to the limitations and directions for extension and modification of extant theory (Abbott 1991; Abrams 1982; J. R. Hall 1991; Ragin 1987; Tilly 1981). This chapter presents one such cycle.

One of the thorniest problems is the creation, transformation, and destruction of frontiers. I want to extend Richard Slatta's (1990a, 1992a) metaphor of the frontier as a membrane. Viewed from a global perspective the frontier is relatively narrow and sharp. Viewed more closely it is a broad zone with considerable internal differentiation both spatially and temporally. From either level, the "membrane" varies in its permeability and symmetry with respect to goods and individuals flowing through it.

There are few systematic theories of frontier formation and transformation. World-system theory, an account of the rise and expansion of European powers during the last five hundred years, should be useful for this task (Chase-Dunn 1989; Shannon 1996; Taylor 1993). Because expansion of the European world-system entailed incorporation of new areas and peoples, it also created frontiers. Unfortunately, many world-system accounts of frontiers proceed from the large to the local forces, and fail to take into account how local forces and actors shape the process. Issues of class, gender, and race or ethnicity have been neglected. The point is *not* that this approach is wrong, but that it is incomplete.[1]

Based on my study of the incorporation of what we now know as the U.S. or American Southwest into Spain, Mexico, and the United States, I have begun to develop a world-system-theory–based account of incorporation and frontier formation. It focuses on zones of incorporation of formerly external areas and peoples into the growing world-system, since this is where the formation, transformation, and destruction of frontiers occurs. From this perspective, the *interactions* of local, regional, colonial or national, and global forces are all examined, with attention to differences in processes by race or ethnicity, class, and gender (Dunaway 1994, 1996a, 1996b, 1996c; T. Hall 1989a, 1989b, 1996b; Harris 1990; Kardulias 1990; Meyer 1990, 1991, 1994). This is one way of bridging the *frontier-region dichotomy* and other oppositional dualisms that have plagued Western history (for a detailed review of these issues, see Klein 1996 and Wrobel 1996).

Recent attempts to expand world-system theory to precapitalist settings have given rise to many elaborations and modifications of the theory (see Chase-Dunn and Hall 1997; T. Hall 1996a, 1996b; Hall and Chase-Dunn 1994). Relevant to this discussion are the further elaborations of the concepts of incorporation and frontier formation (Chase-Dunn and Hall 1997: chap. 4). Most germane here are the distinctions among tributary world-systems (i.e., precapitalist, state-based world-systems) and between merchant and production capitalist world-systems, and especially that each type of world-system engenders different types and processes of incorporation, and consequently of frontier formation and transformation.

The comparison of frontier processes in the Greater Southwest (the U.S. Southwest and northern Mexico) with those in the Río de la Plata region of South America provides an opportunity to focus on local and regional forces because the colonial and global forces were approximately the same in both places. The time frame covered by these studies bridges the transformation of the European world-system from merchant to production capitalism. This is the era in which accumulation of capital through exploitation of price differentials across different regions was replaced by accumulation of capital through ownership and control of the production process itself (Chase-Dunn and Hall 1997: chap. 5). Thus, this comparison offers a further opportunity to study how frontier process shaped this transformation.

Before examining these frontiers, I will reconsider a few general issues. First is the concept of *tribe.* The term encompasses a wide range of social organizations, a range that is significantly broader than that encompassed by the term *state* (Fried 1967, 1975; T. Hall 1989a; Kavanagh 1996, especially chaps. 1 and 8). The imprecision in this term is rooted in the relations between indigenous peoples and Europeans. Eric Wolf (1982) has demonstrated that European contact typically transformed indigenous nonstate societies in a variety of ways. Ferguson and Whitehead (1992) extended his analysis to show that state interactions with nonstate societies usually provoke a drastic increase in violence throughout the zone of contact, both between the state and nonstate societies and beyond the frontier among nonstate societies. They present evidence that this effect is nearly universal.[2] Their observations suggest that Hobbesian images of tribal peoples are rarely accurate reflections of precontact conditions, but typically are reflections of the effects of their contacts with state societies.

In addition to increasing the level of violence, such interactions often transformed indigenous social organizations, sometimes amalgamating tribes from a collection of related bands, at other times fragmenting tribes into competing bands. Thus, most tribes are products of interaction between state and nonstate societies. This means that in studying indigenous societies scholars must pay attention to how indigenous peoples actually made their living, their actual forms of social and political organization, and the degree of coincidence between their concept of themselves and their organizational structures. Scholars must be cautious in reading descriptions of even the very earliest European observers into the precontact setting, unless they have independent evidence for doing so. Such evidence will be archaeological, not archival.

The coincidence between society and polity is often problematic. As a rule of thumb, among nonstate societies the people encompassed within any self-appellation, such as the Navajo term *Diné* (the people), is typically larger than the political organizations found within the group.[3] Padden ([1957] 1985: 328–31), among others, shows how ethnocentricism often blinded Spaniards to such differences. Spaniards often projected their own social organization onto newly encountered groups, or saw them as barbarians without social organization.

European colonizers are not the only ones to read currently observed social organizations into the distant past. Contemporary writers sometimes extend present group organizations and identities into the past, a practice known as *ethnographic upstreaming.* As Thomas Sheridan (1988a) cautions, avoiding ethnographic upstreaming is especially important in frontier settings because of tremendous changes that occur beyond the frontier, long before literate observers document them. Conversely, scholars also need to be cautious about *ethnographic downstreaming* (K. Jones 1994a); that is, presuming historical practices continue unchanged.

Exchanges between representatives of states and tribal peoples are another problematic issue. Are such exchanges really "gifts" as state officials typically call them? Or, are they "tribute" or "extortion payments," as they might be described from the nonstate side of the exchange? There are two intertwined problems here. First, states seldom admit defeat by less-developed groups. Chinese documents are notorious for describing tribute payments to steppe warlords as gifts (Barfield 1989; T. Hall 1991). Second, what may seem relatively inconsequential to a state may be of major significance to tribal recipients in terms of building political alliances, validating status, or even providing basic subsistence. The point is to be cautious in accepting the labels of historical observers and to remain attuned to the asymmetries in such exchanges.

With these cautions in mind, I now turn to comparisons of these two frontiers.

Viceroyalty of the Río de la Plata and Northern New Spain as Frontiers

Modern cartographic practice and political realities make it far too easy to accept precise boundaries for all sorts of geographic boundaries. However, empirically most boundaries are not sharp lines but gradients of transition or fuzzy zones that, like membranes, often change shape. Thus, defining a region requires considerable care.

Following the assumptions of this volume, I define the Greater Southwest as the northern frontier of New Spain, the viceroyalty encompassing Mexico, the U.S. Southwest, and much of Central America. Beginning in 1776, the political, military, cultural, and geographic distinctiveness of northern New Spain was recognized by the Spanish Crown with the creation of the Provincias Internas ("interior provinces") encompassing Sonora-Sinaloa (including southern Arizona), Texas y Coahuila, the Californias, Nueva Vizcaya, Nuevo México, Nuevo Léon, and Nuevo Santander (Tamaulipas). A comandante general with broad political and military authority and direct access to Spain governed the Provincias Internas.[4] This streamlined the administration of the northern provinces and allowed the comandante general to respond quickly to threats to the security of northern New Spain from both Native American and European foes.

The Río de la Plata region includes modern Argentina, Uruguay, Paraguay, and most of Bolivia. The northern part of Argentina and southern Bolivia is semidesert, known as the Chaco (Morris 1981: 48). The region immediately south of Buenos Aires to the Río Salado is known as the pampas húmedas. Further south and west are the pampas secas, while south of the Río Negro are the Patagonian steppes (J. Cole 1965; Morris 1981: 52).

A major physiographic difference between the Río de la Plata region and the Greater Southwest is that in the former the plains front on the ocean and are transected by navigable rivers. From a Spanish point of view, the mountains bordering the pampas were an "empty quarter."[5] This is the reverse in the Greater Southwest, where the highest population densities occurred in the foothills of the Sierra Madre and the mountainous river valleys of Sonora, where the plains were a relatively "empty quarter," where no rivers were navigated on a regular basis, and where the nearest oceanic port was nearly a thousand miles away.[6]

The two regions also differ in the types of terrain that separate them from more populated areas. Mountains and jungles divided most of the Río de la Plata region from Peruvian silver mines and their Hispanic and indio populations. While difficult to traverse, much of this terrain was capable of some development. The Incas developed a road linking much of the Andean region to northern Argentina. Many towns were founded during the colonial era to facilitate trade (Rock 1985). The Greater Southwest, on the other hand, was isolated from central Mexico by the "Chichimec Sea," the vast desert and semidesert areas of what is now north-central Mexico. Overland transportation to the capital was arduous and hazardous, rendering shipment of goods very expensive.

Finally, there is much more variability in the terrain of the Río de la Plata—jungles, plains, mountains, deserts, and a major river system—than in that of the Greater Southwest. If only what is now the U.S. Southwest, or even New Mexico, is compared with the pampean region, however, the reverse is true. Six of the seven commonly differentiated climatic zones exist in New Mexico alone; only the arctic zone is missing (Beck 1962). Furthermore, variation in the U.S. Southwest seems to be more close-grained than in the pampas. Mountains run through New Mexico and Arizona, there are true deserts (Sonoran and Chihuahuan), and much of the region is in the Basin and Range province, marked by relatively small mountainous areas scattered through desert areas. The Great Plains mark the eastern and northeastern border of the region. Lesser La Plata is made up of vast plains, the pampas, which become nearly desert as they merge into foothills, then mountains in the west, while they gradually become moister, changing into jungle areas to the northeast. One consequence of these differences is greater variability in human adaptations to the land *over short distances* throughout the U.S. Southwest. These differences had, and continue to have, important consequences for human use and development of these two regions.

The pampean region and the U.S. Southwest shared a large number of similarities and a few major differences. Initially, both regions were explored and colonized due to rumors of wealth—stories of Trapalanda in La Plata and Cíbola in New Mexico—and to block European rivals from access to known silver-producing areas—Portuguese from Potosí and French and British from Zacatecas (Bolton 1929; T. Hall 1989a: 75–109; Rock 1985: 8, 27–28). In noting the parallel rumors of riches, I cannot help but wonder whether these were either manufactured, or at least fueled, by the Spanish Crown in order to convince wealthy *hidalgos* to invest in entradas and colonization efforts. A situation of new discoveries with little or no concrete knowledge is ripe for rapid spread of rumors—and for state manipulation of them.

Neither region proved to have wealth either in the form of minerals or abundant Indians suitable for labor.[7] Disease and resistance quickly exhausted labor extracted from local Indians. Consequently, Indian labor never played a major role in these economies as it had in Peru or Mexico. Both regions had initial colonies that were destroyed by Indians and then redeveloped. Both were plagued by contraband trade. The pampas supplied almost nothing to the mines; that was the role of the Argentine northwest. The seventeenth and early eighteenth centuries were marked by relative neglect and slow, if sporadic, local economic and political growth. Both regions were major conduits of horses to indigenous peoples, and in the pampean region, for cattle.

Spain imposed similar changes, the Bourbon Reforms, on both regions in the late eighteenth century. In both regions, the reforms led to increased prosperity, followed in the Southwest by increasing neglect as Spain became more deeply embroiled in European wars and agitation for independence began. The movements for independence occurred in the early nineteenth century. After independence, however, with stronger incorporation into a world-system now dominated by production capitalism, the histories of the two regions diverged.

Within these broad similarities there were important differences. First, the European rivals who threatened the early colonies were different. More important within the New World, Europe, and globally, their geopolitical positions were different (see Collins 1981; Wallerstein 1991). The Portuguese were next door to the pampas region. For many years, by special agreement, they were major suppliers to early Buenos Aires (Rock 1985). The bandeirantes of São

Paulo also mounted enormous organized slave raids that stripped away thousands of Indians from the Jesuit Guaraní missions, while Portuguese in Brazil periodically wrested territory away from the Spanish Crown. French and British rivals in North America, on the other hand, were distant from northern New Spain and, in the early centuries, were more of a potential than a real threat.

Second, the roles of Indians differed. In Peru and Bolivia sedentary agricultural Indians were pressed into service on encomiendas and repartimientos, as happened to a lesser extent in Sinaloa, Sonora, and Nueva Vizcaya. In both the pampean region and New Mexico, such labor was not very important, although New Mexican Pueblos were occasionally subjected to forced labor. In New Mexico, trade in captive Indians seems to have played a more significant role. Moreover, Indian resistance was significantly different. The first Spanish colony in the pampean region, Buenos Aires, never really became established until it was refounded in 1580. For many years this outpost played a peripheral role in the region. In New Mexico, the Pueblo Revolt (1680) was a major regional event that destroyed a colony already eight decades old.

A third difference was their roles in the silver trade and silver production. The upper reaches of the Río de la Plata region—Tucumán, Salta, and Santiago del Estero—were also intended to supply necessary materials for the mines. Sinaloa, Sonora, Nueva Vizcaya, and Nuevo León performed a similar role, while Arizona, New Mexico, Texas, and later Alta California supplied only a few goods and captive Indians for the mines during the seventeenth and eighteenth centuries. While such trade was important for New Mexico, it was of marginal importance for the mining economy. Occasionally silver was smuggled through Buenos Aires, whereas little or no silver left through the far north before Mexican independence. Both the Río de la Plata and the Provincias Internas were rumps of the Spanish Empire. In the case of the pampean region, this changed with the establishment of the Viceroyalty of the Río de la Plata in 1776 to protect the region against the Portuguese. In contrast, New Mexico and the far north were "the periphery of the periphery" (Weber 1982: 282).

For both regions, accidental transfers of technology produced dramatic changes. On the pampas, the presence of feral cattle and horses facilitated massive transformations of Indian culture, subsistence, and probably population densities (Baretta and Markoff 1978; Nichols 1939; Worcester 1945). In North America, horses enabled equally spectacular changes—especially among Plains groups (Lowie 1954; Mishkin [1940] 1992; Secoy [1953] 1992).

In the sixteenth and seventeenth centuries, nomadic Indians were serious threats to both regions. Through the late seventeenth or some time in the eighteenth century, nomadic Indians remained a major threat in New Mexico, Arizona, and Texas as well as in the pampas. However, this threat was crosscut by extensive trading relations with nomadic Indians. The trading-raiding-endemic warfare complex that characterized New Mexico and surrounding areas for centuries (T. Hall 1989a: chaps. 4 and 5) also became endemic in the pampas region as the "Araucanization of the desert" took place (see Jones, this volume).

A major difference was the rise of the hide trade in the Río de la Plata in the late eighteenth century. The region became more tightly incorporated into the European world-economy through the hide trade and silver smuggling, whereas the Southwest, with the possible exception of Alta California, remained a rump of the empire. This growth led in turn to the development of an extremely strong merchant class, a somewhat weaker land controlling class, and more urban development. These factors, as well as the prospects of increased international commerce for the pampean region, consequently set the stage for very different paths to independence.

The impact of the Bourbon Reforms dramatically changed the often parallel history of the two peripheries of the Spanish Empire. In 1776, the Viceroyalty of the Río de la Plata was carved out of the Viceroyalty of Peru. In New Spain the Provincias Internas were organized and reorganized several times, but they remained part of the Viceroyalty of New Spain. During the independence movements, both regions experienced regional revolts. While the Viceroyalty of the Río de la Plata fragmented after independence, Mexico remained relatively intact. Texas was a major exception. However, the majority of its inhabitants had recently come from the United States (Weber 1982).

For the nineteenth century, the major difference between Argentina and Mexico is captured in Porfirio Díaz's lament, "Alas, poor Mexico! So far from God, so close to the United States." Argentina did not lose half its land and a tenth of its population to a more populous, more powerful, rising core power. While independence increased trade in both regions, and the Viceroyalty of the Río de la Plata ultimately became four separate nations, Buenos Aires already was a major entrepôt. Santa Fe became an important trading center with the opening the Santa Fe Trail in 1821, but no community in New Mexico, Arizona, Texas, or even Alta California remotely approached Buenos Aires in size or economic importance. After independence the portion of the Southwest annexed into the United States became part of a rising core power, whereas Argentina remained at best semiperipheral, and the remaining countries peripheral.

The Mexican government generally was less stable than was the case for Argentina. In the first decades of independence, the average Mexican government lasted less than one year (Simpson 1966). Consequently, Mexico had few resources with which to develop or defend its northern provinces. In the 1870s, in contrast, Argentina finally managed the "conquest of the desert," which bears a closer resemblance to the United States' pacification of nomadic Indians in the decades after its annexation of the Southwest than it does to Mexico's desultory and ineffective attempts to control its northern provinces (K. Jones 1993, 1994b).

To account for all these similarities and differences would take more pages than can be allotted to this chapter. Nevertheless, it is possible to explain some of the differences and to trace the different trajectories of these frontiers. I begin with relations to and with indigenous populations.

Both the Viceroyalty of the Río de la Plata and the Greater Southwest show broadly similar ranges of variation with respect to types of indigenous organization. In both regions, societies ranged from elementary bands through chiefdoms.[8] In the pampean region, the range of types *seems* narrower, which is congruent with less geographical variation. Whether this is due to relative paucity of information on the Pampas Indian groups or to effects of state-nonstate interactions remains unclear.

A second difference between the two regions appears in the ways in which Spaniards related to groups at either end of the range of types of nonstate societies. In the U.S. Southwest and Sonora the general rule was to attempt to exploit the agricultural, sedentary peoples, either through tribute demands in goods or through labor, and generally to exclude nomadic hunter-gatherers. To be sure there were many attempts to force nomads into reducciones, but these, with the temporary exception of the Apache peace camps, were most notable in their failure (Griffen 1988a; O. Jones 1979). The major exception to exclusion of nomads was the Comanche peace established in New Mexico in 1786 (John 1975; Kavanagh 1996).

Throughout the Río de la Plata, by contrast, there were many attempts to enslave agricultural Indians. Indeed, Jesuit missionaries had to organize a systematic defense against Portuguese bandeirante slavers (Rock 1985). Eventually disease undercut these attempts as Indian populations declined. Slave raiding, encomiendas, and forced labor all provoked Indian resistance. Nomadic Indians were systematically and forcefully excluded from Spanish society. Spaniards seldom attempted to missionize nomadic Indians, especially on the southern pampas, and until the time of Rosas in the 1830s, made little attempt to conquer them. Finally, one phenomenon occurred in the pampean region that seems not to have occurred or to have been very rare in the Southwest, namely voluntary migration *into* Indian societies by Spaniards, especially by gauchos (Padden [1957] 1985; Slatta 1983).

Both regions seem to have shared a condition of endemic warfare engendered by broadly similar, but not identical, processes. These consist of the spread of horses, and later guns; involvement in trade relations; and by the late eighteenth century increasing scarcity of resources. Often, nomadic foragers had little or nothing of interest to Spaniards other than captives taken from enemies or, later, goods stolen from other Spaniards. Kinship obligations required raided groups to exact vengeance on the raiders, thus they needed to obtain horses and guns. Endemic warfare very quickly became the norm. Alliances shifted rapidly and feuds constantly rekindled due to the need for vengeance and access to Spanish goods.

The most significant difference between the two regions is the apparent direction in which the majority of captives moved.[9] In New Mexico, Spaniards took far more captives than they gave up; on the pampas, Spaniards appear to have given up more captives than they took. The explanation for this difference is found in the nature of captives taken.

In both regions, captives seem to have been overwhelmingly women and children (T. Hall 1989a; K. Jones 1994b; Socolow 1992). This preference is quite common in state-nonstate conflicts. Regardless of the direction of flow of captives, adult males are seen as problematic. First, the nearly universal male obligation of warfare, defense, and resistance makes adult male captives particularly intractable and hazardous, especially when held captive near their homeland. Second, adults are much harder to resocialize than children, especially if the resocialization is coerced.

Third, when the captive "exchange" is between nomadic hunter-gatherers and sedentary agriculturists, adult males are not particularly useful as laborers, but for different reasons according to the direction of captivity. Adult males taken from foraging societies do not make very good coerced laborers in agricultural settings. Spaniards all over the Western Hemisphere complained of this. This complaint was also found among farmers in the United States (Hurtado 1988; Knack 1987). Adult males taken from sedentary societies are not particularly useful in nomadic societies. The nature of life and work in nomadic societies necessarily entails a great deal of individual freedom. Supervision of captives costs more effort than the work they could be forced to do, so it is easier to kill them.

For women and children, however, there was an entirely different calculation of value. In any society with high infant mortality rates (which means *all* societies before the mid-nineteenth century), adult women are especially valuable for their reproductive capacity. Since many societies indigenous to both regions preferred polygyny, the role of secondary wife was readily available. The Spanish preoccupation with the sexual fidelity of women is one reason why many

European women chose to stay with Indian captors (Socolow 1992). Furthermore, secondary wives performed the bulk of menial labor, often under the supervision of the primary wife. At times this labor may have been the primary motive for capturing women. Ties of affection for children born in captivity would have tempered the women's desire to flee.[10]

Captured Indian women presented an entirely different problem in Spanish society. They could be forced into the role of servant—both in daily labor and in sexual services—yet there was no acceptable role for them. Also, children born to captured Indian women had a lower caste status, even on extreme frontiers where such distinctions were sometimes not so tightly drawn (R. Gutiérrez 1991). Here, too, attachment to children could keep captive women from running away.

In both New Mexico and on the pampas, offspring of captured Spanish women were accepted more readily into Indian societies than were mixed-blooded children in Spanish society. The relatively greater acceptance of their children may have been an incentive for captured Spanish women to remain in Indian societies. The same differential acceptance was accorded captured children. Among most nomadic foragers, a child raised in captivity often was adopted and became a full-fledged member of the group. The best a captured Indian child raised in Spanish society could hope for (in New Mexico at least) was to be considered *genízaro* (T. Hall 1989a, 1989b; Horvath 1977, 1979).

There appears to have been no equivalent of the genízaros on the pampas, except possibly gauchos. It is especially revealing that in her recounting of the role of Indian frontier trade, Kristine Jones (this volume) does not report development of new ethnic communities (ethnogenesis) based on intercultural trade or warfare. Similarly, in her account of women on the pampas, Susan Socolow does not find mixed-blood, transitional communities—unless, of course, one considers gauchos such a group.

Finally, for children raised in captivity, the possibilities of returning to their native group were limited. They would have been socialized in a completely inappropriate manner, and their emotional ties would have been to their captors. The general acceptance of such children within Indian societies obviated the pressure to form distinctive communities. Two cautions are in order. First, differences in degree of acceptance of non-native children are relative, not absolute. Second, while the patterns hold as rules of thumb, there are exceptions in some Hispanic and Indian communities. A number of Mexican boys captured by the Apaches while they were children later rejoined Mexican society and served as scouts in campaigns against their former captors.

All of these processes took place in somewhat different geopolitical contexts, each of which contained significant internal variations. Thus, this brief discussion of captives illustrates how general processes—frontier expansion, intercultural slave raiding, gender preferences among slaves, and so on—varied from region to region and were shaped by local differences, including needs for labor, for reproductive capacity, for household servants, for ethnic soldiers, and so on.

A major difference between the Greater Southwest and the Río de la Plata was in the barrier and buffer roles of nomadic groups. During the early and mid-eighteenth century, Comanche bands posed a serious threat to the security of New Mexico and Texas. Comanches allied with other enemies of the Spaniards sacked the new mission and presidio of San Sabá in central Texas in 1758. The following year, armed with French muskets, Comanches and their Wichita allies defeated a Spanish punitive expedition led by Colonel Diego Ortiz Parrilla in a fortified village of the Taovayas on the Red River. After Governor Juan Bautista de Anza of New Mexico hammered out the "Comanche Peace" in 1786, however, Comanches provided a singularly effective "border patrol" for New Mexico. The interior nomads, notably Apache bands, became a barrier to internal commerce and communication between northern New Spain and the interior. This in large part explains their differential treatment by Spanish officials. Comanches experienced tremendous pressure for political centralization and for a while actually formed a unitary tribe.[11] Apaches experienced tremendous pressures for further decentralization and fragmentation (John 1975; Weber 1992).

In the pampean region, Indians seemed to play neither role, with the possible exception of east bank Indians early in the colonial era, who may have buffered Spanish-Portuguese rivalry. Rather, the Indians of the pampas were a barrier to Spanish expansion. That is, they retarded the outward spread of the frontier—as the term is typically used in the United States. While nomadic Indians certainly hampered trade and communication with frontier areas and occasionally hampered access to salt mines, they did not form a barrier to communication and commerce between the frontier and the center. And in some cases, as Kristine Jones argues (this volume), they may actually have accelerated expansion via trade.

A possible parallel between Araucanians and Comanches does exist in the late-eighteenth- and early-nineteenth-century expansions of both groups. Comanches became the "Lords of the South Plains" (Wallace and Hoebel 1952); Araucanians seem to have been well on the way to becoming the "Lords of the South Pampas" (see Jones this volume). Comanches achieved such preeminence primarily through their buffering role and their trade with New Mexicans. Araucanians did the same through their middleman role in frontier trade, taking advantage of the increase in trade that accompanied the Bourbon Reforms in the late eighteenth century.

Nevertheless, intertribal relations that developed under these conditions differed. After the Comanche peace (1786), the employment of Comanches as allies against Apaches became the norm. The Araucanians typically allied with southern Pampas tribes in trade relations. Later, Rosas was singularly effective in using southern Pampas groups against one another.

The Bourbon Reforms brought to both regions an increase in trade, an attendant increase in prosperity, and changes in Indian relations at similar times and through the efforts of special Spanish leaders. These leaders shared three vital characteristics: (1) they knew the frontier well and understood Indian organization and leadership; (2) they had an interest in promoting peace and expanding settled territory; and (3) they had resources with which to do this. These three conditions converged in both regions, but at different times and for somewhat different reasons.

In New Mexico, Governors Anza and Concha put their extensive knowledge to work to build a peace treaty with the Comanche bands (John 1975, 1984). The Comanche peace was enduring and lasted well into Mexican era. On the pampas, independence, the growing cattle trade, and the need to build a constituency from which to make a bid for national leadership enabled Juan Manuel de Rosas to make a significant expansion of Argentine territory, but this did not occur until the first half of the nineteenth century.

During the nineteenth century Pax Britannica, the final Indian wars were fought. Cowboys spread widely in the hemisphere and nearly as rapidly disappeared from the scene (Slatta 1983, 1990b). Massive migrations increased the number of European settlers in the New World. The slave trade and slavery were abolished throughout most of the world, the costs of transportation dropped radically, and agriculture began to be mechanized. These processes played out differently in the U.S. Southwest and Argentina.

California, Arizona, New Mexico, and Texas became part of the United States. The factors and forces that motivated this imperialistic land grab involved closely balanced international, national, and regional forces and counterforces that slowly, if seemingly inexorably, tilted toward war (T. Hall 1988, 1989a). These changes set the conditions for internal differentiation of development in what now actually became the U.S. Southwest. Texas and California became states in 1845 and 1850 respectively, while New Mexico languished as a territory for another six decades. In 1863, its western half became Arizona during the U.S. Civil War as means of blocking a potential Confederate land bridge from Texas to the California ports. Once the Civil War was over, the conquest of indigenous populations in the United States was rapidly accomplished (Utley 1984).

The relationships of Comanche and Apache bands to the United States reversed their former relationships to New Spain and Mexico: Comanches became a barrier to internal commerce in the United States, whereas Apache groups became nuisances along a relatively unimportant border until the construction of the Atlantic & Pacific and Southern Pacific transcontinental railroads and the resulting expansion of the livestock and mining industries made Arizona and New Mexico more valuable pieces of real estate.

Within the United States railroads crossed the continent, grain agriculture converted the "Great American Desert" into the great American breadbasket, the buffalo herds were all but destroyed, and Indians were transformed from "red menaces" to quaint "tourist attractions." In New Mexico and Arizona, nomadic Indians were finally turned into sedentary groups on reservations. Former Confederate officers, carpetbaggers, and fortune seekers found prosperity for a while in supplying both Indians on reservations and the armies that put and kept them there. The Hispanic residents of New Mexico, southern Colorado, and Arizona became second-class citizens in their own homeland as their lands were seized in a variety of schemes. Meanwhile, many Indians maintained somewhat better control of their land because of their special relationship with the federal government (Briggs and Van Ness 1987).

For both Indians and Hispanics, however, the process of incorporation was not as rapid or as traumatic as it was in California or Texas, where Anglo immigrants overwhelmed Mexican communities and all but destroyed the indigenous population (Hurtado 1988). Until the construction of the railroads, Anglo-Americans did not flock to either Arizona or New Mexico as they did to California. An unintended, but somewhat benign, side effect of this relative neglect was that the pressures to assimilate and acculturate were far less on southwestern Indians than on nearly all other Indians in the United States. This gave them time to adjust, to adapt, and to modify Anglo customs to meet their needs.

The processes in the Viceroyalty of the Río de la Plata region were different. Independence brought the breakup of former administrative units into separate countries. There was an initial spate of British investment in Argentina, then withdrawal that was not reinstituted until the last third of the century. There were two major waves of Indian wars. The first, led by Juan Manuel de Rosas in the 1830s, pushed the frontier south of the Río Salado and opened the humid pampas to development. The second, Julio Roca's "conquest of the desert" in the 1870s, opened the entire Argentine pampas and Patagonia to development. Both wars found their impetus in growing trade, which itself was part of larger, systematic changes in the world-system.

The continuing "Araucanization of the pampas" had important consequences for the courses and results of these wars. At first, participation in frontier trade gave Indians greater access to Spanish goods and better knowledge of Spanish customs, making them more formidable foes (K. Jones 1989, this volume). But as the process continued during the nineteenth century, Indians became increasingly dependent on trade supplies due to population growth and more intensive harvesting of feral animals. This dependence made them more liable to Argentine control through coercion or disruption of trade networks. Rosas, but especially Roca, used trade dependence against Indians and explicitly imitated the procedures the United States had used against the Plains Indians (K. Jones 1994b).

As industrialization and urbanization proceeded in the core (or "first world"), the demand for raw materials—hides, meat, and wool—from peripheral areas (or "third world") increased dramatically. Price increases were sufficient to make the opening of the pampas economically attractive. In the mid-nineteenth century, sheep began to displace cattle ranches further into the pampas. By late in the century, demand for these products increased even more as transportation technology made it economically feasible to transport Argentinean products, especially meat, over long distances.

The second wave of British investment brought railroads that facilitated transportation of interior products to Buenos Aires for transoceanic shipping. As in the United States, grain production began to expand on the pampas in the 1870s as new farming techniques, machinery, and improved transportation facilitated the transformation of the meat locker into a granary. Each of these changes required more extensive and intensive use of land.[12] It also meant the displacement of Indians and the active recruitment of European farmers to work the land. In this era not only Indians, but gauchos began to disappear (Slatta 1983, 1990b). Gauchos were increasingly forced into lower-class laboring positions. It is not entirely clear what happened to the Indian communities.

Conclusions

First and most obvious is the major role played in the history of both regions by their involvement in, or their degree of incorporation into, the world-system. The ways and extent to which the Viceroyalty of the Río de la Plata region and the Greater Southwest were explored, colonized, administered, and developed were largely—but not entirely—shaped by global geopolitical and geoeconomic forces and processes. In the sixteenth and seventeenth centuries, demand for precious metals and preemptive colonization seemed to be major motives for empire. Consequently, regions that had few precious metals remained "peripheries of peripheries." Later, the Bourbons sought to promote development and to abate the cost of endemic warfare. Trade became freer, stimulating development, and enormous social dislocations began to build toward the crisis of empire and the various independence movements.

During the independence era, the trajectories of incorporation of the two regions diverged sharply: California, Arizona, New Mexico, and Texas were incorporated into the United States while Baja California, Sonora, Sinaloa, Chihuahua, Durango, Coahuila, and Tamaulipas remained part of a peripheral state. Argentina eventually became one of the more prosperous new republics. Still, global processes transcended these differences by influencing the moment when Indian wars would end and nomadic groups would become sedentary. This included the free-spirited gauchos and cowboys. These changes came a little more slowly in Mexico. All this underscores the significance of the difference between merchant and production capitalism, and illustrates how the effects of this transition permeated even the remotest peripheries of the world-system. Within these broad similarities, however, regional and local factors and processes shaped particular changes.

There are several caveats that must be considered when making these types of comparisons. Besides the limitations of availability of evidence—which is a serious problem when dealing with nomadic groups—there are other inherent limitations. First, comparative strategies entail neglect of some local features that are important in narrative histories. Second, there are limitations imposed by the variations found in both regions. There are no groups in the pampean region directly comparable to the Pueblos in New Mexico. Third, the Viceroyalty of the Río de la Plata region ends at the Andes, the ocean, and the jungle whereas the Greater Southwest ends at the Great Plains, the eastern woodlands (Louisiana), and the ocean. Fourth, as noted several times already, the archival sources for the Greater Southwest have been more thoroughly mined than those for the Río de la Plata region—at least with respect to many of the topics discussed here.

Still, there are some benefits from this comparison. First, the comparison underscores that frontiers cannot be explained solely through processes and events that occurred within the frontier zone. They are created, transformed, and closed by larger sociopolitical processes and forces. Second and conversely, these larger processes and forces cannot explain all changes of and on the frontier. Rather, they set a context within which local factors and processes operate. Third, accounts of frontiers must examine the *interaction* of local factors, such as ethnicity, gender, and class, with global factors and processes. This interaction is the real subject of study. Fourth, that frontiers are created and transformed in such interactions explains why all frontiers seem to be the same, until examined closely, and then appear to be immensely different. Even a small number of factors can give rise to many divergent results.

11

The Frontier as an Arena of Social and Economic Change

Wealth Distribution in Nineteenth-Century Buenos Aires Province

LYMAN L. JOHNSON

One of the intriguing questions associated with the history of frontiers in the United States relates to the assumption that these areas are sites of economic and social mobility. Johnson examines the ways in which contemporary and historical commentators have viewed Buenos Aires during the Rosas era (1829–1852) as a time of economic backwardness and social immobility. Using probate records, Johnson constructs a sophisticated statistical model indicating that not only did the Buenos Aires economy grow significantly during this time, it seems to have been a place where wealth inequality was less evident than in similar ranching frontiers of the United States, such as Texas.

SINCE THE nineteenth century, grazing frontiers have exercised a powerful hold on the popular imagination across the Western Hemisphere. The cowboys of the United States and Canada as well as the vaqueros, llaneros, and gauchos of Latin America have all come to hold a special place in the highly romanticized visions of the past that inform both political discourse and national mythology in their respective countries. In the United States, in particular, frontier images found in movies and popular literature endlessly rehearse the politically utilitarian themes of rough justice, courage, and personal honor.[1] Given the important differences in national histories and cultural practices, it is worth noting that these same themes dominate *Martín Fierro, Don Segundo Sombra* and other enduring examples of Argentine gaucho literature.

Sometimes wilfully disengaged from the usefulness and popularity of these themes, modern scholars now more commonly analyze American frontiers as arenas of cultural exchange between indigenous peoples and an advancing wave of European culture. This intellectual project is built on the solid foundation of social historical achievement over the last three decades. Demography, family history, and gender studies have all contributed to the transformation of frontier studies since the 1970s. The metaphor of contested ground provides a useful, if fragile, bridge between these popular and academic understandings of frontier experience.

In the United States and, to a lesser degree, Latin America writers in both the popular and academic traditions have celebrated the apparent cultural fluidity and egalitarian character of frontier society. As a result, both popular and academic traditions often manifest a common hostility to the "civilizing" intentions of central governments and capitalist development. Bankers, railroad developers, large landowners, and agents of central political authority are commonly portrayed in similarly unflattering terms in movies, popular novels, and the work of academic historians. Despite important differences in the use of sources, style of presentation, and intended audiences, both popular and academic versions of frontier experience commonly portray Indian raids, banditry, and cattle rustling as forms of resistance.

Largely isolated from the arguments of social and cultural historians, a small number of economic historians have examined North American frontier societies as arenas of enterprise, production, and exchange. Many of these academic researchers have used the popular belief that the frontier offered men and women a unique opportunity to transform hard work and courage into wealth as a conceptual foil for quantitative analyses of frontier social realities. Given the fact that nearly every serious investigation of North American frontier wealth distribution has found high levels of inequality, the resilience of the myth of equality is remarkable.

In Latin America, on the other hand, there is widespread agreement that frontier economic development led to inequality and repressive social relations. Focused on the development of *latifundia* (large landed estates) and related themes of class conflict and social injustice, the dominant historiographical tradition views grazing frontiers as pristine examples of oligarchic economic and political power. Neither abundant opportunity nor social mobility are recurrent themes in popular or academic examinations of Latin American frontiers. However, because historians of Latin American economic development have seldom analyzed wealth distribution in frontier regions, these presumptions have not been adequately tested. The major obstacle to the exploration of this issue has been the absence of reliable government estimates of individual wealth for the nineteenth century.

In this chapter, changes in average wealth, in the distribution of wealth, and in total provincial wealth will be reported for Buenos Aires province during the ascendancy of Juan Manuel de Rosas, 1829–1852. These results are based on estimates of individual wealth found in probate inventories. Until now, estimates of regional economic performance during this important period have relied on the statistical summaries produced by customs authorities at the port of Buenos Aires. As a result, changes in the volume and value of exports and imports have been widely used as proxies for regional economic performance (Brown 1979: 80–83; Burgin 1946: 271–72; Lynch 1981: 253–54). These large cycles of commercial activity have been connected to discussions of social justice and distribution of wealth through anecdotal evidence drawn from travelers' accounts and reports of contemporary political actors. Put simply, little is known about the material conditions experienced by the majority of provincial residents during the period.

If used with proper care, probate records provide an opportunity to overcome the absence of aggregate statistics and to develop reliable measures of economic performance. Probate records take three major forms: wills, inventories, and accounts of administration. This study is based on estate inventories.[2] Surviving inventories provide remarkable details about individual wealth holding.[3] Whereas historians of Latin America have seldom made systematic use of probate records, economic historians interested in the United States have pioneered the use of probate records to generate measures of economic performance for the pre-statistical era (Carr and Walsh 1980; Alice Jones 1970; Main 1975; Shammas 1977).

Nevertheless, there are inherent problems in using probate records in the ways proposed here. The segment of the population found in probate records is both older and richer than the living population in any society. The young and the poor, often single and living alone, as well as those living in isolation in the countryside, were much less likely than wealthy men and women living in cities and towns or in well-established rural villages to involve the courts in the division of their property.[4] Fortunately, these problems of bias are not disabling. U.S. and European economic historians have developed statistical techniques for adjusting probate records to accurately reflect the demographic and economic characteristics of the larger society. In this study of Buenos Aires province, statistical weights derived from contemporary censuses and burial records were used to compensate for age bias and to estimate the wealth of the non-probate population.[5]

In order to estimate changes in average wealth holding and in the distribution of wealth during the Rosas period, two data sets based on the universe of cases found for two two-year cohorts were created (Alice Jones 1982; Main 1978; McCuster 1981).[6] All surviving probate inventories for the years 1829–30 (N = 169) and 1855–56 (N = 273) were analyzed and coded. The number of surviving inventories found for these two-year cohorts may appear to be a weak foundation for an effort to measure changes in wealth holding in a provincial population that rose from approximately 135,000 in 1829 to 275,000 in 1855. Yet, Alice Hanson Jones used a sample of 919 cases for her well-respected study of the thirteen British North American colonies in 1774, a region with a population of approximately 2,300,000 (Jones 1980: Appendix A). A more important consideration in assessing the utility of these sources is the actual coverage of the population of decedent wealth holders found in the probate records. After examining burials recorded in surviving parish registers, I was able to estimate that 23 percent of all potential wealth holders for 1829–30 and 28 percent of potential wealth holders for 1855–56 were probated.[7]

The history of Argentina to 1860 is still commonly framed in the mythic terms imposed by Domingo Sarmiento's novel, *Facundo* (*Life in the Argentine Republic in the Days of the Tyrants; or Civilization and Barbarism*) (Sarmiento, [1845] 1971). According to Sarmiento's enduring trope, the failure by 1820 of the first Republican experiments led inexorably to a bloody conflict between "civilization and barbarism." Central to this dramatic representation of the region's history is the assertion of a fundamental rivalry between rural and urban cultures. The federalism of Rosas and the unitarianism of his rivals in the city of Buenos Aires have often been portrayed as ideological expressions of antithetical cultural traditions. According to this tradition, the brutality, cruelty, and personalism of Juan Manuel de Rosas were natural and predictable given the brutishness, isolation, and pure physicality of life on the livestock frontier that spawned his political movement.[8]

Important contributions to the historical literature over the last two decades have expanded and revised our understanding of both the political and economic history of this period. Modern historians of the early national economy reject the idea of a zero-sum economic competition between city and countryside (Brown 1979; Halperín Donghi 1963; Lynch 1981). There is now general agreement that the regional economy grew substantially during the Rosas years. From the 1820s, a rising tide of hides; beef, both salted and dried; and other livestock byproducts flowed through the port of Buenos Aires to Europe, the United States, and the slave societies of Brazil and Cuba. Agricultural and livestock production expanded while both the urban and rural population grew substantially.

But historians of Argentina disagree about the effect of this expansion on the nation's long-term economic development. Many scholars view the export-led expansion of the Rosas years as having benefited only the livestock sector. Some have asserted that agricultural and manufacturing sectors actually contracted as a result of the policies of Rosas. Scholars exploring the period from Marxist and dependency perspectives accept that the economy grew, but associate this growth with increased structural dependence on more developed economies. The common subtext in these analyses is the assumption that the ranching elite monopolized the benefits of economic growth while rural and urban workers experienced a decline in living standards. Until now, however, it has been difficult to assess the impact of Rosas' policies on wealth distribution and living standards because we lacked even rudimentary measures of economic performance during the era.

At the outset of the Rosas period in 1829, the city of Buenos Aires and its rural hinterland had suffered from more than twenty years of political and fiscal chaos as well as from periodic military violence (Szuchman 1988).[9] Yet, despite political instability and administrative mismanagement, the grazing sector, linked after 1810 to the markets of Europe and the United States by liberalized commercial regulations at the port of Buenos Aires, expanded steadily.[10] The livestock frontier was pushed south and east as indigenous peoples were pacified episodically through a combination of military campaigns and subsidies. This territorial expansion coincided with an increase in the average size of estancias (cattle ranches) and with the appearance of a few enormous latifundia measuring in excess of 120,000 acres. By the end of the Rosas dictatorship in 1852, 28 percent of all ranchers owned 60 percent of the largest holdings (estates of ten square leagues or larger) (Cárcano 1972: chap. 3; Carretero 1972).

Between 1820 and midcentury, the region diversified its export mix and found new markets. Cattle byproducts (especially hides, tallow, jerked beef, and animal hair) dominated exports through the end of the Rosas period. Hides alone accounted for more than 60 percent of the total value of exports in 1852. Beginning in the 1840s, however, the region's landowners dramatically expanded wool production to meet growing demand in Europe and North America (Sabato 1989). During the Rosas period, wool exports grew from a marginal position in 1830 to roughly 10 percent of total exports, or 1.1 million gold pesos, in 1851. Only tallow exports, valued at 1.2 million gold pesos, and hides, at 6.9 million, remained more important (Burgin 1946: 271).

Export diversification coincided with the appearance of new trading partners and with the expansion of imports. Great Britain received nearly 50 percent of all exports from the port of Buenos Aires in 1820, but this domination was of short duration (Brown 1979: 59, 66). During the 1840s, France briefly supplanted Britain as the region's primary trading partner. Between 1840 and 1850, exports to France fell more than 50 percent and Britain regained its position as the province's best customer, although it now received less than 30 percent of total exports. Argentine exports were sent to increasingly diverse destinations, including important new linkages with the markets of the United States, Belgium, and Germany.

Augmented earnings from exports helped pay for an enlarged volume and expanded array of imported manufactured goods and agricultural products. Yet, although this expansion coincided with the proliferation of new manufacturing technology in Europe, machines, tools, and other producer goods were almost completely absent from the import mix during the Rosas years. Instead, the region's export earnings were used to pay for imported textiles and other consumer goods that altered regional material culture while undermining traditional producers, both locally and in the interior.[11] The wealthiest sectors of the society were the primary consumers of imported goods, but the itinerant peddlers and shopkeepers of the countryside found ready markets for imported textiles, metal wares, and inexpensive luxuries like yerba and tobacco among small farmers, rural workers, and indigenous communities as well (Brown 1979: 142–45; Halperín Donghi 1963: 77–80).

This dramatic expansion in the volume and value of exports also increased the economic and political power of the grazing elite. Although land values on the province's southern frontier were periodically depressed by the government's sale of land following military campaigns against native peoples, the cattle ranching elite generally continued to support and promote territorial expansion. At the same time, complaints about high wages and labor scarcity from cattle ranchers and urban employers led to the implementation of harsh new laws that required the rural poor to find steady employment or face conscription or jail (Lynch 1981: 115–16; Slatta 1983: 109–13).

Does this mean that the rich grew richer while the poor grew poorer? And, if inequality increased during the Rosas period, what was the impact on the overall distribution of wealth and on average wealth? This study attempts to answer these questions by providing more reliable measures of inequality and average wealth. In the analysis that follows, levels of wealth inequality will be expressed as Gini coefficients.[12] The Gini coefficient summarizes inequality in a convenient number ranging from 0.0 to 1.0. A zero value indicates perfect equality; a value of 1.0 indicates maximum inequality. At the beginning of the Rosas period in 1829, the Gini coefficient for the Province of Buenos Aires was 0.63.[13]

This level of wealth inequality compares favorably with the Gini coefficient of 0.73 found by Alice Hanson Jones for Britain's thirteen North American colonies in 1774 (Jones 1980: 169). Jones' conclusions are generally supported by social historians of colonial North America, who have found widespread evidence of growing wealth concentration and declining living conditions for the poor after 1760 (Nash 1979: 233–63). Nevertheless, it is unlikely that someone familiar with the historical literatures of both the British North American colonies and early national Argentina would suspect that the Province of Buenos Aires had substantially lower levels of wealth inequality in 1829 than did the thirteen colonies in 1774.

The province's comparatively low level of inequality was certainly not the result of a pattern of highly dispersed landholding. As early as 1830, sixty large-scale cattle ranchers held 76 percent of the province's settled areas (Lynch 1981: 68–69). In fact, the level of land concentration in Buenos Aires province in 1830 was greater than that found for Texas in 1860 (Campbell and Lowe 1977: 127). By the end of the Rosas period, landholding was even more concentrated. In 1852 Nicolás de Anchorena, Rosas' kinsman and political ally, held 306 square leagues (approximately 1.8 million acres) of land.

An explanation for the relatively low Gini coefficient must, therefore, be sought elsewhere. It appears that the pace of wealth concentration before 1830 was retarded by two factors. First, from the late colonial era into the 1880s the region experienced a chronic labor shortage and resulting high wages (Burgin 1946: 267–68; L. Johnson 1990; Sabato 1985). Effective full employment and relatively high wages lifted the material circumstances of the lowest levels of the social pyramid even while the wealth of the rural elite grew rapidly. And second, the impact of expanding latifundia on the distribution of provincial wealth after 1820 was somewhat mitigated by the coincidental erosion of the economic power of those elite families that had depended on monopoly commercial arrangements and administrative posts in the late colonial period. These sectors lost wealth shares during the period from 1810 to 1820 due to the leveling effects of political violence and confiscatory taxes.

During the period covered by this study, both silver and paper pesos circulated in the Province of Buenos Aires, but probate values were almost always expressed in *moneda corriente,* or paper pesos. In 1830, mean wealth for the province was 9,499 paper pesos. Median wealth, on the other hand, was 5,103 paper pesos.[14] To facilitate comparison, these peso values can be converted to 1830 U.S. dollars. Mean wealth was 1,581 dollars and median wealth 849 dollars.[15] Total provincial wealth in 1830 can be estimated, then, as approximately 744 million paper pesos or slightly more than 123 million dollars.[16]

The wealthiest 10 percent of the 1830 probate population held an average wealth of 121,718 paper pesos or 20,152 dollars. Although the top 10 percent was overwhelmingly native-born, three of the richest six members of this elite group were foreign-born. Despite the central importance of livestock raising to the provincial economy in 1830, the propertied elite retained the urban character of the late colonial period, with less than 20 percent of its membership maintaining their primary residence in the countryside. Although some members of the elite found in the probate population owned substantial amounts of rural property while residing in the city, none of the wealthiest individuals (estates larger than 100,000 paper pesos) owned any rural property.

This had been the colonial pattern as well. But the commercial and bureaucratic basis of the colonial social hierarchy had been eroded by the city's loss of administrative authority over and access to fiscal resources of the vast territory included in the old viceroyalty. The arrival of representatives of British and North American commercial houses and the reorientation of the city's trade away from Spain contributed as well to the declining position of the commercial families that had once dominated the city. Unlike their colonial antecedents, members of the urban economic elite in 1830 owed their dominant positions to real estate investments, especially urban residential and business properties, rather than to monopoly trade, bureaucratic positions, and control of credit markets. Among the richest 10 percent of probate decedents in 1830, real estate made up 57 percent of total wealth.

By 1855, provincial population had grown to 275,000. During the three decades covered by this study, rural settlements had expanded, as had both the volume and value of provincial exports. Before comparing average wealth holding and levels of wealth inequality for 1830 and 1855, it is worthwhile to recall the central characteristics of the Sarmiento trope and more modern scholarly variants. For Sarmiento, the dark era of the Rosas dictatorship had dire consequences for both political culture and the economy. The triumph of the countryside had retarded material progress relative to that experienced by what he saw as more-enlightened societies such as the United States and Britain. By preventing full integration in international markets, the acquisition of new technology, and the full utilization of local economic resources, Rosas had caused stagnation.[17]

Some revisionist historians have turned Sarmiento's interpretation on its head without essentially altering his summary judgement that Rosas slowed regional economic development. Little deterred by the overwhelming evidence of growing wealth concentration and implementation of repressive labor laws, Bradford Burns judged Rosas to have been an ally of the rural and urban masses, stating that "the gauchos enjoyed an access to land, freedom of movement, greater economic alternatives, and better living conditions during the

Rosas period than any time afterward" (Burns 1980: 146). According to this argument, it was Rosas' success in resisting full integration into the Atlantic market that created a golden period of prosperity for the masses.

This opinion has found little support among historians who have closely examined rural life during the Rosas period. These historians instead provide convincing evidence of both export-led economic expansion and a fiercely repressive labor regime. The harsh discipline and coercive work requirements experienced by rural workers appear indisputable. The historical literature commonly associates this combination of growth and repression with the structural form of the region's integration in the Atlantic economy. Two of our most reliable guides to the period, Halperín Donghi and Slatta, have suggested that rural workers actually experienced declining standards of living under Rosas due to punitive labor laws and the eroding value of the paper peso (Halperín Donghi 1963: 95–98; Slatta 1983: 30–37).

In his subtle analysis of the Rosas period, John Lynch explored the cultural context within which the regime's repressive labor relations developed. Although his summary judgement about labor conditions reinforced that offered by Slatta, Lynch broadened his analysis to explore the reciprocal obligations between estancieros and peones. In his examination of economic performance during the Rosas period, Lynch argued that, although the livestock export sector had experienced significant growth, structural impediments to continued progress had appeared prior to Rosas' overthrow in 1852 (Lynch 1981: 88):

> There was a limit beyond which the Rosas economy could not grow. Lack of technology meant that the *estancia* could only expand by acquiring more and more land; and its specialization worked in a number of commodities—hides, jerked beef—for which overseas demand was limited and, in the slave markets of Brazil and Cuba, was more likely to contract than to grow. In the final analysis, therefore, the Rosas system was economically stagnant.

Analysis of probate records suggests a somewhat different summary of economic performance during the Rosas period. Average wealth grew to 148,383 paper pesos in 1855 from the 9,499 pesos of 1830. However, this increase in average wealth is misleading because of currency devaluation. Rosas pursued an inflationary monetary policy throughout his regime and, as a result, the paper pesos of 1855 were worth much less than those of 1830. Contemporary conversion tables permit us to deflate 1855 peso values to 1830 levels.

Mean wealth in 1855, expressed in 1830 pesos, was an impressive 45,377 pesos or 7,550 U.S. dollars. Median wealth in 1855, deflated to constant pesos, had risen more slowly, from 5,103 to 14,178 pesos. Put another way, mean wealth in Buenos Aires province increased more than 4.7 times while median wealth increased approximately 2.7 times during the Rosas period. Although the poorest 50 percent of provincial residents experienced a substantial improvement in their material circumstances during the Rosas period, they clearly lost ground relative to wealthier segments of the population.

Total provincial wealth in 1855 reached an estimated 7.24 billion pesos (deflated) or 1,204,225,000 dollars. That is, between 1830 and 1855, the province's economically active population doubled while total provincial wealth increased nearly 10 times. It is worth recalling that this remarkable growth occurred despite British and French blockades, war in Uruguay, and civil war in the interior provinces. If this was the "barbarism" of Sarmiento, it was a barbarism capable of producing significant amounts of wealth.

Yet wealth was clearly more concentrated in 1855 than in 1830. Between 1830 and 1855 wealth concentration, as measured by the Gini coefficient, rose from 0.63 to 0.72 in Buenos Aires province. Among the wealthiest 10 percent of the probate population, average wealth had grown from 121,718 paper pesos in 1830 to 740,085 paper pesos (deflated) or 123,142 dollars in 1855. In comparison with median wealth, which had increased 2.7 times, the average wealth of the richest 10 percent of the probate population had multiplied roughly 6 times between 1830 and 1855. The richest 10 percent, then, increased their wealth nearly 3 times faster than those located in the middle of provincial wealth distribution.

The preponderance of Creoles among the elite, already evident in 1830, had increased by 1855. Only six of the thirty wealthiest probate decedents in 1855 were foreign-born and the ten richest were all local-born. There were, however, some important changes in the relationship between the city of Buenos Aires and the countryside. By the end of the Rosas period nearly every member of the provincial elite held substantial amounts of rural real estate. Only five of the thirty wealthiest decedents in the probate records in 1855 owned no rural property. Eighteen members of this group, on the other hand, owned more than one million deflated paper pesos in rural property. Generally, ranchers who maintained their primary residences in the city were wealthier and owned more valuable rural property than those who lived in the countryside. In fact, six of the seven wealthiest ranchers in 1855 maintained their primary residences in the city of Buenos Aires (Lynch 1981: 88).

In addition to Gini coefficients for 1829–30 and 1855–56, I have calculated a second statistic for measuring levels of wealth concentration. Increases in the percentage of all wealth held by the richest 10 percent of the population confirm the tendency towards greater wealth inequality reflected in the 1855 Gini coefficient. The wealth of the richest 10 percent of the population increased substantially, rising from 51 percent to 59.8 percent of total provincial wealth. Thus, nearly 60 percent of the province's total wealth in 1855 was concentrated in the hands of a small elite.[18]

The land policies of the Rosas government obviously promoted this tendency toward increased inequality but, as noted earlier, rural property was already highly concentrated. Nevertheless, new military campaigns against Amerindian populations in the south of the province in the 1830s allowed Rosas to promote greater concentration by distributing vast new estates to political allies and kinsmen. However, increasingly concentrated rural land ownership alone cannot account for the rise in wealth inequality between 1830 and 1855. It appears instead that the growing profitability of livestock raising attracted investments from the wealthiest members of the urban elite and led to the creation of a single integrated elite that dominated both rural and urban real estate markets and exercised effective control of credit (Halperín Donghi 1963: 92; Lynch 1981: 44).

With the exception of the government's policies for land distribution, the provincial government's monetary policy was the most important contributor to wealth concentration. Unwilling to cut expenditures, especially for the military, the Rosas government papered over its revenue shortfalls with currency issues. Between 1836 and 1851, the provincial government issued 109,980,854 pesos in paper money (Burgin 1946: 216). Livestock producers who operated in the hard currency export market were clearly advantaged relative to urban commercial and manufacturing sectors and wage earners, who received paper pesos for their goods and services and paid for their imports in silver or gold.

As pointed out by Burgin and Lynch, the fiscal policy of the Rosas regime also contributed to the enrichment of the livestock sector. Port duties remained the government's primary source of revenues through this period, providing 81.9 percent of the provincial government's revenues in 1829 and 93.1 percent in 1850 (Burgin 1946: 49, 195; Lynch 1981: 60). However, since port duties were not adjusted for inflation in the Rosas era, rural producers floating upward on rapidly rising real estate and livestock values were little inconvenienced by these assessments. Nor were they affected by the *contribución directa,* a property tax introduced in 1822 that actually placed heavier burdens on urban commercial sectors than on livestock producers.[19]

This brief summary of economic change during the Rosas years can be further illuminated by comparing the city and Province of Buenos Aires with selected regions of the United States. Among economic historians of the United States there is general agreement that wealth holding became more concentrated during the nineteenth century (Soltow 1971a).[20] Both Robert Gallman and Lee Soltow found high levels of concentration for the United States in 1860; however, they disagree about the direction of change after 1860 (Gallman 1965; Soltow 1971a).

Soltow found a Gini coefficient of 0.83 for all adult free men in 1860 (Soltow 1975a: 103).[21] He has argued that this high level of wealth inequality remained fairly stable to the end of the century, despite the destruction caused by the Civil War, the economic consequences of emancipation in the South, and increased levels of industrialization and urbanization in the Northeast and Midwest. Gallman and others agree generally with Soltow's 1860 estimate, but argue for a second round of wealth concentration near the end of the century (Gallman 1965: 320–21).

These national-level studies of the U.S. suggest that the tendency towards greater wealth concentration associated with nineteenth-century industrialization and urbanization was somewhat offset by the opening of new communities in the West, where lower land values promoted more equitable wealth distribution. For the United States, there is clear evidence that wealth tended to be most concentrated in the older cities and towns of the East and Midwest (Gallman 1969: 22–23, 1979: 2–3; Pessen 1973: 30–40). In 1860, Philadelphia had a Gini coefficient of 0.93, Boston one of 0.94, and Chicago one of 0.92 (Soltow 1975a: 236–37). That is, during the nineteenth century, wealth inequality in the U.S. appears to have been strongly associated with the proliferation of commercial and manufacturing activities and with the growth of urban populations. Nevertheless, most analyses of North American frontier communities have also found significant levels of inequality. Although his results are not directly comparable to those of Soltow and Gallman, Robert A. Burchell (1987) found similarly high levels of concentration in California during the period from 1848 to 1880. Since California experienced its gold rush during this period and developed only a limited grazing sector, comparison with Buenos Aires province would yield only questionable results. An effort to compare this Argentine province with frontier regions of the United States necessarily requires some care in controlling for important differences in social and economic character.

Of all the regions of the United States for which comparable data exist, Texas on the eve of the Civil War may provide the best candidate for comparison with Buenos Aires province in 1855. Both Texas and Buenos Aires had important grazing sectors, abundant and inexpensive land, and similar population densities. Yet there were important differences as well.

There was no city in Texas in 1860 with the population size or commercial importance of the city of Buenos Aires. There were, however, four Texas towns of some consequence (Houston, Galveston, San Antonio, and Austin). None of these Texas towns was as heavily integrated in the rapidly developing Atlantic economy as Buenos Aires, however (Campbell and Lowe 1977). The Texas cattle frontier in 1860 was only tenuously tied to external markets through the port of Galveston or over long-distance overland routes. The mature era of the long drive to distant markets developed only after the Civil War (Bloom 1966; T. Jordan 1994: chap. 7; Utley 1965–66). An even more important difference between this rapidly developing American frontier state and Buenos Aires province was the significance of cotton agriculture and the presence of a substantial slave population in Texas. As a result, the comparison of wealth concentration is made more difficult, because slaves were both a form of wealth and potential wealth holders.

Using wealth information provided in the 1860 U.S. census, Campbell and Lowe (1977: 127) found a Gini coefficient of 0.74 for Texas. This is nearly identical to the Gini of 0.72 here established for the Province of Buenos Aires in 1855 using probate inventories. When wealth concentration is compared for urban and rural settings in Buenos Aires province and Texas some of this broad similarity disappears. While Campbell and Lowe estimated a Gini of 0.85 for the four Texas towns in 1860, provincial probate records yield a somewhat lower Gini of 0.78 for the city of Buenos Aires in 1855. The Texas cattle frontier, identified as Region III in the Campbell and Lowe study, was found to have a Gini coefficient of 0.76 in 1860. The livestock-dominated countryside of the Province of Buenos Aires, on the other hand, had a substantially lower Gini coefficient of 0.64 in 1855. Despite the unambiguous evidence that rural landownership and wealth holding had become much more concentrated during the Rosas period, among full-time rural residents, wealth was much less concentrated in the Province of Buenos Aires than in Texas.

Wisconsin was another rapidly developing frontier state in 1860. It was distinguished from Texas by its free labor force, by a larger percentage of immigrants in its population, and by the earlier development of manufacturing in its largest city, Milwaukee. Lee Soltow (1971b) found a Gini coefficient of 0.75 for Wisconsin in 1860. The Gini for highly urbanized Milwaukee County was 0.89 while the state's combined rural counties had a Gini coefficient of 0.73. Again, both urban and rural Gini coefficients for Wisconsin in 1860 were higher than those established for Buenos Aires in 1855.

Any effort to comparatively interpret variations in these levels of inequality would be compromised by differences in sources, sampling techniques, and coding decisions that preceded these calculations.[22] North American census estimates were collected for different purposes and by different means than were the estimates based on Argentine probate inventories. As a result, it is probably best to avoid any attempt at this time to associate Gini coefficients for these three frontier societies with the form and pace of economic development. Although Buenos Aires province had the lowest levels of wealth concentration of these three frontier regions, general similarities in levels of inequality are, perhaps, more important to our understanding of frontiers. Despite important differences in labor forms, the scale of rural holdings, regional products and markets, and cultural and political characteristics, all three frontier societies experienced high levels of wealth inequality.

The relative prosperity of these three frontier societies can be estimated by examining average wealth (measured in dollars). While Campbell and Lowe and Soltow estimated average wealth in 1860 for Texas and Wisconsin as 6,393 and 1,486 dollars, respectively, I found an average wealth of 7,327 dollars for the Province of Buenos Aires in 1855. The results of this comparison are startling. Certainly, differences in sources and methods used by researchers are partially responsible for these differences in average wealth. It seems unlikely, however, that an effort to control for the effects of these factors would alter the surprising outcome that the average wealth of Buenos Aires province in 1855 was as great or greater than that of Texas or Wisconsin in 1860. If wealth levels in Buenos Aires at midcentury compared favorably with fast-growing frontier regions in the United States, many of our assumptions about economic development in nineteenth-century Argentina will have to be revised.

At this stage of my analysis, I am able to tentatively suggest a periodization for changes in wealth concentration in the Province of Buenos Aires during the first half of the nineteenth century. Using a limited sample of probate records weighted for age bias only, I calculated a Gini coefficient of 0.67 for 1800. This suggests a level of wealth concentration slightly lower than that found by Alice Hanson Jones (1980) for Britain's North American colonies on the eve of independence.[23] This pattern of wealth distribution appears to have been associated—as in the North American case—with the expansion of long-distance trade, with the relative growth of urban population, and with the articulation of commercial marketing and credit networks that increasingly linked and subordinated the interior to the capital city.

In the two decades that followed the *cabildo abierto* (emergency town council meeting that declared Argentina's independence from Spain) of May 25, 1810, this tendency toward increased inequality was temporarily reversed. Despite the growth of the grazing and agricultural sectors of the province after 1810, the city of Buenos Aires experienced a period of stagnation or, at best, slow growth. In the city it appears that wealth was redistributed away from traditional commercial and government elites toward new middle and skilled working groups. Novel fiscal mechanisms, altered commercial arrangements, and the vagaries of the political process all played a role in this wealth transfer. The combined effects of these forces explain most of the reduction in the Gini coefficient by 1829–30. Bureaucrats, Spanish and Creole merchants linked to the traditional trade with Spain and Potosí, and ultimately artisans and small manufacturers lost wealth shares relative to new groups, such as revolutionary officials, the military, and especially rural landowners.

The Rosas era reversed this trend towards reduced wealth concentration. The relative stability of his long rule permitted the maturation and diversification of the grazing sector and led to significantly increased levels of inequality, a Gini of 0.73. That is, the Buenos Aires province experienced a pattern of increasing wealth concentration similar to what has been found by most studies of the North American frontier. Although a small number of frontier historians continue to assert the Frederick Jackson Turner (1994) version of North American history, in which frontier expansion is associated with enhanced opportunity and greater social mobility, the most respected studies of U.S. census samples demonstrate that frontier regions had uniformly high levels of wealth concentration. The southern expansion of the Rosas era was characterized by the creation of enormous cattle ranches as well as by government-sanctioned efforts to form a disciplined, subordinate rural labor force. The two measures of inequality offered in this essay provide limited support for those authors who have emphasized the social costs of this process (Slatta 1983: chap. 3).[24] Yet the results of this process of wealth concentration are difficult to interpret given the high average wealth found for the Province of Buenos Aires when compared with Texas and Wisconsin. The poorest 50 percent of the provincial population clearly lost wealth share during the Rosas period, but the actual wealth of this group measured in constant pesos (or dollars) grew significantly.

The economic and social policies that promoted inequality by redistributing wealth shares away from the rural and urban masses, urban commercial and artisan sectors, and small farmers to the rural grazing elite also led to an important increase in average wealth and total provincial wealth. This suggests that the Rosas years were, in fact, anticipatory to the well-known prosperity and growth of the late-nineteenth-century economy, rather than a period of stagnation and lost opportunity.

12

Two, Three, Many Barbarisms?

The Chihuahuan Frontier in Transition from Society to Politics

DANIEL NUGENT

Complementing Radding, Nugent describes the formation of a colonial pact between the Spanish Crown and non-Indian military settlers of Namiquipa, Chihuahua, during the late eighteenth century. Like the indigenous villagers of highland Sonora, Namiquipans were granted land in return for defending northern New Spain against its "barbaric" Indian enemies, the Apaches. This "civilizing" process of colonization became a part of their popular consciousness—a "grand and beneficent project" they carried out in collaboration with the colonial state.

By the late nineteenth century, however, the Apaches had been conquered and exiled, and northern Mexico had become a frontier of capitalist penetration and expansion. The Mexican state of Porfirio Díaz mounted a sustained assault on the lands of indigenous communities and former military colonies alike. The colonial compact that had united Namiquipans with the state on a frontier of civilization broke down on the new frontier of capitalism, transforming peasants in Namiquipa and other northern Mexican communities into obstacles to capitalist progress rather than defenders of colonial civilization.

THIS CHAPTER draws on a more general study of the construction of social relationships and social identities during the nineteenth and twentieth centuries in former military settlement colonies in Chihuahua, Mexico.[1] Focusing on the town of Namiquipa, one such colony, it demonstrates how these settlements were located at the end of the eighteenth century on a social, cultural, and geographical frontier, and at the end of the nineteenth century on a political and economic frontier. Despite the genuine ethnic diversity of these settlements during the late colonial and early national periods of Mexican history (Alonso 1995), structurally they are best described as *white settlement colonies*. In the closing decades of the eighteenth century, settlers were encouraged by military governors of northern New Spain to migrate to this region. Assuming residence in abandoned missions or estates, they were given land by the colonial state in exchange for fighting Apache Indians, who were also moving into the region at the time.

As a result of this process of tenuous settlement and protracted conquest, communities were formed whose inhabitants were wedded to a notion of privileged connection to the center—to imperial Spain, to European "civilization." That notion proved illusory by the end of the nineteenth century. Their initially exalted status position within a colonial social structure of power was ultimately eroded when a new and devalued class or structural position was forcibly imposed on the communities' residents as a consequence of the development of capitalist relations of production and property in the region and a redrawing of the boundary between Mexico and the United States. This later outcome was, in turn, the result of a contradictory, but not at all ambiguous, process of transformation that went in two opposite directions simultaneously. As the peripheral locales and the spaces they inhabited were drawn concretely into the center, the residents of this region were denied—and were no longer able to legitimately assert—the central role they had previously assumed abstractly in a "civilizing" process.[2] They were reidentified from without as the barbarians of a new(er) world order.

The "without" from which the residents of these communities were earlier identified was a European system of territorial conquest and administration. Throughout the period under discussion, these towns were located on the periphery of a capitalist world-system: specifically, the northern frontier of nineteenth-century Mexico. Yet however peripheral their physical location, from the very outset in the late eighteenth century, these communities provided for their residents a locus of sentiment, affinity, knowledge, and experience that was organized materially, socially, and historically in terms of the settlers' vision of participating in a colonizing and civilizing process. The forms of social consciousness that emerged in this peripheral locale—forms through and in terms of which work, residence, and livelihood were comprehended and transformed—were initially linked to ideological projects rooted in a "civilizing process" called colonialism that originated elsewhere. By the end of the nineteenth century, however, those popular forms of social consciousness were no longer commensurate with the new identifications imputed to the colonists' descendants by the agents and agencies of the bourgeois state in Mexico.

One possible starting point for analyzing these changes is the observation that Mexico—like most of Latin America—has long been a "postcolonial society." In other words, it has moved along temporally—if not developmentally—from an earlier "colonial" condition for almost two centuries. Yet one of the most striking features of the ways political power is organized socially and experienced subjectively in much of Mexico today is that it is and remains a profoundly colonial or, in a pinch, *neo*-colonial—rather than unequivocally postcolonial—form of power. Neither the Wars of Independence and the Wars of the Reform during the nineteenth century, nor the revolution of 1910 and the "reforms" of Salinastroika in the period from 1988 to 1994 during the twentieth century, signaled irreversible, radical breaks with the past. Rather, they served as sustained moments of transformation, linking instead of separating prior events and relationships to an indefinite future.

This chapter examines a related series of transformations in a specific region of Mexico's northern frontier (see also Nugent 1989). The transformations that occurred in people's livelihoods and relations to the state, and the character of the links between the past and the present, had, and still are marked by, features that are simultaneously structural and meaningful, pragmatic and discursive. Hence, to understand this frontier region we should remain skeptical of the claims embodied (and embedded) in assertions to the effect that a world-historical situation identified by Georges Balandier (1951) in the early 1950s as "colonial" has been supplanted by another situation, variously termed "postcolonial" or "postmodern."

In turning to the material I consider below, the pedestrian (and perhaps empirical) point is that there is not much that is particularly "post" about the present forms through which power is organized in Mexico.[3] An additional point is that we have to develop an appreciation of historical process as a series of transformations rather than a sequence of ruptures. Instead of examining change in light of rigid binary contrasts between past and present, between here continuities and there discontinuities, between now this and then that, we should instead devote greater attention to the mutual imbrication of the past and the present. We should explore the fluidity and changeability of our criteria for distinguishing between which phenomena are "continuous" and which are "discontinuous," and the relational character of constructions of "then" and "now" (alongside the recognition that such constructions are always already contested and contentious). In looking at a frontier, such an approach requires developing our analyses through the historiographic and ethnographic examination of local and regional archives, popular resources, and social memories. Further, these should be regarded not as abstracted texts, but as elements and evidence of human experience which frame sociohistorical process in terms of periodizations that are alternatives to either official or scholarly discourse (Post 1978; Stern 1987).

What occurred in Namiquipa, as I discuss in this chapter, provides an example (not a case study) of the instantiation, actualization, and active construction of social values and relationships that could be uncontroversially characterized as "modern," "colonial," "core" . . . or even "metropolitan." An intriguing feature of these core or colonial values, relationships, and understandings, though, is that they emerged in a physical, geographical locale and region that is unequivocally peripheral. Furthermore, the "core" values, forms of relationship, and so on, were actively worked out and elaborated by people within the periphery over a much longer period of time than routinely figures in analyses of the postmodern or postcolonial situation in the late twentieth century. Despite this discursive and pragmatic elaboration largely internal to the communities of ex-military colonists, by the start of the twentieth century those people, their towns, and the mode of livelihood they had developed were regarded as backward, even barbaric from the perspective of landlords and rulers of state in Mexico (see Nugent 1989). In light of this violent reidentification from the (newly redefined) center, it is not surprising that the first popular contingents of fighters who initiated the Mexican revolution in 1910 came from communities such as these (see especially Alonso 1995; Calzadíaz Barrera 1979; Duarte Morales 1968; Katz 1981: 7ff; Knight 1986: 115–27; Nugent 1993; Olea Arias 1961). I will, however, restrict the account presented here to what happened during the long nineteenth century (1780s–1900s) preceding the revolution.

The Struggle Against Barbarism from the Periphery

The social anthropology of twentieth-century Mexico by Anglophone and Mexican anthropologists (see Hewitt de Alcantara 1984) for a long time concentrated on understanding the languages, livelihoods, forms of social organization, mythologies, and different fates of Amerindian societies. Where anthropology in South Asia produced boatloads of "village studies" through the 1960s and 1970s, we produced boatloads of "community studies" frequently (though not always) focused on indigenous peoples. Not many indigenous peoples remained in northern Mexico by the end of the twentieth century, however, and those who had lived in what is now the state of Chihuahua from the time Spanish-speaking colonists began to penetrate the region had only infrequently lived in fixed communities in any event.

Most of the earlier inhabitants of this region had, by the middle of the eighteenth century, been exterminated, assimilated or, in Gonzalo Aguirre Beltrán's ([1957] 1970) telling phrase, driven into "regions of refuge." The Tarahumaras, for example, were forced from the river valleys and plains on the eastern slope of the Sierra Madre Occidental to the most inhospitable heights and rugged canyons of the same sierra (see F. Jordan [1956] 1981; Kennedy 1979; Lartigue 1984). The Conchos, whose settlements had ranged across a territory extending from the upper reaches of the Santa María River valley in the northwest to the lower reaches of the Río Conchos in the east, and to the confluence of the Conchos and Florido Rivers in the south, were, like most other inhabitants of Chihuahua with the exception of the Tarahumaras, "near the end of their existence as distinctive cultural systems or societies" by the 1730s (Griffen 1979: 23). More nomadic groups such as the Sumas, Janos, and Jocomes living to the north and northwest of the Conchos fared even worse in the wake of Franciscan and Jesuit missionization on the one hand and violent suppression of uprisings and revolts by Spanish forces (usually reliant on foreign Indian auxiliaries) on the other. "The result, for all Indians, was biological extermination, emigration from the province, or assimilation either into Spanish society or into Apache groups who moved in from the north" (Griffen 1979: 19).

It was roughly during this period—the middle decades of the eighteenth century—that various bands of Athapaskan raiders from the north started to plunder the region and its inhabited settlements—both Spanish and Indian. These new raiders were identified as "Apaches" by colonial officials. One Spanish response to Apache raiding during the colonial period was to establish towns on the eastern slope of the Sierra Madre Occidental as military outposts. These towns were inhabited by soldiers and civilian settlers, who formed the vanguard of the Spanish, and later Mexican, states' war against the Apaches. As a result, much of Chihuahua became a militarized zone in the second half of the eighteenth century. Notwithstanding the tenuous peace achieved with some Apache bands from the 1790s until the 1820s, Chihuahua remained a militarized zone until 1886, when the last armed band of Apaches led by Geronimo was driven north across the U.S.-Mexican border.

The town of Namiquipa, where I did fieldwork in the 1980s with non-Indian peasants—most of them descendants of settler-colonists—had been the site of a ranchería of Conchos Indians in the seventeenth century prior to a Franciscan mission being established there in 1663 (Gerhard 1982: 187; Griffen 1979: 82). In the early eighteenth century, Spanish and criollo[4] families acquired properties in the region and developed agricultural and cattle estates. By the 1760s, however, attacks by Apaches on the "civilized" settlements were so generalized and devastating in their effect that the region was largely abandoned by non-Indian civilian settlers.[5] By March 1778, Namiquipa was home to eleven wretched families, the nearby haciendas abandoned, its future in doubt.[6]

The names of the twenty-eight individuals in those eleven families indicate that they were all Indians, bearing last names—if any—such as de la Cruz or Domingo. The first entry in the March 1778 census is "Don Lazaro, Gobernador," the last part being the title routinely bestowed on "native chiefs" of northern New Spain by missionary priests and colonial officials. The oldest individual, a man of ninety, was named Pedro Llepomera, which suggests that he was a Tarahumara who moved to Namiquipa from the pueblo of that name (Yepomera) in the neighboring Papigochic Valley. One forty-five-year-old man was named Antonio Concho, a brutal irony since his identifying badge—a family (not a place) name that follows a personal name, in the Spanish fashion—is identical to the name given to the group of people—the Conchos Indians—who, by that point in time, appear to have been completely exterminated or absorbed into frontier Hispanic society (Barnes, Naylor, and Polzer 1981: 129; Spicer 1962: 39).

Namiquipa was resettled after November 1778 by Spanish, criollo, mestizo, and mulatto military settlement colonists from outside the region, people who called themselves gente de razón.[7] Teodoro de Croix, governor and commanding general of the Provincias Internas, ordered soldiers and encouraged civilians to settle in Namiquipa, Cruces, Casas Grandes, Janos, and Galeana (the latter two towns were at that time already the sites of presidios). To each of these five towns Croix assigned 112,000 hectares of land for use by the colonists. Soldiers and civilians alike were given rights to land by the Spanish colonial state in exchange for their working upon the land and establishing viable communities in the region and, most important, for doing battle against the Apaches—called indios bárbaros in colonial and nineteenth-century documents—who were also moving into (and through) the region from the north.

Also taking up residence in Namiquipa were soldiers assigned to the 2a Compañía Volante (the Second Flying Company of presidial soldiers), headquartered at Namiquipa until 1821.[8] Presidial captains initially assumed responsibility for local governance, and many soldiers remained resident in the town after their formal tours of duty were up. By the early 1820s, when Mexico achieved independence from Spain, there were almost three hundred families living in Namiquipa. While a few families of local Indians remained—primarily Tarahumaras though at times also some Apaches—most of the residents had settled in Namiquipa in the four decades prior to independence, responding to Croix's offer of rights to land in exchange for fighting the indios bárbaros.

As Friedrich Katz (1981: 8) writes:

> The inhabitants of the colonies [such as Namiquipa] were privileged in many respects compared to the free villagers of central and southern Mexico. Unlike the villagers, they were not wards of the crown during the colonial period but enjoyed

> rights generally reserved for Spaniards and their descendants, the criollos. They owned their land individually and were allowed to sell it, or buy additional land. They usually owned more land and more cattle than the free peasants of Mexico's other areas. Their communities were entitled to greater internal autonomy, and the military colonists had not only the right but the duty to bear arms.

The very presence of towns such as Namiquipa on the frontline of armed struggle against the Apaches was linked to, indeed predicated upon, a colonial project of the Spanish Empire in the Americas, which marked their distinctiveness vis-à-vis communities of indígenas and free villagers in other regions of Mexico. The basic problem confronting the colonial state in Chihuahua at the end of the eighteenth century may be synthesized in a phrase: securing the control of a territory. Peoples inhabiting the region had to be identified and mechanisms for an orderly exploitation and transformation of the region established.

Hence, the colonists were involved in a "civilizing" mission at the service of the colonial state, an ideological project oriented toward the taming of putatively uncivil behavior or the erasure of particular forms of difference—in language, custom, beliefs, and lifestyle generally—on the frontier. The civilizing mission was conducted simultaneously in relation to three domains of action and experience: social structural, "metropolitical" (i.e., as that ultimately political mission was conceived from the metropole), and local (i.e., in the way the central plan figured in popular, local experience and consciousness).

The first of these domains—which I call social structural—involved the replacement of one way of life with another. The nomadic and sedentary bands and tribes of indigenes were to be converted to Christianity and brought together to live in fixed settlements under the watchful gaze of missionary priests and soldiers in the service of the Spanish Crown. Groups such as the Sumas in the late seventeenth and early eighteenth centuries or the Apaches somewhat later, who refused to settle down and in fact carried on the practice of raiding Spanish and other Indian settlements, were to be pursued by soldiers and contained or exterminated. The missionaries' policy of congregating groups of Indians (sometimes of varying provenance and speaking different languages) in towns—and then often relying on Indian labor to construct a church—was called reducción.

The reduction of earlier forms of living was registered not only spatially through concentrated rather than dispersed settlement, but also socially and culturally, through the "end of their existence as distinctive cultural systems or societies" (Griffen 1979: 23). Instead of living in semi-sedentary or nomadic bands, carrying on rude and technically unsophisticated traditions, and being illiterate or, in short, savage, people were expected as a result of the civilizing mission to reside in nucleated settlements and be able to transform a harsh landscape by the application of human labor and modern instruments of production. Further, they would now be in communication with bureaucrats and courts halfway across the globe. In short, people would be civilized.

The second dimension through which action and experience were organized and regulated involved the civilizing mission as it was conceived from the center. On November 15, 1778, Teodoro de Croix issued an order for the "creation and firm establishment of towns in the most important sites on the frontier," each of which would be assigned more than 100,000 hectares of land. Croix did so in order to bring the Apaches to peace, to provide work and property for people who had neither, and to "expand commerce, encourage agriculture, and bring knowledge of industry" to the region. Settlers, regardless of their "class, caste or quality" (the latter terms referring to ethnicity) could join the community and secure rights to land. Also assigned to the new towns were soldiers, "under whose protection the happy settlers might make use of the fertility and beauty of the lands assigned to the new pueblos, of the abundance of waters, of the promise of mineral wealth . . . and of the fruits of their labor and Industry." "The primary obligation of the Spanish settlers," Croix went on, "was to have small arms and horses, . . . to defend themselves from, and to direct themselves against, the enemies."[9]

A new wave of settlers from outside the region proved responsive to the offer of lands in exchange for fighting the Apaches. In addition to soldiers assigned to the five towns,[10] hundreds of civilian settlers went there as well, and retired soldiers maintained residence after their tours of duty were completed.[11] It is highly significant that the landlords and owners of large estates that had been developed and consolidated during the first half of the eighteenth century but abandoned by the 1760s did not immediately return to the region. Parts of the land grants that Croix issued to the colonists of Namiquipa and Galeana comprised the former estates of Aranzazú, Carmen, and Santana del Torreón belonging to the González de Almoyna family.[12] Croix offered in 1778 to return a sixth of the properties abandoned a decade and a half earlier to their former owners provided they immediately occupied and worked the land.[13] However the González de Almoyna descendants did not indicate any interest in those properties until thirty years later, during one of the periods when the Apaches were at peace. When the family tried to reassume possession of land in Namiquipa, their efforts were thwarted by the new residents, backed by the authority of the colonial state.[14]

This introduces the third domain in relation to which the civilizing mission was conducted; namely, the way the cultural struggle outlined in Croix's Bando of 1778 figured in the settlers' popular representations of their own history. In the aftermath of Mexico's independence from Spain, most presidios were no longer supported, either directly or indirectly, by the state. Just as state support for the presidios fell off in the 1820s,[15] so did Apache raiding increase dramatically starting in the 1830s (Escudero 1839). More large estates in Chihuahua were abandoned; for example, the 16,000-hectare Hacienda de Ortega northeast of Namiquipa in the Santa Clara Valley. Decades later the German-American entrepreneur Enrique Müller paid only four hundred pesos for Ortega, the low purchase price possible because the lands were "worth no more than that, by virtue of the fact they have been completely abandoned for more than 30 years as a consequence of the frequent incursions of the Barbarians."[16] During the 1840s, rural Chihuahuans were also ravaged by mercenary scalp hunters from the United States, who sometimes did not bother to distinguish between Apache and Mexican scalps (R. Smith 1963, 1965). Those events were almost coincident in time with the external wrench of the U.S.-Mexican war, during which Chihuahua was invaded by U.S. soldiers and after which the United States seized about half of Mexico's territory. By the 1850s, hundreds of Apaches lived in the Sierra de Santa Clara east of Namiquipa.[17] By 1863 there were only 127 families still living in Namiquipa, where there had been 300 in the past. That, wrote the municipal president (mayor), was the result of "los ataques de los bárbaros."[18]

The experiences of those Chihuahuans who survived the Apache wars left a lasting impression in popular consciousness. The colonists and their descendants were manifestly aware of their historical mission of "civilizing" the frontier. The Proyecto de Restitución de Ejidos for Cruces (now in the municipio of Namiquipa), for example, includes a history "obtained from the inhabitants of this place." This history remarks, "in the course of the 18th and 19th centuries and part of the 20th, there were many difficulties, primarily having to do with defending their households and their lands against Apache Indians."[19] In 1894, a statement by the popular Municipal Council of Namiquipa affirms that "since the year 1778 and until very recently, the descendants [of the original colonists] and those who actually possess the aforementioned land [of the pueblo] have defended it . . . against the frequent and tenacious attacks of the barbaric Indians, irrigating with their own blood, as with that of their ancestors, the land which until now they have peacefully possessed."[20]

In petitions for land written in the 1900s and 1920s, and indeed in discussions during the 1980s, Namiquipans refer to Croix's bando and the compact between the colonial state and the colonists of Namiquipa as a "grand and beneficent project."[21] In 1922, while petitioning the postrevolutionary state for the restitution of their lands threatened with invasion by the owners of large estates, Namiquipans wrote:

> The traditional History of our pueblo as that of the State [of Chihuahua] marks a period of continuous War against Apache tribes, and the settlers of these isolated regions had to withstand this struggle with true stoicism and abnegation for more than seventy years, and even though they frequently fell beneath the knife of the Savage, they never abandoned their *posesiones* [fields and houses] because this signified losing them, a condition imposed by the Decree of Colonization [i.e., the Bando of 1778].[22]

What is demonstrated by these (and many other) testimonies in the historical memory of Namiquipans in the nineteenth and twentieth centuries is basically a popular recension of an official project of colonization. Alongside the conquest and structural transformation of the region, and the way that transformation was conceived and planned from the center, there occurred a reading and experience of that "grand and beneficent project" from the standpoint of the people themselves, that is, a reading from the periphery.

There was an undeniable consistency and coherence to the manner in which Namiquipans understood and represented their experiences living on Mexico's northern frontier from the colonial period through the Mexican revolution —with many of the idioms and terms describing work, identity, and livelihood derived directly from an unashamed and programmatic colonial project. Nonetheless, that frontier had been transformed considerably in the decades before the 1910 revolution. Toward the end of the nineteenth century, the social and historical conditions in the region were very different from what they had been at the end of the eighteenth century; further, those conditions had been changed and redefined in no small measure as a result of military settlement colonists' actions.[23] In other words, neither the structural nor the metropolitical frameworks or domains were the same. The "indios bárbaros" were gone and the colonial state was gone. But landlords were back now, not with a vengeance, but with a hearty confidence that property rights would be respected and investments protected. And the state (albeit a different one) was back as well.

The Struggle Against Barbarism from the Center

The social structural and political changes in the region during the nineteenth century—bound up as they were with the process of bourgeois state formation in Mexico (Corrigan and Sayer 1985; Joseph and Nugent 1994)—were unevenly and contradictorily articulated with the development (or, as I have argued elsewhere, the "devolution"; Nugent 1989) of forms of relationship largely internal to the ongoing formation of the community. This is most strikingly evident in the differentiated notions of the meaning and value of land from the standpoint either of the colonists or of a new wave of outsiders intent on recolonizing the territory to the end of establishing capitalist enterprises rather than self-sustaining military settlement colonies.

The land of Namiquipa has always been on one or another kind of frontier. Initially a frontier of a "civilization" threatened by the forces of "barbarism" represented by the Apaches, it later became a frontier of socioeconomic expansion. As the frontier changed from a sociocultural and geographic one to a historical frontier on which contrasting developmental trajectories of elite and subaltern social groups confronted one another (a change that Katz [1981: 7] describes eloquently and concisely as "the transformation of the frontier into the border"), the lands assumed new and different meanings from the perspectives of the colonists on the one hand and, on the other, those groups and classes (above all estate owners and agents of the modern state) who coveted the same lands.

During the earlier period, land had been one of the raw materials for a new society, in a space where "civilized" people grazed cattle, planted trees and crops, and built towns. Putting aside for the moment the fact that these civilized people did not immediately exercise the option to set themselves up as independent entrepreneurs or capitalists, initially the settlers of Namiquipa were the beneficiaries and instruments of "the so-called primitive accumulation" of capital. That was described by Marx as "nothing else than the historical process of divorcing the producer from the means of production" (Marx [1867] 1906: 786). During the colonial period, settlers of Namiquipa were in fact invested with control of means of production (particularly land); the social groups being divorced from the means of production included the indigenous inhabitants of the region and, significantly, landlords such as the González de Almoyna family and others who abandoned properties in the region because they could not protect them against Apache attacks. The Conchos Indians had been "divorced" in that most incontrovertible manner, through physical extermination.

But that only points to the features of the "secret of primitive accumulation" in those many examples—particularly from colonized regions—that do not correspond to its "classic form" (Marx [1867] 1906: 787); namely the extermination of entire societies, entire ways of living. Another feature, though, is the possibility that the initial beneficiaries of the primitive accumulation process—again, particularly in the colonies (see Marx [1867] 1906: 838–48)—may not immediately set themselves up as a capitalist class. As Marx wrote, "The history of this expropriation [of the peasant from the soil], in different countries, assumes different aspects, and runs through its various phases in different orders of succession, and at different periods" (Marx [1867] 1906: 787). In Namiquipa colonists were invested with control of means of production to the end of establishing communities the very existence of which required a high degree of militarization and common defense of land and livelihood. These were hardly social practices and organizations commensurate with the development of capitalist relations of production.

By the time of the defeat of the Apaches in 1885 during the first half of the Porfiriato,[24] however, the location and identity of Namiquipans and other settlement colonists as subjects in the process of primitive accumulation had been inverted. They now faced the prospect of being alienated from their land—which they had taken earlier from the Conchos, the Sumas, and the Janos, or from estate owners, and for which they fought against the Apaches. Land policies backed by laws implemented in Mexico in the 1880s and 1890s mandated the sale of all national and "vacant" lands, and authorized surveying companies to assume ownership of one-third of the lands they surveyed (Bellingeri and Gil Sánchez 1980). The Municipal Lands Law imposed in Chihuahua by Governor Enrique C. Creel in 1905 ordered local authorities to sell off all land, including house lots, agricultural fields, and pasturelands claimed by residents of the towns (Lloyd 1987, 1988).

In the later period, then (i.e., after the defeat of the Apaches and the elimination of indigenous threats to the establishment of capitalist relations of production and enterprises throughout the region), the inhabitants of towns such as Namiquipa, who still controlled extensive lands in the 1880s, became themselves the object of an assault by the state. The dispossession of peasants in Chihuahua during the two and a half decades following 1885 was especially violent and thoroughgoing in the ex-colonies, because their residents were able to claim considerably more land than other communities in the region, or indeed anywhere in Mexico (Lloyd 1983, 1988; Nugent 1993: 69; Wasserman 1980).

In relation to the broader process of socioeconomic transformation that had redefined the frontier from a "frontier of civilization" to a "frontier of capitalism," then, the land assumed new and different meanings for social groups (landlords, petty bourgeois speculators) from outside the community. These new meanings contrasted with the ones recognized by Namiquipan colonists and their descendants who, although they had worked upon the land and defended it for more than a century, now stood to lose it. This did not go unnoticed by Namiquipans, who wrote to President Díaz in 1908, "We see with deep sorrow that those lands which we justly esteem to be ours, received from our fathers and fecundated with over a century's constant work, are passing into the hands of strangers through a simple petition and the payment of a few pesos. . . . If you do not grant us your protection, we will have to abandon our homes in order to subsist." [25]

Marx's discussion of primitive accumulation of capital in part VIII of volume 1 of *Capital* provides an accessible, resonant, and recognizable account of historical processes affecting laboring masses of the Mexican countryside during the late nineteenth century. As Mario Cerutti (1989) among others points out, primitive accumulation involved more than just the celebrated "separation of producers from means of production," however. It also involved the growth and consolidation of political and economic power by a particular class, the bourgeoisie (for prerevolutionary Chihuahua, see Wasserman 1984). Along with that came the growth of the internal market, an amplification of available means of production—unequally distributed—and, as an outcome, a recasting of the social relations of production.

A critical feature of the primitive accumulation of capital in Mexico was the commodification of land. By encouraging the sale of "national," "vacant," and "untitled" land, the state permitted elites to secure control of massive estates (the process of land concentration) while peasants were compelled to rent or sharecrop land they had worked in the past (as they rarely had enough money to purchase their own land) or to sell their labor power to the large estates. In other words, from the standpoint of the peasantry (including the residents of Namiquipa and other military settlement colonies in Chihuahua whose lands were under attack as a result of porfirian land laws), this later moment of the primitive accumulation of capital had consequences that were simultaneously structural (separation of producers from means of production) and cultural or subjective.

If the former consequences were transparent and obvious, the latter were somewhat more opaque, and are sometimes overlooked and neglected in analysis. But they are no less important and are perhaps more interesting from the standpoint of developing an understanding of how structural effects are registered and apprehended within popular culture. Peasants were compelled to reorient their practices in light of the transformation of land from a subject of labor in their communities into a commodity—which they could not afford to purchase—that circulated in spheres of exchange having little to do with community life (Cardoso 1980; Marx [1857–58] 1973: 471–72, [1867] 1906: 198–201, 784–805; Nugent 1988: 16; Roseberry 1989: 80–121).

Arguments that the agrarian struggle in Namiquipa—in the twentieth century as much as at the end of the nineteenth—is best understood as a struggle to maintain the land as a subject of labor for the agriculturalist, rather than merely as a more immediate, almost technical, struggle for control of a given territory or means of production, have been published elsewhere (Nugent 1991, 1993; Nugent and Alonso 1994). The point demonstrated here is simply this: Namiquipans and other settler-colonists had earlier advanced a colonial project by securing the territory for an external political power (and had received enormous grants of land in exchange for that service). By the end of the nineteenth century, however, they were found to be an obstacle to the reordering of social relations of production and property underway throughout Mexico in those circumstances where they were still able to hold, work, and collectively maintain extensive tracts of land, which they regarded as commons. This was particularly the case in the north, and especially after the end of the Apache wars, in which Namiquipans and others (indígena and gente de razón alike) had been on the frontlines (compare Katz 1988). But ironically, with the defeat of the Apaches, their former combatants were converted into the new backward "barbarians" whose way of living required reform or merited elimination.

Great landlord families, both Mexicans such as the Terrazas and foreigners such as the Müllers, consolidated million-acre estates through the purchase of national and (supposedly) vacant lands. Foreigners such as William Greene, William Randolph Hearst, and Yves Limantour secured mining and timber concessions, built railroads and company towns, and operated cattle and sheep ranches encompassing territories that had previously been parts of communities in the sierra of Chihuahua. Even though Namiquipans secured recognition of the legality of Croix's land grant from President Díaz himself in 1889 and from the Ministry of Government in 1893, that information was not passed along to the residents of Cruces, Galeana, Casas Grandes, and Janos. By the turn of the century, as much as 90 percent of the land of those towns was controlled by estate owners from outside the communities (see Nugent 1993: 69).

This whole ugly, violent process of peasant dispossession was justified in the terms of a logic that exalted the privatization of land as the surest guarantee for the orderly progress of society. Díaz insisted that "to divide the villagers' commons [*ejidos*] among the heads of families [would have] a very beneficial outcome for that indigent class of people, for it would assure them small private properties."[26] Unfortunately, the division—if not the outright invasion—

of village lands assumed priority over any guarantees regarding to whom the lands would devolve; in most cases "that indigent class of people" lost out.

In 1904, Governor Enrique C. Creel—nephew and son-in-law of Luis Terrazas, patriarch of the grand family that had politically and economically dominated the state of Chihuahua for the prior half century—eliminated the last vestiges of peasant control over local politics through revisions to the Chihuahuan constitution. He also imposed a municipal tax law that substantially increased the state's share of peasant surpluses (Almada 1964: 21–26, 81–83). Then Creel's Municipal Land Law of 1905 put on the market whatever land was still controlled by the residents of rural communities in the state. Wealthy ranchers, hacendados, officials at the municipal and district levels, and petty bourgeois immigrants purchased grazing land, agricultural fields, and even house lots out from under existing residents. These residents, even though they were descendants of colonial-period settlers, could not produce what were regarded by local and state officials as legitimate titles to their properties (see Alonso 1995; Lloyd 1987, 1988; Nugent 1993: 69–71).

Next to the violence of these actions, the most striking feature of this whole process was the condescension with which the victims of state-mandated expropriations of peasant lands were regarded. Luis J. Comadurán, the Porfirian cacique who carried out a survey of Namiquipan land prior to the division and sales that occurred after 1905 (during which he secured control of more than three hundred hectares of prime agricultural land—twelve times the legal limit), could not understand what he evidently regarded as the Namiquipans' baseless refusal to accept new immigrants to the community in the decades after the end of the Apache wars.[27] Victoriano Torres, the *presidente municipal* (mayor) during much of the decade from 1900 to 1910, presided over the sales of "municipal" lands. He complained bitterly throughout his correspondence with district and state officials about the ignorance that made the Namiquipans reluctant to accept the terms of a logic according to which land they and their ancestors had fought to defend should be put on the market.[28] Overall, the image of the descendants of settler-colonists that emerges from the correspondence of the state officials who engineered the expropriation of the peasantry is one of backwardness, childishness, and ignorance, an ignorance sharpened and inflamed by the rustic conditions they tolerated and by their reluctance to accept an alternative, modernizing future.

Writing about nineteenth-century Argentina in a discussion of "the antinomies of ruling class culture," the geographer Michael Johns (1993: 83) describes how in 1845, "writer and statesman Domingo Sarmiento made a clarion call to replace barbarism (the countryside, Latin America) with civilization (the city, Europe). The civilizing process involved purging the country both of Indians and of gauchos, who were viewed as obstacles to progress." In Chihuahua, the lumping together of Apache fighters with Apaches had to wait until the Indians who still resisted northward movements of (now Mexican) settlers were completely exterminated or driven north across the U.S.-Mexican border to a future of prison camps or relocation to distant reservations. Another important difference is that in Chihuahua it was precisely the non-Indian settlers and frontiersmen and women—analogues of the Argentine gauchos—who were employed to drive off the barbarians. That mission accomplished, their lands came under the lustful gaze of landlords, surveying companies, and the development orientation of state officials. By the start of the twentieth century, this lumping of "barbarians" and frontiersmen (and women) was complete. Also firmly in place were the categories describing "the future" of capitalism and neocolonial relations of power and production for the region.

A compelling example of this new recognition of a putative identity for the people of the countryside of Chihuahua appeared in the closing lines of a short book written by Enrique C. Creel in 1928. Creel, the governor of Chihuahua in the six years preceding the revolution of 1910, was also a (corrupt) banker, (fabulously successful) businessman, and national government minister during the close of the Porfiriato. His essay on Chihuahua was originally presented as a series of talks to the Sociedad Mexicana de Geografía y Estadística, and subtitled "its history, geography, and natural resources." People (the inhabitants of Chihuahua) are mentioned and discussed primarily in the latter sections of his study, that is, the parts devoted to "geography" and "natural resources." His book concludes with the following passages:

> Seeing as how I have gone beyond the boundaries of Chihuahua, and begun to touch on a few of the grand problems of the fatherland, I will end by highlighting the dangers our nation faces, and the means of saving it.
>
> | DANGERS: | SOLUTIONS: |
> |---|---|
> | 1. Hatred of religion. | 1. Peace. |
> | 2. Hatred of capital. | 2. Justice. |
> | 3. Hatred of foreigners. | 3. Love of Capital. |
> | 4. Civil War. | 4. Love of Work. |
> | | 5. Respect for property. |
>
> GOD SAVE THE FATHERLAND!!
>
> (1928: 78–79)

Creel's "solutions" present an impressive condensation of ruling class ideology; the very notions of peace, justice, work, and property that he invokes are all predicated on the "love of capital." More significant for the present argument is that these notions render peasants invisible even as they assume the disappearance of Indians. The property for which Creel demands respect is capitalist property, not the common lands that Namiquipans and others worked and transformed during the prior century and a half. Indeed, the work of defending the land and transforming it through human labor—the work that the colonists had already performed—does not even figure in Creel's vision, which appears to be focused on wage work alone.

As for the notions of peace and justice, compare Creel's optimistic confidence in 1928 to the remarks of a Namiquipan peasant responding to a query about whether people in Chihuahua had joined the revolution in 1910 to recover control of their land. "Put it that we now have land," replied Cruz Chávez in 1986, "but that was a fight. And justice? And freedom? When will we get that? Can you tell me?"[29]

By Way of Conclusion

Unable to answer such questions, I indulge in the standard retreat of scholars by insisting that that is not what I intended to do. In this chapter, I have tried to explain how a community that was earlier established by a colonial state as a military settlement colony dedicated, among other things, to the extermination or pacification of indios bárbaros should later occupy a structural position vis-à-vis the state curiously similar to that of the indigenous peoples the settlers were originally commissioned to suppress. The putative "barbarity" of the Namiquipans from the standpoint of the state by the start of the twentieth century, though, was no longer so much a "lifestyle" issue as it was a function of the fact that they stood—with their extensive lands—in the way of the "rational" reordering of relations of property and production that were a requirement for the successful accumulation of capital. Arguably, of course, the dispossession between the 1880s and 1910 of peasant communities in western Chihuahua by Mexican and North American landlords, surveying companies, and the state itself was the truly barbaric process. But that's another argument.

The present argument has offered an analysis of discourses of civility and barbarity that insists on always situating those discourses in the historical contexts of specific practices that occurred on a particular frontier. This chapter provides an example of how popular representations may appropriate and transform the language of official or dominant representations, but that appropriation and transformation are always mediated by the particular experiences of specific groups of people trying to live their lives under trying circumstances. In other words, the very discourses are grounded in material social processes.

Notes

Chapter 2. The Jesuit Mission Frontier

1. This denial of Amerindian culture is evident in the landscape paintings and sketches of the American West by artists such as Bodner, Catlin, and Remington; Indians are either absent altogether or are "naturalized"—objects worthy of study like the buffalo (rather than owners or prior claimants to the land).

2. This is not to deny the significant discussion and debate over Indian identity that took place in Spain during the sixteenth century. The debate notwithstanding, the vast majority of Europeans, beginning with Columbus, saw themselves as far superior to the Indians, owing to their possession not only of the "truth" about God, but of "true" government, town life, commerce, and a host of other behaviors, beliefs, and items of material culture that the Indians were said to have lacked.

3. Of course, it is difficult to compare technologies. Is a metal knife better than one of stone? If one compares knives in terms of ease of cutting, durability, etc., the metal knife generally is more efficient. However, the making of a metal knife implies various technologies (e.g., mining, forging) as well as social relations of production whose costs, particularly environmental and social, are much higher than those associated with the making of a stone knife.

4. See the chapter by Mary Karasch in this volume, which discusses instances where Jesuits were successful with hunter-gatherer groups in Brazil.

5. While it is true that the Jesuits in northwestern Mexico did not organize, train, or lead an Indian militia, the priests often raised Indian armies numbering in the hundreds, if not thousands. This was accomplished through Indian governors and war captains who were controlled, or at least influenced, by the Jesuits. One or more Jesuits usually accompanied the militia, which was led by a Spanish captain and soldiers. At no time, however, did the Jesuits of northwestern Mexico try to secure firearms for their neophytes (see Pérez de Ribas 1645: 65–67).

6. Of course, the precise link between mosquitoes and malaria was not understood. Jesuits and other Spaniards did, however, correlate certain diseases with particular environments (e.g., lowlands) and insects such as mosquitoes (Reff 1991: 106–7, 198).

7. Note that one cannot compare cattle with carpinchos, armadillos, or capybaras simply in terms of the number of calories (or "nourishment") they provided. Obviously a cow provides more food than an armadillo. But cows and other domesticated animals require large grazing areas and irrevocably alter (simplify) complex ecosystems, often

leading to their destruction. For instance, cattle grazing has degraded or destroyed millions of acres of land in southern Arizona and Sonora, Mexico (Dobyns 1981: 79–90; Dunbier 1968).

8. This point was made in a somewhat indirect way by Mörner (1953: 200–1), who noted that the Guaraní "were the most culturally advanced people in the eastern part of the La Plata region, . . . yet they lacked the cultural and religious traditions and the political consciousness of the Andean peoples."

9. The Jesuit Constitutions prescribed the teaching of St. Thomas' doctrines (Ganss 1970: 219). In his *Summa contra gentiles* (McInerny 1990: 63–65), St. Thomas held that all men could acquire through the natural light of reason a limited and imperfect knowledge of God.

10. As an example, in his *Historia,* Pérez de Ribas (1645) suggested that, after several Spanish military expeditions had failed to subdue the Yaqui, "good angels" interceded, frightening the Yaqui into accepting missionization.

11. Note that it was not uncommon for religious, when they retained native languages, to nevertheless employ non-native terms for God.

12. Interestingly, figures compiled by Aspurz (1946: 278–319) show that a minimum of 954 missionaries of non-Spanish origin emigrated to the New World prior to 1767. Of these 954, 874 were Jesuits. The first three Jesuits who arrived in Asunción were a Catalonian, an Irishman, and a Portuguese; eventually priests from thirty-one different countries worked in the missions of Paraguay (McNaspy 1984: 22; Storni 1980).

13. The Sinaloa mission was founded by Gonzalo de Tapia, from León, Spain, and Martin Pérez, who was born and raised on the frontier in San Martín, Nueva Vizcaya. The first two Jesuits to work on the eastern slopes of the Sierra Madre Occidental, out of Durango, were Gerónimo Ramírez, from Sevilla, and Juan Agustín de Espinosa, who was born and raised in Zacatecas.

14. This pattern was also true of secular clergy. In 1575, only sixteen peninsular priests in the Diocese of Mexico spoke Nahuatl whereas forty-four Creoles spoke the language (Poole 1987: 48).

15. Polzer (1976: 56–57) has suggested that the Franciscan practice of moving their missionaries at regular intervals often made it difficult or impossible for priests to master native languages.

16. Rodrigo de Cabredo, "Ordenaciones del Padre Rodrigo de Cabredo para las Misiones, January 1, 1611. Durango." Latin American Manuscripts, Mexico II, Lilly Library, Indiana University.

Chapter 3. Indigenous Rebellions on the Mission Frontier

The author would like to thank the contributors to this volume for their suggestions. She is also indebted to students in her fall 1995 graduate seminar on Comparative Frontier History. This work was partially supported by Northern Arizona University Organized Research grants in 1991 and 1992.

1. Pratt denotes these as contact zones.

2. I have not included here other uprisings and continuous raiding carried out by indigenous groups that were more successful in resisting missionization and other attempts at incorporation (e.g., Seris, Conchos, Tobosos, Apaches).

3. I have analyzed three other early revolts in "First-Generation Rebellions in Seventeenth-Century Nueva Vizcaya" (forthcoming 1998a). It should be noted that my sources for the Acaxee uprising (which has not been studied in detail by historians) are primarily archival and for the later Yaqui Revolt, largely secondary accounts.

4. Coatsworth produces a useful typology of rural revolts. Nonetheless his category of "mission" revolts does not reflect the differences among these.

5. Reff argues that Jesuits encountered the aftermath of drastic population reduction by disease in societies which had been far denser, more sociopolitically complex until the sixteenth century.

6. The correspondence between the evolution of encomienda/repartimiento in Nueva Vizcaya and the *encomienda originaria/encomienda mitaya* in Paraguay is striking.

7. Cartas ánuas of 1597 and 1607 in, respectively, Archivo General de la Nación, Mexico City (hereafter cited as AGN), Historia, vol. 19, exp. 6.

8. Since only a few Franciscans remained in Topia, Bishop Mota y Escobar assigned the area to Jesuits; carta de P. Hernando de Santarén, n.d., AGN, Jesuitas II-4.

9. "Relación de la entrada que hizo el gobernador de la Nueva Vizcaya . . . , 1610," University of Texas, Nettie Lee Benson Library (hereafter cited as UTNLB), Joaquín García Icazbalceta Collection, Varias Relaciones, I-1; "Carta ánua de P. Juan Font, 1608," in González Rodríguez, *Crónicas,* 160–65.

10. "Testimonio jurídico de las poblaciones y conversiones de los serranos acaxees . . . ," AGN, Historia 20, exp. 19.

11. Within pueblos, the *parcialidades* distinguished by Jesuits certainly correspond to former rancherías. The term is used to distinguish a barrio or neighborhood probably with kinship ties.

12. P. Nicolás de Arnaya to P. Prov. Francisco Baez, 9 February 1601, *Documentos para la historia de México* [hereafter cited as DHM] (México, 1853–57), 4th series, III, 61.

13. Pérez de Ribas discusses how this silver was used in betting on ball games. The custom was established early in Sinaloa.

14. "Testimonio jurídico . . . , 1600," AGN, Historia 20, exp. 19.

15. "Carta ánua, P. Prov. Francisco Báez, April 1602," in Thomas H. Naylor and Charles W. Polzer, S.J., eds. (1986: I:154–63); P. Nicolás de Arnaya to P. Prov. Báez, 9 February 1601, DHM, III, 61.

16. Much of the following account of the Acaxee Revolt is taken from Pérez de Ribas and the following sources: "Relación de P. Prov. Francisco Baez, April 1602" and other documents in Archivo General de Indias, Sevilla (hereafter cited as AGI), Audiencia de México, 1254, published in Naylor and Polzer (1986: 154–99); and Urdiñola to King, Durango, 31 March 1604, in Hackett, Bandelier, and Bandelier (1926–1937: II:89–93).

17. Ibid.

18. "Relación de P. Diego Ximénez, San Andrés, 1633," AGN, Jesuitas, III-15, exp. 4.

19. Francisco de Urdiñola to king, 31 March 1604, Hackett, Bandelier, and Bandelier (1926–1937: II: 89–93).

20. "Carta ánua, P. Prov. Francisco Báez, April 1602," in Naylor and Polzer (1986: 159). Dunne recounts many examples of the targeting of young people. For example, when Padre Santarén attempted to negotiate with the rebels asserting that he was "their father," they responded that "he was not their father and they were not his sons." Gutiérrez discusses how these practices upset traditional hierarchical relations in Pueblo society.

21. Carta ánua de 1607 and carta de P. Luis de Ahumada to P. Martín Pelaez, 13 November 1608, both in AGN, Historia 19. Halley's comet would most likely have been seen in northern Mexico in September or October 1607; personal communication from astronomers Kathy Eastwood and David Schleicher, 30 October 1995.

22. P. Andrés Pérez de Ribas to P. Hernando de Villafane, Tesamo, 13 June 1617, AGN, Archivo Provisional, Misiones, caja 2.

23. See, for example, "Apologético defensorio," November 1657, AGN, Historia, vol. 316, f. 359–425.

24. Report of P. Vis. Juan Antonio Balthasar to Viceroy, n.p., n.d., UTNLB, W. B. Stephens Collection, #1719.

25. "Decree of Gov. Ignacio Francisco de Barrutia," 18 June 1729, in marriage registers, Santiago Papasquiaro, microfilmed records of the Genealogical Society of Utah, microfilm #658011.

26. Spicer relied on Navarro García's narrative account taken from documents in the AGI; Hu-Dehart used Mexican documents.

27. P. Joseph Toral to P. Provincial Joseph de Barra, 25 March 1736, UTNLB, W. B. Stephens Collection, #1747; letters of Huidobro, August 1735, University of California, H. E. Bolton Collection, microfilm #1875.

28. For Nueva Vizcaya, see Archivo de la Parroquia de Santiago Papasquiaro, burial records, 1659–1750; and Archivo de la Parroquia de Santa Catalina de Tepehuanes, 1728–58 (filmed by the Genealogical Society of Utah). For Guadalajara, see Audiencia de Guadalajara to king, 16 July 1739, AGI, Guadalajara. leg. 104; and MacLeod.

29. Various autos of 1740 in University of California, H. E. Bolton Collection, microfilm #1875; and in AGI, Audiencia of Guadalajara, leg. 89.

30. P. Prov. Juan Antonio Balthasar to Gov. Diego Ortiz de Parrilla, México, 23 January 1752, AGN, Jesuitas II-7, exp. 15. Balthasar blamed both the Yaqui and Pima rebellions on betrayal by Indians who had been overly trusted and feted by Spaniards.

31. Stern discusses resistant adaptation as a long-term process which encompasses resistant and self-protective acts along with partial accommodations to colonial authority.

32. Indians in other parts of colonial Mexico formed specific associations based on images of Saint James pictured with his powerful horse surrounded by thunder and lightning.

33. Junta de Guerra report on Nueva Vizcaya to Viceroy, México, 4 August 1704, AGN, Historia, vol. 20, exp. 1.

34. Scott develops the idea of hidden space or the "hidden transcript."

Chapter 4. The Colonial Pact

The author acknowledges the American Philosophical Society, the University of Missouri-St. Louis, the University of Illinois at Urbana-Champaign, and the American Council of Learned Societies for financial support that contributed to researching and writing this chapter.

1. The concept of ethnic space is developed by Marcello Carmagnani (1988: 15, 52–108). John Tutino (1986: 25–29) identifies mobility as a value defended by peasants in different cultural milieux.

2. These three terms refer to non-Indians of different racial categories in colonial society. Vecinos were landholding residents of a given locality; whether or not they were actually of Spanish origin, they were Hispanic in their cultural and political orientation. Gente de razón ("people of reason") were distinguished from Indians in their civil status and legal obligations; racially they could be Spanish, criollo (whites born in the New World), or mestizo (a mixture of white and Indian). *Castas,* a term that appeared frequently in colonial documents generated in Sonora, included persons of mixed racial composition with Amerindian, European, and African antecedents.

3. *Recopilación de las leyes de Indias,* 1680, Título doce. De la venta, composición, y repartimiento de tierras, solares y aguas, ley V; Título tercero. De las reducciones y pueblos de indios, ley VIII, Madrid, Marcialo Pons, 1973.

4. Fray Antonio Angel Núñez, "Carta edificante histórico-curiosa," Biblioteca Nacional Fondo Franciscano (hereafter BNFF) *Noticias de Varias Misiones,* vol. 76.

5. Juan Bautista de Anza to Brigadier Teodoro de Croix, Comandante General de Provincias Internas, 30 June 1777, BNFF 34/734, f. 1–5; Pedro Garrido y Durán, Intendente de Sonora to Don Ygnacio de Noperi, Capitán General de la Nación Opata, BNFF 35/767; "Representación del Padre Comisario de las misiones fray Juan Prestamero sobre quejas de los ópatas contra el padre ministro de Opodepe," 17 July 1777, BNFF 34/735.

6. Figures for Sonora are sketchy at best, because of the general mobility of this frontier population and the absence of systematic tribute collection. Although a few well-documented Jesuit and diocesan visitations produced estimates of the number of families and "souls" in each mission pueblo, these are not exact and, more to the point, do not account for an indeterminate number of Indian *naborías* and mestizos living outside the missions.

7. Bishop Reyes, 1784, BNFF 34/759, f. 31.

8. Evidence of composiciones comes from the archives of the Audiencia de Guadalajara, conserved in the Archivo de Instrumentos Públicos (hereafter AIPJ) and in the Biblioteca Pública del Estado de Jalisco (BPEJ), and the Archivo de Hidalgo de Parral (AHP), the latter consulted in microfilm at the University of Arizona.

9. AIPJ Libros de Gobierno de la Audiencia de Guadalajara, Libro 47, f. 218–20; Archivo de la Mitra, Hermosillo (AMH), Archivo del Sagrario 1, 1666–1828.

10. BPEJ Real Audiencia de Guadalajara RC 27-9-259, 15ff, 1716.

11. My analysis is based on the following sources: AGN, Tierras [AHGES TP], and Archivo Histórico del Gobierno del Estado de Sonora, Títulos Primordiales. Romero (1991) analyzes a similar body of material.

12. BNFF 34/738, 740, 741.

13. Military reports on the movements of Sibubapas and presidial captains' negotiations with them are in AGN, Provincias Internas, vols. 48 and 86.

14. During the wars of independence, Sonora remained nominally under the administration of the Intendencia de Arispe and the Comandancia de Provincias Internas de Occidente. After 1821, the northwestern provinces sent delegates to the Deputación Provincial convened under the auspices of Iturbide. In 1824, Sonora and Sinaloa became part of the constitutional Republic of Mexico as the unified Estado de Occidente, but they divided into two separate states in 1831.

15. "Decreto No. 89 del Estado de Occidente, Alamos, 30 de septiembre de 1828: Ley para el repartimiento de los pueblos indígenas, reduciéndolos a propiedad particular," in F. Pesqueira, *Documentos para la historia de Sonora,* Serie II, Tomo I, 1821–1845.

16. Juan de Gándara, Protector de indios de Opodepe, to Fiscal Protector General de Indios, 24 July 1818, BPEJ ARAG RC 264-5-3600; Fernando Ma. Grande, Visitador de las misiones de la Pimería Alta, to gobernador del Estado de Occidente, 1828. I consulted a copy of this document through the courtesy of Kieran R. McCarty.

17. Sonoran state decrees were consulted in AHGES caja 36-1, exp. 1052. Laws directly concerning land tenure are 3 (1833), 10 (1834), 41, 47, 62, and 75 (1835).

18. BNFF 32/659, 1803; Governor Manuel Escalante y Arvizu used the term *proletario* in a letter to the president of Mexico, 4 June 1836, in AGN, Gobernación, caja 3, exp. s/n.; AHGES TP Tomo IV, exp. 40, f. 899–947; leg. 1, exp. 1, 1831; leg. 7, exp. 87, f. 1304–1350; exp. 83, f. 1188–1218; exp. 84, 85, f. 1219–1289; AGN, Tierras, leg. 1416, exp. 11, 18; leg. 1422, exp. 3; leg. 1424, exp. 7, 10.

19. AGN, Gobernación caja 3, exp. s/c, s/n, 1837. Governor Escalante to the Secretary of State and of the Interior.

20. The language of Anrríquez's and Bohórquez's petitions illustrates well the tenets of the moral economy literature. See especially Hobsbawm (1973), J. Scott (1985, 1990), G. Smith (1989), and Stavig (1988).

Chapter 5. Women of the Buenos Aires Frontier

1. Fernando O. Assunção (1978–79) believes the gaucho first appeared in the Banda Oriental during the eighteenth century; Emilio A. Coni (1969) finds no gauchos in eighteenth-century Río de la Plata, while Leon Pomer (1971) sees the gaucho as emerging from the landless peasantry in the region to the west of Buenos Aires in the eighteenth century. See also Rodríguez Molas (1968). Regardless of how or when they

believe the gaucho emerged, none of these historians addresses the issue of women on the frontier.

2. Bonifacio de Carril (1978: 27), for example, mentions that the 1778 census reflected a significant increase in the rural female population, but sees this only as "clear proof that rural life was becoming more sedentary."

3. The Guardia del Zanjón, in the pago of Magdalena, and the forts of Luján and Salto were all constructed between 1753 and 1756. Between 1770 and 1777, additional forts at Areco, Matanza and Laguna de los Ranchos completed the frontier defenses.

4. According to Urbano de Iriondo (1936: 44), by 1722 not one estancia in Santa Fé had escaped attack by Indians, loss of property and lives, and the taking of captives.

5. In 1784 Indians raided the estancias in the Mendoza region, and in 1786 and 1806 they attacked across the San Luis frontier. In 1784 the priest in charge of the Charruan mission of Cayastá requested that the mission be moved to Los Manânciales, a site near the original settlement of the city of Santa Fé, in order to free his wards from "the invasions of the infidel [Indians] of the Chaco." Archivo General de la Nación Argentina, Buenos Aires (hereafter AGNA), Justicia, leg. 15, exp. 363, Sala IX-31-4-4. As late as 1802 Toba Indian tribes were making incursions along the Río Dorado. AGNA, Testimonio del expediente sobre la gratificación hecha a los indios fieles . . . , Hacienda, Leg. 122, exp. 3081, Sala IX-34-5-8. On Spanish-Indian illegal trade see K. Jones (1993, 1986). For information on population growth see Comadrán Ruiz (1969: 97–114); for increased agricultural and pastoral production see Garavaglia (1985).

6. Cabildo de Buenos Aires, Acuerdo de 3 de agosto de 1744, in *Documentos para la Historia Argentina,* vol. 10, *Padrones de la Ciudad y Campaña de Buenos Aires (1726–1810)* (Buenos Aires: Peuser, 1920), 30–31. This volume also contains the census data.

7. Although reference to the pago of Magdalena dates from the beginning of the seventeenth century, up to the beginning of the eighteenth century it was a region populated only by wild horses and cattle (Caride 1992: 3).

8. According to Lynch (1958: 166-67), "The general situation was that only the rich could buy, and as it cost almost as much to buy a small amount as a large one, they bought huge areas which they could not themselves exploit, but rented to the poor."

9. *Padrones de la Ciudad y Campaña de Buenos Aires (1726–1810),* "Padrón de 1744," p. 707.

10. Archivo de la Provincia de Buenos Aires, La Plata (hereafter referred to as APBA), Criminales, 1793, 34-1-18, Narcisa Cordero contra su yerno Calisto Baigorria por haverla pegado.

11. APBA, Criminales, 1783–84, 34-1-12, María Antonia Josefa de Aguilar sobre los malos tratamientos de su marido Simón Launar.

12. APBA, Criminales, 1790, 32-1-16, Alonso Domingo contra Feliz Fernández por haver violado y querido forzar a su mujer.

13. APBA, Criminales, 1780, 34-1-10, Causa criminal contra Ignacio Urreta por ilícita amistad con una mujer casada.

14. APBA, Criminales, 1785–86, 34-1-13, Causa criminal contra Miguel Godoy por

haberse querido robar una niña de poder de su madre, y después de casa de su cura don Luis de Tagle, que lo es de capilla del Pilar; 1785, 34-1-13, Sumaria contra Basilio Bustamante y María de los Santos por amancebados.

15. The following discussion is based on a reading of the rich historiography produced during the last fifteen years on frontier women in the United States. For the colonial period see Laurel Thatcher Ulrich's extraordinary works (Ulrich 1982, 1990). One of the most important figures of the recent historiography on American rural women has been Glenda Riley and her pathbreaking studies (G. Riley 1981, 1984, 1988). Among other interesting studies dealing with the experiences of American women on the frontier see John Mack Faragher (1979) and Johana L. Stratton (1981). For nineteenth-century rural women see Nancy Grey Osterud (1991) and the volume edited by Lillian Schlissel, Vicki L. Ruiz, and Janice Monk (1988).

16. For an interesting discussion of how and why the gaucho became an icon of national self-image see Richard Slatta (1985).

Chapter 7. Comparative Raiding Economies

Material in this chapter will be included in a larger work in progress, tentatively entitled, *Frontier Economies: Argentina, Araucanía, and Chile.*

1. A note about terms. I try to avoid the word *Indian,* an invention of the European world, and instead use the less loaded if awkward terms *indigenous* or *native* (in the sense of preexisting) or the self-ascribed names. By the nineteenth century, however, the term Indian was commonly shared by Creole and native people alike. Today, in most cases, tribal names are the preferred terms used by the people themselves.

2. These groups are also known as Querandís, Serranos, or according to the *Handbook of South American Indians,* Puelches. I will use the inclusive term Pampas Indians to refer to the groups north of the Río Negro and Tehuelches to refer to the southern Patagonian groups (Steward 1946: I: 160–68).

3. For linguistic evidence about these people, see Casamiquela (1969) and Manelis Klein (1985).

4. These relations were commented on by several early Spanish chroniclers of Chilean Araucanians in the sixteenth century, and the archeological record also documents the *transandino* movement of goods. For the eighteenth century, see Leonardo Leon Solís, (1990: 65–142).

5. Ramón Gutiérrez (1991: 153) and John Kessell (1979) discuss this process as it occurred on the northern frontier. A similar rationale motivated the military forces in Chile.

6. In 1780 Apaches disguised themselves as Spanish soldiers by donning leather jackets, hats, and muskets. They completely surprised Pima Indians in Gila River, Arizona, villages and killed or captured 120 persons. See Powell (1952: 45–46) and Officer (1987: 56).

7. These groups were sometimes called *Auca,* the Inca word for *enemy,* in colonial sources.

8. The parallels to the high northern plains of North America are obvious, and are treated in a chapter of my dissertation (see K. Jones 1984).

9. Recognizing the deadliness of indigenous weapons, gaucho cavalrymen on the frontier soon adopted them.

10. The author is indebted to Richard Slatta for details regarding comparative warfare tactics.

11. The translation is mine. In contrast to Leon Solís, who depicts intercultural relations as mostly hostile and outside the concerns of state or society, Richard White (1991) uses comparable material about the intercultural arena in the Great Lakes region of North America to come to quite different conclusions about the formation of the new republic.

12. See, for example, Archivo General de la Nación Argentina (AGNA), Sala IX, 1-4-3, "Comandancia de Fronteras de Chacras, Chascomús, Chivilcoy, et al. 1780–1809."

13. This is not to say that ranching efforts had not always existed in the frontier, only that the balance shifted in their favor.

14. AGNA, Sala 9, 24-2-6, leg. 14, exp. 26, 1790. See also K. Jones (1994b: 109).

15. Figures abstracted from unpublished research data compiled by Argentine historian Claudia Wentzel for a larger study tracing the development of internal commerce in Argentina in the decades following independence. Original data are in AGNA, Sala III, Hacienda; Entradas 20-7-7, 20-7-8 and Salidas 20-7-10, 20-8-1.

16. These generalizations of course say little about the wide range of cultural differences among the different groups and even less about the scope of activities. For instance, it would be a mistake to compare the scale of Tehuelche raids, in which a few dozen head of livestock were taken at a time, to the malones carried out by Calfucurá's troops, in which thousands of cattle and horses were driven off. Likewise, it would do a disservice to both the Apaches and the Comanches to suggest anything other than broad similarities between these traditional enemies. Given this caveat, however, the fact remains that native participation in thriving commercial markets and frontier economies through trading and raiding was fundamental to the formation of a capitalist system.

17. The documents that detail the system, including the amounts raised from individual landowners, can be found in the provincial archives at La Plata, Provincia de Buenos Aires, "Negocio pacífico con el indio (1825–1828)."

18. AGNA, Sala III, 17-8-5 (1835–39); 17-8-6 (1840–58), "Negocio pacífico con los indios, rendiciones de cuentas." These records provide detailed information about the amounts remitted from the Comisaría General to provide specific goods ("*yeguas, alimentos, vicios*") to the Indians and includes the names of each of the caciques.

19. See Recart Novión (1971: 133) for population data.

Chapter 8. Interethnic Conflict and Resistance

1. My thanks to Vera Blinn Reber for calling my attention to this essay on intercultural frontiers, which helped me to conceptualize my chapter.

2. Chagas' disease (trypanosomiasis, trypanosomiasis cruzi) is an untreatable disease

transmitted to humans by insects. It is marked by fever, edemas, enlargement of the lymph nodes, megacolon, megaesophagus, and cardiac enlargement and failure. It is the leading cause of cardiac death among young adults in parts of South America.

3. The Portuguese used *nação* (nation) to define African political units and new Afro-Brazilian identities. Hence the Angola and Mina nations of Goiás referred to Africans. The Portuguese also employed "nation" and semiaccurate names, which were often newly constructed ethnic indicators such as *Canoeiro,* which means canoer. I have, therefore, retained the colonial usage of nação. Only with the conquests of the 1750s does more extensive information on the indigenous "nations" appear.

4. See governors' reports and narratives of exploratory voyages in the late eighteenth and nineteenth centuries. What was once the Captaincy of Goiás (province of Goiás in the nineteenth century) has been divided into two states: Goiás in the south and Tocantins in the north.

5. Goiânia, Arquivo Histórico Estadual (hereafter AHG) caixa 9, "Relação dos Habitantes a situados no termo da Freguesia d'Nossa Senhora do Rozario, Minas d'Meia ponte, Comarca de Villa boa d'Goyaz, 1818." This document records the number of slaves owned by small farmers, including female heads of households.

6. In 1955 the Xerente told anthropologist David Maybury-Lewis that "they regretted their decision" to make peace and remain on the Tocantins. "Perhaps if we too had fought the whites . . . perhaps then we would now be strong like the Chavante." (Hemming 1987: 192). For excellent pictures of the assimilated Xerente of the late nineteenth century see Carneiro da Cunha (1992: 238–39).

7. The Karajá had been attacked by a slaving expedition in 1755, but their official pacification took place in 1775, when José Pinto da Fonseca used musicians to attract them. On Karajá trade with merchants of Pará, see Goiânia, AHG, Seção de Municípios, Niquelândia, Letter of Alex.e de Souza Von Ar.o J., São José de Tocantins, 5 February 1776, to Rmo. Snr. Vig.ro José Pires dos Santos e Sousa.

8. In 1783 only 591 brancas (white women) lived in Vila Boa; they comprised 7.3 percent of the total population of 8,159. Other women included 644 pardas and 535 *pretas forras* (freed black women). Slave women were not identified separately. Rio de Janeiro, Biblioteca Nacional, Manuscript collection (hereafter RJBN), 16, 3, 2, Notícia Geral da Capitania de Goiás, 1783, Freguesia de Villaboa.

9. One of the best sources on the trade in Indian women is RJBN, Manuscript Collection, I-31, 21, 9, Goiás (Capitania), Cópia da Memória oferecida pelo Capitam d'ordenanças Francisco José Pinto de Mangalhens [sic] em 3 de Janeiro de 1813; with notes dated 1815.

10. 1783 census: RJBN, 16, 3, 2, Notícia, Freguesia de Villaboa.

11. Since some priests formed illicit liaisons with Indian or African slave women, the genealogies of white families in Goiás recognize them as founding "fathers."

12. Complaints about the contraband trade in gold are ubiquitous in the correspondence of the governors of Goiás with the Overseas Council and the Tribuanal de Contas in Lisbon. Those often accused of the contraband trade were the men of color who traveled throughout the backlands.

13. RJBN, I-28, 31, 26, Goiás (Província), "Ofício de Miguel Lino de Moraes dirigido aos Snrs. do Conselho Geral da Província do Goiaz, expondo o estado econômico [e político] da província do Goiaz" (Goiás, 1830).

14. Pedroso argues on pp. 144–48 that the Avá-Canoeiro lived in the lower Rio Tocantins region in the seventeenth century and are linguistically different from the Karijó Indians.

15. According to Survival International, Urgent Action Bulletin of 14 November 1988 (which includes a picture by André Toral), the Avá-Canoeiro were being threatened by a major dam project because the authorities claimed they no longer existed in the Tocantins region. My thanks to André Toral for a copy of this bulletin.

Chapter 9. North to the Yerbales

1. Governor Agustín Fernando de Pinedo to Viceroy Pedro de Ceballos, Plaza de Ygatimí, 30 October 1777, two letters, both in Archivo General de Indias, Audiencia de Buenos Aires, legs. 57 and 543. (Hereafter cited as AGI-BA).

2. For the founding, administration, and spatial configurations of these new settlements, see "Copia de reparto de tierras de la Pob.ón de Quarepoty," Governor Joaquín de Alós, Asunción, 25 May 1789 in Archivo Nacional de Asunción, Sección Histórica, vol. 151. (Hereafter cited as ANA-SH.) Comisionado D. Roque de Acosita, Asunción, 3 July 1787 in ANA-SH 151. For Yguamandiyú, see Decree of Governor Alós, Asunción, 19 May 1789 in ANA-SH 151.

3. See, for instance, the report of "indios monteses" of new yerbales some fifty leagues from Villa Real de la Concepción. Luis Bernardo Ramírez to Governor Joaquín de Alós, Villa Real de la Concepción, 4 March 1794, in Archivo Nacional de Asunción-Nueva Encuadernación, vol. 3379. (Hereafter cited as ANA-NE.)

4. A good description of the different types of beneficiadores is found in the Informe of Rafael Requejo, Asunción, 18 January 1801 in ANA-SH 183.

5. Contrato of the troperos, father and son, D.n Judas Tadeo Duarte and D.n Vizente Amancio Duarte, with the benificiador D.n Juan Carso, Villarica, 1806 in ANA-NE 1783.

6. "Expediente que trata del modo con que los Beneficiadores de Yerba contratan con sus Peones," Asunción, año de 1804 in ANA-NE 2514.

7. A typical contract and one that listed fomentos was that of Juan Horite with beneficiador Lorenzo Flecha, Asunción, 1 December 1795 in ANA-NE 410. An extensive listing of fomentos to peones is found in the books of the beneficiador Anacleto Cazeres, Yguamandiyú, 15 (?) 1812 in Archivo Nacional de Asunción-Sección Judicial Criminal, vol. 1910. (Hereafter cited as ANA-SJC.)

8. "Causa criminal formada contra Simón Sanquina por . . . bestialidad," Asunción, año de 1810 in ANA-SJC 1452.

9. See "Demanda contra Juana Bautista Almada," Villa Real de la Concepción, 30 September 1806 in ANA-SJC 1740.

10. José Ruiz to Governor Alós, Trinidad, 28 February 1788 in ANA-NE 3370.

11. Acuerdo of the Cabildo de Asunción, Asunción, 18 June 1791 in Archivo Nacional de Asunción-Actas del Cabildo, XXVIII.

12. Auto of Interim Governor Manuel Gutiérrez, Asunción, 1 September 1808 in ANA-SH 206; and Comandante José de Espínola to Interim Governor Gutiérrez, Villa Real de la Concepción, 26 September 1808 in ANA-SH 206.

13. Comandante of Villa Real de la Concepción Espínola to Interim Governor Eustaquio Gianini, Villa Real de la Concepción, 9 February 1809 in ANA-SH 366. For similar practices in the region of Curuguatí see Teniente Asesor Letrado Pedro Somellera, Asunción, 1 September 1808 in ANA-SH 206.

14. Ministros of the Real Hacienda Pedro de Ozcariz and José Elizalde to Interim Governor Gianini, Asunción, 28 June 1809 in ANA-SH 207.

15. Declaración of Juan José Benites de Portugal, Beneficiador of Arancanque (partido of Curuguatí), 6 March 1800 in ANA-SH 179. Also see Luis Vargas Machuca and Juan Ignacio Villasanti to Governor Lázaro de Ribera, Asunción, (?) March 1800 in ANA-SH 175.

16. Ibid.; and Miguel José de Aguayo to Governor Ribera, Asunción, March (?) 1800 in ANA-SH 183. That limitation appears to have been a vestige of encomienda days and in all justice, that rule had little validity in the new yerba industry of the Intendencia era.

17. "Declaración" of Antonio de (?) (capataz of Lieutenant Colonel Benancio de la Rosa of Cuarepotí), Beneficio of Ytavará, 16 February 1800 in ANA-SH 183.

18. Oficio of Governor Ribera, Asunción, 20 December 1799 in ANA-SH 179. However, smuggling continued unabated in that poorly policed region. See "Razón de los Tercios de yerba que salieron de esta Provincia en el ultimo quinquenio," Ministros Prales de R.l Hacienda Oscariz and Elizalde, Asunción, 28 November 1808 in ANA-NE 1790.

19. "Informe sobre los yerbales de Curuguaty," Síndico Procurador Severino Acosta, Asunción, 1 September 1806 in ANA-SJC 2192; and Manuel Antonio Villalva to Governor Bernardo de Velazco, Curuguatí, 8 August 1806 in ANA-NE 1783.

20. Ministros de la Real Hacienda Martín José Aramburu and José de Elizalde to Governor Ribera, Asunción, 10 May 1805 in ANA-NE 3402.

21. "Guias," 1808 in ANA-NE 2900.

22. "Expediente sobre el arreglo de la navegación del Paraguay," in Archivo General de la Nación Argentina (Buenos Aires), leg. 9-4-7-4 (Consulado de Buenos Ayres, Expedientes 1794–1797). (Hereafter cited as AGNA.)

23. Viceroy marqués of Sobremonte to Ministro de Hacienda Miguel Cayetano Soler, Buenos Aires, 29 August 1804 in Manuel Gondra Manuscript Collection, University of Texas, No. 294. (Hereafter cited as MG.)

24. See "Lizencias de Beneficios," Asunción, año de 1793 in ANA-NE 545. It appears that this payment to the Ramo de Guerra also exempted his capataz and peones from militia service, but sources are not clear on this point.

25. Emergency taxes might be imposed upon yerba exports as well. See "Expediente sobre derechos patriotos," Asunción, 18 November 1809 in ANA-SH 210.

26. "Caxa R.l del Paraguay: su cuenta del año de 1777," Buenos Aires, 1 December 1783 in AGI-BA 451. And "Libro mayor de la R.l Caxa del Paraguay . . . año de 1809," Ministro de R.l Hacienda Elizalde, Asunción, 4 January 1810 in typescript of account of the Para-

guayan Treasury, 1803–10 held in the Patterson Rare Book Collection, Ekstrom Library, University of Louisville, Louisville, Kentucky.

27. Martín José Yegros and José Marcos Yegros to Governor Pedro Melo de Portugal, Asunción, 28 September 1784 in ANA-SH 151.

28. "Interrogatorio" of Capitán Andrés de Orué, Asunción, 31 August 1789 in ANA-NE 388.

29. Ministros Prales de la R.l Hacienda Martín José de Aramburu and José Joaquín Goyburi to Governor Ribera, Asunción, 7 March 1803 in ANA-SH 190.

30. Protector de Pobres Juan Bautista de Achard to Governor Alós, Asunción, (?) October 1787 in ANA-SH 151.

31. "Razón de los sugetos que han pagado el Derecho de Alcabala . . . ," Asunción, 1804 in ANA-SH 193.

32. Informe of Ministros Prales de la R.l Hacienda Barnabé González Bueno and José Joaquín Goyburi, Asunción, 13 August 1804 in ANA-SH 193.

33. See, for example, Governor Ribera to the Comandante of Villa Real de la Concepción Espínola, Asunción, 30 May 1799 in ANA-SH 175. The Cabildo de Asunción was also concerned about the high cost of Indian wars. See Acuerdos of that body relative to Indian raids on the northern frontier in the years 1795–96 in ANA-Actas del Cabildo de Asunción, XXXII, 1795–1796.

34. Governor Alós to Viceroy Nicolás Arredondo, Asunción, 13 January 1793 in ANA-NE 3382.

35. Governor Ribera to Viceroy marqués de Avilés, Asunción, 18 April 1801 in MG 2074 m; and Comandante de la Cordillera Juan Bautista Rivarola to Governor Ribera, Yacaví, 10 December 1799 in ANA-SH 176.

36. "Expediente sobre la visita del Señor Director de la Real Renta de Tabacos," Asunción, años de 1800 y 1801 in ANA-NE 3395.

37. Juan Manuel Gamarra to Governor Ribera, Asunción, (?) April 1806 in AGNA 9-5-5-1. Also see Comandante de Villa Real de la Concepción Espínola to Interim Governor Gutiérrez, Villa Real de la Concepción, 9 May 1808 in ANA-SH 365.

Chapter 10. The Río de la Plata and the Greater Southwest

I would like to thank all the participants in the Contested Ground project for their advice and criticism, especially Kristine Jones, Richard Slatta, and Thomas Sheridan. At DePauw University the Faculty Development Fund and the John and Janice Fisher Fund for Faculty Development provided funds and time that enabled me to pursue this project in a timely manner.

1. This is changing. For brief overviews of the new work in these areas from the world-system tradition see Hall (1996a, 1996b).

2. Earlier, Owen Lattimore said that "civilization gave birth to barbarism" (1962: 99 cited in Wallerstein 1974: 98), meaning that it is the interaction between state and non-state societies that often produces those characteristics state officials are wont to call "barbarous."

3. Among modern states the reverse holds. The state encompasses groups that, at least initially, do *not* have a shared sense of identity. Hence the problem of nation-building. We should keep in mind that the European states had only recently begun their own nation-building processes in the colonial era.

4. The Provincias Internas were initially comprised of Sonora-Sinaloa, Texas, Coahuila, the Californias, Nueva Vizcaya, and Nuevo México (Nuevo Léon and Nuevo Santander were added in 1786).

5. Of course these were not truly "empty quarters." Nomadic Indians used them for hunting grounds, for gathering, and for refuge. The were "empty" only from a European point of view.

6. It is interesting to note that until sometime in the nineteenth century Europeans referred to much of the pampas, Patagonia, and Great Plains as "deserts." See, for example, Morris (1981: 48).

7. As Kristine Jones states (this volume, note 1) the term *Indian* is a misnomer. Among peoples descended from those people who already occupied the land when Europeans arrived, tribal or national names are preferred. However, in the United States at least, the terms *Native American* and *Indian* are used somewhat interchangeably. For an excellent discussion of the politics of naming see Churchill (1994).

8. All but chiefdoms were found in the American Southwest. Some would argue that the Pueblos verged on chiefdoms, others demur.

9. As both Kristine Jones and Susan Socolow demonstrate in their chapters this difference could be an artifact of the extent to which archival sources have been studied. A valuable contribution to comparative frontier studies would be more thorough research on this topic.

10. Socolow (1992) notes that Indians were more tolerant of women using a different language. The root of this was in rules of exogamy that often required marriage to women from groups who spoke a different language. For the later period this tendency was no doubt exaggerated as part of the "Araucanization of the pampas" (Jones, 1994b).

11. According to Thomas Kavanagh (1996) the unitary organization, though lasting through several successive leaders, did not encompass all those who spoke Comanche dialects or practiced Comanche culture, but did include the largest groups.

12. Lyman Johnson's (1994) analysis of wealth distribution demonstrates the effects of these changes. Wilma Dunaway's (1996a) analysis of southern Appalachia in the southeastern United States shows parallel changes. Both Johnson and Dunaway show that these regions did not "stagnate," but experienced considerable development. Dunaway shows, however, that this development was distorted by world-systemic relations and contributed to subsequent underdevelopment, which was often misinterpreted as stagnation. Much of her analysis, *mutatis mutandis,* fits Argentina.

Chapter 11. The Frontier as an Arena of Social and Economic Change

This research was supported by the Tinker Foundation, Social Science Research Council, National Endowment for the Humanities, American Philosophical Society, and the University of North Carolina at Charlotte Foundation. I also want to acknowledge the crucial statistical support and analytical advice provided by Dr. Nancy Schoeps, my colleague in the Department of Mathematics.

1. I write this at the end of a year that welcomed two new movie versions of the gunfight at the OK Corral. In both versions the completely dissolute gunfighter and gambler Doc Holliday, rather than the marginally upright Wyatt Earp, clearly held audience attention and affection.

2. In normal judicial supervision of the probate process, court-appointed expert assessors produced detailed inventories of all decedent wealth at the time of death. When the estate included real estate, it was examined separately by a mason, a carpenter, and a blacksmith. Depending on the mix of goods found in an estate, other experts would be appointed as needed. Artisan shops, small manufactories, and retail shops were also subject to detailed inventories. Separate assessments were made for land and for improvements. Household furnishings, tools, and other utensils were also itemized and evaluated.

Because a similar level of specificity was applied to producer goods and financial assets, these records are of particular value to economic historians. Commercial and factory inventories, livestock, tools, machinery, carts and wagons, buildings used in rural and urban production, even fruit trees, unharvested crops, and unsold rural products such as hides were counted and assessed. In addition, loans owed the decedent, cash (both metallic and paper) stocks and bonds, and debts were also regularly included in inventories.

3. Personal variables used in this study are sex, birthplace, primary occupation, birth legitimacy, marital status, age, race, secondary occupation, number of children, location of primary residence, location of secondary residence, and membership in a lay brotherhood. Economic variables (coded in paper pesos) are value of slaves, number of slaves, value of clothing, jewelry, gold and silver furnishings, furniture, household utensils, urban residence/land, urban residence/improvements, business/land, business/improvements, rental property, tools and machinery, raw materials, inventory, cash/paper, cash/coin, rural residence/land, rural residence/improvements, livestock, farm and ranch tools and machinery, corrals, rural inventory, trees, wagons and carts, boats, stocks, bonds, debts, credits, books, paintings, and area of rural estate.

4. Because I found adequate geographic and occupational coverage in the probate records no weights were necessary for these variables. My research uncovered inventories for fifty-three provincial towns plus the city of Buenos Aires and for fifty-one separate occupations.

5. Unfortunately, some parish records have been destroyed. These parishes are Mer-

ced, Piedad, Balvanera, Pilar, San Telmo, Socorro, Monserrat, San José, and Concepción. I examined copies of the surviving records held by the Genealogical Library of the Church of the Latter Day Saints, Salt Lake City, Utah, in order to estimate the characteristics of decedents not found in the probate records. The age distributions for contemporary census records were provided by Mark D. Szuchman.

6. Although I am primarily interested in measuring changes in wealth concentration over time, I decided against using a stratified random sample of probate records for each year because the limitations of surviving census records and the low number of probate records for some years made sophisticated sampling impossible. In fact, although Alice Hanson Jones' (1980) study of the thirteen colonies is justly celebrated as a model for using probate records, there was widespread criticism of her sample design. For the debate, please refer to the cited sources.

7. Potential wealth holders are defined as free men and women eighteen years of age and older.

8. Burgin (1946) is an important exception. He offers a substantial and thoughtful analysis of the era. An important recent addition to the discussion of fiscal policy is Halperín Donghi (1982).

9. Szuchman altered in important ways our discussion of the social and cultural consequences of this period, but he did not attempt to systematically assess economic performance on the provincial level.

10. This expansion is well documented in Registro Oficial de la Provincia de Buenos Aires, 1821–51 (Buenos Aires); Registro Estadístico de Provincia de Buenos Aires, 1821–23 (Buenos Aires); Gaceta Mercantil (Buenos Aires, 1830–1852), and Woodbine Parish (1852).

11. It is clear now that this decline in textiles and artisan manufacturing began in the late colonial period rather than with the free traders of the independence era. In fact, Rosas was willing to provide some protection for provincial manufacturers (e.g., tariff of 1835) and his inflationary issues of paper money also retarded the progress of imports. Nevertheless, by 1852 little manufacturing remained in the province. See Burgin (1946), especially chapter x.

12. The Gini coefficient summarizes inequality in a convenient number ranging from 0.0 to 1.0. A zero value indicates perfect equality; a value of 1.0 indicates maximum inequality. This statistic is based on the Lorenz curve, which displays graphically the cumulative percentage of wealth owned from the poorest to the wealthiest in comparison with a forty-five-degree line of hypothetical perfect equality. If each wealth holder had the same wealth all points would be on this forty-five-degree line. The Gini coefficient is the ratio of the inequality area lying between the forty-five-degree line and the concave or upper side of the Lorenz curve to the total triangular area enclosed by the forty-five-degree line and the two boundary lines at the base and right side of the graph.

13. The Gini coefficients published in this essay are based on the probate records adjusted by two statistical weights to compensate for problems of representativeness. They differ slightly from the Gini coefficients I recently published in Andrien and Johnson

(1994: 197–214). In the earlier analysis I adjusted the raw data using a preliminary weight to compensate for age bias. For this essay an improved age adjustment and a weight for the non-probate population were developed prior to the calculation of Gini coefficients.

14. Mean or average wealth as used here is total wealth divided by the number of potential wealth holders. Median wealth is the midpoint in the distribution of all individual wealth holders.

15. To convert paper pesos to silver, I averaged the annual exchange rates for 1829–1831. As a result, paper peso values were divided by 6.04 to produce the 1830 values. The rate of exchange between the silver peso and the U.S. dollar was approximately one to one throughout this long period. Each was assumed to be equivalent to one ounce of silver. Since the silver peso was often adulterated, the dollar was traded with a slight premium. However, in this study I have considered the two coins equivalents. Professor Samuel Amaral of Northern Illinois University very generously helped me through the numerous problems of currency conversion.

16. I estimate that 58 percent of the total provincial population of 135,000 was over age eighteen and held some wealth. The exact calculation for total provincial wealth was 733,905,900 pesos, or 121,521,600 dollars.

17. Roberto Cortés Conde, one of Argentina's most talented economic historians, recently summarized the period in similar terms: "Four decades after independence the volume of exports had not varied significantly, except for a few particular years. Apart from the expansion of the frontier in Buenos Aires, no new urban centers or transportation networks had appeared. This relative stagnation was aggravated by internal conflicts and by external blockades. Nor did the order Rosas established succeed in making the panorama of the Argentine economy a more promising one" (Cortés Conde 1993: 326).

18. In Andrien and Johnson (1994: 207), I provided estimates for the top 1 percent of wealth holders. I now believe that a reliable estimate of the percentage of wealth held by the top 1 percent cannot be calculated from the weighted data set used in this analysis. However, the estimate provided in this essay for the top decile is statistically sound.

19. As pointed out by Burgin (1946), capital invested in goods imported on consignment accounted for 56 percent of all revenues obtained from this tax in 1849.

20. Lee Soltow has argued that wealth concentration among slaveholders in selected regions of the South remained unchanged from 1790 to 1860. Because censuses before 1850 did not provide wealth data it has been difficult to measure changes in wealth concentration in the early national period. In this study he uses slave ownership as a proxy for wealth holding before 1850, a decision he justifies by demonstrating a strong correlation between slave ownership and wealth of all kinds from the 1860 census.

21. Soltow (1971a: 839) established a nearly identical Gini of 0.84 for 1850. This was based on the U.S. census estimates for real estate only.

22. Some of the difference in results found for Wisconsin by Soltow (1971b) and for Texas by Campbell and Lowe (1977) result from sampling decisions. Soltow's study of Wisconsin is based on a sample of adult males twenty years of age and older. Camp-

bell and Lowe used a sample of heads of households. Census enumerators commonly assigned all real and personal property controlled by a family to the head of household. Soltow's sampling method, therefore, might select a young man living at home in a fairly affluent household and code him as having no wealth. Campbell and Lowe's method, on the other hand, would always select the head of household. Campbell and Lowe tested the effects of these differences in sampling technique and found only limited variation in Gini coefficients. The effect on estimates of average wealth, however, was not explored. See Randolph Campbell and Richard Lowe (1976: note 6).

23. I constructed a sample of probate records for 1800 (82 cases) and adjusted it for age bias using the census of 1810. This resource is limited in its utility because of underrepresentation of rural districts and the fragmentary character of the census used to generate the age weight. The Gini, therefore, is less reliable than those for 1830 and 1855.

24. Slatta and I have looked at very different sources and came to different conclusions. It is, in fact, possible that the general prosperity and high average wealth holding found in my research coincided with low wages and earnings among the sectors of the population studied by Slatta. Before this issue can be clarified the wages and earnings of rural workers will have to be studied in a more systematic manner. At present we have two contradictory summaries: Slatta asserts that landowners forced rural wages downward while Burgin (1946), in his earlier study, argued for high average wages in the countryside.

Chapter 12. Two, Three, Many Barbarisms?

Earlier versions of this paper were presented to the University of Arizona Geography Department in Tucson, Arizona, and the American Anthropological Association Annual Meetings in San Francisco, California, in November and December 1992 and to the CIESAS de Occidente in Guadalajara, Jalisco, Mexico, in January 1993. Ana Alonso, Ellen Basso, John Calagione, Carmen Castañeda, Guillermo de la Peña, Donna Guy, Sally Marston, Stephen Nugent, Tom Sheridan, Marvin Waterstone, and Eva Zorrilla Tessler commented on earlier drafts; I appreciate each of their suggestions and criticisms, even if I failed to follow up all of them.

A note on archival references where they appear: caja = caja [box]; doc. = document; exp. = expediente [file]; f. = folio(s); leg. = legajo; vol. = volume.

1. Historical and anthropological studies of towns in this region include Alonso (1988, 1995), Griffen (1988a), Katz (1981), Lloyd (1987, 1988), Nugent (1993), Nugent and Alonso (1994), and Orozco (1995).

2. This term is placed in quotes to underline the irony of characterizing a process for forming subjects, creating subjectivities, and establishing subjection (here drawing on the multiple senses of *subject* mapped out by Michel Foucault 1982) such as European colonization of the New World which, in light of its characteristically mind-numbing violence and brutality is in many respects devoid of elements the least bit "civil."

3. Elsewhere I mention in greater detail the vacuity of certain discussions of postcoloniality and postcolonialism in Latin America (Nugent 1994, 1995)—an issue hardly pertinent to the present volume. Among the most lucid discussions of postcoloniality in its literary and political variants is the work of Aijaz Ahmad (1992; see also 1995a, 1995b).

4. Descendants of Spaniards born in the New World.

5. A history of non-Indian settlement of the region may be gleaned from a reading of documents in the Archivo General de las Indias (ramo Audiencia de Guadalajara, leg, 120) and from the "Dictamen del Perito Paleografo," included as an appendix to documents related to the request from the people of Namiquipa in 1922 for recognition of their rights to the land in question in the Archivo General del Cuerpo Consultativo Agrario (AGCCA), Gómez Palacio, Durango, Bienes Comunales, exp. 24/432 (721.1).

6. The following information is taken from the "Census of the families in the pueblo of Sainapuchi, Visita de San Andrés" under the heading "The pueblo of Namiquipa, attached to Sainapuchi." The author was Fray Ignacio Jimenez, priest of San Andrés when the census was taken in March 1778. Archivo Franciscano, Manuscrito 16/328.1, f. 1–5 (Biblioteca Nacional, Mexico, D.F.).

7. Literally "people of reason" or capable of reasoning, in contrast, that is, to the "indios bárbaros," though in point of fact gente de razón was initially an ethnic term intermediate between españoles (Spaniards) or blancos (whites) and indígenas (indigenes) or bárbaros (barbarians) within the regime of castes in colonial New Spain. Gente de razón was often used to refer to castas, or peoples of mixed race who were neither peninsular Spaniards nor of solely Indian blood, who were presuming to adopt a fundamentally white or Spanish identity. But on the northern frontier, there was a breakdown of the in places highly elaborate *régimen de castas* (see Barnes, Naylor, and Polzer 1981: 90–93), so that by the early nineteenth century, even before independence in 1821, the only relevant ethnic distinction was between indios and non-indios (see Von Humboldt; O. Jones 1979; Archivo Parocial de Namiquipa).

8. Archivo General de la Nación (AGN), Provincias Internas, vol. 188, 2-iii-1819; vol. 189, x-1820; AGN, Carceles y Presidios, vol. 7, exp. 1, f. 39–49, 1-vii-1819.

9. All quotations in this paragraph are from Croix's November 15, 1778 Bando, quoted in AGCCA, exp. 24/432 (721/1) and copied in the Archivo del Ejido de Namiquipa (AEN). I was first given a typescript copy of this document by José Muñoz Franco of Armera, Namiquipa. Compare Griffen (1979: 82).

10. A piquete of thirty soldiers at Cruces, the Fourth Flying Company at Casas Grandes, the Second Flying Company at Namiquipa, and the existing presidial companies at Galeana and Janos. Bando of Teodoro de Croix, 15-xi-1778, copy in AEN.

11. Ten years of tax-free residence was a prerequisite for securing unambiguous rights to agricultural lands and use of commons, a point mentioned in the Bando, 15-xi-1778 (AEN) and discussed in a series of letters from 1807–8 between María Martina Salazar (Chihuahua City), Francisco Vásquez and Comandante Facundo Melgares (Namiquipa), and Governor Salcedo (Chihuahua City), in AEN.

12. This is discussed in Nugent (1993: 40–42, 49).

13. Croix to Nicolás Gil, captain of the presidial company at San Buenaventura (Galeana), Nov. 15, 1778, AEN.

14. See the Vásquez-Salazar correspondence of 1807–8 mentioned in note 11 (AEN); see also Nugent (1993: 47–49).

15. "Decreto de la Secretaria de Guerra y Marina, Sección 2a" Mexico, 21-iii-1826, Manuel Gómez Pedraza, copy at Arizona Historical Society; compare Griffen (1988a: 119ff).

16. Archivo General de Notarías del Estado de Chihuahua, Protocolos, vol. 72, September 9, 1861.

17. Archivo Municipal de Ciudad Guerrero (AMCG) caja 7, passim.

18. Municipal president Ramón Sotelo to the Jefe Político del Distrito Guerrero, AMCG caja 8, exp. 94, Namiquipa, 28-viii-1863.

19. AGCCA, exp. 24/434, 8-viii-1923.

20. Archivo Municipal de Namiquipa (AMN) 1-iv-1894.

21. AMN, caja 5-C, "Acuerdo referente al terreno de común repartimiento," Nam., 3-ii-1918. Interview with Perpetuo Ruiz, El Molino, Namiquipa, Chih., July 1986.

22. AGCCA, exp. 24/432 (721.1), Nam., 18-xi-1922.

23. Compare in this connection Tom Sheridan's study (1986) of Tucson, Arizona, another military settlement colony established in the 1770s.

24. A period of headlong capitalist development in Mexico in the decades leading up to the revolution of 1910 named after President Porfirio Díaz who was in power from 1876 until 1911. On the Porfiriato see, e.g., Carbó and Sánchez (1983), Cockcroft (1983: 85–99), and Katz (1986),

25. Letter from inhabitants of Namiquipa to President Porfirio Díaz, Archivo de Terrenos Nacionales, exp. 178, 28-vii-1908.

26. Porfirio Díaz in Mexico City to Lic. Gabriel Aguirre in Chihuahua City, Colección Porfirio Díaz 1.41, caja 7.16, doc. 346, f. 170–72, 10-ix-1889.

27. Letter by Luis J. Comadurán to the Jefe Municipal of Namiquipa, AMCG caja 59, exp. 535, 8-x-1907.

28. AMCG cajas 56–65; AMN cajas 3–3b (1906–1910), passim. In 1906 Torres himself claimed control of some two hundred hectares of land (eight times the legal limit) under the terms of the Municipal Land Law (Anuario Estadístico 1906, denuncia #925, 22-viii-1906). Later, during the revolution, Torres was pulled from a jail cell in Chihuahua City and executed by Manuel Vaca, a native of Namiquipa.

29. Interview by Ana Alonso, Daniel Nugent and Ruben Osorio with Cruz Chávez Gutiérrez, El Tascate, Municipio de Namiquipa, July 1986.

Bibliography

Abbott, Andrew

1991 History and Sociology: The Lost Synthesis. *Social Science History* 15(2): 201–38.

Abrams, Philip

1982 *Historical Sociology.* Ithaca: Cornell University Press.

Academia Nacional de la Historia

1979 *Relación de los cristianos salvados del cautiverio por la División Izquierda del Ejército Expedicionario contra los bárbaros, al mando del Sr. Brigadier General Juan Manuel de Rosas.* Buenos Aires: Academia Nacional de la Historia.

Aguirre, Juan Francisco

1949 Diario del capitán de Fragata D. Juan Francisco Aguirre, tomo II—primera parte. *Revista de la Biblioteca Nacional* (Buenos Aires) 18:45–46.

1950 Diario del Capitán de Fragata D. Juan Francisco Aguirre, tomo II—segunda parte. *Revista de la Biblioteca Nacional* (Buenos Aires) 19(47–48).

1951 Diario del Capitán de Fragata D. Juan Francisco Aguirre, tomo III—continuación. *Revista de la Biblioteca Nacional* (Buenos Aires) 20(49–50).

Aguirre Beltrán, Gonzalo

[1957] 1970 *El proceso de adulturación y el cambio socio-cultural en México.* México, D.F.: Universidad Iberoamericano.

Ahmad, Aijaz

1992 *In Theory.* London: Verso.

1995a The Politics of Literary Postcoloniality. *Race and Class* 36(3):1–20.

1995b Postcolonialism: What's in a Name? In *The Late Imperial Culture.* Ed. de la Campa et al., 11–32. London: Verso.

Alchon, Suzanne

1991 *Native Society and Disease in Colonial Ecuador.* New York: Cambridge University Press.

Alegre, Francisco Javier, S.J.

1956–60 *Historia de la Provincia de la Compañía de Jesús de Nueva España (1780).* 4 vols. Annotated by Ernest J. Burrus and Felix Zubillaga. Rome: Jesuit Historical Institute.

Allison, Marvin J.

1993 Chagas' Disease. In *The Cambridge World History of Human Disease.* Ed. Kenneth F. Kiple, 636–638. Cambridge: Cambridge University Press.

Almada, Francisco

1964 *La revolución en el estado de Chihuahua.* Chihuahua: Biblioteca del Instituto Nacional de Estudios Históricos de la Revolución Mexicana.

Alonso, Ana María

1988 The Effects of Truth: Re-presentations of the Past and the Imagining of Community. *Journal of Historical Sociology* 1(1):33–57.

1995 *Thread of Blood. Colonialism, Revolution and Gender on Mexico's Northern Frontier.* Tucson: University of Arizona Press.

Alvarez, Salvador

1992 Chiametla: Una provincia olvidada del siglo XVI. *Trace* 22:5–23.

Amaral, Samuel

1987 Rural Production and Labor in Colonial Buenos Aires. *Journal of Latin American Studies* 19:235–78.

Amundsen, Darrel W.

1986 The Medical Catholic Tradition. In *Caring and Curing, Health and Medicine in the Western Religious Traditions.* Ed. R. L. Numbers and D. W. Amundsen, 65–107. New York: Macmillan.

Andrien, Kenneth, and Lyman L. Johnson

1994 *The Political Economy of Spanish America in the Age of Revolution.* Albuquerque: University of New Mexico Press.

Angelis, Pedro de

[1836–37] 1969 *Colección de obras y documentos relativos a la historia antigua y moderna de las provincias del Río de la Plata.* 6 vols. Buenos Aires: Plus Ultra.

Annino, Antonio, et al.

1987 *América Latina: Del estado colonial al estado nación, 1750–1940.* 2 vols. Milano: Franco Angeli.

Archivo Histórico de la Provincia de Buenos Aires

1938 *Cedulario de la Real Audiencia de Buenos Aires.* Vol. 3. La Plata: Provincia de Buenos Aires.

Archivo Histórico de la Provincia de Mendoza

1985 *La frontera interna de Mendoza, 1810–1820.* Mendoza: Ministerio de Cultura y Educación.

Argentine Republic, Comando en Jefe

1973 *Política seguida con el aborigen, 1750–1819.* Buenos Aires: Círculo Militar.

Aspurz, Lazaro de, O.F.M.

1946 *La aportación extranjera a las misiones españoles del Patronato Regio.* Madrid: Consejo de la Hispanidad.

Assunção, Fernando O.

1978–79 *El gaucho: Estudio socio-cultural.* 2 vols. Montevideo: Dirección General de Extensión Universitaria.

Astrain, Antonio

1902 *Historia de la Compañía de Jesús en la asistencia de España.* 7 vols. Madrid.

Aufderheide, Patricia Ann

1976 Order and Violence: Social Deviance and Social Control in Brazil, 1780–1840. Ph.D. diss., University of Minnesota.

Avilés y del Fierro, D. G. de.

1945 Memoria de D. G. Avilés y del Fierro, marqués de Avilés, Buenos Aires, 21 de mayo de 1801. In *Memorias de los virreyes del Río de la Plata.* Ed. Sigfrido Radaelli. Buenos Aires: Bajel.

Azara, Félix de

1847 *Descripción e historia del Paraguay y del Río de la Plata.* Vol. 1. Madrid: Sánchez.

1943 Memoria sobre el estado rural del Río de la Plata, Batoví, 9 de mayo de 1801. *Memoria sobre el estado rural del Río de la Plata.* Buenos Aires: Bajel.

1969a Diario de un reconocimiento de las guardias y fortines que guarnecen la línea de frontera de Buenos Aires para ensancharla. In *Colección de obras y documentos.* Vol. 5. Comp. Pedro de Angelis, 1–16. Buenos Aires: Le Plus Ultra.

1969b *Viajes por la América Meridional.* Madrid: Espasa-Calpe.

Azcuy Ameghino, Eduardo

1991 La propiedad de la tierra en los campos bonaerenses y el censo de hacendados de 1789. *Revista ciclos* 1(1):199–208.

Baiocchi, Mari de Nasaré

1983 *Negros de Cedro: Estudo antropológico de um bairro rural de negros em Goiás.* São Paulo: Ática.

Balandier, Georges

[1951] 1970 The Colonial Situation: A Theoretical Approach. In *The Sociology of Black African Social Dynamics in Central Africa.* Trans. D. Garman, 34–61. New York.

Baretta, Silvio R. D., and John Markoff

1978 Civilization and Barbarism: Cattle Frontiers in Latin America. *Comparative Studies in Society and History* 20(4):587–620.

Barfield, Thomas J.

1989 *The Perilous Frontier.* London: Blackwell.

Barnes, Thomas, Thomas Naylor, and Charles Polzer

1981 *Northern New Spain: A Research Guide.* Tucson: University of Arizona Press.

Basso, Keith H.

1983 Western Apache. In *Handbook of North American Indians.* Vol. 11. Ed. William C. Sturtevant. Washington, D.C.: Smithsonian Institution.

Bastos, Uacury Ribeiro de Assis

1962 Nota previa sobre os governadores do Paraguay: Eustaquio Gianini y Bentallol e Manuel Gutiérrez. *Revista de Historia* 25 (Oct./Dic.):448–50.

1979 *Expansão territorial do Brasil colonial no vale do paraguai (1767–1801).* São Paulo: Universidade de São Paulo.

Beals, Ralph

1932 *The Comparative Ethnology of Northwestern Mexico before 1750.* Ibero-Americana 2. Berkeley: University of California Press.

1933 *The Acaxee: A Mountain Tribe of Durango and Sinaloa.* Berkeley: University of California Press.

Beck, Warren A.

1962 *New Mexico: A History of Four Centuries.* Norman: University of Oklahoma Press.

Beckett, Patrick H., and Terry L. Corbett

1992 *The Manso Indians.* COAS Monograph No. 9. Las Cruces, N.Mex.: COAS Publishing and Research.

Bellingeri, Marco, and Isabel Gil Sánchez

1980 Las estructuras agrarias bajo el porfiriato. In *México en el siglo XIX (1821–1910): Historia económica y de la estructura social.* Ed. Ciro Cardoso. México, D.F.: Nueva Imagen.

Benítez, Luis G.

1985 *Historia del Paraguay: Época colonial.* Asunción: Impr. Comuneros.

Bertran, Paulo

1978 *Formação Econômica de Goiás.* Goiânia: Oriente.

Bloom, Aaron M.

1966 Texas in the 1850s, as Viewed by a Recent Arrival. *Southwestern Historical Quarterly* 70:281–88.

Blujacki, Agustin

1972 *Un gran paraguayo: Presbítero Juan Francisco Amancio González Escobar.* Asunción: Escuela Técnica Salesiana.

Bolton, Herbert E.

1917 The Mission as a Frontier Institution in the Spanish-American Colonies. *American Historical Review* 23:42–61.

1929 Defensive Spanish Expansion and the Significance of the Borderlands. In *The Trans-Mississippi West.* Ed. J. F. Willard and C. B. Goodykoontz, 1–42. Boulder: University of Colorado Press.

Borges Moran, Pedro

1960 *Métodos misionales en la cristianización de América, siglo XVI.* Madrid: Departamento de Misionología Española.

1977 *El envío de misioneros a América durante la época española.* Series Biblioteca Salamanticensis, 20. Salamanca: Universidad Pontífica.

Boxer, C. R.

1975 *Women in Iberian Expansion Overseas, 1415–1815: Some Facts, Fancies and Personalities.* New York: Oxford University Press.

Brading, David A.

1984 Bourbon Spain and Its American Empire. *The Cambridge History of Latin America.* Vol. 1, *Colonial Latin America.* Ed. Leslie Bethell, 389–439. Cambridge: Cambridge University Press.

Briggs, Charles, and John R. Van Ness, eds.

1987 *Land, Water, and Culture: New Perspectives on Hispanic Land Grants.* Albuquerque: University of New Mexico Press.

Brown, Jonathan C.

1979 *A Socioeconomic History of Argentina, 1776–1860.* Cambridge: Cambridge University Press.

Burchell, Robert A.

1987 Opportunity and the Frontier: Wealth Holding in Twenty-Six Northern California Counties, 1848–1880. *The Western Historical Review* 18(2):177–96.

Burgin, Miron

1946 *The Economic Aspects of Argentine Federalism, 1820–1852.* Cambridge: Harvard University Press.

Burkholder, Mark A., and Lyman L. Johnson

1994 *Colonial Latin America.* 2d ed. New York: Oxford University Press.

Burns, E. Bradford

1980 *The Poverty of Progress.* Berkeley: University of California Press.

Butzer, Karl W., ed.

1992 The Americas before and after 1492: Current Geographical Research. Special Issue of the *Annals of the Association of American Geographers* 82(3).

Caldcleugh, Alexander

1825 *Travels in South America during the Years 1819, 20, 21: Containing an Account of the Present State of Brazil, Buenos Ayres, and Chile.* 2 vols. London: John Murray.

Calzadíaz Barrera, Alberto

1979 [1958] *Hechos reales de la revolución.* Vol. 1. México, D.F.: Editorial Patria.

Campbell, Randolph B., and Richard E. Lowe

1976 Slave Property and the Distribution of Wealth in Texas, 1860. *Journal of American History* 63(2):318–19.

1977 *Wealth and Power in Antebellum Texas.* College Station: University of Texas Press.

Cantón, Eliseo

1921 *Historia de la Universidad de Buenos Aires y de su influencia en la cultura Argentina: La Facultad de Medicina y sus escuelas.* Buenos Aires: Casa Editora.

Carbó, Margarita, and Andrea Sánchez

1983 México bajo la dictadura porfiriana. In *Un pueblo en la historia.* Vol. 2. Ed. Enrique Semo. México, D.F.: Universidad Autónoma de Puebla and Editorial Nueva Imagen.

Cárcano, Miguel A.

1972 *Evolución histórica del régimen de la tierra pública 1810–1916.* Buenos Aires: EUDEBA.

Cardiel, José

[1767] 1989 *Breve relación de las misiones del Paraguay.* Madrid: Gráficas Nilo.

Cardoso, Ciro, ed.

1980 *México en el siglo XIX (1821–1910): Historia económica y de la estructura social.* México, D.F.: Nueva Imagen.

Cardozo, Efraim

1959 *El Paraguay colonial: Las raíses de la nacionalidad.* Buenos Aires: Nizza.

Caride, Horacio Eduardo

1992 Divisiones administrativas de la campaña de Buenos Aires (1730–1864). *Medio Ambiente y Urbanización* 41:1–16.

Carmagnani, Marcello

1988 *El regreso de los dioses. El proceso de reconstitución de la identidad étnica en Oaxaca. Siglos XVII y XVIII.* México, D.F.: Fondo de Cultura Económica.

Carneiro da Cunha, Manuela, ed.

1992 *História dos Índios no Brasil.* São Paulo: Companhia das Letras.

Carr, Lois Green, and Lorena S. Walsh

1980 Inventories and the Analysis of Wealth and Consumption Patterns in St. Mary's County, Maryland, 1658–1777. *Historical Methods* 13(2):81–104.

Carretero, Andrés M.

1972 *La propiedad de la tierra en la época de Rosas.* Buenos Aires: El Coloquio.

Carril, Bonifacio de

1978 *El gaucho a través de la iconografía.* Buenos Aires: Emecé Editores.

Casamiquela, Rodolfo M.

1969 *Un nuevo panorama etnológico del área pan-pampeano y patagónica adyacente.* Santiago, Chile: Ediciones del Museo Nacional de Historia Natural, Dirección de Bibliotecas, Archivos y Museos.

Certeau, Michel de

1992 *The Mystic Fable.* Chicago: University of Chicago Press.

Cerutti, Mario

1989 El noroeste Mexicano en el siglo XIX. Ph.D. diss, University of Leiden, The Netherlands.

Cervantes, Francisco

1994 *The Devil in the New World: The Impact of Diabolism in New Spain.* New Haven: Yale University Press.

Chaim, Marivone Matos

1974 *Os Aldeamentos Indígenas na Capitania de Goiás.* Goiânia: Oriente.

Chappell, David A.

1990 The Crisis of Bipolar Ethnicity on the Great Frontier: Nativist "Democracy" in Fiji, Malaysia, and New Caledonia. *Journal of World History* 1(2): 171–98.

Chase-Dunn, Christopher

1989 *Global Formation: Structures of the World-Economy.* London: Basil Blackwell.

Chase-Dunn, Christopher, and Thomas D. Hall

1997 *Rise and Demise: Comparing World-Systems.* Boulder: Westview Press.

Chipman, Donald E.

1992 *Spanish Texas 1519–1821.* Austin: University of Texas Press.

Christian, William A., Jr.

1981 *Local Religion in Sixteenth-Century Spain.* Princeton: Princeton University Press.

Churchill, Ward

1994 *Indians R Us: Culture and Genocide in Native North America.* Monroe, Maine: Common Courage Press.

Clastres, Pierre

1981 *Investigaciones en antropología política.* Barcelona: Gedisa.

Clendinnen, Inga

1982 Yucatec Maya Women and the Spanish Conquest: Role and Ritual in Historical Reconstruction. *Journal of Social History* (Spring):427–42.

1987 *Ambivalent Conquests: Maya and Spaniard in Yucatán, 1517–1570.* Cambridge: Cambridge University Press.

Clifford, James

1986 Introduction: Partial Truths. In *Writing Culture: The Poetics and Politics of Ethnography.* Ed. J. Clifford and G. Marcus, 1–26. Berkeley: University of California Press.

Coatsworth, John

1988 Patterns of Rural Rebellion in Latin America: Mexico in Comparative Perspective. In *Riot, Rebellion, and Revolution: Rural Social Conflict in Mexico.* Ed. Friedrich Katz, 21–62. Princeton: Princeton University Press.

Cockroft, James

1983 *Mexico: Class Formation, Capital Accumulation and the State.* New York: Monthly Review Press.

Cole, D. C.

1988 *The Chiricahua Apache, 1846–1876: From War to Reservation.* Albuquerque: University of New Mexico Press.

Cole, John P.

1965 *Latin America: An Economic and Social Geography.* Washington: Butterworths.

Collins, Randall

1981 Long-Term Social Change and the Territorial Power of States. In *Sociology Since Midcentury.* Ed. Randall Collins, 71–106. New York: Academic Press.

Comadrán Ruiz, Jorge

1969 *Evolución demográfica Argentina durante el período hispano.* Buenos Aires: EUDEBA.

Comaroff, John, and Jean Comaroff

1992 *Ethnography and the Historical Imagination.* Boulder: Westview Press.

Concolorcovo

[1773] 1942 *El lazarillo de ciegos caminantes: Desde Buenos Aires hasta Lima.* Buenos Aires: Solar.

Coni, Emilio

1930 *Historia de las vaquerías del Río de la Plata (1555–1750).* Madrid: Tipografía Archivos.

1969 *El gaucho: Argentina, Brasil, Uruguay.* Buenos Aires: Solar-Hachette.

Cook, Nobel D.

1981 *Demographic Collapse: Indian Peru, 1520–1620.* New York: Cambridge University Press.

1992 Impact of Disease in the Andean World. In *Disease and Demography in the Americas.* Ed. J. Verano and D. Ubelaker, 207–14. Washington, D.C.: Smithsonian Institution Press.

Cook, Nobel David, and W. George Lovell

1991 *Secret Judgments of God: Old World Disease in Spanish Colonial America.* Norman: University of Oklahoma Press.

Cook, Sherburne F., and W. W. Borah

1971–79 *Essays in Population History.* 3 vols. Berkeley: University of California Press.

Cooney, Jerry W.

1982 Smallpox Treatment in Colonial Paraguay. *South Eastern Latin Americanist* 26:1–11.

1990 *Economía y sociedad en la Intendencia del Paraguay.* Asunción: CPES.

n.d. The Population of Paraguay—History and Problems "La Gente Guaraní." In *The Peopling of Latin America.*

Corominas, Joan

1980 *Diccionario crítico etimológico castellano y hispánico.* 5 vols. Madrid: Editorial Gredos.

Correa Filho, Virgilio

1925 *As rais do Matto Grosso. Fronteira meridonal.* Vol. 3. São Paulo: Secção de obras d' O Estado de S. Paulo.

Corrigan, Philip, and Derek Sayer

1985 *The Great Arch: English State Formation as Cultural Revolution.* Oxford: Basil Blackwell.

Cortés Conde, Roberto

1993 The Export Economy of Argentina, 1880–1920. In *The Latin American Economies, Growth and the Export Sector, 1880–1930.* Ed. Roberto Cortés Conde and Shane J. Hunt, 319–81. New York: Holmes and Meier.

Cortesão, Jaime

1952 *Manuscritos da coleção de Angelis, Jesuítas e Bandeirantes no Itatim (1596–1760).* Rio de Janeiro: Biblioteca Nacional, Divisão de Publicações e Divulgação.

Couto de Magalhães, José Vieira

[1863] 1975 *Viagem ao Araguaia.* 7th ed. São Paulo: Companhia Editora Nacional.

Cramaussel, Chantal

1990 *La provincia de Santa Bárbara en Nueva Vizcaya, 1563–1631.* Ciudad Juárez: Universidad Autónoma de Ciudad Juárez.

1991 Encomiendas, repartimientos y conquista en Nueva Vizcaya. *Historia* 25: 73–90.

Creel, Enrique C.

1928 *El estado de Chihuahua.* México, D.F.: El Progreso.

Crosby, Alfred

1972 *The Columbian Exchange: Biological and Cultural Consequences of 1492.* Westport, Conn.: Greenwood Press.

Cuello, José

1988 The Persistence of Indian Slavery and Encomienda in the Northeast of Colonial Mexico, 1577–1723. *Journal of Social History* 21(4):683–700.

Deeds, Susan M.

1979 Las relaciones entre los jesuitas y los oficiales reales en Sinaloa y Sonora a mediados del siglo XVIII. In *Memoria del IV Simposio de Historia de Sonora,* 94–108. Hermosillo: Instituto de Investigaciones Históricas, Universidad de Sonora.

1981 Rendering unto Caesar: The Secularization of Jesuit Missions in Mid-eighteenth Century Durango. Ph.D. diss., University of Arizona.

1989 Rural Work in Nueva Vizcaya: Forms of Labor Coercion on the Periphery. *Hispanic American Historical Review* 69(3):425–49.

1995 Indigenous Responses to Mission Settlement in Nueva Vizcaya. In *The New Latin American Mission History.* Ed. Erick Langer and Robert H. Jackson, 77–108. Lincoln: University of Nebraska Press.

1998a First-Generation Rebellions in Seventeenth-Century Nueva Vizcaya. In

The Pax Colonial: Native Resistance in New Spain. Ed. Susan Schroeder. Lincoln: University of Nebraska (forthcoming).

1998b Legacies of Resistance, Adaptation and Tenacity: History of the Native Peoples of Northwest Mexico. In *The Cambridge History of the Native Peoples of the Americas.* Vol. 4, *Mesoamerica.* Ed. Murdo J. MacLeod. Cambridge: Cambridge University Press (forthcoming).

Denevan, William M.

1992a The Pristine Myth: The Landscape of the Americas in 1492. *Annals of the Association of American Geographers* 82(3):369–85.

1992b *The Native Population of the Americas in 1492.* 2d ed. Madison: University of Wisconsin Press.

Dening, Greg

1980 *Islands and Beaches: Discourse on a Silent Land, Marquesas, 1774–1880.* Honolulu: University Press of Hawaii.

Deutsch, Sarah

1987 *No Separate Refuge: Culture, Class and Gender on an Anglo-Hispanic Frontier in the American Southwest, 1880–1940.* New York: Oxford University Press.

Dobyns, Henry F.

1966 Estimating Aboriginal American Population: An Appraisal of Techniques with a New Hemispheric Estimate. *Current Anthropology* 7(4):395–449.

1976 *Native American Historical Demography.* Bloomington: Indiana University Press.

1981 *From Fire to Flood: Historic Human Destruction of Sonoran Desert Riverine Oases.* Anthropological Papers No. 20. Socorro, N.Mex.: Ballena Press.

1983 *Their Number Become Thinned: Native American Population Dynamics in Eastern North America.* Knoxville: University of Tennessee Press.

Doles, Dalísia Elizabeth Martins

1973 *As Comunicações Fluviais pelo Tocantins e Araguaia no Século XIX.* Goiânia: Oriente.

Doolittle, William E.

1988 *Oasis in the Gran Chichimeca: Pre-Hispanic Occupance in the Valley of Sonora.* Anthropological Papers of the University of Arizona No. 48. Tucson: University of Arizona Press.

Dos Quilombos Fez-se Kalunga

1992 *Goianidade,* edição especial, dezembro, documentários, 12–13.

Duarte Morales, Teodosio

1968 *El rugir del cañon.* Juárez: B. Herrera.

Dunaway, Wilma

1994 The Southern Fur Trade and the Incorporation of Southern Appalachia into the World-Economy, 1690–1763. *Review* 18(2):215–42.

1996a *The First American Frontier: Transition to Capitalism in Southern Appalachia, 1700–1860.* Chapel Hill: University of North Carolina Press.

1996b Incorporation as an Interactive Process: Cherokee Resistance to Expansion of the Capitalist World-System, 1560–1763. *Sociological Inquiry* 66(4): 455–70.

1996c The Incorporation of Mountain Ecosystems into the Capitalist World-System. *Review* 19(4):355–381.

Dunbier, Roger

1968 *The Sonoran Desert.* Tucson: University of Arizona Press.

Dunigan, Peter

1958 Early Jesuit Missionaries: A Suggestion for Further Study. *American Anthropologist* 60:725–32.

Dunne, Peter Masten, S.J.

1951 *Andres Pérez de Ribas.* New York: United States Catholic Historical Society.

1944 *Pioneer Jesuits in Northern Mexico.* Berkeley: University of California Press.

1948 *Early Jesuit Missions in Tarahumara.* Berkeley: University of California Press.

Elliott, J. H.

1984 The Spanish Conquest and Settlement of America. In *The Cambridge History of Latin America.* Vol. 1, *Colonial Latin America.* Ed. Leslie Bethell, 149–206. Cambridge: Cambridge University Press.

1989 *Spain and Its World, 1500–1700.* New Haven: Yale University Press.

Escandón, Patricia

1985 Economía y sociedad en Sonora, 1767–1821. In *Historia general de Sonora.* Vol. 2, *De la conquista al estado libre y soberano de Sonora,* 258–64. México, D.F.: Gobierno del Estado de Sonora.

Escudero, José Agustín

1839 *Observaciones sobre el estado actual del departamento de Chihuahua y los medios de ponerla a cubierto de las incursiones de los bárbaros.* México, D.F.: Impreso por Juan Ojeda.

Estrada, Marcos de

1981 *Apuntes sobre el gaucho argentino.* Buenos Aires: Ministerio de Cultura y Educación.

Evans, Brian M.

1991 Death in Amaya of Upper Peru, 1580–1623. In *Secrets Judgments of God: Old World Disease in Spanish Colonial America.* Ed. N. D. Cook and W. G. Lovell, 142–58. Norman: University of Oklahoma Press.

Fajardo, José del Rey, S. J.

1974 *Bio-Bibliografía de los Jesuitas en la Venezuela colonial.* Caracas: Instituto de Investigaciones Históricas, Universidad Católica Andres Bello.

Falkner, Thomas

[1744] 1976 *A Description of Patagonia and the Adjoining Parts of South America (1744).* 1st ed. Reprint. New York: AMS Press.

Faragher, John Mack

1979 *Women and Men on the Overland Trail.* New Haven: Yale University Press.

Faulk, Odie B.

1979 The Presidio: Force or Farce? In *New Spain's Far Northern Frontier: Essays on Spain in the American West, 1540–1821.* Ed. David J. Weber. Albuquerque: University of New Mexico Press.

Ferguson, R. Brian, and Neil L. Whitehead.

1992 The Violent Edge of Empire. In *War in the Tribal Zone.* Ed. R. B. Ferguson and N. L. Whitehead, 1–30. Santa Fe: School of American Research Press.

Ferrer de Arrellaga, Renee

1985 *Un siglo de expansión colonizadora: Los orígenes de Concepción.* Asunción: Editorial Histórica.

Figueroa Valenzuela, Alejandro

1986 *Los que hablan fuerte. El desarrollo de la sociedad yaqui.* Noroeste de México No. 7. Hermosillo: Instituto Nacional de Antropología e Historia.

Flint, Valerie I. J.

1991 *The Rise of Magic in Early Medieval Europe.* Princeton: Princeton University Press.

Foote, Cheryl J.

1990 *Women of the New Mexico Frontier, 1846–1912.* Niwot, Colo.: University Press of Colorado.

Forbes, Jack D.

1960 *Apache, Navajo, and Spaniard.* Norman: University of Oklahoma Press.

Foster, George M.

1952 The Significance to Anthropological Studies of the Places of Origin of Spanish Emigrants to the New World. In *Acculturation in the Americas, Proceedings and Selected Papers of the XXIX International Congress of Americanists.* Ed. Sol Tax, 292–338. Chicago: University of Chicago Press.

1960 *Culture and Conquest: America's Spanish Heritage.* New York: Wenner-Gren Foundation.

Foucault, Michel

1982 The Subject and Power. In *Michel Foucault: Beyond Structuralism and Hermeneutics.* Ed. Hubert L. Dreyfus and Paul Rabinow. Brighton: Harvester Press.

Frakes, Mark

1989 Governor Ribera and the War of Oranges on Paraguay's Frontiers. *The Americas* 45(4):489–508.

Fried, Morton

1967 *The Evolution of Political Society.* New York: Random House.

1975 *The Notion of a Tribe.* Menlo Park, Calif.: Cummings.

Furlong, Guillermo

1962 *Misiones y sus pueblos guaranís.* Buenos Aires: Balmes.

Gallais, Estevão-Maria

1942 *O Apóstolo do Araguaia.* Trans. Pedro Secondy e Soares de Azevedo. São Paulo: Conceição do Araguaia.

Gallman, Robert

1965 The Social Distribution of Wealth in the United States of America. *Proceedings of the Third International Conference of Economic History, Munich.* The Hague: Mouton.

1969 Trends in the Size Distribution of Wealth in the Nineteenth Century. In *Six Papers on the Size Distribution of Wealth and Income.* Ed. Lee Soltow, 1–24. New York.

1979 The Effects of Changes in Economic and Demographic Structure on the Size Distribution of Wealth in the Antebellum U.S. Comment on session "Historical Implications of 19th Century Wealth Data." Social Science History Association, November.

Galloway, Patricia.

1991 The Archaeology of Ethnohistorical Narrative. In *Columbian Consequences.* Vol. 3, *The Spanish Borderlands in Pan-American Perspective.* Ed. D. H. Thomas, 453–71. Washington, D.C.: Smithsonian Institution Press.

Ganss, George E., S.J.

1970 *The Constitutions of the Society of Jesus.* St. Louis: Institute of Jesuit Sources.

Garavaglia, Juan Carlos

1983 *Mercado interno y economía colonial (tres siglos de historia de yerba mate).* Buenos Aires: Grijalbo.

1985 Economic Growth and Regional Differentiations: The River Plate Region at the End of the Eighteenth Century. *Hispanic American Historical Review* 65:51–89.

Gelman, Jorge

1989 New Perspectives on an Old Problem and the Same Source: The Gaucho and the Rural History of the Colonial Río de la Plata. *Hispanic American Historical Review* 69:714–46.

1992 Formas de explotación agraria y estructura de la población en un medio rural colonial: El Río de la Plata al fines del siglo XVIII. *El poblamiento de las Américas* Actas (Veracruz) 1:105–22.

Gerhard, Peter

1982 *The North Frontier of Spain.* Princeton: Princeton University Press.

1993 *The North Frontier of New Spain.* Rev. ed. Norman: University of Oklahoma Press.

Getty, Harry T.

1963 *The San Carlos Indian Cattle Industry.* Anthropological Papers of the University of Arizona No. 7. Tucson: University of Arizona Press.

Giberti, Horacio C. E.

1970 [1954] *Historia económica de la ganadería argentina.* Buenos Aires: Solar-Hachette.

Gomes, Horieste, and Antônio Teixeira Neto

1993 *Geografia: Goiás-Tocantins.* Goiânia: Centro Editorial e Gráfico/UFG.

Gómez Canedo, Lino

1977 *Evangelización y conquista, experiencia franciscana en Hispanoamérica.* México, D.F.: Editorial Porrua.

González Rodríguez, Luis

1984 *Crónicas de la sierra tarahumara.* México, D.F.: Secretaría de Educación Pública.

Gosner, Kevin

1992 *Soldiers of the Virgin: The Moral Economy of a Colonial Maya Rebellion.* Tucson: University of Arizona Press.

Gregg, Josiah

1966 [1844] *Commerce of the Prairies.* 2 vols. Ann Arbor, Mich.: University Microfilms.

Griffen, William B.

1969 *Culture Change and Shifting Populations in Central Northern Mexico.* Anthropological Papers of the University of Arizona No. 13. Tucson: University of Arizona Press.

1979 *Indian Assimilation in the Franciscan Area of Nueva Vizcaya.* Anthropological Papers of the University of Arizona No. 33. Tucson: University of Arizona Press.

1988a *Apaches at War and Peace: The Janos Presidio, 1750–1858.* Albuquerque: University of New Mexico Press.

1988b *Utmost Good Faith: Patterns of Apache-Mexican Hostilities in Northern Chihuahua Border Warfare, 1821–1848.* Albuquerque: University of New Mexico Press.

Guevara-Gil, Armando, and Frank Salomon

1994 A "Personal Visit": Colonial Political Ritual and the Making of Indians in the Andes. *Colonial Latin American Review* 3:3–36.

Guha, Ranajit

1983 *Elementary Aspects of Peasant Insurgency in Colonial India.* Delhi: Oxford University Press.

Gutiérrez, Leandro

1968 *Fortines y malones.* Buenos Aires: Centro Editorial de América Latina.

Gutiérrez, Ramón A.

1991 *When Jesus Came, the Corn Mothers Went Away: Marriage, Sexuality, and Power in New Mexico, 1500–1846.* Stanford: Stanford University Press.

Gutiérrez Castillas, José

1961 *Santarén: Conquistador Pacífico.* Guadalajara: Ediciones Canisio.

Hackett, Charles W., Adolf Francis Alphonse Bandelier, and Fanny R. Bandelier, eds.

1926–1937 *Historical Documents Relating to New Mexico, Nueva Vizcaya, and Approaches Thereto, to 1773,* 3 vols. Washington: Carnegie Institution of Washington.

Hadley, Diana, and Thomas E. Sheridan

1995 Land Use History of the San Rafael Valley, Arizona (1540–1960). General Technical Report RM-GTR-269. Fort Collins, Colo.: United States Department of Agriculture, National Forest Service, Rocky Mountain Forest and Range Experiment Station.

Hall, John R.

1991 The Patrimonial Dynamic in Colonial Brazil. In *Brazil in the World System.* Ed. Richard Graham, 57–88. Austin: University of Texas Press.

Hall, Thomas D.

1988 The Transformation of the Mexican Northwest into the American Southwest: Three Paths of Internal Development. In *Rethinking the Nineteenth Century: Contradictions and Movements.* Ed. Francisco O. Ramirez, 21–42. Westport, Conn: Greenwood Press.

1989a *Social Change in the Southwest, 1350–1880.* Lawrence: University Press of Kansas.

1989b Is Historical Sociology of Peripheral Regions Peripheral? In *Studies of Development and Change in the Modern World.* Ed. Michael T. Martin and Terry R. Kandal, 349–72. New York: Oxford University Press.

1991 The Role of Nomads in Core/Periphery Relations. In *Core/Periphery Relations in Precapitalist Worlds.* Ed. Christopher Chase-Dunn and Thomas D. Hall, 212–39. Boulder, Colo.: Westview Press.

1996a World-Systems and Evolution: An Appraisal. *Journal of World-System Research* 2(5):1–109 [electronic journal http://csf.colorado.edu/wsystems/jwsr.html]

1996b The World-System Perspective: A Small Sample from a Large Universe. *Sociological Inquiry* 66(4):440–54.

n.d. Frontiers and Incorporation into the Modern World-System: Northern New Spain and Southwestern United States, 1598–1880. In *Geographic Perspectives on Social Change.* Ed. Carville Earle and Leonard Hochberg. Stanford: Stanford University Press. Forthcoming.

Hall, Thomas D., and Christopher Chase-Dunn
1994 Forward into the Past: World-Systems Before 1500. *Sociological Forum* 9:(2):295–306.
Halperín Donghi, Tulio
1963 La expansión ganadera en la campaña de Buenos Aires, 1810–1852. *Desarrollo Económico* 3(1–2):57–110.
1982 *Guerra y finanzas en los orígines del estado argentino (1791–1850).* Buenos Aires: Editorial Belgrano.
Hammond, George, and Agapito Rey, trans.
1928 *Obregón's History of 16th Century Exploration in Western America.* Los Angeles: Wetzel Publishing Company.
Harris, Betty J.
1990 Ethnicity and Gender in the Global Periphery: A Comparison of Basotho and Navajo Women. *American Indian Culture and Research Journal* 14(4): 15–38.
Hemming, John
1987 *Amazon Frontier: The Defeat of the Brazilian Indians.* Cambridge: Harvard University Press.
Hernández, Pablo, S.J.
1913 *Organización social de las doctrinas guaranís de la Compañía de Jesús.* 2 vols. Barcelona: Guastavo Gili.
Herreros, Miguel de
1899 Estado de defensa de la provincia del Paraguay, Asunción, 13 de marzo de 1810. *Revista del Instituto Paraguayo* 3(15):234–47.
Hewitt de Alcantara, Cynthia
1984 *Anthropological Perspectives on Rural Mexico.* London: Routledge & Kegan Paul.
Hobsbawm, Eric
1973 Peasants and Politics. *Journal of Peasant Studies* 1(1):3–22.
Holder, Preston
1970 *The Hoe and the Horse on the Plains: A Study of Cultural Development Among North American Indians.* Lincoln: University of Nebraska Press.
Horvath, Steven
1977 The Genízaro of Eighteenth-Century New Mexico: A Reexamination. *Discovery,* 25–40. Santa Fe: School of American Research.
1979 The Social and Political Organization of the Genízaros of Plaza de Nuestra Señora de los Dolores de Belén, New Mexico, 1740–1812. Ph.D. diss., Brown University.
Hu-DeHart, Evelyn
1981 *Missionaries, Miners, and Indians: Spanish Contact with the Yaqui Nation of Northwestern New Spain, 1533–1820.* Tucson: University of Arizona Press.
1988 Peasant Rebellion in the Northwest: The Yaqui Indians of Sonora, 1740–

1976: Rural Social Conflict in Mexico. In *Riot, Rebellion, and Revolution.* Ed. Friedrich Katz, 141–75. Princeton: Princeton University Press.

Huerta Preciado, María Teresa

1966 *Rebeliones indígenas en el noreste de México en la época colonial.* México, D.F.: INAH.

Hurtado, Albert L.

1988 *Indian Survival on the California Frontier.* New Haven: Yale University Press.

Jackson, Robert H.

1994 *Indian Population Decline: The Missions of Northwestern New Spain, 1687–1840.* Albuquerque: University of New Mexico Press.

Jacobsen, Nils

1991 Campesinos y tenencia de la tierra en el altiplano peruano en la transición de la Colonia a la República. *Allpanchis* 23:25–93.

Jayme, Jarbas

1973 *Famílias Pirenopolinas (Ensaios genealógicos).* 5 vols. Pirenópolis: Estado de Goiás.

Jennings, Francis

1976 *The Invasion of America.* New York: Norton Press.

John, Elizabeth A. H.

1975 *Storms Brewed in Other Men's Worlds: The Confrontation of Indians, Spanish, and French in the Southwest, 1540–1795.* College Station: Texas A&M University Press.

1984 Nurturing the Peace: Spanish and Comanche Cooperation in the Early Nineteenth Century. *New Mexico Historical Review* 59:345–69.

1989 [1799] *Views from the Apache Frontier. Report on the Northern Provinces of New Spain by José Cortés.* Norman: University of Oklahoma Press.

Johns, Michael

1993 The Autonomies of Ruling Class Culture: The Buenos Aires Elite, 1880–1910. *Journal of Historical Sociology* 6(1):74–101.

Johnson, Elizabeth A.

1987 Marian Devotion in the Western Church. In *Christian Spirituality, High Middle Ages and Reformation.* Ed. Jill Raitt, 392–414. New York: Crossroad.

Johnson, Lyman L.

1990 Salarios, precios y costo de vida en el Buenos Aires colonial tardío. *Boletín de Historia Argentina y América* 3(1):133–58.

1994 Distribution of Wealth in Nineteenth-Century Buenos Aires Province: The Issue of Social Justice in a Changing Economy. In *The Political Economy of Spanish America in the Age of Revolution, 1750–1850.* Ed. Kenneth J. Andrien and Lyman L. Johnson, 197–214. Albuquerque: University of New Mexico Press.

Jones, Alice Hanson

1970 Wealth Estimates for the American Middle Colonies, 1774. *Economic Development and Cultural Change* 18(4):1–48.

1980 *Wealth of a Nation to Be.* New York: Columbia University Press.

1982 Estimating Wealth of the Living from a Probate Sample. *Journal of Interdisciplinary History* 13(2):273–300.

Jones, Archer

1987 *The Art of War in the Western World.* Urbana: University of Illinois Press.

Jones, Grant D.

1989 *Maya Resistance to Spanish Rule: Time and History on a Colonial Frontier.* Albuquerque: University of New Mexico Press.

Jones, Kristine L.

1984 Conflict and Adaptation in the Argentine Pampas. Ph.D. diss., University of Chicago, Chicago.

1986 Nineteenth-Century British Travel Accounts of Argentina. *Ethnohistory* 33:195–211.

1989 Calfucurá and Namuncurá: Nation Builders of the Pampas. In *The Human Tradition in Latin America.* Vol. 2, *Historical Silhouettes: Latin Americans in the Nineteenth Century.* Ed. Judith Ewell and William Beezeley, 175–86. Wilmington, Del.: Scholarly Resources.

1993 Civilization and Barbarism and Sarmiento's Indian Policy. In *Sarmiento and His Argentina.* Ed. Joseph Criscenti, 35–43. Boulder: Lynne Rienner Publishers.

1994a Comparative Ethnohistory and the Southern Cone. *Latin American Research Review* 29(1):107–18.

1994b Indian-Creole Negotiations in the Southern Frontier. In *Revolution and Restoration: The Rearrangement of Power in Argentina, 1776–1860.* Ed. Mark D. Szuchman and Jonathan C. Brown, 103–23. Lincoln: University of Nebraska Press.

Jones, Oakah L.

1979 *Los paisanos.* Norman: University of Oklahoma Press.

Jordan, Fernando

[1956] 1981 *Crónica de un país bárbaro.* 6th ed. Chihuahua: Centro Librero la Prensa.

Jordan, Terry G.

1994 *North American Cattle-Ranching Frontiers: Origins, Diffusion, and Differentiation.* Albuquerque: University of New Mexico Press.

Joseph, Gilbert M.

1990 On the Trail of Latin American Bandits: A Reexamination of Peasant Resistance. *Latin American Research Review* 25(3):7–53.

Joseph, Gilbert, and Daniel Nugent

1994 Popular Culture and State Formation in Revolutionary Mexico. In *Everyday Forms of State Formation: Revolution and the Negotiation of Rule in*

Modern Mexico. Ed. Gilbert Joseph and Daniel Nugent, 3–23. Durham: Duke University Press.

Karasch, Mary

1981 Damiana da Cunha: Catechist and Sertanista. In *Struggle and Survival in Colonial America.* Ed. David G. Sweet and Gary B. Nash, 102–20. Berkeley: University of California Press.

1992 Catequese e cativeiro: Política indigenista em Goiás, 1780–1889. Trans. Beatriz Perrone-Moisés. In *História dos Índios no Brasil.* Ed. Manuela Carneiro da Cunha, 397–412. São Paulo: Companhia das Letras.

1996 Slave Women on the Brazilian Frontier in the Nineteenth Century. In *More than Chattel: Black Women and Slavery in the Americas.* Ed. David Barry Gaspar and Darlene Clark Hine, 79–96. Bloomington: Indiana University Press.

Kardulias, P. Nick

1990 Fur Production as a Specialized Activity in a World System: Indians in the North American Fur Trade. *American Indian Culture and Research Journal* 14:(1):25–60.

Katz, Friedrich

1981 *The Secret War in Mexico.* Chicago: University of Chicago Press.

1986 The Porfiriato. In *The Cambridge History of Latin America.* Vol. 5. Ed. Leslie Bethell. Cambridge: Cambridge University Press.

1988 Rural Rebellions after 1810. In *Riot, Rebellion, and Revolution: Rural Social Conflict in Mexico.* Ed. Friedrich Katz, 521–60. Princeton: Princeton University Press.

Kavanagh, Thomas W.

1996 *Comanche Political History: An Ethnohistorical Perspective 1706–1875.* Lincoln: University of Nebraska Press.

Kennedy, John G.

1979 *The Tarahumara of the Sierra Madre.* Arlington Heights: AHM Publishing Co.

Kenner, Charles L.

1969 *A History of New Mexican-Plains Indians Relations.* Norman: University of Oklahoma Press.

Kessell, John L.

1970 *Mission of Sorrows: Jesuit Guevavi and the Pimas, 1691–1767.* Tucson: University of Arizona Press.

1976 *Friars, Soldiers, and Reformers.* Tucson: University of Arizona Press.

1979 *Kiva, Cross, and Crown.* Albuquerque: University of New Mexico Press.

1991 Spanish Exploration in the Western Borderlands. *Montana: The Magazine of Western History* 41(4):68–75.

Klein, Kerwin Lee

1996 Reclaiming the 'F' Word, Or Being and Becoming Postwestern. *Pacific Historical Review* 65(2):179–215.

Knack, Martha C.
1987 The Role of Credit in Native Adaptation to the Great Basin Ranching Economy. *American Indian Culture and Research Journal* 11(1):43–65.

Knight, Alan
1986 *The Mexican Revolution.* Vol. 1. Cambridge: Cambridge University Press.

Lange, Charles H., Carroll L. Riley, Elizabeth M. Lange, ed.
1970 *The Southwestern Journals of Adolph F. Bandelier, 1883–1884.* Albuquerque: University of New Mexico Press.

Lartigue, Francois
1984 *Indios y bosques.* México, D.F.: Casa Chata.

Lastarria, Miguel
1914 Colonias orientales del Río Paraguay o de la Plata, Madrid, 30 de mayo de 1805. In *Documentos para la historia argentina.* Vol. 3. Buenos Aires: Compañía Sudamericana de Billetes de Banco.

Lattimore, Owen
1962 La civilisation, mère de barbarie? *Annales E.S.C.* 17(1):95–108.

Leite, Brazilisso
1970 *Generalidades das missoes jesuíticas, 1531–1759.* Porto Alegre: Internacional Gráfica.

Lejeune, Louis
1984 *La guerra apache en Sonora.* Ed. Michel Antochiew. Hermosillo: Gobierno del Estado de Sonora.

Leon Solís, Leonardo
1990 *Maloqueros y conchavadores en Araucanía y las pampas, 1700–1800.* Temuco: Ediciones Universidad de la Frontera.

Limerick, Patricia
1995 Turnerians All: The Dream of a Helpful History in an Intelligible World. *American Historical Review* 100:697–716.

Lloyd, Jane-Dale
1983 La crisis económica de 1905 a 1907 en el Noroeste de Chihuahua. *Humanidades Anuario VII.* México: Universidad Iberoamericana.
1987 *El proceso de modernización capitalista del noroeste de Chihuahua, 1880–1910.* México, D.F.: Universidad Iberoamericana.
1988 Rancheros and Rebellion: The Case of Northwestern Chihuahua 1905–1909. In *Rural Revolt in Mexico and U.S. Intervention.* Ed. Daniel Nugent, 87–112. San Diego: Center for U.S.-Mexican Studies.

Lockhart, James
1968 *Spanish Peru, 1532–1560.* Madison: University of Wisconsin Press.

Lombardi, Cathryn L., and John V. Lombardi, eds.
1983 *Latin American History: A Teaching Atlas.* Madison: CLAH, The University of Wisconsin Press.

López, Adalberto

1976 *The Revolt of the Comuneros, 1721–1735.* Cambridge: Schenkman.

Lowie, Robert H.

1954 *Indians of the Plains.* Garden City, N.Y.: Natural History Press.

Lumholtz, Carl

1902 *Unknown Mexico: Explorations in the Sierra Madre and Other Regions, 1890–1898.* New York: Scribner's.

Lynch, John

1958 *Spanish Colonial Administration, 1782–1810: The Intendant System in the Viceroyalty of the Río de la Plata.* London: Athlone Press.

1981 *Argentine Dictator, Juan Manuel de Rosas, 1829–1852.* Oxford: Oxford University Press.

MacLeod, Murdo J.

1986 The Matlazáhuatl of 1737–38: Some Villages in the Guadalajara Region. In *Investigating Natural Hazards in Latin American History.* Ed. Robert H. Claxton, 7–15. Carrollton, Ga.: West Georgia College.

1991 Indian Riots and Rebellions in Colonial Central America, 1530–1720. In *Columbian Consequences.* Vol. 3, *The Spanish Borderlands in Pan-American Perspective.* Ed. D. H. Thomas, 375–88. Washington: Smithsonian Institution Press.

Maeder, Ernesto J. A.

1977 La producción ganadera de Corrientes entre 1700 y 1810. In *Bicentenario del Virreinato del Río de la Plata.* Vol I. Buenos Aires: Imprenta del Congreso de la Nación.

Main, Gloria L.

1975 Probate Records as a Source for Early American History. *William and Mary Quarterly* 43:(1):89–99.

1978 Review of Alice Hanson Jones' *American Colonial Wealth: Documents and Methods,* Vols. 1–3. *Business History Review,* LII:(3):408–10.

Manelis Klein, Harriet E.

1985 Current Status of Argentine Indigenous Languages. *Occasional Publications in Anthropology,* Linguistic Series No. 9. Greeley: Museum of Anthropology, University of Northern Colorado.

Manje, Juan Mateo

1985 *Diario de las exploraciones en Sonora. Luz de tierra incógnita.* Hermosillo: Gobierno del Estado de Sonora.

Marfany, Robert

1940a *El indio en la colonización de Buenos Aires.* Buenos Aires: Comisión Nacional de Cultura.

1940b Frontera con los indios en el sud y fundación de pueblos. In *Historia de la nación Argentina.* Vol. 4(1a). 2d ed. Ed. Ricardo Levene, 307–33. Buenos Aires: Imprenta de la Universidade.

Martin, A. Lynn

1988 *The Jesuit Mind, The Mentality of an Elite in Early Modern France.* Ithaca: Cornell University Press.

Martín, Luis

1983 *Daughters of the Conquistadores.* Albuquerque: University of New Mexico Press.

Martin, Paul S., and Richard G. Klein, ed.

1984 *Quaternary Extinctions: A Prehistoric Revolution.* Tucson: University of Arizona Press.

Martin, Paul S., and Christine R. Szuter

n.d. After Overkill: Game Sinks and Overhunting. Ms.

Martins de Lima, Raimundo, ed.

[1738–1739] 1986 *Autos da Devassa Contra os Índios Mura do Rio Madeira e Nações do Rio Tocantins (1738–1739): Facsimiles e transcriçoes paleográficas.* Manaus: Universidade do Amazonas/MINC-Pró-Memória, Instituto Nacional do Livro.

Marx, Karl

[1857–1858] 1973 *Grundrisse.* Trans. M. Nicolaus. New York: Vintage.

[1867] 1906 *Capital.* Vol. 1. Trans. Samuel Moore and Edward Aveling. Chicago: Charles Kerr & Co.

Matson, Daniel S., and Bernard L. Fontana, ed.

1977 *Friar Bringas Reports to the King.* Tucson: University of Arizona Press.

Mayo, Carlos A.

1984 Estancia y peonaje en la región pampeana en la segunda mitad del siglo XVIII. *Desarrollo Económico* 92:609–16.

Mayo, Carlos A., Samuel Amaral, Juan Carlos Garavaglia, and Jorge Gelman

1987 Polémica: Gauchos, campesinos y fuerza de trabajo en la campaña rioplatense colonial. *Anuario del IEHS* (Tandil) 2:23–70.

McCuster, John J.

1981 Review of Alice Hanson Jones' synthesis *Wealth of a Nation to Be. The Journal of American History* 68:(1):113.

McInerny, Ralph

1990 *A First Glance at St. Thomas Aquinas: A Handbook for Peeping Thomists.* Notre Dame: University of Notre Dame Press.

McNaspy, G. J., S.J.

1984 *Conquistador without a Sword.* Chicago: Loyola University Press.

McNeill, William

1976 *Plagues and Peoples.* New York: Doubleday.

Meinig, Donald W.

1971 *Southwest: Three Peoples in Geographical Change, 1600–1970.* London: Oxford University Press.

Melatti, Julio Cezar

1967 *Índios e criadores: a situação dos Krahô na área pastoril do Tocantins.* Rio de Janeiro: Instituto de Ciências Sociais da Universidade Federal do Rio de Janeiro.

Melia, Bartomeu

1988 *El Guaraní conquistado y reducido.* Asunción: Universidad de Asunción.

Méndez Beltrán, Luz María

1982 La organización de los parlamentos de indios en el siglo XVIII. In *Relaciones fronterizas en la Araucanía.* Ed. Sergio Villalobos et al., 109–73. Santiago: Ediciones Universidad Católica de Chile.

Merrill, William

1983 God's Saviors in the Sierra Madre. *Natural History* 92(3):58–67.

Métraux, Alfred

1949 Jesuit Missions in South America, Part 2. In *Handbook of South American Indians.* Vol. 5, *Comparative Ethnology of South American Indians.* Ed. J. Steward, 645–53. Washington, D.C.: Smithsonian Institution Press.

Meyer, Melissa L.

1990 Signatures and Thumbprints: Ethnicity among the White Earth Anishinaabeg, 1889–1920. *Social Science History* 14:(3):305–45.

1991 "We Can Not Get a Living as We Used To": Dispossession and the White Earth Anishinaabeg, 1889–1920. *American Historical Review* 96:2:368–94.

1994 *The White Earth Tragedy: Ethnicity and Dispossession at a Minnesota Anishinaabeg Reservation, 1889–1920.* Lincoln: University of Nebraska Press.

Millau, Francisco

[1772] 1947 *Descripción de la provincia del Río de la Plata (1772).* Buenos Aires: Espasa-Calpe Argentina.

Mintz, Sidney W.

1985 *Sweetness and Power: The Place of Sugar in Modern History.* New York: Viking.

Mirafuentes Galván, José Luis

1987a Seris, apaches y españoles en Sonora. Consideraciones sobre su confrontación militar en el siglo XVIII. *Historias* 22:18–29.

1987b Elite y defensa en la provincia de Sonora, siglo XVIII. *Memoria del XI Simposio de Historia y Antropología de Sonora* 22:411–23.

1989 El "enemigo de las casas de adobe," Luis de Sáric y la rebelión de los pimas altos en 1751. *Memoria del XIII Simposio de Historia y Antropología de Sonora* I:103–24. Hermosillo: Universidad de Sonora.

1992 Identidad india, legitimidad y emancipación política en el noroeste de México (Copala 1771). In *Patterns of Contention in Mexican History.* Ed. Jaime E. Rodríguez O., 49–67. Wilmington, Del.: Scholarly Resources.

1993 Estructuras de poder político, fuerzas sociales y rebeliones indígenas en Sonora (siglo XVIII). *Estudios de Historia Novohispana* 14(2):117–143

Mishkin, Bernard

[1940] 1992 *Rank and Warfare among the Plains Indians.* American Ethnological Society Monograph No. 3. Seattle: University of Washington Press. Reprint, Lincoln: University of Nebraska Press.

Molina, Ignatius

[1808] 1973 *The Geographical, Natural and Civil History of Chile.* Vol. 2. New York: AMS Press.

Moncaut, Carlos Antonio

1978 *Los más remotos orígenes de Ranchos.* General Paz: Municipalidad de General Paz.

Monteiro, Ofélia Sócrates do Nascimento

1951 História de S. José de Mossâmedes. Goiânia, 8 June 1951. Typescript.

Moore, James T.

1982 *Indian and Jesuit.* Loyola City: Loyola University Press.

Moorhead, Max L.

1968 *The Apache Frontier: Jacobo Ugarte and Spanish-Indian Relations in Northern New Spain, 1769–1791.* Norman: University of Oklahoma Press.

1975a *The Presidio: Bastion of the Spanish Borderlands.* Norman: University of Oklahoma Press.

1975b Spanish Deportation of Hostile Apaches: The Policy and the Practice. *Arizona and the West* 17(3):205–20.

Morales, Francisco, O.F.M.

1973 *Ethnic and Social Background of the Franciscan Friars in Seventeenth Century Mexico.* Washington, D.C.: Academy of American Franciscan History.

Moreno, José Luis

1989 Población y sociedad en el Buenos Aires rural a mediados del siglo XVIII. *Desarrollo Económico* 29:265–82.

Mörner, Magnus

1953 *The Political and Economic Activities of the Jesuits in the La Plata Region, The Hapsburg Era.* Stockholm: Library and Institute of Ibero-American Studies.

1967 *Race Mixture in the History of Latin America.* Boston: Little, Brown & Co.

Morris, Arthur

1981 *Latin America: Economic Development and Regional Differentiation.* Totawa, N.J.: Barnes & Noble Books.

Moynihan, Ruth Barnes, Susan H. Armitage, and Christiane Fischer

1990 *So Much to Be Done: Women Settlers on the Mining and Ranching Frontier.* Lincoln: University of Nebraska Press.

Myres, Sandra
1982 *Westering Women and the Frontier Experience, 1800–1915.* Albuquerque: University of New Mexico Press.

Nader, Helen
1990 *Liberty in Absolutist Spain, The Hapsburg Sale of Towns, 1516–1700.* Baltimore: Johns Hopkins University Press.

Nakayama, Antonio, ed.
1974 *Relación de Antonio Ruiz.* México, D.F.: Instituto Nacional de Antropología e Historia.

Nash, Gary B.
1979 *The Urban Crucible.* Cambridge: Cambridge University Press.

Navarro García, Luis
1966 *La sublevación yaqui de 1740.* Seville: Escuela de Estudios Hispano-Americanos.

Naylor, Thomas
1981 Athapaskans They Weren't: The Suma Rebels Executed at Casas Grandes in 1685. In *The Protohistoric Period in the North American Southwest, A.D. 1540–1700.* Ed. David R. Wilcox and W. Bruce Masse, 275–81. Anthropological Research Papers No. 24. Tempe: Arizona State University.

Naylor, Thomas N., and Charles Polzer, eds.
1986 *The Presidio and Militia on the Northern Frontier of New Spain: A Documentary History,* Vol. 1, *1570–1700.* Tucson: University of Arizona Press.

Nentvig, Juan, S.J.
[1764] 1980 *Rudo Ensayo: A Description of Sonora and Arizona in 1764.* Trans. Alberto F. Pradeau and Roberto R. Rasmussen. Tucson: University of Arizona Press.
1971 *Descripción geográfica de Sonora.* Ed. Germán Viveros. México, D.F.: Archivo General de la Nación.

Nichols, Madaline Wallace
1939 The Spanish Horse of the Pampas. *American Anthropologies* 41:(1):119–29.
1968 *The Gaucho: Cattle Hunter, Calvaryman, Ideal of Romance.* Reprint. New York: Gordian Press.

Nimuendajú, Curt
[1942] 1979 *The Šerente.* Trans. Robert H. Lowie. New York: AMS Press.

Nugent, Daniel
1988 Rural Revolt in Mexico, Nationalism and the State, and Forms of U.S. Intervention. In *Rural Revolt in Mexico and U.S. Intervention.* Ed. Daniel Nugent. San Diego: Center for U.S.-Mexican Studies.
1989 Are We Not (Civilized) Men?: The Formation and Devolution of Community in Northern Mexico. *Journal of Historical Sociology* 2(3):206–39.
1991 Revolutionary Posturing, Bourgeois Land "Reform": Reflections on the Agrarian Reform in Northern Mexico. *Labour, Capital and Society* 24(1): 90–108.

1993 *Spent Cartridges of Revolution: An Anthropological History of Namiquipa, Chihuahua.* Chicago: University of Chicago Press.

1994 The Center at the Periphery: Civilization and Barbarism on the Northern Mexican Frontier. *Identities: Global Studies in Culture and Power* 1(2–3): 151–72.

1995 Northern Intellectuals and the EZLN. *Monthly Review* 47(3):124–38.

Nugent, Daniel, and Ana María Alonso

1994 Multiple Selective Traditions in Agrarian Reform and Agrarian Struggle: Popular Culture and State Formation in the *Ejido* of Namiquipa, Chihuahua. In *Everyday Forms of State Formation: Revolution and the Negotiation of Rule in Modern Mexico.* Ed. G. Joseph and D. Nugent, 209–246. Durham, N.C.: Duke University Press.

Officer, James E.

1987 *Hispanic Arizona, 1536–1856.* Tucson: University of Arizona Press.

Olea Arias, Heliodoro

1961 *Apuntes históricos del 20 de noviembre de 1910 en Bachiniva.* Chihuahua: Impresora AIFFER.

O'Malley, John W.

1993 *The First Jesuits.* Cambridge: Harvard University Press.

Opler, Morris E.

1978 The Apachean Culture Pattern and Its Origins. In *Handbook of North American Indians.* Vol. 11. Ed. William C. Sturtevant, 368–92. Washington, D.C.: Smithsonian Institution.

Orozco y Orozco, Victor

1995 *Historia general de Chihuahua III.* Primera parte. *Tierra de libres. Los pueblos del Distrito Guerrero en el siglo XIX.* Ciudad Juárez: Universidad Autónoma de Ciudad Juárez y Gobierno del Estado de Chihuahua.

Ortega Noriega, Sergio

1985 El sistema de misiones jesuíticas, 1591–1699. *Historia general de Sonora.* II, *De la conquista al estado libre y soberano de Sonora,* 37–75. México, D.F.: Gobierno del Estado de Sonora.

1993 *Un ensayo de historia regional: El noroeste de México, 1530–1880.* México, D.F.: UNAM.

Osterud, Nancy Grey

1991 *Bonds of Community: The Lives of Farm Women in Nineteenth-Century New York.* Ithaca: Cornell University Press.

Padden, Robert Charles

[1957] 1985 Cultural Change and Military Resistance in Araucanian Chile, 1550–1773. *Southwestern Journal of Anthropology* 13:(Spring):103–21. Reprinted in *Native South Americans: Ethnology of the Least Known Continent.* Ed. Patricia J. Lyon, 327–47. Prospect Heights, Ill.: Waveland Press.

Palacios, Silvio, and Ena Zoffoli

1991 *Gloria y tragedia de las misiones guaraníes.* Bibao: Mensajero.

Pastells, Pablo, S.J.

1912–49 *Historia de la Compañía de Jesús en la Provincia del Paraguay según documentos del Archivo General de Indias, extractados y anotados.* Madrid: Victoriano Suárez.

Pedroso, Dulce Madalena Rios

1992 Avá-Canoeiro: A história do povo invisível—Séculos XVIII e XIX. Master's thesis, Universidade Federal de Goiás, Goiânia.

Pennington, Campbell W.,

1982 La cultura de los eudeve del noroeste de México. *Noroeste de México* No. 6. Hermosillo: INAH.

Pennington, Campbell W., ed.

1981 *Arte y vocabulario de la lengua dohema, heve o eudeva. Anónimo (siglo XVII).* México, D.F.: UNAM.

Pérez de Ribas, Andres

1645 *Historia de los triunfos de nuestra santa fe entre gentes las más bárbaras y fieras del nuevo orbe, 1645.* Libro 2. Madrid: Por Alonso de Paredes junto a los estudios de la Compañía.

1896 *Crónica e historia religiosa de la Provincia de la Compañía de Jesús de México.* 2 vols. México, D.F.: Impr. del Sagrado Corazón de Jesús.

1985 [1645] *Historia de los triunfos de nuestra santa fé entre gentes las más bárbaras y fieras del nuevo orbe.* Hermosillo: Gobierno del Estado de Sonora.

1992 *Historia de los triunfos de nuestra santa fe entre gentes las más bárbaras y fieras del nuevo orbe [1645].* México, D.F.: Siglo Veintiuno Editores.

Pesqueira, Fernando

n.d. *Documentos para la historia de Sonora.* Serie II, Tomo II, *1821–1845.*

Pessen, Edward

1973 *Riches, Class, and Power Before the Civil War.* Lexington, Mass.: D. C. Heath.

Pfefferkorn, Ignaz

1983–84 [1794–95] *Descripción de la Provincia de Sonora.* ed. Armando Hopkins Durazo. Hermosillo: Gobierno del Estado de Sonora.

Philips, Paul Chrisler

1961 *The Fur Trade.* Vol. 2. Norman: University of Oklahoma Press.

Pohl, Johann Emanuel

1976 *Viagem no interior do Brasil.* Trans. Milton Amado and Eugênio Amado. Belo Horizonte: Itatiaia.

Polzer, Charles W., S.J.

1976 *Rules and Precepts of the Jesuit Missions of Northwestern New Spain, 1600–1767.* Tucson: University of Arizona Press.

Polzer, Charles W., T.C. Barnes, and T.H. Naylor

1977 *The Documentary Relations of the Southwest Project Manual.* Tucson: Arizona State Museum.

Polzer, Charles W., and Thomas E. Sheridan

in press *The Presidio and Militia on the Northern Frontier of New Spain.* Tucson: University of Arizona Press.

Pomer, León

1971 *El gaucho.* Buenos Aires: Centro Editor de América Latina.

Poole, Stafford, C.M.

1981 Church Law on the Ordination of Indians and Castas in New Spain. *Hispanic American Historical Review* 61:637–650.

1987 *Pedro Montoya de Contreras, Catholic Reform and Royal Power in New Spain.* Berkeley: University of California Press.

Post, Ken

1978 *Arise, Ye Starvelings!* The Hague: Martinus Nijhoff.

Potthast-Jutkeit, Barbara

1994 *"Paradies Mohammends" oder "Land der Frauen"? Zur Rolle von Frau and Familie in Paraguay im 19. Jahrhundert.* Köln: Böhlau Verlag.

Powell, Philip W.

1952 *Soldiers, Indians, and Silver: The Northward Advance of Northern Spain, 1550–1600.* Berkeley: University of California Press.

Pratt, Mary Louise

1992 *Imperial Eyes: Travel Writing and Transculturation.* London: Routledge & Kegan Paul.

Primerio, Frei Fidelis M. de

1942 *Capuchinhos em Terras de Santa Cruz nos Séculos XVII, XVIII, e XIX.* São Paulo.

Pyne, Stephen F.

1982 *Fire in America: A Cultural History of Wildland and Rural Fire.* Princeton: Princeton University Press.

Quevedo, Roberto C.

1959–60 El gobernador Pinedo y su fundación de Villa Real de la Concepción. *Historia Paraguaya* 4/5:17–25.

Radding, Cynthia

1979 *Las estructuras socioeconómicas de las misiones de la Pimería Alta, 1768–1850.* Noroeste de México 3. México, D.F.: Instituto Nacional de Antropología e Historia.

1982 Las misiones de Ostimuri y la sublevación indígena de 1740. In *Memoria del VII Simposio de Historia de Sonora.* Hermosillo: Gobierno del Estado de Sonora.

1990 *Ethnicity and the Emerging Peasant Class of Northwestern New Spain, 1760–1840.* Ph.D. diss. San Diego: University of California.

1992 Población, tierra y la persistencia de comunidad en la Provincia de Sonora, 1750–1800. *Historia Mexicana* 41(4):551–578.

1995 *Entre el desierto y la sierra. Las naciones o'odham y tegüima de Sonora, 1530–1840.* México, D.F.: Centro de Investigaciones y Estudios Superiores en Antropología Social, Instituto Nacional Indigenista.

1997 *Wandering Peoples: Colonialism, Ethnic Spaces, and Ecological Frontiers in Northwestern Mexico, 1700–1850.* Durham and London: Duke University Press.

Ragin, Charles

1987 *The Comparative Method: Moving Beyond Qualitative and Quantitative Strategies.* Berkeley: University of California Press.

Ramenofsky, Ann F.

1987 *Vectors of Death: The Archaeology of European Contact.* Albuquerque: University of New Mexico Press.

Rausch, Jane M.

1984 *A Tropical Plains Frontier: The Llanos of Colombia, 1531–1831.* Albuquerque: University of New Mexico Press.

Recart Novión, Alberto

1971 *El laja: Un río creador.* Santiago: Editorial Jeronimo de Vivar.

Recopilación de las leyes de Indias

1973 [1680] Madrid: Marcialo Pons.

Reed, Erik K.

1964 The Greater Southwest. In *Prehistoric Man in the New World.* ed. Jesse D. Jennings and E. Nordbeck, 175–191. Chicago: University of Chicago Press.

Reff, Daniel T.

1991 *Disease, Depopulation and Culture Change in Northwestern New Spain, 1518–1764.* Salt Lake City: University of Utah Press.

1992 Contact Shock in Northwestern Spain, 1518–1764. In *Disease and Demography in the Americas.* Ed. J. Verano and D. Ubelaker, 265–277. Washington, D.C.: Smithsonian Institution Press.

1994 Contextualizing Missionary Discourse: The Benavides Memorials of 1630 and 1634. *Journal of Anthropological Research* 50:51–67.

1995 The "Predicament of Culture" and Spanish Missionary Accounts of the Tepehuan and Pueblo Revolts. *Ethnohistory:*63–90.

Ribeiro, Darcy

1983 *As Américas e a Civilização, Estudos de Antropologia da Civilização.* Petrópolis: Vozes.

Riley, Carroll

1987 *The Frontier People. The Greater Southwest in the Protohistoric Period.* Albuquerque: University of New Mexico Press.

Riley, Glenda

1981 *Frontierswomen: The Iowa Experience.* Ames: The Iowa State University Press.

1984 *Women and Indians on the Frontier, 1825–1915.* Albuquerque: University of New Mexico Press.

1988 *The Female Frontier: A Comparative View of Women on the Prairie and the Plains.* Lawrence: University of Kansas Press.

Río, Ignacio del

1979 Sobre la aparición y desarrollo del trabajo libre asalariado en el norte de Nueva España (siglos XVI–XVII). In *El trabajo y los trabajadores en la historia de México.* Ed. Elsa Cecilia Frost, Michael Meyer, and Josefina Vázquez, 92–111. México, D.F.: El Colegio de México and Tucson: University of Arizona Press.

1985 El noroeste novohispano y la nueva política imperial española. *Historia general de Sonora* II: *De la conquista al estado libre y soberano de Sonora,* 209–219. México, D.F.: Gobierno del Estado de Sonora.

Rivera Marín de Iturbe, Guadalupe

1983 *La propiedad territorial en México 1301–1810.* México, D.F.: Siglo Veintiuno Editores.

Robertson, J. P., and W. P. Robertson

1839 *Letters on Paraguay: Comprising an Account of a Four Years' Residence in that Republic under the Government of the Dictator Francia.* Vol. 2. 2d ed. London: J. Murray

Rock, David

1985 *Argentina, 1516–1982: From Spanish Colonization to the Falklands War.* Berkeley: University of California Press.

1987 *Argentina, 1516–1987: From Spanish Colonization to Alfonsín.* 2d ed. Berkeley: University of California Press.

Rodríguez Molas, Ricardo

1968 *Historia social del gaucho.* 2d ed. Buenos Aires: Marú.

Romano, Ruggiero

1987 Algunas consideraciones alrededor de nación, estado, y libertad en europa y America centro-meridional. In *America Latino: del estado colonial al estado nación (1750–1940).* Vol. 1. Ed. Antonio Annino et al., 1–24. Milano: Franco Angeli.

Romero, Saul Gerónimo

1991 *De las misiones a los ranchos y haciendas: La privatización de la tenencia de la tierra en Sonora, 1740–1860.* Hermosillo: Gobierno del Estado de Sonora.

Roseberry, William

1989 *Anthropologies and Histories.* New Brunswick, N.J.: Rutgers University Press.

Rubert de Ventos, Xavier

1991 *The Hispanic Labyrinth, Tradition and Modernity in the Colonization of the Americas.* Trans. M. A. Newman. New Brunswick, N.J.: Transaction Publishers.

Ruiz, Comadrán

1969 *Evolución demográfica (1513–1810).* Buenos Aires: EUDEBA.

Ruiz de Montoya, Antonio, S.J.

[1639] 1892 *Conquista espiritual.* Bilbao: Mensajero.

Sabato, Hilda

1985 La formación del mercado de trabajo en Buenos Aires, 1850–1880. *Desarrollo Económico* 24(96):561–92

Sabato, Hilda, et al.

1981 *Los trabajadores y el mercado de trabajo en Buenos Aires, ciudad y campaña, 1850–1880.* Buenos Aires: Editorial Sudamericana.

1989 *Capitalismo y gandería en Buenos Aires: La fiebre del lanar, 1850–1890.* Buenos Aires: Editorial Sudamericana.

Saeger, James S.

1981 Survival and Abolition: The Eighteenth Century Paraguayan Encomienda. *The Americas* 38(1):59–85.

1989 Eighteenth-Century Guaycurú Missions in Paraguay. In *Indian Religious Relations in Colonial Spanish America.* Ed. Susan E. Ramírez. Syracuse: Syracuse University.

Sahlins, Peter

1989 *Boundaries: The Making of France and Spain in the Pyrenees.* Berkeley: University of California Press.

Salvatore, Ricardo, and Jonathan Brown

1987 Trade and Proletarianization in Latin Colonial Banda Oriental: Evidence from the Estancia de las Vacas, 1791–1805. *Hispanic American Historical Review* 67:431–59.

Sarmiento, Domingo F.

[1845] 1971 *Life in the Argentine Republic in the Days of the Tyrants; or Civilization and Barbarism.* New York: Hafner Press.

Sauer, Carl O.

1935 *Aboriginal Population of Northwestern Mexico.* Ibero-Americana 10. Berkeley: University of California Press.

Scadron, Arlene, ed.

1988 *On Their Own: Widows and Widowhood in the American Southwest.* Urbana: University of Illinois Press.

Schlissel, Lillian, Vicki L. Ruiz, and Janice Monk, eds.

1988 *Western Women: Their Land, Their Lives.* Albuquerque: University of New Mexico Press.

Schmidel, Ulrico

1986 *Relatos de la Conquista del Río de la Plata y Paraguay 1534–55.* Madrid: Alianza.

Scott, James C.

1985 *Weapons of the Weak: Everyday Forms of Peasant Resistance.* New Haven: Yale University Press.

1990 *Domination and the Arts of Resistance: Hidden Transcripts.* New Haven: Yale University Press.

Secoy, Frank

[1953] 1992 *Changing Military Patterns on the Great Plains: Seventeenth Century through the Early Nineteenth Century.* Locust Valley, N.Y.: Monographs of the American Ethnological Society 21. Reprint Lincoln: University of Nebraska.

Serrano, Antonio

1947 *Los aborígenes argentinos: síntesis etnográfica.* Buenos Aires: Editorial Nova.

Service, Elman R.

1951 The *Encomienda* in Paraguay. *Hispanic American Historical Review* 31(2): 230–52.

Shammas, Carole

1977 The Determinants of Personal Wealth in Seventeenth-Century England and America. *The Journal of Economic History* 33:(3):675–89.

Shannon, Thomas R.

1996 *An Introduction to the World-System Perspective.* 2d ed. Boulder, Colo.: Westview Press.

Sheridan, Thomas E.

1986 *Los Tucsonenses.* Tucson: University of Arizona Press.

1988a How to Tell the Story of a "People without History": Narrative Versus Ethnohistorical Approaches to the Study of Yaqui Indians through Time. *Journal of the Southwest* 30:(2):168–89.

1988b Kino's Unforeseen Legacy: The Material Consequences of Missionization among the Northern Piman Indians of Arizona and Sonora. *The Smoke Signal* 49 & 50. Tucson: Tucson Corral of Westerners.

1988c *Where the Dove Calls: The Political Ecology of a Peasant Corporate Community in Northwestern Mexico.* Tucson: University of Arizona Press.

1992 The Limits of Power: The Political Ecology of the Spanish Empire in the Greater Southwest. *Antiquity* 66:153–71.

1995 *Arizona: A History.* Tucson: University of Arizona Press.

Shetler, Stanwyn G.

1991 Three Faces of Eden. In *Seeds of Change: A Quincentennial Commemoration.* Ed. Herman J. Viola and Carolyn Margolis, 225–47. Washington and London: Smithsonian Institution Press.

Silva, Aracy Lopes da

1992 Dois Séculos e Meio de História Xavante. In *História dos Índios no Brasil.* Ed. Manuela Carneiro da Cunha, 357–78. São Paulo: Companhia das Letras.

Silva, Martiniano José da

1974 *Sombra dos Quilombos.* Goiânia: Editora Barão de Itararé e Editora Cultura Goiana.

Simmons, Marc

1968 *Spanish Government in New Mexico.* Albuquerque: University of New Mexico Press.

1991 *Coronado's Land: Essays on Daily Life in Colonial New Mexico.* Albuquerque: University of New Mexico Press.

Simpson, Lesley Byrd

1966 *Many Mexicos.* 4th ed. Berkeley: University of California Press.

Slatta, Richard W.

1983 *Gauchos and the Vanishing Frontier.* Lincoln: University of Nebraska Press.

1985 The Gaucho in Argentina's Quest for National Identity. *Canadian Review of Studies in Nationalism* 12:99–112.

1989 "Civilization" Battles "Barbarism": Argentine Frontier Strategies, 1516–1880. *Inter-American Review of Bibliography* 39(2):177–94.

1990a *Cowboys of the Americas.* New Haven: Yale University Press.

1990b Historical Frontier Imagery in the Americas. In *Latin American Frontiers, Borders, and Hinterlands: Research Needs and Resources,* 5–25. Albuquerque: SALALM Secretariat.

1992a Far Frontiers: Spanish Colonial Military Policy in Northern New Spain and Southern Río de la Plata. Paper presented at the Rocky Mountain Committee on Latin American Studies meeting, El Paso, Texas, Feb.

1992b Historical Frontier Imagery in the Americas. In *Changing Boundaries in the Americas: New Perspectives on the U.S.-Mexican, Central American, and South American Borders.* Ed. Lawrence A. Herzog, 25–48. San Diego: Center for U.S.-Mexican Studies.

Smith, Gavin

1989 *Livelihood and Resistance. Peasants and the Politics of Land in Peru.* Berkeley: University of California Press.

Smith, Ralph

1963 Indians in American-Mexican Relations before the War of 1846. *Hispanic American Historical Review* 43(1).

1965 The Scalphunt in Chihuahua, 1849. *New Mexico Historical Review* 40(2).

Socolow, Susan

1987 Los cautivos españoles en las sociedades indígenas: El contacto cultural a través de la frontera argentina. *Anuario IEHS* (Tandil) 2:99–136.

1992 Spanish Captives in Indian Societies: Cultural Contact along the Argentine Frontier, 1600–1835. *Hispanic American Historical Review* 72(1):73–99.

Soltow, Lee
1971a Economic Inequality in the United States in the Period 1790 to 1860. *Journal of Economic History* 31:822–39.
1971b *Patterns of Wealthholding in Wisconsin Since 1850.* Madison: University of Wisconsin Press.
1975a The Wealth, Income, and Social Class of Men in Large Northern Cities of the United States in 1860. In *The Personal Distribution of Income and Wealth.* Ed. James D. Smith. New York: National Bureau of Economic Research.
1975b *Men and Wealth in the United States, 1860–1870.* New Haven: Yale University Press.

Spicer, Edward H.
1962 *Cycles of Conquest.* Tucson: University of Arizona Press.
1972 *Plural Society in the Southwest.* New York: Interbook, Weatherhead Foundation.
1980 *The Yaquis: A Cultural History.* Tucson: University of Arizona Press.

Spicer, Edward, and Raymond H. Thompson, ed.
1969 Northwest Mexico: Introduction. In *Handbook of Middle American Indians.* Vol. 8, *Ethnology,* Pt. 2, 777–91. Washington D.C.: Smithsonian Institution Press.
1972 *Plural Society in the Southwest.* New York: Interbook, Weatherhead Foundation.

Spielmann, Katherine A.
1991 *Interdependence in the Prehistoric Southwest: An Ecological Analysis of Plains-Pueblo Interaction.* New York: Garland Publishing.

Stannard, David E.
1992 *American Holocaust, Columbus and the Conquest of the New World.* New York: Oxford University Press.

Stavig, Ward
1988 Ethnic Conflict, Moral Economy, and Population in Rural Cuzco on the Eve of the Tupac Amaro II Rebellion. *Hispanic American Historical Review* 68(4):737–70.

Stern, Steve J., ed.
1987 *Resistance, Rebellion, and Consciousness in the Andean Peasant World, 18th to 20th Centuries.* Madison: University of Wisconsin Press.
1988 Feudalism, Capitalism, and the World-System in the Perspective of Latin America and the Caribbean. *American Historical Review* 93:4.

Steward, Julian, H. ed.
1946 *Handbook of South American Indians.* Smithsonian Institution Bureau of Applied Ethnology Bulletin 143. Washington, D.C.: Government Printing Office.

Storni, Hugo, S.J.

1980 *Catálogo de los Jesuitas de la Provincia del Paraguay, 1585–1768*. Rome: Jesuit Historical Institute.

Stratton, Joanna L.

1981 *Pioneer Women: Voices from the Kansas Frontier*. New York: Simon and Schuster.

Sweeney, Edwin R.

1991 *Cochise, Chiricahua Apache Chief*. Norman: University of Oklahoma Press.

Szuchman, Mark D.

1988 *Order, Family, and Community in Buenos Aires, 1810–1860*. Stanford: Stanford University Press.

Szuter, Christine R.

1991 *Hunting by Prehistoric Horticulturalists in the American Southwest*. New York and London: Garland Publishing.

Tapson, Alfred

1952 The Indian Problem on the Argentine Pampas, 1750–1880. Ph.D. diss., University of Chicago.

1962 Indian Warfare on the Pampa during the Colonial Period. *Hispanic American Historical Review* 42:1–28.

Taylor, Peter J.

1993 *Political Geography: World-Economy, Nation-State, and Locality*. 3d ed. Longman: Harlow, Essex, England.

Taylor, William B.

1979 *Drinking, Homicide and Rebellion in Colonial Mexican Villages*. Stanford: Stanford University Press.

1994 Santiago's Horse: Christianity and Colonial Indian Resistance in the Heartland of New Spain. In *Violence, Resistance, and Survival in the Americas: Native Americans and the Legacy of Conquest*. Ed. William B. Taylor and Franklin Pease. Washington: Smithsonian Institution Press.

Teja, Jesús Frank de la

1990 Indians, Soldiers, and Canary Islanders. *Locus* Fall.

Tenenbaum, Barbara

1993 The Making of a Fait Accompli: Mexico and the Provincias Internas, 1776–1846. In *The Evolution of the Mexican Political System*. Ed. Jaime E. Rodriguez O., 91–115. Wilmington: Scholarly Resources.

TePaske, John J., and Herbert S. Klein

1986 *Ingresos y egresos de la Real Hacienda de Nueva España*. México, D.F.: Colección Fuentes del Instituto Nacional de Antropología e Historia.

Tilly, Charles

1981 *As Sociology Meets History*. New York: Academic Press.

Toral, André A. de

1984–85 Os Indios Negros ou os Carijó de Goiás: A História dos Avá-Canoeiro. *Revista de Antropologia* 27–28:287–326.

Treutlein, Theodore E.

1939 The Economic Regime of the Jesuit Missions in the Eighteenth Century. *Pacific Historical Review* 8:284–300.

Treutlein, Theodore E., trans.

1949 *Sonora, A Description of the Province,* by Ignaz Pfefferkorn. Albuquerque: University of New Mexico Press.

1965 *Missionary in Sonora, The Travel Reports of Joseph Och, S.J., 1755–1767.* San Francisco: California Historical Society.

Turner, Frederick Jackson

1994 The Significance of the Frontier in American History. In *Where Cultures Meet: Frontiers in Latin American History.* Ed. David Weber and Jane Rausch. Jaguar Books on Latin America, No. 6. Wilmington, Del.: Scholarly Resources.

Turner, Terence

1992 Os Mebengokre Kayapó: História e mudança social, de comunidades autônomas para a coexistência interétnica. Trans. Beatriz Perrone-Moisés. In *História dos Índios no Brasil.* Ed. Manuela Carneiro da Cunha, 311–38. São Paulo: Companhia das Letras.

Tutino, John

1986 *From Insurrection to Revolution. Social Bases of Agrarian Violence, 1750–1940.* Princeton: Princeton University Press.

Ulrich, Laurel Thatcher

1982 *Good Wives: Image and Reality in the Lives of Women in Northern New England, 1650–1750.* New York: Knopf.

1990 *A Midwife's Tale: The Life of Martha Ballard Based on Her Diary, 1785–1812.* New York: Knopf.

Urbano de Iriondo, José

1936 Apuntes para la historia de la provincia de Santa Fé. *Revista de la Junta de Estudios Históricos de Santa Fé* I:35–64.

Utley, Robert M.

1965–66 The Range Cattle Industry in the Big Bend of Texas. *Southwestern Historical Quarterly* 69:419–41.

1984 *The Indian Frontier of the American West, 1846–1890.* Albuquerque: University of New Mexico Press.

Van Young, Eric

1986 Millennium on the Northern Marches: The Mad Messiah of Durango and Popular Rebellion in Mexico, 1800–1815. *Comparative Studies in Society and History* 28(3):385–413.

1992 Mentalities and Collectivities: A Comment. In *Patterns of Contention in Mexican History.* Ed. Jaime E. Rodriguez O., 337–53. Wilmington, Del.: Scholarly Resources.

Vanderwood, Paul J.

1989 Teresa de Urrea: Mexico's Joan of Arc. In *The Human Condition in 19th Century Latin America.* Ed. Judith Ewell and William Beezley, 215–32. Wilmington, Del.: Scholarly Resources.

Vedoya, Juan Carlos, et al.

1979 *La campaña del desierto y la tecnificación ganadera.* Buenos Aires: EUDEBA.

Velázquez, Rafael Eladio

1965 *El Paraguay en 1811: Estado político, social, económico y cultural en las postrimerías del período colonial.* Asunción: Self-published.

1980 Carácteres del poblamiento paraguayo del siglo XVIII. *Congreso Internacional de Historia de América* 6(3):265–301.

Verano, J., and D. Ubelaker, ed.

1992 *Disease and Demography in the Americas.* Washington, D.C.: Smithsonian Institution Press.

Vidal, Emeric Essex

[1820] 1944 *Picturesque Illustrations of Buenos Ayres and Montevideo.* Buenos Aires: Mitchell's English Book-Store.

Vidargas del Moral, Juan Domingo

1985 Sonora y Sinaloa como provincias independientes y como estado interno de occidente. *Historia general de Sonora,* II, *De la conquista al estado libre y soberano de Sonora,* 321–57. México, D.F.: Gobierno del Estado de Sonora.

Villa, Eduardo W.

1984 *Historia del Estado de Sonora.* Hermosillo: Gobierno del Estado de Sonora.

Villa Real, Thomaz de Souza

[1792–1793] 1848 Viagem de Thomaz de Souza Villa Real pelos Rios Tocantins, Araguaya e Vermelho. *Revista do Instituto Histórico e Geográphico Brasileiro* 11:401–44.

Viola, Alfredo

1986 *Orígen de pueblos del Paraguay.* Asunción: Ediciones Comuneras.

Vives Azancot, Pedro A.

1980 Demografía paraguaya, 1782–1800. Bases históricas y primera aproximación para su análisis sobre datas aportados por Félix de Azara. *Revista de Indias* 40:(159/162):159–217.

Voss, Stuart

1982 *On the Periphery of Nineteenth-Century Mexico.* Tucson: University of Arizona Press.

1984 Northwest Mexico. In *Notable Family Networks in Latin America.* Ed. Diane Balmori, Stuart F. Voss, and Miles Wortman, 79–128. Chicago: University of Chicago Press.

Wallace, Anthony F. C.

1956 Revitalization Movements. *American Anthropologist* 58:264–81.

Wallace, Ernest, and E. A. Hoebel

1952 *Lords of the South Plains.* Norman: University of Oklahoma Press.

Wallerstein, Immanuel

1974 *The Modern World-System: Capitalist Agriculture and the Origins of European World-Economy in the Sixteenth Century.* Vol 1. New York: Academic Press.

1991 *Geopolitics and Geoculture.* Cambridge: Cambridge University Press.

Wallis Nichols, Madaline

1968 *The Gaucho: Cattle Hunter, Calvaryman, Ideal of Romance.* Reprint. New York: Gordian Press.

Walther, Juan Carlos

1964 *La conquista del desierto.* 2d ed. Buenos Aires: Círculo Militar.

Wasserman, Mark

1980 The Social Origins of the 1910 Revolution in Chihuahua. *Latin American Research Review* 15(1):15–38.

1984 *Capitalists, Caciques, and Revolutions.* Chapel Hill: University of North Carolina Press.

Weber, David J.

1982 *The Mexican Frontier, 1821–1846: The Southwest under Mexico.* Albuquerque: University of New Mexico Press.

1992 *The Spanish Frontier in North America.* New Haven: Yale University Press.

Weber, David J., and Jane M. Rausch, eds.

1994 *Where Cultures Meet: Frontiers in Latin American History.* Jaguar Books on Latin America, No. 6. Wilmington, Del.: Scholarly Resources.

Weinstein, Donald, and R. M. Bell

1982 *Saints and Society, The Two Worlds of Western Christendom, 1000–1700.* Chicago: University of Chicago Press.

West, Robert C.

1949 *The Mining Community in Northern New Spain: The Parral Mining District.* Ibero-Americana 30. Berkeley: University of California Press.

Whigham, Thomas

1991a *The Politics of River Trade: Tradition and Development in the Upper Plata, 1780–1870.* Albuquerque: University of New Mexico Press.

1991b *La yerba mate del Paraguay (1780–1870).* Asunción: CPES.

White, Richard

1991 *The Middle Ground: Indians, Empires and Republic.* New York: Cambridge University Press.

Williams, John Hoyt

1973 Paraguay's Nineteenth-Century Estancias de la República. *Agricultural History* 47(3):206–15.

Wolf, Eric R.

1982 *Europe and the People without History.* Berkeley: University of California Press.

Worcester, Donald

1945 The Spread of Spanish Horses in the Southwest, 1700–1800. *New Mexico Historical Review* 20(1):1–13.

Wrobel, David M.

1996 Beyond the Frontier-Region Dichotomy. *Pacific Historical Review* 65(3): 401–29.

Zambrano, P. Francisco, S.J.

1961–77 *Diccionario bio-bibiliográfico de la Compañía de Jesús en México.* Vols. 12, 15, 16. México, D.F.: Editorial JUS.

Zubillaga, Felix, S.J.

1968–73 *Monumenta Mexicana.* Vols. 3–5. Rome: Jesuit Historical Institute.

Zúñiga, Ignacio

1985 [1835] *Rápida ojeada al Estado de Sonora.* Hermosillo: Gobierno del Estado de Sonora.

About the Contributors

JERRY W. COONEY is professor emeritus of the University of Louisville. Recent publications are *A Guide to Collections on Paraguay in the United States* (in collaboration with Thomas Whigham, 1995), *Paraguay: A Bibliography of Immigration and Emigration,* and *El Paraguay bajo el Doctor Francia: Ensayos sobre la sociedad patrimonial (1814–1840)* (also in collaboration with Thomas Whigham, 1996).

SUSAN M. DEEDS is associate professor of history at Northern Arizona University. She has published a number of articles on the effects of colonialism on northern Mexican Indians, including "Indigenous Responses to Mission Settlement in Nueva Vizcaya," in Erick Langer and Robert H. Jackson, eds., *The New Latin American Mission History* (1995).

THOMAS D. HALL is Lester M. Jones Professor of Sociology at DePauw University. He is author of *Social Change in the Southwest, 1350–1880* (1989) and coauthor, with Christopher Chase-Dunn, of *Rise and Demise: Comparing World-Systems* (1997). His research interests include relations of nonstate peoples with state and ancient world-systems.

LYMAN L. JOHNSON is professor of history at the University of North Carolina at Charlotte. His most recent publications include *The Political Economy of Spanish America in the Age of Revolution* (edited with Kenneth J. Andrien) and *The Earth and Its Peoples* (written with Richard W. Bulliet, Pamela Kyle Crossley, Daniel Headrick, Steven W. Hirsch, and David Northrup). He is now researching a late colonial slave conspiracy in Buenos Aires.

KRISTINE L. JONES is currently resident director of the Council Study Center at the Pontificia Universidad Católica Madre y Maestra in Santiago de los Caballeros, Dominican Republic, directing the Academic Program in Spanish and Caribbean Studies for students and participating in academic activities. She has published numerous articles on Indians of the Southern Cone pampas region. Her current research interests have expanded from a focus on native peoples, frontiers, and state formation in the Southern Cone to a more hemispheric perspective.

MARY KARASCH is professor of history at Oakland University. Her recent publications include "Slave Women on the Brazilian Frontier of Goiás," in *More than Chattel: Black*

Women and Slavery in the Americas (edited by Darlene Clark Hine and David Barry Gaspar, 1996), and "Os quilombos do ouro na capitania de Goiás," in *Liberdade por um fio: História dos quilombos no Brasil* (edited by José José Reis and Flávio dos Santos Gomes, 1996). Karasch also served as the Brazil editor for the *Encyclopedia of Latin American History and Culture* (1996) and is currently writing a book on the social history of Goiás.

DANIEL NUGENT taught anthropology and Latin American history for ten years. A managing editor of the *Journal of Historical Sociology,* he authored *Spent Cartridges of Revolution* (1993), edited *Rural Revolt in Mexico: U.S. Intervention and the Domain of Subaltern Politics* (1998), and coauthored the play *13 Días/13 Days: How the New Zapatistas Shook the World.* He died suddenly in October 1997.

CYNTHIA RADDING is assistant professor of history at the University of Illinois at Urbana-Champaign. She recently published *Entre el desierto y la sierra. Las naciones o'odham y tegüima de Sonora, 1530–1840* (1995) and *Wandering Peoples: Colonialism, Ethnic Spaces, and Ecological Frontiers in Northwestern Mexico, 1700–1850* (1997). Her current research focuses on the comparative environmental and cultural history of northwestern Mexico and eastern Bolivia in the late colonial and early national periods.

DANIEL T. REFF is associate professor in the Division of Comparative Studies at Ohio State University. He is currently working on a comparative study of missionary texts and the mission frontier in early medieval Europe and colonial Mexico. He is coauthor (with Maureen Ahern and Richard Danford) of a forthcoming critical edition of Perez de Ribas' history of the Jesuit missions of New Spain (1645).

RICHARD W. SLATTA is professor of history at North Carolina State University. Recent books include *The Cowboy Encyclopedia* (1994, 1996) and *Comparing Cowboys and Frontiers* (1997).

SUSAN MIGDEN SOCOLOW, Dobbs Professor of Latin American History at Emory University, is the author of *The Merchants of Viceregal Buenos Aires: Family and Commerce, 1778–1810* and *The Bureaucrats of Buenos Aires, 1769–1810: Amor al Real Servicio.* She also coedited *The Countryside in Colonial Latin America, Cities and Society in Colonial Latin America,* and *The Atlantic Staple Trade.* She is currently studying women in Buenos Aires in the period immediately before independence.

About the Editors

DONNA J. GUY is professor of history at the University of Arizona. A specialist in Argentine economic and gender history, her recent publications include *Sex and Danger in Buenos Aires: Prostitution, Family and Nation in Argentina* (1991) and a volume coedited with Daniel Balderston entitled *Sex and Sexuality in Latin America* (1997). Currently she is researching state policies toward marginal children in Argentina from 1880 to 1955.

THOMAS E. SHERIDAN is curator of ethnohistory at the Arizona State Museum of the University of Arizona. Recent publications include *Arizona: A History* (1995), *Paths of Life: American Indians of the Southwest and Northern Mexico* (coedited with Nancy Parezo, 1996), and *The Presidio and Militia on the Northern Frontier of New Spain: A Documentary History*, Volume II, Part I: *The Californias and Sinaloa-Sonora, 1700–1765* (coedited with Charles W. Polzer, 1997), all published by the University of Arizona Press. Editor of the SMRC-*Newsletter*, his current research focuses on ranching and rural development in Arizona.

Index